1997

THE COMPLETE HANDBOOK OF

PRO BASKETBALL

W9-BFY-763

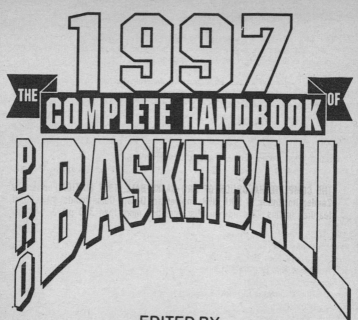

1997

THE COMPLETE HANDBOOK OF

PRO BASKETBALL

EDITED BY
ZANDER HOLLANDER

AN ASSOCIATED FEATURES BOOK

A SIGNET BOOK

ACKNOWLEDGMENTS

Never . . . but never in 50 years of NBA history has there been a preseason like this one. And there were players still on the move as the 23rd edition of *The Complete Handbook of Pro Basketball* went to press.

We especially acknowledge the under-the-gun contributions of managing editor Eric Compton, art director Dot Gordineer and the writers listed on the contents page. We also thank Lee Stowbridge, Nat Andriani, Phyllis Hollander, Linda Spain, Jennifer Arnold, Amy Greenagle, Deb Brody, Sandra Mapp, Carl Galian, the NBA's Matt Winick, Marty Blake and the team publicity directors, the CBA's Brent Meister, Elias Sports Bureau and Bill Foley, Laura Courtney and the crew at Westchester Book Composition.

PHOTO CREDITS: Cover: Wide World. Inside Photos: Michael Hirsch, Vic Milton, Wide World, Sports Photo Source, Nathaniel Butler/NBA Photos and the various club and college photographers.

CONTENTS

Editor's Note: The material herein includes trades and rosters up to the final printing deadline.

MICHAEL JORDAN OUTHITS BABE RUTH

Michael Jordan with Bulls' fourth championship trophy.

By STEVE JACOBSON

It was on the romantic Greek island of Santorini, all set about with spectacular sunsets, chalky white houses, a smoldering volcano just off shore, and young people with romance in their hearts. We were sitting at a sidewalk table enjoying some tzaziki and a bottle of throat-tightening retsina watching the people-watching scene.

So this young man strikes up a conversation with this attractive young woman in English. Now English, we could tell from the accents, was not the primary language of either participant in this game of soft-nosed competitors, but it is the *lingua franca* of boy-meets-girl the world over. And one little word leads to another and he says to her, "My name is Michael Jordan."

And she laughs, and he laughs, and the ice is broken. Michael Jordan had once again demonstrated another unexpected spectacular contribution to world culture. He is the lingua franca of our era.

More than any athlete the world has ever known, he needs no translation on Santorini, the Dizengoff, the Rue de la Paix, Stroeget, the Grand Canal, Red Square, the Strand or Unter der Linden.

Babe Ruth was the Michael Jordan of his time, but not even in the same league. He was the American hero, and the Japanese knew him well. Japanese troops in World War II would seek to inflame passions of American troops on Pacific islands by shouting "unprint Babe Ruth!" in the dark, as if it were an insult tantamount to slurring the Emperor. It didn't work very well. Nobody unprinted Babe Ruth in the South Pacific.

Making the comparisons across time, when television constitutes 90 percent of personality advertising, is like comparing Jordan's Bulls with the Boston Celtics of the late '60s. Who knows?

For his time, Pele, the deity of soccer, was one to cross the international nameline, but not to the U$A, where the bucks are biggest. And Muhammad Ali was the world's most famous athlete for a long time, but his appeal was largely limited to ring appearances and magazine covers.

Steve Jacobson, a sports columnist for Newsday, *has toiled in the trenches since the year of Bill Mazeroski's home run. If you don't know when that was, it's your problem. He has covered NBA championships, Olympic Games, World Series . . . He refuses to cover boxing. If you don't understand that, he says, it's your problem.*

Jordan endorses "The Breakfast of Champions."

Then came Arnold Palmer, who was the first to cross the international marketing line, in sports-related topics and those entirely unrelated. He touched a more upscale, more adult demographic than the others, with Hertz, John Deere, Pennzoil and more. He was the first in golf to make the huge bucks.

"If Ruth got what he did in his time, put him 50 years later and it wouldn't be a great leap of faith to put him in Jordan's category," says Marty Blackman of the firm of Blackman and Raber, which puts athletes with advertisers. "But he didn't have the international sweep Jordan has."

Who else knew Ruth? The Ruth the Italians knew was to be

Babe Ruth told the kids to eat their Wheaties.

pinched on the Via Veneto. The Germans couldn't have cared less.

Michael Jordan? See them down in Soho Square, wearing Air Jordans everywhere.

Open *The New York Times Magazine* featuring the global revolution of female athletes. In a double-spread—even before the contents page—like a Playmate centerfold, lounging in jeans, a denim shirt and no hair at all is His Airness, himself, selling ambisexual handbags. "He carries the Olympic Games Collection Lightweight Backpack from Coach," the ad proclaims. Look at the catlike gleam in Jordan's eyes, the sly smile. He's enjoying the best of everything, and if he has a little private joke about putting something over on the world, why not?

Michael Jordan can sell anything. McDonald's fast food, Quaker Oats, Nike, Gatorade, Wheaties. He can make a movie with Bugs Bunny, helping the wascally wabbit stop aliens from kidnapping earthlings.

He can sell—for goodness sake—a perfume with his name on it. Bijan Fragrances—you should know you need an appointment to shop at the Bijan men's store in New York—named its men's perfume for the great man. "We have captured the essence of Michael Jordan," Sandra Love, executive vice-president of the company, said in a statement. "This is a fragrance that will envelop the varied aspects of Michael Jordan's lifestyle off the court and will highlight each in the most unique way."

Such corporate balderdash. Anyone who would say she had captured the essence of Michael Jordan in a perfume doesn't have the faintest idea of what the aroma is in an NBA locker room. Uuuuh. Even Michael.

But the world is covered with people who would dab it behind their ears because he tells them to. Well, maybe the Chinese and Indians wouldn't, but their time will come later.

A company named WorldCom, which is the fourth-largest long-distance telecommunications company in the U.S. but largely unknown, wants to be be known by everybody. So Jordan was sold on joining the corporate team. "This announcement demonstrates that WorldCom is serious about it's long-term strategy to aggressively compete," Bernard Ebbers, the company president said.

Because Jordan says so, you should switch to WorldCom? So who else should they use? Candice Bergen? She shills for Sprint. Whoopi Goldberg puts her name with MCI. You have to understand that in the U.S. the World Series still outpulls the NBA Finals on TV, but the NBA playoffs were telecast in more than 120 countries. You should see the legions of people in Tel Aviv drinking in the coffee bars in the middle of the night and watching the NBA. "Michael Jordan makes a whole lot more sense overseas than Candice Bergen or Whoopi Goldberg," Ebbers said.

And so he does. "He is a once-in-50-years phenomenon," Blackman said.

This is very big stuff, you know. And we haven't even so much as mentioned a scoring championship, a gravity-defying dunk or returning from the field of dreams of baseball to encore three championships with a fourth. This is bigger.

Babe Ruth was very big in his time. He made more money

than the President, Herbert Hoover, you know, and Ruth did explain that he had a better year than the President, which he did. Ruth always had a better year than anybody.

Ruth sold his name to Spalding baseball equipment, a board game named Babe Ruth's Baseball Game, Wheaties, Quaker Puffed Wheat and Quaker Puffed Rice, DM Sporting Goods, All-American Athletic Underwear, Bambino Smoking Tobacco, Barbasol Shaving Cream, Remington Shotguns, Gilbert Paper products, Babe Ruth Gum and—honest—Ruth's Home Run Candy Bar. That's not to be mistaken for Baby Ruth, which was named after Grover Cleveland's daughter, born in the White House, nor mistaken for the Reggie Bar.

In 1985, however, Babe Ruth's image was put on a $2 stamp by St. Vincent Island as the first in its Hall of Fame series.

Don't forget, the enormous development of TV marketing wasn't available to Ruth's agent because TV hadn't yet been invented. Radio was only just beginning its coverage of sports. What Ruth got was print and billboard advertising. And people weren't yet wearing athletic shoes on the street because Nike in Ruth's time was still the name of a Greek god.

What Ruth and Jordan have most in common was championships. They were absolutely the best at what they did. There is no other comparison in any sport. No athletes were so clearly superior to the competition. Between 1921 and 1932 Ruth's Yankees won seven pennants.

More significantly, he saved his sport and transformed it into what was clearly the nation's game for 60 or 70 years. Ruth's home-run dynamism came right after the shame of the 1919 Black Sox scandal, at a time when baseball very badly needed something—someone—to transform its image. He remade the game from a single-and-a-cloud-of dust of Ty Cobb to the game where one man swung the bat and touched all the bases. It's still the game in vogue.

You may have seen the classic photo of Ruth playing first base in Japan on tour in 1934, leaning intently toward the plate, holding a Japanese umbrella over his head to protect him from a light rain.

Ruth was the man with his fun-loving image and his zest for living. Nobody asked Ruth to live in a monastery, and he didn't. Neither does Jordan.

Jordan came along when the NBA had already been lifted from the brink of insolvency by Magic Johnson and Larry Bird. They merely played the existing game better than others. Jordan gave basketball's growth real emphasis, playing in a manner that was

Jordan co-starred with Bugs Bunny in Space Jam.

merely hinted by Elgin Baylor and Julius Erving, who first discovered a man in sneakers could fly, and took sports marketing to a new dimension.

This is bigger than a championship or any one sport. Nike hitched its wagon to Jordan before he had won a championship, when he was merely the human who could fly, and Jordan's presence elevated the brand to the top. He took the whole casual shoe industry to a new level—creating a market for sneakers that cost $14 to make and up to $115 to buy, for people who rarely take more than three consecutive running steps. You don't have to play basketball to walk a mile in Jordan's shoes. Half the kids who wear them don't even tie the laces. But they buy them. Kids have been known to kill for them.

There is some moral question in the fact that Jordan's aura has created a demand among kids and families that have little money for shoes at that price, money that would be better spent on necessities, but that's not the issue of today. Hakeem Olajuwon deliberately put his name on lower-priced Spaldings. Jordan's name is at the top.

He's entitled to rake in the money with either hand like ambidextrous moves to the basket. He's entitled to his smile. He's earned all of it. He's that superior.

He plays on the outer edge of basketball at a time the game of basketball is conquering the world, driving the centuries-old tradition of soccer into a secondary position. Just see all the NBA-licensed stuff all over Europe—especially Bulls on it—and the counterfeit goods like caps emblazoned, "Bulls Chicago Los Angeles," which doesn't make any sense or any money for the NBA but sure does indicate its influence.

Those Nike ads are so good—posters and banners and signboards a block long and a mile high—that they sell shoes and Jordan's image—and the inherent message is that basketball must be a terrific game if this person enjoys it so much. The NBA gets only richer. All the players benefit from what Jordan has done to make basketball thrive worldwide.

What he does, however, is not solely the product of some marketing genius sitting down with the thought that nobody ever went broke underestimating the intelligence of the buying public. Unlike Shaquille O'Neal, who struts like a rock star/movie star and has won no championship in college or professional basketball, Jordan has real credentials. Like, nobody else has won an NCAA championship, two Olympic golds, and four NBA championships. You could look it up.

Jordan has been an extraordinary ambassador for the game, Ruthian in his own way. It's impossible to imagine any player displaying more sheer love and enthusiasm for the game he was playing than Magic Johnson did, but Jordan does his bit. He's there before every game in the locker room talking with media and dealing with questions that range from alpha to omega, and he makes himself available after every game and every practice. Well, not every time. There are occasions when he does close himself off, but rarely. Every time he speaks, he sells basketball and his merchandise.

You might think it was no big deal to be courteously available to the press on a regular basis, but it's startling to consider the athletes in all sports who refuse to the point of hostility. Consider that the Cleveland Indians are one of baseball's showcase teams, but the players have made the Indians very hard to embrace. Albert Belle may be baseball's best player and he has driven away fans rather than drawn them.

Jordan does it all. Plus, he has the astounding showcase of instant replay. Ruth's home runs had to be seen, or at least visualized; Jordan can raise himself above the world, twist and turn, stick out his tongue and spin the ball into the basket, and TV shows it over and over as if he'd been airborne 30 seconds. And then it shows that sly smile.

Give David Stern, the commissioner, a bit of credit for Jordan's place in history. His league, which Jordan dominates, has achieved labor peace. Players make enormous salaries, but they

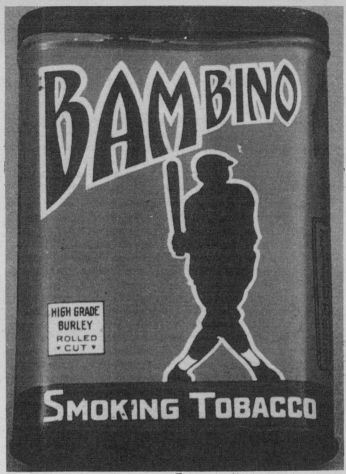

Don't expect to find it in the tobacco shop.

don't appear as greedy as do the baseball players who strike, even if the owners are more at fault. "Don't underestimate what that means in the marketplace," Blackman said.

The basic standard advertising people use to decide whether they'll tap an athlete as a spokesman is the subjective evaluation: Is this athlete someone the potential buyer would like to share the product with? Would you like to sit down and drink a beer with him? Would you like to walk a mile with Michael Jordan in his shoes?

Jordan meets the standards. He is bright, articulate, handsome and his appeal has no racial limitation. Even the gambling business that appeared in his alphabet soup a couple of years ago—when he went to the tables at Atlantic City the night before a playoff game with the Knickerbockers, the well-documented stories of his golfing losses that reached into hundreds of thousands of dollars—have slid off his persona like so much wine out of a Frenchman's glass. He remains unstained. No evidence has been turned up that his baseball interlude was, in effect, a suspension from the NBA.

Not even Jordan's failure to become a big-league baseball player can be regarded as a failure. To the contrary, it actually enhanced his image as all-conquering basketball god. It lent a flavor of vulnerability that makes him that much more appealing.

The Bulls couldn't win without him. Then he came back and they won. Whatta story!

The night he came back to New York after that two-year break was one of the magical moments of sports. He had his two warm-up games in March 1995, and then he came to New York, which is really New York, New York, in the business of sports. Chicago is Second City—or, one might argue, the whole world is Second City to New York. "My one night on Broadway," Magic used to say, "You got to make the most of your one night on Broadway." If you haven't come back in New York, you haven't come back anywhere.

Jordan had 20 points by the end of the first quarter. There was one point in the third period when Jordan put up a shot and it went in and the crowd laughed. He was so good that they laughed, as if they needed to be reminded. The people had come to see the Knicks win, but they had come with the schizophrenia of wanting to see THE Michael Jordan again.

"He reminds us of something," Stern said from a good seat in the front row. "He reminds us of how we want our sports to be. He is back to expanding the possibilities."

Jordan scored 55 that night, made 21 of 37 shots, and the greatest laugh was that he passed off for the winning basket with 3.1 seconds remaining. Nike couldn't have produced a better plotline.

What might have been possible? "That's the fun thing about it," he said afterward. "Tomorrow, you don't know what I might do."

Indeed, that evening he had provided one of the memorable moments for the year and for the history of the building that bills itself as the world's most famous arena. He laughed. He was bright and amiable before the game, too. Tickets were being scalped for $500 for a pair of $45 tickets and there were 300 media credentials issued, compared to a normal high demand of 150, to media people from Japan, Belgium, Israel, Italy, Croatia, Portugal, Australia, Brazil, Holland, England and Staten Island—any place a young man might say his name was Michael Jordan as an ice-breaker.

Itzhak Perlman was at courtside and so were Oprah and Gunther Gabel Williams, who set records training lions. Jordan was the lion king of the NBA; he was Mufassa returned to claim his throne.

He had left basketball as a supremely confident athlete and found that baseball was a different game. He wanted to play baseball because he wanted to play baseball. Simple as that. He'd conquered basketball but there was this childhood daydream nurtured by his father. As fascinated by baseball as he was, baseball was more fascinated by him.

He worked so hard. He hit in the cage until his hands bled. Scouts from other teams came by to gawk. "If I could have said no, I wouldn't have," Gene Lamont, then the Sox manager said, answering both questions at once.

And then there was White Sox broadcaster Ken Harrelson to explain how he had left baseball to be a golfer—and never made expenses. He cited a newspaper story that said with his baseball background he should have no trouble handling the pressure. "They were wrong," Harrelson said. "You can handle pressure only if you're confident in what you can do. I wasn't confident in golfing skills; at times I got total braincramps."

And there was Jordan, who had no more reason to be confident in baseball other than the knowledge that even if he failed he'd still be Michael Jordan. What he revealed was that even his wonderful body didn't translate to baseball. However much he improved in baseball, he didn't sting the ball in batting practice. He couldn't snap the bat in that six-inch piece of the arc where he made contact.

He noted the hands and wrists and forearms on what he called the "real" baseball players. "Look at me," he said. "From here to here, I'm flimsy."

When he came back to basketball he was welcomed as if from unjust exile. His aura was enhanced. He had gone to baseball, not for the money, but for the romance of trying. Now he had come back, not for the money but because he loved the game. That's a nice sweet story.

He was coming back after the murder of his father on a lonely roadside in North Carolina, a random victim with his son's championship ring on his finger. For anyone who was a father or every had one, Jordan was a more appealing figure.

But there was nothing sweet about his approach to basketball that night in Madison Square Garden. His eyes narrowed to slits and he was going to go out and die trying. He didn't exactly have to prove himself again; he did have to demonstrate himself.

The Orlando Magic can explain that from first-hand experience in the spring of 1996. And the Seattle Sonics, too. He couldn't be ready for the playoffs in 1995 after such a brief turnaround. By 1996 he was honed sharp for his fourth championship.

If you studied his game closely, he didn't go to the basket with quite the same inevitability. He did it on occasion. He didn't have the gift for levitation at such ready availability; he couldn't fly. But he was as good a basketball player as ever. He was a better shooter than they remembered; he didn't need the sleight of hand to cover that flaw. If possible, he played smarter. His desire was maybe even keener.

What happened was that the Bulls won 72 games—more than any team in the history of the league. The argument was valid that the Bulls weren't the greatest team in history, but they had the greatest player and there was no limit to what he could make his team into this time. He was Most Valuable Player again.

"I had a lot of doubt in myself," Jordan reflected on coming back to basketball after the baseball struggle, "because I had never experienced that on this level. Again, I've always tried to cover the holes in my game and last year my holes were exposed. It led to revelations about my age and my ability and what I could do and couldn't do. That was the motivation I needed to get myself back in the gym to refresh my mind and my body.

"It was a blessing in disguise, really, the way I struggled in the playoffs. It was a driving force. I'm very blessed to have had the opportunity to come back to my level of basketball and lead this team to where I feel it belongs."

It was as if he willed himself to succeed again. Babe Ruth, legend says, took two strikes in the World Series, waggled his finger in the direction of the fence, and hit the next pitch out. Nobody is quite sure what he intended, except that he was the man of legend. We all know what Jordan intended. He made his own legend.

Nothing sells like a legend.

A Dream Game Celebrates the NBA's 50th Birthday

By JOE GERGEN

Seeking a true line of demarkation between the most significant eras in National Basketball Association history, between the game that was and the game that is, David Stern settled on the three-point arc. The establishment of a bonus for distant field goals carried a symbolism far beyond the awarding of an additional point. It so happened the rule change was adopted for the 1979-80 season, the same one in which the league welcomed Magic Johnson and Larry Bird to its ranks.

Thus did the NBA embark on a period of unprecedented prosperity, one characterized by Michael Jordan's ascent to the level of American cultural icon. It proved to be the ideal cutoff point from which to divide the two teams selected for Stern's grandest promotion. In celebration of the league's 50th anniversary, the NBA planned to stage a Dream Game as the centerpiece of its annual All-Star Weekend.

This wouldn't be East against West but an all-encompassing battle of the ages, between the great performers of the NBA's first three decades and those representing the latter two. Former coaches and players were invited to nominate candidates, who then were selected by a blue-ribbon Hall of Fame committee, the results announced on national television from the shrine in Springfield, Mass. It remained for the league's hierarchy to properly distribute the 24 honorees.

Stern and his assistants finally evened the sides by assigning Rick Barry and Walt Frazier to the older group. The youngest

As a sports columnist for Newsday *and a longtime follower of the NBA, Joe Gergen sometimes has flights of fantasy.*

Red Auerbach

Phil Jackson

members of the pioneer team, their professional careers had nonetheless concluded in that landmark 1979-80 season. Ever the conciliator, the commissioner designated the transaction as a trade. In return for the services of the forward and guard, he awarded Red Holzman to the staff of the contemporaries at the suggestion of head coach Phil Jackson.

As coach of the Chicago Bulls, who won their fourth title in the 1990s last season, the latter was the popular choice to lead the modern athletes. But the hip Jackson, spouting his theory of *Sacred Hoops*, had been profoundly influenced by Holzman during his playing days with the New York Knicks, champions in 1970 and 1973. Besides, Holzman was able to compile a firsthand scouting report on every member of the opposition since his

Wilt Chamberlain

Hakeem Olajuwon

Bob Cousy

Michael Jordan

service to pro basketball dated back to the dawn of the NBA and he had the unassuming personality to deal with Pat Riley, the other assistant who had earned four championship rings with the Los Angeles Lakers in the 1980s but had a testy relationship with Jackson.

There was never any doubt about the head coach of the Originals, as they called themselves. It had to be Red Auerbach, the man who constructed the Boston Celtics' dynasty and coached nine championship teams, including eight in succession from 1958-59 through 1965-66. He would be assisted by one of his great former players, Bill Sharman, whose 1971-72 Los Angeles Lakers set the NBA standard of 33 consecutive victories and compiled a regular-season record (69-13) that wasn't surpassed until

Charles Barkley

Bob Pettit

John Stockton

Oscar Robertson

1996. The other coach, Lenny Wilkens, had exceeded Auerbach's record for career victories and directed Dream Team III at the Atlanta Olympics.

A firm believer in gamesmanship, Auerbach demanded concessions for his team in addition to the temporary restoration of players to their prime physical condition, no problem for a league that had succeeded in teaming Jordan and Bugs Bunny in a motion picture for marketing exposure. Although the game was scheduled for Cleveland's Gund Arena, the man insisted the parquet floor from the old Boston Garden be employed "for historical purposes." Jackson wouldn't give his permission until he was assured that the ear-splitting sound system from the old Chicago Stadium would be installed. Auerbach opted for green uniforms,

John Havlicek

Karl Malone

Kareem Abdul-Jabbar

Scottie Pippen

similar in style to that warn by the Celtics. His counterpart chose red, the color of the Bulls.

Because Jordan and Chicago teammate Scottie Pippen, Hakeem Olajuwon, John Stockton, Karl Malone and Charles Barkley still were actively employed in the league, practices of the Explorers were limited to one full session and a series of scattered workouts by Magic Johnson, Isiah Thomas, Kareem Abdul-Jabbar, Moses Malone, Larry Bird and Julius Erving under the supervision of Holzman. The Originals had no such limitations, and Auerbach took maximum advantage, convening a week-long camp in Boston before the team appeared in New York for a day of promotional appearances.

For a final edge, the coach arranged for the party to board a

Elgin Baylor

Magic Johnson

Julius Erving

Walt Frazier

special edition of the 20th Century Limited out of Grand Central Station, retracing the route that carried so many teams west in the early years of the NBA. The train made whistle stops in Syracuse, home of the 1955 champion Nationals and Hall of Famer Dolph Schayes, and Rochester, where Holzman helped the Royals to the league title in 1951. "At least," Bob Cousy explained to Oscar Robertson and Jerry West in a private dining car, "we don't have to go to Fort Wayne."

They didn't believe it when he explained how players in the '50s were dropped at a siding in northern Indiana, hiked to the nearest watering hole and waited for automobiles to transport them an hour south to the home of the Zollner Pistons. "Ask George," Cousy said aloud, picking up a roll and hitting George

Rick Barry

Moses Malone

Larry Bird

Dolph Schayes

Mikan in the hands with a nifty behind-the-back pass.

"Oh, yeah, it's the truth," said George Mikan, seated across the aisle at a table with Bob Pettit and Elgin Baylor. "And we had to play in a high-school gym until they built the Coliseum."

Overhearing the conversation, Wilt Chamberlain called out, "George, you never saw Hershey."

"It didn't seem to bother you too much," said his dinner companion, Bill Russell. "Did you score those 100 points against a high-school team?"

"What can you expect from the Knicks?" interjected John Havlicek, winking at his old rival Frazier.

At the end of dinner, Auerbach banged a spoon against his water glass, calling the team to order. "I have one last thing to

George Mikan

Bill Russell

Isiah Thomas

Jerry West

tell you guys," he said, rising to his feet. "You built this league. You're responsible for the success it enjoys today. And you're not going to lose to a bunch of guys who have been pampered their entire lives." He then reached into the inside pocket of his suit, theatrically removed a cigar and lit it to wild applause, even from those who once recoiled at the sight.

Without the time to form a strong bond or formulate much strategy, Jackson relied on the competitiveness of Jordan, Johnson and Bird, who had earned a combined 11 championship rings in 17 years. They had reigned as the NBA's secular trinity during a time of spectacular growth and were the headliners of the first Dream Team at the 1992 Olympic Games in Barcelona. Now they would have the opportunity to do what everyone said was impossible: to measure themselves against the past.

They had spent enough time with each other, as well as with Barkley, Pippen, Stockton and Malone, to function as a unit. They were boosted by the presence of Abdul-Jabbar, the most prolific scorer in league history and a center whose sky hook had spanned two generations of players, as well as rebounding marvel Malone and Olajuwon, whose turnaround jump shot in the post had become as dependable a weapon as there was in the sport. They also had the sublime Dr. J to fill the air lanes in tandem with Jordan and the strong-minded, quicksilver Thomas to set a tempo in the backcourt.

Against any other team ever assembled, they would have been prohibitive favorites. But their opponents were a collection of basketball immortals, every one a Hall of Famer. It's true that many of the Originals hadn't played at the same breakneck pace prevalent in the 1990s but they were better grounded in fundamentals. And they believed they would do just fine with the new rules, particularly the three-point shot.

Indeed, in their very first practice session, the 6-8 Schayes had walked to a position two feet behind the arc and sunk the first 10 of his trademark two-hand set shots. The former college center had evolved into one of pro game's great perimeter shooters. "Dolph," Russell said, "I do believe you were born 30 years too soon."

Another who found the line intriguing was the 6-3 West, who practiced launching his trademark jump shot inches beyond the arc. It was well within his range, he decided. West, whose form was so perfect he was chosen as the model for the NBA logo, had a particularly difficult task. The consummate backcourt defender, he would be matched against the 6-6 Jordan. "Just don't let him dunk on your head," warned Frazier, who would draw the assignment when West was on the bench.

"Don't worry about me," West replied. "I got Russ behind me for a change." The 6-9 Russell had been the driving force behind 11 Celtics' championships, often denying West's Lakers in the process. He had literally changed the course of basketball with his superbly-timed shot-blocking.

While the Originals held an open shoot-around on the day before the contest, bantering not only with each other but with the media, the unpredictable Jackson held a private workout for his players. However, he cut it short in order to lead them on a tour of the nearby Rock 'n Roll Hall of Fame, paying particular emphasis to the exhibit honoring the Grateful Dead.

The pregame ceremony on Saturday night featured a video tribute to the NBA and a moment of silence for such deceased stars as Joe Fulks, Bob Davies, Jim Pollard, Maurice Stokes and Pistol Pete Maravich. Meanwhile, in the Originals' locker room, Auerbach waved a fedora that had helped Frazier earn his nickname of Clyde (after the movie treatment of gangster Clyde Barrow) and from which, he told the team, he was going to pick his starting lineup.

"Arnold, is that the same hat from the dispersal draft?" inquired Cousy, the only player allowed to address him by his given name. In his first season as Boston coach, Auerbach had rejected the notion of drafting Cousy as a territorial pick. The guard from Holy Cross with the fancy-dan reputation was taken by Chicago, instead, but when the Stags folded before the start of the 1950-51 season, he was included in a special draft. His name was placed in a hat along with those of veterans Max Zaslofsky and Andy Phillip. The Knicks were delighted to come up with native New Yorker Zaslofsky, Philadelphia was pleased with the blind selection of Phillip and the Celtics were "stuck" with Cooz, who became the greatest drawing card of the decade.

"This hat's not that old," Auerbach replied. "And tonight, neither are you." Then he pretended to read the slips he removed from the haberdashery: "Robertson . . . West . . . Pettit . . . Baylor . . . and Russ." One by one, each man rose and slapped palms with his teammates. Except for Russell. He was fulfilling an old ritual, vomiting before the start of another big game. As soon as they heard the flush, the Originals knew their captain was ready.

Jackson posted his starting lineup on a blackboard and it contained no surprises. Forwards Bird and Erving, Abdul-Jabbar at center, Johnson and Jordan at guard. Jordan, the captain, introduced his movie partner to his teammates. Turning to Erving, Bugs Bunny said, "Eh, what's up, doc?" The Explorers, entering unchartered territory, left their locker room with a smile.

Russell and Jordan shook hands at midcourt in the company of officials Sid Borgia, Earl Strom and Jake O'Donnell, who wore black armbands in memory of deceased colleagues Pat Kennedy, Mendy Rudolph and others, Thousands of fans, led by Jack Nicholson and Spike Lee at courtside, stood as Kareem and Russell prepared for the opening jump. Nicholson rooted for the Explorers while Lee, attired in an old Sweetwater Clifton jersey, favored the Originals.

The tap went to Johnson, who quickly passed to a cutting Erving for a thunderous dunk. "Now that's Showtime," Nicholson bellowed. The Originals responded with a basket by Baylor, who hung in the air after all the defenders—Erving included— returned to earth. Jordan posted up West for a turnaround but, seconds later, Robertson maneuvered into the lane and sank a short jump shot, drawing a foul by Johnson and sinking the free throw for a 5-4 lead.

Two sky hooks by Jabbar and a long three-point shot by Bird ignited a 9-2 run by the Explorers. Just when it appeared the youngsters were about to assume control, however, Russell deflected consecutive attempts by Jordan and Erving. Emboldened by the defensive stand, Pettit and West scored the next eight points and the Originals opened a 15-13 advantage. Jackson called a timeout and both teams substituted for the first time.

John Havlicek, who defined the position of Sixth Man, quickly hit a running bank shot and the Cousy whipped a blind pass inside to Chamberlain for a stuff. "Dipper dunk," shouted the public

Jack Nicholson led the celebrity cheering section.

address announcer in imitation of Dave Zinkoff's immortal call. But Karl Malone scored off a classic pick and roll with Stockton, Barkley muscled Barry inside and Olajuwon beat Chamberlain across the lane. A Pippen trey beat the first-period buzzer, tying the score at 28.

Johnson, Jordan and Erving succeeded in revving the running game in the second period while the Originals worked the ball inside to Chamberlain and then Mikan, who benefitted from accurate outside shooting by Schayes and Barry. Schayes was particularly effective against the 6-9 Bird, who was slow to grasp the notion of a big man with greater range. Bird took it as a challenge and hit a pair of long jumpers of his own. When Moses Malone rammed home two offensive rebounds, the Explorers opened their largest lead of the game, at 45-38.

But with Russell back at center, swatting shots into the corners, and Cousy triggering a fast break, the Originals stormed back. After Frazier deftly stole the ball from Thomas in the backcourt, he fed Russell for a layup that cut the deficit to a single point. Jordan's jump shot pushed the Explorers' lead to 59-56 at halftime.

A baby hook by Johnson sparked an 8-2 salvo by the red team at the outset of the second half. The Big O led the Originals back with a pair of baskets and a nifty pass to Baylor. Erving then lifted the fans out of their seats. After appearing to be trapped in the right corner, he faked left and began a drive along the baseline. "Remember this move?" said Johnson, who was taking a breather on the bench alongside Abdul-Jabbar. "I'll never forget it," said the center. "He left me hanging in the air."

This time, the victim was Russell, who rose to challenge Erving's shot. But the 6-7 forward pulled the ball down, floated underneath the backboard and reemerged on the other side, flipping the ball off the backboard for an astonishing reverse layup. Russell shook his head, then took a seat as Auerbach sent Chamberlain into the game. Wilt hit a fadeaway, then scored on a finger roll. The Originals forged into the lead for the first time since the opening quarter as West and Frazier sank jump shots, Schayes scored a driving basket with his left hand and hit the ensuing free throw and Pettit tapped in an offensive rebound. Rick Barry's slick pass to Chamberlain raised the margin to 86-80 after three periods.

Two assists by Stockton, the all-time leader, and a thundering dunk by Barkley soon reversed the direction of the game. Olajuwon scored twice and Thomas fed a streaking Pippen for a breakaway midway through the fourth period, enabling the Explorers to push their lead to eight points. Auerbach reinserted his starting lineup with four minutes remaining in the hope of overcoming the disadvantage.

Slowly but surely, the Originals cut into the deficit. West intercepted a Johnson pass intended for Jordan and set up a Robertson basket. Russell blocked an Erving drive from behind and Baylor scored at the other end. After Bird set up a Jordan dunk with a behind-the-ear pass, Pettit hit a baseline jumper and Rob-

Ref Sid Borgia deals with Bob Cousy and Bill Russell.

ertson scored in traffic.

Chamberlain, with two free throws, had a chance to forge a tie in the final minute. Despite hours of practice with Barry, who used the same funky underhanded style to convert a record 90 percent during his career, the big man sank the first and missed the second. The Explorers thought they wrapped up the game when Bird scored on a scoop shot while tumbling across the lane.

Auerbach didn't bother calling a time-out. His players knew exactly what to do. Russell inbounded to Robertson, who hit West heading upcourt. The former Laker star took two dribbled and launched a long shot from behind halfcourt. "Deja vu, baby," yelled out Frazier, whose Knicks had been stunned by a similar West heave that tied the third game of the 1970 championship series. The clock was at zero when the ball snapped the net. Standing underneath the basket, Erving crumbled to the floor in astonishment.

Inspired by the stunning three-pointer, the Originals swept into the lead in overtime. They built the margin to six points but Thomas brought back the Explorers, hitting a three-point jump shot and leading Pippen on the break. When Barkley slammed home an offensive rebound and was fouled by Mikan, Jackson's team appeared certain of victory for a second time. But with one second remaining, Mikan rumbled across the lane and was fouled in his attempt at a hook shot. The call was made by Borgia just as the clock hit 0:00.

"Remind you of 1954?" asked Borgia, handing the ball to Mikan. Ol' No. 99 simply nodded. He had been in a similar position at the conclusion of the 1954 All-Star Game at Madison Square Garden and sank both free throws to force an extra period. Bowing at the knees and dipping the ball underhanded, he did so again and the fans gasped and sat down.

The lead seesawed in the second overtime and the Originals carried a 140-138 advantage into the waning seconds. After Russell slapped a Johnson drive out of bounds, the Explorers lined up for an out-of-bounds play. Bird attempted to pass the ball to Johnson but Havlicek jumped in front and intercepted. while television announcer Bob Costas repeated the Johnny Most mantra—"Havlicek stole the ball! Havlicek stole the ball!"—from the 1965 playoffs, Auerbach clutched a cigar in his hands and appeared to light it with contempt for Ohio laws.

But when Havlicek signalled a timeout, Bird assured his teammates in the Explorers' huddle that the setback was only temporary. "I can do that, too," he said. "Tell them, Isiah." Thomas smiled ruefully at the memory of Bird's theft in Game Five of the 1987 Eastern Conference finals between the Celtics and Pistons. Sure enough, when Havlicek threw his own inbounds pass in the direction of Robertson, Bird slapped the ball to Jordan as he fell to the court. Jordan banked a shot off the glass and it fell into the basket as time expired, knotting the score once again as a third overtime loomed.

Just when it seemed the players had run out of thrills, Havlicek threw in a shot from an impossible angle as he had done in Boston's historic three-overtime triumph over Phoenix in the 1976

Patented Kareem Abdul-Jabbar skyhook breaks final tie.

Finals to create a final tie. But Jabbar answered with a sweet sky hook over Russell and Jordan punctuated an exhausting but ex-hilirating 152-148 triumph with a reverse slam following a Pippen steal.

As the fans stood and cheered for five minutes, Russell sought out Jordan. "Let's not wait 50 years to do this again," said the captain of the Originals. "Next time," his Airness replied, "let's make it best-of-seven."

ORIGINALS

	FGA	FGM	FTA	FTM	Reb.	Ast.	Pts.
Baylor	10	4	5	4	5	1	12
Pettit	9	4	4	4	6	8	12
Russell	6	3	4	2	15	2	8
West	20	8	4	4	5	1	22
Robertson	20	10	6	5	10	7	25
Havlicek	10	4	2	2	4	2	10
Chamberlain	13	6	6	2	12	0	14
Mikan	8	3	2	2	6	0	8
Cousy	6	2	4	3	1	6	7
Schayes	7	4	1	1	4	2	12
Barry	5	3	2	2	3	4	10
Frazier	4	3	2	2	2	3	8
Totals	118	54	42	33	73	36	148

EXPLORERS

	FGA	FGM	FTA	FTM	Reb.	Ast.	Pts.
Bird	18	8	2	1	7	5	20
Erving	12	6	4	2	6	2	14
Abdul-Jabbar	15	9	2	1	8	2	19
Johnson	8	5	2	2	5	12	12
Jordan	22	12	2	2	2	3	28
Pippen	8	4	2	1	6	2	11
Stockton	4	1	0	0	1	10	3
K. Malone	9	3	4	2	8	0	8
Olajuwon	10	4	4	3	6	2	11
M. Malone	5	3	2	2	10	1	8
Barkley	16	6	6	3	9	0	15
Thomas	4	1	0	0	2	4	3
Totals	131	62	30	19	70	43	152

Score by Periods:

Originals	28	28	30	26	14	14	8—148
Explorers	28	31	21	32	14	14	12—152

Blocked shots: Russell 7, Chamberlain 4, Abdul-Jabbar 3, Erving, Jordan. 3-Pt. Field goals: Schayes 3-5, Barry 2-3, West 2-2; Bird 3-6, Jordan 2-4, Pippen 2-5, Stockton 1-3, Thomas 1-2. Officials: Borgia, Strom, O'Donnell. Att: 20,562.

Hannah Storm Soars to the Top In The TV World

By STAN ISAACS

Hannah Storm was in a terrific bind. The New York Knicks had just lost the seventh game to the Houston Rockets in the 1994 NBA championships, and she was waiting in the hall outside the Knicks' locker room unable to get to coach Pat Riley for a quick postgame interview.

"The Knicks were devastated," Storm said, "and Riley was destroyed. No one was coming out of the locker room, yet I had to get the interview and we were running out of time. I finally told the cameraman to follow me and I went inside. I burst out to Riley that 'we are live on the air and could you answer some questions?'

"He was really cool. He understood the situation and talked to me. It worked out fine after all."

Dick Ebersol, the head of NBC Sports who brought Storm to NBC in 1992, was tickled. He told her it was great.

You could almost say that Hannah Storm was bred to be outside that and other locker rooms and in front of a camera at sporting venues. She is the daughter of Mike Storin, a significant figure in the American Basketball Association. He was involved with the Chicago Zephyrs, the Cincinnati Royals, the Indiana Pacers and the Kentucky Colonels.

As commissioner of the ABA he faciliated the merger with the NBA, was involved with football and tennis endeavors and was vice president of the Houston Astros.

Stan Isaacs, a former Newsday *TV columnist, writes a media column for the* ESPN *Sports Zone.*

Hannah Storm is not singing The Star Spangled Banner.

"He's involved with real estate in Houston right now," Storm said, and "is also working to put an investment group in Mexico City for a major-league baseball franchise."

Storm, 34, said recently, "I always went to basketball games on non-school nights. I remember little things like my mom making basketball Christmas ornaments for people involved with our teams. We always had players around the house. At Louisville I particularly remember Artis Gilmore, Dan Issel and Louis Dampier."

As early as her freshman year at Notre Dame, Storm knew she wanted to get into television, into TV sports. "I had always been

Pregame at the NBA Finals with Shawn Kemp.

around sports and had this comfort zone about it. I thought this would be a lot more fun than news. And I think I had a really good perspective by being on the inside of it because of my father. He and my mother were, of course, very supportive even though it wasn't a common dream for women to be sportscasters at the time.''

While at Notre Dame she worked at the South Bend station WNDU. She toiled behind the scenes and on the air. ''The first thing I did was a four-part documentary about Bookstore Basketball—which was what intramural basketball was called.''

When she graduated there was no great demand for women sportscasters. ''I couldn't for the life of me find a job in television. My dad encouraged me to get into radio.'' She hooked on as a disc jockey at a rock radio station in Corpus Christi, Tex. where Storin became Storm ''because,'' she said, ''Storin doesn't translate on the air.''

She did sports on a part-time basis for two radio stations in Houston and moved into TV hosting Houston Rockets halftime and postgame telecasts. "Now I was doing what I really wanted to do," she said. She also hosted Houston Astros pregame telecasts, still on a part-time basis. She then moved on to Charlotte full time. "That was the first year of the Hornets and that was a huge deal."

Storm was the No. 2 sports anchor, on the air frequently. "I also got involved hosting half-hour NASCAR specials. I showed up knowing nothing, but the drivers were really good ol' boys who explained things. Richard Petty was great. I still love and follow auto racing."

She went on to CNN for three years, becoming their first female sports anchor. She debuted at NBC during its 1992 Wimbledon coverage. She has been a jacqueline-of-all-sports since then, a solid, respected professional.

For all that, it was the Albert Belle incident that gave her an eminence that she didn't particularly want. This was the infamous incident at Game 3 of the 1995 World Series at Cleveland. She recalled it this way:

"It happened hours before the game. I had asked to interview Kenny Lofton in the dugout and I was waiting there for Kenny to return after he had gone out to hit in batting practice. I was sitting there going over my script.

"Belle had been in a slump and he came into the dugout screaming for all the reporters there to leave. Everyone who was there had a right to be there because it was before the time everybody had to clear out. The others left, but I stayed because I was there to do a job. It was just me and two ballboys. I had promised Kenny to meet him.

"So I didn't leave and I got it from Belle, who I hadn't asked for an interview. A big earful of shouting and obscenities. He was right in front of me walking back and forth, extremely angry. Finally, Albert left and Lofton came back and I did the interview and then hosted the pregame show.

"I didn't refer to it on the air," she said, "because I was not the story. This was the World Series. But I was hard and I was shaken. In a way it made me feel self-conscious like when I was younger and sensitive about my looks. I have a birthmark, a port wine stain under my left eye. I was self-conscious about it until I discovered makeup.

"You don't see it when I'm on the air because of the makeup, but that's the only time I wear makeup now. I'm no longer self-conscious about it. And my husband likes it."

Her list of credits is impressive.

She has been the co-host of the pregame and half-time telecasts of Notre Dame football; hosted the studio coverage of football bowl games; was a sideline reporter at the Cotton Bowl and the 1994 major league All-Star Game; she has become a familiar face as a reporter on NBA regular-season action, All-Star Games, playoffs and finals. She has served as a substitute host for the "NBA Showtime" pregame show.

With Bob Costas taking a sabbatical, her star will continue to rise as she replaces him in that chair next spring. She regards this as no small honor, calling Costas "the Michael Jordan of broadcasting."

She served as a reporter and studio host at the 1992 Olympics in Barcelona and was the co-host of the evening coverage at the Games in Atlanta last summer. In 1995 she broke new ground, becoming the first woman to serve as the regular network host of a professional sports telecast when she hosted "Baseball Night in America", the weekly wraparound show for the late, uunlamented Baseball Network. She anchored pregame and postgame segments and did interviews for the 1995 World Series that included the tete-a-tete with Gentleman Albert Belle.

Storm is still identified with that incident mostly because Belle's ongoing misbehavior keeps it in the news. She has put it well behind her, though, in continuing to make her mark as a sound professional. With all the NBA work and the recent Olympics assignment exposure, she is, arguably, at the top rank of women sportscasters—over Mary Carillo, who is Ms Tennis, and ESPN's all-around Robin Roberts.

Storm is a thorough pro. "I go overboard to be professional," she said. "I think I am very thorough, very fair."

She credits CNN with "having trained me. They hammered home that I have to be objective." In relation to her Notre Dame background, she says her boss once warned her, "If I ever see even a glint in your eye when you mention Notre Dame . . ."

Storm's professionalism may have been best evidenced in her work as a sideline reporter during last year's NBA championships. Sideline reporting is one of the toughest jobs in television because it requires the ability to think and speak quickly, to ask good questions under the gun, to be relevant, to be intrusive without seeming to be intrusive and to, at times, negotiate tense interviews with losing athletes and coaches.

Storm covered the Seattle SuperSonics in the NBA Finals. "I covered the Western Conference all year so I developed really good relationships with the Sonics. I think I have a really good rapport with players. I repect them but I am not awed by them, so I don't think you ever see me being syrupy with them. I think that may be from having grown up around them.''

Mark Wolff, the NBC producer on last year's NBA Finals, has worked with Storm often. ''She is a terrific reporter with great tenacity,'' he said. ''She is one of the most buttoned-up reporters I know. She keeps a computer file on every athlete she has been around. It is so extensive that when a player is injured or is in the news, she can dip into her file to come up with valuable tidbits of information about him.''

Storm said, ''Before the first game of the Chicago-Seattle series there was a lot of question about who would guard Michael Jordan. One of the players told me I wouldn't believe who it was. He said it's Detlef Schrempf. He was afraid that it would look as if he told me, so I told him I would make sure to get it from some other people, and I did.''

Marv Albert, NBC's ace play-by-play man, labeled her work ''terrific. There was nothing from an information standpoint she didn't have. The players trusted her and she used that trust correctly.''

Storm talked to the players the day before a game, went back to a particular three or four and the coach right before the tipoff. When she knew what she would report, she informed the producer and the annoncers.

''I tried to think what Marv and Bill [Walton] and Matt [Guokas] wouldn't be talking about. I tried to be their investigative reporter and come up with tidbits that people would find interesting.''

Before the fifth game she talked about Xs and Os and then came up with the sweet scene involving the Karl family. Seattle coach George Karl's wife brought his frail, aged father to the game and NBC covered the drama with Storm talking to Karl. He was so moved it made for rich viewing.

She listened in on the timeout huddles of the Sonics, one of the teams that allowed her to do it. ''I try to report what's going on. I don't repeat profanity and I don't talk about what plays they will use because I really don't think that is very interesting,'' she said.

In the Seattle-Utah series, when Chris Morris threw his towel after being yanked from the game, Utah coach Jerry Sloan let him have it. Storm reported that, ''because it was interesting and it was something the people in the third row behind the bench could see.''

She is a tough cookie in the near free-for-all involved in get-

ting players on camera after a game. "They are high-fiving, cel-
ebrating, so you have to physically grab the player until the
camera is ready to put you on the air. I always grab on to arms
and jersey and hold on.'

When Shawn Kemp, a key Sonic, was hurt and walked off
before she could get to him after Game 5, she had to react quickly.
She said, "Jim Gray had Gary Payton so I thought who had the
next best game, and I grabbed Hersey Hawkins."

She hit Hawkins with, "Hersey, you have shown you can beat
these guys both ways, in a high-scoring game and in a defensive
battle. How did you hold them to 78 points?"

Storm is so knowledgeable she breaks down any chauvinistic
feelings that a woman wouldn't understand the intricacies of a
game. At one point after Seattle won two games to narrow Chicago's lead to 3-2, she asked Karl if his team's "postups started
working for you in the fourth quarter" She went on to ask, "So
what's the key? You guys got great rebounding, you played great
defense. What are you going to do there [in Chicago]?"

Storm has thought long and hard about how to interview.
"You have to ask tough questions," she said, "but you can ask
them in a way that is not abrasive. I don't ask softballs, I ask
what people want to know, but in a tone that doesn't alienate."

She avoids the irritating practice of too many TV interviewers
who elicit a response by throwing out a statement. "I don't believe in making a statement. I believe in the short question, in not
answering the question before you ask it. And you ask a question
that won't be answered with just a yes or no."

In view of Storm having done well with the last four losing
coaches of NBA Finals, is it possible that athletes other than
yuggs like Albert Belle are more sympathetic to women?

Storm disagrees. "NBA players are the best with women.
There are a lot of women covering them and they have had
women covering them in college. I don't see that I get different
treatment. I like to think they treat me well because of my work.
Because I don't ask obnoxious or bad questions. You have men
reporters who are friends and socialize with athletes and have that
advantage."

Wolff said, "As a producer I don't even look at her as a
woman. I evaluate her as a reporter who works hard and who
knows that the criteria for her are probably higher than it would
be for somebody else. This shows on the air. There are no
blemishes."

Storm is married to Dan Hicks, a colleague at NBC. He does
football play-by-play, is the No. 2 golf host behind Dick Enberg

As studio host for CNN's 1992 Olympic coverage.

and covered swimming at the Olympics. They evaluate each other's work. "We are each our biggest supporters," she said.

They met when they both worked at CNN. She said, "Our desks were next to each other. I told him where the makeup room was, helped him find an apartment, that kind of stuff. We became good friends, fast friends and it developed from there."

They were married Jan. 2, 1994. The Storms are expecting their first child this December.

Hannah is a big name in her family. Her mother and her grandmother were named Hannah. Her brother Duke develops welfare programs for the state of New Jersey, while brother Mark, who is in international trade, used to do good work with refugees.

When Storm wondered about her work, she was heartened by a priest who said what she did was important, too. "He told me that if you are a good example, particularly for other young women, and conducted yourself in a moral and ethical way, you were a shining light who affected people in a positive way."

INSIDE THE NBA

By FRED KERBER, CONRAD BRUNNER
and
SCOTT HOWARD-COOPER

PREDICTED ORDER OF FINISH

ATLANTIC	CENTRAL	MIDWEST	PACIFIC
New York	Chicago	Houston	L.A. Lakers
Miami	Indiana	San Antonio	Seattle
Orlando	Atlanta	Utah	Phoenix
Washington	Cleveland	Dallas	Sacramento
Philadelphia	Charlotte	Denver	Portland
New Jersey	Detroit	Minnesota	Golden State
Boston	Milwaukee	Vancouver	L.A. Clippers
	Toronto		

EASTERN CONFERENCE: Chicago
WESTERN CONFERENCE: L.A. Lakers
CHAMPION: Chicago

Those rumblings you hear in southern California are not earthquake aftershocks or tremors. They're just echoes reverberating from Shaquille O'Neal running up and down the Great Western Forum floor.

Those screams traveling through the streets of New York are

Fred Kerber is a veteran NBA writer for the New York Post, *Conrad Brunner follows the Pacers for the* Indianapolis Star-News *and Scott Howard-Cooper does the Lakers for the* Los Angeles Times. *Brunner wrote the Central Division, Cooper the Midwest and Pacific, and Kerber the Atlantic and the introduction after going one-on-two with his counterparts.*

It seemed fitting for Shaq O'Neal to go Hollywood.

not coming from more crime victims. They're howls of delight emanating from Madison Square Garden, where the Knicks not only rearmed and reloaded, but built their own darn arsenal with savvy moves that brought in Larry Johnson, Allan Houston and Chris Childs.

Those oohs and aahs filtering through Miami are not coming from another South Beach model parade—although they could be. No, they're coming from Miami Arena, where the local populace is learning to love the high-caliber game brought by Pat Riley, whose front-office gamesmanship made headlines in the offseason when he signed Bullet free-agent Juwan Howard

($100.8 million for seven years) and then ran into a roadblock. The NBA voided the deal, saying the Heat had gone over the salary cap. So Howard returned to Washington even richer ($105 million for seven years).

And all those yawns you hear across the land are not coming from boredom. No, they're coming from the largest group of underclassmen in history, 17 kids who bypassed collegiate eligibility to jump on the NBA gravy train but are being kept up past bedtime.

The yawns, though, may be loudest in Chicago. That's where the Bulls are smiling and assessing threats to their title stranglehold, threats that, as long as Michael Jordan draws a competitive breath, may not be threats at all.

"I think we can consider ourselves the greatest team ever," said Scottie Pippen after the Bulls culminated an unprecedented 72-victory season by eliminating Western Conference champ Seattle in six games to claim their fourth NBA championship in six years.

"This team is very amazing," said the amazing Jordan who was regular-season, All-Star Game and playoff MVP. "We came together in such a short amount of time and accomplished a major feat. I don't know if it is the best team, but it is the most amazing."

As coach Phil Jackson, who signed on for one more season, noted, "We set a new level for teams to play toward, a new standard for teams to chase."

So despite all the retooling, all the free-agent signings that reached an unparalleled frenzy, everyone should again be chasing the Bulls. Last season, some considered the Bulls the greatest team ever because of their astonishing 72-10 record. Great teams don't disappear. And they certainly don't stop being great, not when they have Jordan, Pippen and the strange but great Dennis Rodman back among the fold.

Figure the Bulls will prevail again.

In the East, where the Bulls and Knicks are the likely division winners, the top threats will be Miami in the Atlantic and Indiana in the Central. After those four teams, everybody else will scramble.

In the West, the big question will be whether or not the addition of O'Neal will be enough to carry the Lakers past the Sonics in the Pacific and the Spurs or the Rockets in the Midwest. Los Angeles had a major revamping to clear up cap space in order to sign Shaq: Magic Johnson retired, Anthony Peeler and George Lynch were given away to Vancouver and Vlade Divac was traded to Charlotte for high-school wunderkind draft pick Kobe Bryant.

The Lakers in the past acquired two other great centers via trades, Wilt Chamberlain and Kareem Abdul-Jabbar, and the results were extraordinary. The same should happen here, although the Lakers shouldn't think title immediately. They should get to the Finals, which would please TV and the NBA, but they're not ready to get past Michael yet. Not when, because of cap moves, they are left with a reserve backcourt of Bryant, the high-schooler who'll open the season as an 18-year-old, and rookie Derek Fisher from Arkansas-Little Rock as the backup guards. So the biggest problem the Lakers will face is depth. And while they could dominate the Bulls in the middle, there are four other spots on the floor. Jordan will fill one of them for the Bulls. Title five.

The East has undergone a major transformation. There are super teams in the Bulls, Knicks, Heat and Pacers. There are very good teams in the Magic and Hawks. Then there are also-rans. In New York, whatever the Knicks do don't mean a thing if they ain't got that ring. So team brass plotted, dumping contracts and saving enough money to buy a title. Johnson joins a frontline populated by Patrick Ewing, Charles Oakley and Buck Williams. Add a new backcourt of Childs and Houston and the Knicks, with Jeff Van Gundy in his first full season, rate as favorites over Pat Riley's group in Miami which brought in free agents P.J. Brown from the Nets and Dan Majerle from the Cavaliers.

Riley's deals make the Heat more solid, yet still with scant depth. But once the playoffs start, never bet against Riley. Especially with shortened rotations in postseason.

Orlando still should be quality, despite the absence of Shaq, whose departure Penny Hardaway labeled "devastating." They still have the outside threats of Nick Anderson and Dennis Scott, plus the formidable inside strength of Horace Grant. Hardaway should run the show completely so the Magic figure to be even more wide open, even more exciting than before. But there's no way Felton Spencer, imported from Utah, can fill the hole in the middle.

In Washington, there is joy over the return of Howard. The Bullets also brought back Harvey Grant from the Blazers. More importantly, Washington landed the usually brilliant playmaking of Rod Strickland in the same deal. Add on free-agent Tracy Murray to a group that includes Chris Webber and vastly improved giant Gheorghe Muresan and the Bullets (soon to be Wizards) could make some noise and make a playoff bid.

The playoffs don't loom in the immediate future for the Sixers,

Nets or Celtics. In Philadelphia, first-year coach Johnny Davis welcomes the No. 1 pick, Allen Iverson, the dazzling Georgetown point guard who will need a lesson in NBA ball distribution. But he has quality to distribute to in last year's rookie ace Jerry Stackhouse, the universally underappreciated Clarence Weatherspoon and perennial enigma Derrick Coleman. If Davis gets Coleman to play to his potential, the Sixers may have the start of something.

In New Jersey, the Nets have invested the future in a 37-year-old coach, John Calipari, who performed a miracle at UMass. He'll need another after the Nets took major free-agent hits, losing Childs and Brown. For starters on the road to respectability, they have Shawn Bradley, Kendall Gill and Jayson Williams. Robert Pack was signed to replace Childs, and they opted for free agent David Benoit of the Jazz for his all-around play. In addition, the Nets boast highly touted Kerry Kittles, No. 8 pick and the first senior in the draft.

In Boston, M.L. Carr brought himself back as coach after the Celtics finished nine games out of the playoff field. It may be even tougher staying that close this season, but the Celtics, with the likes of Dino Radja and Dana Barros as the inside-outside threats, landed a good one in Antoine Walker from Kentucky in the draft.

Giving the closest chase to the Bulls in the Central should be the Pacers again. Indiana kept hopes high by re-signing both Davis guys, Dale and Antonio, on the free-agent market. Reggie Miller figured to be back and the Pacers added more quality up front with 6-11 draft pick Erick Dampier of Mississippi State. Mark Jackson was traded to Denver for Jalen Rose, who provides more versatility in the backcourt. Travis Best assumes the point.

Atlanta made the biggest—literally and figuratively—free-agent improvement in the Central by signing center Dikembe Mutombo away from Denver. The Hawks re-signed Steve Smith to go along with defensive whiz Mookie Blaylock in the backcourt. Add on a Christian Laettner, obtained last season, plus the direction of Lenny Wilkens, and the Hawks appear headed for the 50-victory neighborhood. But the Hawks could be in trouble at small forward.

Cleveland may be hard-pressed to duplicate the 47 victories posted last season. But never bet against a Mike Fratello team, especially if the Cavs can get any serious production from first rounders 7-1 Lithuanian Zydrunas Ilgauskas and 6-11 Ukranian, by way of Wright State, Vitaly Potapenko.

In Charlotte, rookie coach Dave Cowens starts a new regime

Marcus Camby was Consensus Player of the Year.

with a decidedly new Hornet look, one that lacks Johnson but has the versatility of Anthony Mason, acquired from the Knicks in the one of the summer's blockbuster deals.

Detroit took a major step back in losing Houston. The Pistons quickly tried to plug the gap with Stacey Augmon from Atlanta. They also landed a nice frontcourt player in Grant Long, but the Pistons lost out in the Mutombo sweepstakes, so one of the game's most exciting players, Grant Hill, could be shut out of the playoffs.

Milwaukee appears on the rebound, acquiring Ray Allen for the rights to Stephon Marbury on draft night. In essence, they earned a center as well as they returned a future draft pick to Minnesota for Andrew Lang. And they beefed up by acquiring Net free agent Armon Gilliam. With Glenn Robinson and Vin Baker at forward posts, the Bucks have a strong, but shallow, nucleus to hand first-year coach Chris Ford, one of six new faces on the sidelines this season.

In Toronto, Darrell Walker takes over as coach for the Raptors' second season. The hope there is for more of the same from Rookie of the Year Damon Stoudamire and a similar coming-out party by No. 2 pick Marcus Camby, the 7-0 versatile star from UMass.

San Antonio, with David Robinson and Sean Elliott still in charge, rates as the favorite again in the Midwest. The Spurs, though, were without a first-round pick, so they'll need even more from the group that made only the conference semis.

Karl Malone re-upped in Utah and longtime running mate John Stockton was expected to follow suit. The Jazz extended Western champ Seattle to seven games but received little offseason help. So Utah will rely again on what always works for them, the league's best pick-and-roll game, some solid halfcourt defense and an overachieving bench.

One year removed from back-to-back titles, the Rockets' grand plan to regain real title hopes has fully taken shape with the trade for the Suns' Charles Barkley (at the price of Sam Cassell, Charles Horry, Mark Bryant and Chucky Brown). With Hakeem Olajuwon, Clyde Drexler and now Barkley, the Rockets are geared to go all the way.

Jim Cleamons, an assistant to Phil Jackson through the titles in Chicago, gets his shot at a head-coaching job in Dallas. His first assignment is to bring harmony to a team dotted with good young talent in Jason Kidd, Jim Jackson, Jamal Mashburn and Eric Montross, acquired by trade with Boston. Add draft pick Samaki Walker from Louisville and veteran point guard Derek Harper, and the Mavs are rising.

Denver's first order of business was to find a replacement for Mutombo and the best they could manage was Ervin Johnson, late of Seattle, a serviceable but unspectacular center. Antonio McDyess figures to provide the most spectacular moments, along with LaPhonso Ellis, if healthy.

Minnesota could be the team of the future with Kevin Garnett and Marbury filling the center and point-guard spots. Garnett was last season's high-school-to-pros wonder while Marbury did one year at Georgia Tech before bolting.

Patience is the word in the early expansion years and Vancouver is no exception, especially after making Shareef Abdur-Rahim, who had a sensational freshman season at Cal, the No. 3 pick. By stealing Lynch and Peeler, the Grizzlies may have fast-tracked respectability.

The Sonics, Pacific and conference champs last season, will be hard-pressed to retain the titles due to the developments in Southern California. But Seattle is a legitimate force. No way you discount a team whose talent includes Shawn Kemp, Gary Payton, Hersey Hawkins and Sam Perkins. The bench took a hit in the offseason through the departures of Vincent Askew (New Jersey) and Johnson but Seattle is still 60-win caliber.

Phoenix won't be the same without Barkley, but Cassell and Horry are welcome additions. The Suns still need a center.

Sacramento hopes Mahmoud Abdul-Rauf is their answer at point guard for a backcourt that already has All-Pro Mitch Richmond. There's quality in the likes of Brian Grant and Michael Smith and if Corliss Williamson stays healthy, the Kings should make another playoff appearance and could surprise in the Pacific standings.

The Warriors should excite again offensively around Joe Smith, the No. 1 pick a year ago. Latrell Sprewell, after all the problems, stayed put with his high-octane game. Rony Seikaly and rookie Todd Fuller are the hopes in the middle. The Warriors are on the right track. Problem is, there are too many teams already lined up ahead of them but if free-agent signee Mark Price can show glimpses of his past, then Golden State could surprise.

In Portland, P.J. Carlesimo did not see Rod Strickland off at the airport, but rather greeted free agent Kenny Anderson to run the show. Can Cliff Robinson, who needs lots of shots, co-exist with Anderson and Rasheed Wallace, the main return for Strickland? Arvydas Sabonis, the 7-3 Lithuanian first drafted over a decade ago, proved most effective in his rookie season. But the cast around him is questionable, as is his durability.

And then there are the Clippers. A resurgent team last season under the direction of Bill Fitch, who led a 12-game jump, the Clips have some nice young, developing talent, such as Slam-Dunk champ Brent Barry. Do they have enough to make a serious challenge for a playoff spot? Probably not, but with the possible ridiculous imbalance in the NBA looming this season, almost anyone can challenge for a playoff spot.

BOSTON CELTICS

TEAM DIRECTORY: Chairman: Paul Gaston; Vice-Chairmen: Paul Dupee, Stephen Schram; Pres.: Red Auerbach; Exec. VP/GM: Jan Volk; Exec. VP/Dir. Basketball Oper./Head Coach: M.L. Carr; Exec. VP-Marketing and Sales: Stuart Lane; Dir. Pub. Rel.: Jeff Twiss; Dir. Publications and Inf.: David Zuccaro; Asst. Coaches: K.C. Jones, John Kuester, Dennis Johnson. Arena: Fleet Center (18,624). Colors: Green, gold, brown, beige, black and white.

SCOUTING REPORT

SHOOTING: One of the things you normally don't want to do is hire a shooting specialist for big money and then don't let him shoot. But that was the rather novel approach taken by the Celtics last season with the free-agent acquisition of Dana Barros. An All-Star in Philadelphia the previous season, which made his stock rise on the open market, Barros rarely received plays called for him and his attempts were down by more than 300. Well, the decoy theory is always popular. Still, Barros hit a .470 accuracy, which was a nice companion to the inside efforts of perennial workhorse forward Dino Radja (.500).

Overall offensively, the Celtics often looked confused and as though they didn't know what they were doing. Bad shots abounded, many by choice, many by necessity as sets broke down and guys were running around or, worse still, standing around. After placing 23rd in the league in field-goal accuracy, the Celtics might want to get back to the offensive-sets drawing board.

The Celtics have their fingers crossed with rookie center Steve Hamer, who has a nice, soft touch but is vastly underbulked for the NBA middle.

PLAYMAKING: As was the case with their shooting, the Celtics were too often confused. And you'd figure a team whose roster seemingly was half-filled with point guards or point-guard types—David Wesley, Dee Brown, Dana Barros (and don't forget Sherman Douglas started the season there)—would be among the leaders in assists. Wrong. Despite being fifth in the league in scoring, the Celtics were 20th in assists. They need cohesiveness on offense, need more direction. And they definitely need better shot selection. This is not the World B Free School of Creating Shots. Having the ball in your possession doesn't mean shoot.

Kentucky's Antoine Walker was No. 6 in the draft.

You can actually pass it. Several times. By gum, it's so crazy, it might just work.

DEFENSE: Let's see, what's the term we're looking for? Oh yeah, rotten. Rotating to the ball became a lost art in Boston, apparently as difficult to grasp and understand as translating the Dead Sea Scrolls. Teams with patience simply moved the ball around and waited for the Celtics to go into their Keystone Kops routines. Transition defense was not bad; it was terrible. Add all the factors together and you had a Celtic team surrendering 107 points a night while allowing .481 shooting. The points mark ranked next-to-last in the league while the shooting figure ranked 26th. The biggest problem with the Celtics' defense? They don't

CELTIC ROSTER

No.	Veterans	Pos.	Ht.	Wt.	Age	Yrs. Pro	College
11	Dana Barros	G	5-11	163	29	7	Boston College
--	Frank Brickowski	F-C	6-9	248	37	12	Penn State
7	Dee Brown	G	6-1	175	27	6	Jacksonville
F-5	Junior Burrough	F	6-8	242	23	1	Virginia
13	Todd Day	F-G	6-6	188	26	4	Arkansas
29	Pervis Ellison	F-C	6-10	235	29	7	Louisville
44	Rick Fox	F-G	6-7	250	27	5	North Carolina
53	Alton Lister	C	7-0	245	38	15	Arizona State
9	Greg Minor	G-F	6-6	210	25	2	Louisville
0	Julius Nwosu	F-C	6-10	255	25	1	Liberty
40	Dino Radja	F	6-11	263	29	3	Croatia
4	David Wesley	G	6-6	196	25	3	Baylor
55	Eric Williams	F	6-8	220	24	1	Providence

F-Free agent

Rd.	Rookies	Sel. No.	Pos.	Ht.	Wt.	College
1	Antoine Walker	6	F	6-8	224	Kentucky
2	Steve Hamer	38	C	7-0	245	Tennessee

have many defensive players. But they can count on some tug-of-war from Frank Brickowski, a new addition from Seattle.

REBOUNDING: The Celtics did have more offensive rebounds than their opponents. Of course, the Celtics missed a helluva lot more shots than their opponents. Overall, though, the Celtics were upper middle class in the rebounding stats. They have some legit boards in Radja and Pervis (when he's healthy) Ellison. Greg Minor, about the only guard who doesn't strain his neck looking up at his opponent every night, supplies some toughness and rebounding from an otherwise pint-sized backcourt. The Celtics are hoping the 7-foot Hamer can negate the loss of Eric Montross, another 7-footer, who was dealt to Dallas so Boston could move up in the draft and snare Antoine Walker, a 6-8 product from Kentucky who the Celts hope will bulk up and handle the three.

OUTLOOK: A little brighter than last year, when it was as dark as roof tar. M.L. Carr's Celtics have individual talent but collectively form a mess. They want to be uptempo but seem to want that style of game only on offense. Unless a serious commitment is made to stopping people on the defensive side, the Celtics will struggle again. They'll beat some teams they shouldn't, lose to a lot of teams they shouldn't. Consistency is merely a myth with this group who, if they are nailed by injuries again like last season, may have trouble even duplicating their 33 victories.

CELTIC PROFILES

DANA BARROS 29 5-11 163   Guard

Brought him in for huge free-agent money. Then rarely ran anything for him . . . Not exactly good utilization of the salary cap, you know? . . . After 20.6 ppg All-Star season with Sixers, he went to Celtics as free agent Sept. 22, 1995, and saw average plunge to 13.0 . . . Minutes took a staggering hit by nearly 1,000 . . . But the guy can score. Maybe not defend, but he can score. Especially from long range . . . Shot .407 on three-pointers . . . Holds NBA record of at least one three-pointer in 89 consecutive games. Streak snapped against Knicks on Jan. 12 when he clanged nine triple tries . . . Set Sixer trifecta record when he shot .464 two seasons ago . . . Sprained ankle in November caused him to sit and it ended a run of 167 straight games . . . Terrific free-throw shooter: career mark .860 . . . This Boston native, Michael Adams and Calvin Murphy are the only sub-6-footers in history of NBA to get 50 points in a game . . . He did it against Houston March 14, 1995 . . . Reared as a two guard, but size necessitated pro switch . . . Despite his own quickness, he's troubled big-time on defense by quick point guards. But then, who isn't? . . . Boston College, 1989. Seattle picked him 16th in '89 draft . . . Went to Charlotte with Eddie Johnson for Kendall Gill Sept. 1, 1993 . . . Then went with Sidney Green and Greg Graham to Sixers in exchange for Hersey Hawkins Sept. 13, 1993 . . . First year of free-agent windfall paid him $3.3 million . . . Born April 13, 1967, in Boston.

Year	Team	G	FG	FG Pct.	FT	FT Pct.	Reb.	Ast.	TP	Avg.
1989-90	Seattle	81	299	.405	89	.809	132	205	782	9.7
1990-91	Seattle	66	154	.495	78	.918	71	111	418	6.3
1991-92	Seattle	75	238	483	60	.759	81	125	619	8.3
1992-93	Seattle	69	214	.451	49	.831	107	151	541	7.8
1993-94	Philadelphia	81	412	.469	116	.800	196	424	1075	13.3
1994-95	Philadelphia	82	571	.490	347	.899	274	619	1648	20.6
1995-96	Boston	80	379	.470	130	.884	192	306	1038	13.0
	Totals	534	2267	.466	869	.860	1053	1941	6159	11.5

DINO RADJA 29 6-11 263 Forward

Wait a minute. He sprained his ankle dunking? . . . So much for grace and beauty . . . Missed 26 games with the bum ankle. Had missed three games with post-concussion syndrome . . . At least he didn't get that dunking . . . Still, a strong statistical year: shot 50 percent, led team in scoring, rebounding and average minutes, and made 30 points three times. Double-figure rebounds 27 times . . . Had season-high 33 points vs. Pacers Feb. 26 . . . No egg of goose for him dat night, eh? . . . At Portland Jan. 3, tied career high with 18 rebounds . . . Strong inside player who is willing to bang and bruise . . . Developing range, but at his best inside 15 feet . . . Defense coming, although at a snail's pace. But it has improved each year . . . Can block some shots . . . Earned 1988 silver medal with Yugoslavian (now Croatian) Olympic team and played again for Croatia in the Atlanta Olympics last summer . . . Wife played for the former Yugoslavian national team . . . Celtics made him a second-round No. 40 overall pick in 1989 . . . It's why he wears No. 40 . . . Attended Technical School Center in Croatia . . . Speaks Italian fluently . . . Made $2.64 million . . . Visited U.S. troops stationed in Trogir, Croatia, in offseason . . . He's from Split, Croatia. Born there April 24, 1967.

Year	Team	G	FG	FG Pct.	FT	FT Pct.	Reb.	Ast.	TP	Avg.
1993-94	Boston	80	491	.521	226	.751	577	114	1208	15.1
1994-95	Boston	66	450	.490	233	.759	573	111	1133	17.2
1995-96	Boston	53	426	.500	191	.695	522	83	1043	19.7
	Totals	199	1367	.504	650	.736	1672	308	3384	17.0

TODD DAY 26 6-6 188 Guard-Forward

Should be an All-Star. But there should also be justice in the world . . . Has the talent. Understands the game . . . Just doesn't seem to do what he should . . . Was spotted playing defence once. Back in high school . . . Takes lots and lots of bad shots . . . Think that might have something to do with that spiffy .366 shooting? . . . But there are always flashes: at Washington April 19, he established a building record for points in any quarter when he went off for 23 in the fourth quarter, making 8-of-10 from the floor . . . Had career-high 41 points vs. T-Wolves Dec. 22. Tied Larry Bird's team record when he scored 24 points in one quarter in that one . . . Began season with Bucks but came to Celtics with Alton Lister in exchange for Sherman Douglas Nov. 26, 1995 . . . Was the No. 8 pick by Bucks in 1992 after a second-team All-American season at Arkansas . . . Was Bucks' first-ever lottery pick . . . Made $2.518 million . . . Born Jan. 7, 1970, in Decatur, Ill.

Year	Team	G	FG	FG Pct.	FT	FT Pct.	Reb.	Ast.	TP	Avg.
1992-93	Milwaukee	71	358	.432	213	.717	291	117	983	13.8
1993-94	Milwaukee	76	351	.415	231	.698	310	138	966	12.7
1994-95	Milwaukee	82	445	.424	257	.754	322	134	1310	16.0
1995-96	Mil.-Bos.	79	299	.366	224	.780	224	107	922	11.7
	Totals	308	1453	.411	925	.736	1147	496	4181	13.6

DEE BROWN 27 6-1 175   Guard

A year in cyberspace . . . Demanded to be traded. Asked to be traded. Begged to be traded. Wasn't traded . . . He was fed up with the Celtics, who got fed up with him and tried hard to trade him. No takers . . . Even got ripped by Larry Bird . . . These things happen when you're supposed to be a big part of the team and you shoot career-low .399, including .301 on trifectas . . . Came on real strong at the end when Celtics were about 300 games out of a playoff spot . . . Missed seven games early because of knee injury or bruised trachea. Later went on the injured list with foot/toe problem . . . Fewest games of any season except his second, when he blew out his knee . . . As usual, had his moments. But far too few . . . Still has the quickness . . . All-Rookie team in 1990-91 after Celts tabbed him at No. 19 out of Jacksonville . . . Won slam-dunk championship at All-Star Weekend as a rookie. He was first Celtic ever to compete . . . In second season, blew out left knee in preseason practice . . . In first game back, Feb. 14, 1992 at Houston, he scored 23 points . . . Real name: DeCovan . . . Born Nov. 29, 1968, in Jacksonville, Fla. . . . Made $3 million.

Year	Team	G	FG	FG Pct.	FT	FT Pct.	Reb.	Ast.	TP	Avg.
1990-91	Boston	82	284	.464	137	.873	182	344	712	8.7
1991-92	Boston	31	149	.426	60	.769	79	164	363	11.7
1992-93	Boston	80	328	.468	192	.793	246	461	874	10.9
1993-94	Boston	77	490	.480	182	.831	300	347	1192	15.5
1994-95	Boston	79	437	.447	236	.852	249	301	1236	15.6
1995-96	Boston	65	246	.399	135	.854	136	146	695	10.7
	Totals	414	1934	.452	942	.833	1192	1763	5072	12.3

PERVIS ELLISON 29 6-10 235   Center

The sun goes up, the sun goes down. Never Nervous Pervis will show promise and be beset with injuries . . . Yawn . . . When he played, he played well. But once again, the tease element figured into the equation . . . Began season on injured list with sore left knee . . . Still, he played the second-most games of his career . . . What can he do? Well, against Charlotte Feb. 28, he had season highs in minutes (43), rebounds (20), assists (5) and blocks (6) . . . Suspended one game for December fight with Miami's Kurt Thomas . . . Has been under 60 games in four of his seven seasons since Kings made him the No. 1 overall pick in 1989 . . . Rookie-season surgery for bone spurs in right foot and ankle. Played just 34 games . . . Kings, Bullets and Jazz converged on a three-team trade June 25, 1990. He went to Bullets, Jeff Malone went to Jazz. Kings got Bobby Hansen, Eric Leckner and draft picks . . . Both knees underwent surgery during days with Bullets . . . Boston signed him as free agent Aug. 1, 1994 . . . Born April 3, 1967, in the Bronx, N.Y. . . . Attended high school in Savannah, Ga. . . . Was the NCAA Tournament MVP as a freshman when Louisville won national title in 1987 . . . Made $1.43 million.

Year	Team	G	FG	FG Pct.	FT	FT Pct.	Reb.	Ast.	TP	Avg.
1989-90	Sacramento	34	111	.442	49	.628	196	65	271	8.0
1990-91	Washington	76	326	.513	139	.650	585	102	791	10.4
1991-92	Washington	66	547	.539	227	.728	740	190	1322	20.0
1992-93	Washington	49	341	.521	170	.702	433	117	852	17.4
1993-94	Washington	47	137	.469	70	.722	242	70	344	7.3
1994-95	Boston	55	152	.507	71	.717	309	34	375	6.8
1995-96	Boston	69	145	.492	75	.641	451	62	365	5.3
	Totals	396	1759	.511	801	.691	2956	640	4320	10.9

ERIC WILLIAMS 24 6-8 220   Forward

He was good, really good as a rookie . . . And he didn't exactly have a real teaching environment . . . Problem was, his game in April was pretty much where it was in November . . . Tremendously aggressive athlete. Very active around the glass . . . Will drive against anyone, anything, any time, any place . . . Remarkable ability to get to the line . . . Didn't do a whole heckuva lot once he got there, though: .671 . . . No range to speak of . . . Season ended with arthroscopic left knee surgery April 16 . . . Personal highs of 31 points and nine rebounds . . . Was the fourth overall pick by Celtics in '95 . . . Averaged 17.7 points for Providence as a senior . . . That was his third collegiate stop . . . Began at Burlington County (N.J.) CC, went to Vincennes U. and then on to Providence for 1993-94 . . . Born July 17, 1972, in Newark, N.J. . . . Made $876,000.

Year	Team	G	FG	FG Pct.	FT	FT Pct.	Reb.	Ast.	TP	Avg.
1995-96	Boston	64	241	.441	200	.671	217	70	685	10.7

JUNIOR BURROUGH 23 6-8 242　　　Forward

There's a place for him in the game. But it's probably in Europe . . . "Now starting for YOUR Bologna Buckaroos" . . . Sat a lot. For a lottery team . . . Started the last three games . . . Has some skills: five rebounds in six minutes March 27 vs. Minnesota . . . But he's undersized at power forward and not skilled enough for small forward . . . Was 33rd pick, on second round, by Celtics in '95 draft . . . Left Virginia as the school's fifth-leading scorer . . . Was only the second player at the school to have 1,900 points and 900 rebounds. Ralph Sampson was the other . . . Born Jan. 18, 1973, in Charlotte, N.C. . . . Made $300,000 as a rookie.

Year	Team	G	FG	FG Pct.	FT	FT Pct.	Reb.	Ast.	TP	Avg.
1995-96	Boston	61	64	.376	61	.656	109	15	189	3.1

RICK FOX 27 6-7 250　　　Forward-Guard

Probably coming off his best year as a pro . . . Shooting was down but his scoring was up as he moved into the starting lineup . . . Started 81 games. Only miss was due to a death in the family . . . Career-high totals across the board, including turnovers, which, in addition to lack of bulk, rate as his biggest drawback . . . Showed what he can do when healthy . . . Frustrating, injury-plagued 1994-95. Missed playoffs after surgery to remove bone spurs . . . Found out last season he suffered from an attention-span disorder... Decent one-on-one defender with quickness and good hands... Solid finisher, slashing type of scorer... Ball-handling has always been a problem... Real name is Ulrich... Tied school mark at North Carolina by playing 140 games in career. Never missed a game... Celtics drafted him at No. 24 on the first round in 1991... All-Rookie second-team selection... Born July 24, 1969, in Toronto... Made $1.75 million.

Year	Team	G	FG	FG Pct.	FT	FT Pct.	Reb.	Ast.	TP	Avg.
1991-92	Boston	81	241	.459	139	.755	220	126	644	8.0
1992-93	Boston	71	184	.484	81	.802	159	113	453	6.4
1993-94	Boston	82	340	.467	174	.757	355	217	887	10.8
1994-95	Boston	53	169	.481	95	.772	155	139	464	8.8
1995-96	Boston	81	421	.454	196	.772	450	369	1137	14.0
	Totals	368	1355	.465	685	.768	1339	964	3585	9.7

DAVID WESLEY 25 6-0 196   Guard

A terrific backup point guard, one of best in league... Problem was, he was the starter. At least from mid-January on... Had a very good, productive season... Averaged seven assists in the last 30 games... He's learning and improving all the time... His 1994-95 season in Boston ended early with a left knee injury, so he still has yet to have a complete campaign as a starter... Good scorer. Showed he can hit the three and penetrate... Shot has always been a question... Showed more instinctive play than ever before... Wasn't drafted coming out of Baylor in 1992... Failed to catch on with Rockets... Hit the CBA for a year and then signed with Nets as free agent. Backed up Kenny Anderson for a year. As often is the case in New Jersey, Nets lost him to free agency... Celtics signed him July 20, 1994... A $300,000 steal last season... Born Nov. 14, 1970, in Longview, Tex.

Year	Team	G	FG	FG Pct.	FT	FT Pct.	Reb.	Ast.	TP	Avg.
1993-94	New Jersey	60	64	.368	44	.830	44	123	183	3.1
1994-95	Boston	51	128	.409	71	.755	117	266	378	7.4
1995-96	Boston	82	338	.459	217	.753	264	390	1009	12.3
	Totals	193	530	.433	332	.763	425	779	1570	8.1

GREG MINOR 25 6-6 210   Guard-Forward

Became the Celtic starter late: started last 26 games and 34 of final 35 ... Guess M.L. got tired of looking at a crew of Munchkins in the backcourt starting the game ... Brought size to the backcourt ... Unfortunately, didn't bring the range so necessary for the two-guard spot ... Good strength, too, makes him an inside force at guard ... Shot an impressive .500. But was .251 on three-pointers. Only tried 27 ... See what we said about range? ... Season-high 24 points ... As a rookie two seasons ago, he broke in impressively: first start produced a career-best 31 points on Jan. 27, 1995, vs. Golden State ... The Clippers made him the 25th pick in 1994 out of Louisville ... He accompanied Mark Jackson to Indiana in the June 30, 1994 trade that placed Pooh Richardson, Malik Sealy and Eric Piatkowski in L.A. ... Pacers renounced him when they couldn't work out a contract ... Celtics signed him as free agent, Oct. 19, 1994 ... Made $325,000 ... Born Sept. 18, 1971, in Sandersville, Ga.

Year	Team	G	FG	FG Pct.	FT	FT Pct.	Reb.	Ast.	TP	Avg.
1994-95	Boston	63	155	.515	65	.833	137	66	377	6.0
1995-96	Boston	78	320	.500	99	.762	257	146	746	9.6
	Totals	141	475	.505	164	.788	394	212	1123	8.0

ALTON LISTER 38 7-0 245   Center

And on the seventh day, The Lord rested. And Lister entered the NBA. Or so it seems ... Played very well for the often-confused Celtics ... Has always been a good rebounder and above-adequate shot-blocker ... Understands the game. That alone made him stand out in Boston ... Started 14 of the last 16 games and probably gave C's their more consistent play of the season at center. Had double-figure rebounds in nine of those starts ... Stands as Milwaukee's all-time leader in blocked shots ... Was the Bucks' first-round pick, No. 21, in 1981 ... Went to Sonics with two first-round picks for Jack Sikma and draft picks July 1, 1986 ... Sonics got a future first-rounder from Warriors for him Aug. 7, 1989 ... Warriors waived him after rash of injuries and Bucks took him back as free agent in October

1994 . . . Came to Celtics with Todd Day in the Sherman Douglas trade Nov. 26, 1995 . . . Member of 1980 U.S. Olympic team . . . Born Oct. 1, 1958, in Dallas . . . Finished at Arizona State after two years at San Jacinto JC . . . Made $300,000.

Year	Team	G	FG	FG Pct.	FT	FT Pct.	Reb.	Ast.	TP	Avg.
1981-82	Milwaukee.	80	149	.519	64	.520	387	84	362	4.5
1982-83	Milwaukee.	80	272	.529	130	.537	568	111	674	8.4
1983-84	Milwaukee.	82	256	.500	114	.626	603	110	626	7.6
1984-85	Milwaukee.	81	322	.538	154	.588	647	127	798	9.9
1985-86	Milwaukee.	81	318	.551	160	.602	592	101	796	9.8
1986-87	Seattle	75	346	.504	179	.675	705	110	871	11.6
1987-88	Seattle	82	173	.504	114	.606	627	58	461	5.6
1988-89	Seattle	82	271	.499	115	.646	545	54	657	8.0
1989-90	Golden State	3	4	.500	4	.571	8	2	12	4.0
1990-91	Golden State	77	188	.478	115	.569	483	93	491	6.4
1991-92	Golden State	26	44	.557	14	.424	92	14	102	3.9
1992-93	Golden State	20	19	.452	7	.538	44	5	45	2.3
1994-95	Milwaukee.	60	66	.493	35	.500	236	12	167	2.8
1995-96	Mil.-Bos.	64	51	.486	41	.641	280	19	143	2.2
	Totals	893	2479	.514	1246	.595	5817	900	6205	6.9

FRANK BRICKOWSKI 37 6-9 248   Forward-Center

Boo! There's Dennis Rodman! . . . Just kidding . . . Their battles became one of the sub-plots of the Finals last spring . . . Rodman was doing a lot of flopping, but why was a veteran like Brick getting caught up in the antics? . . . Ejected twice in a three-game span, hurting a bench already weakened by Nate McMillan's injury . . . Gotta like the way he always competes, even while giving away size at center . . . Released by Sonics, he signed with Celtics last summer . . . Third-round pick, No. 57 overall, by Knicks in '81, but played in Italy, France and Israel before joining NBA with Sonics . . . Bounced around, then returned Sept. 18, 1995, when Byron Houston and Sarunas Marciulionis were sent to Sacramento . . . Born Aug. 14, 1959, in Bayville, N.Y. . . . Made $3.25 million.

Year	Team	G	FG	FG Pct.	FT	FT Pct.	Reb.	Ast.	TP	Avg.
1984-85	Seattle	78	150	.492	85	.669	260	100	385	4.9
1985-86	Seattle	40	30	.517	18	.667	54	21	78	2.0
1986-87	LAL-S.A	44	63	.508	50	.714	116	17	176	4.0
1987-88	San Antonio	70	425	.528	268	.768	483	266	1119	16.0
1988-89	San Antonio	64	337	.515	201	.715	406	131	875	13.7
1989-90	San Antonio	78	211	.545	95	.674	327	105	517	6.6
1990-91	Milwaukee	75	372	.527	198	.798	426	131	942	12.6
1991-92	Milwaukee	65	306	.524	125	.767	344	122	740	11.4
1992-93	Milwaukee	66	456	.545	195	.728	405	196	1115	16.9
1993-94	Mil.-Char.	71	368	.488	195	.768	404	222	935	13.2
1994-95	Sacramento					Injured				
1995-96	Seattle	63	123	.488	61	.709	151	58	339	5.4
	Totals	714	2841	.520	1491	.740	3376	1369	7221	10.1

THE ROOKIES

ANTOINE WALKER 20 6-8 224   Forward
The Celtics traded up to No. 6 to get him. And still held their breath for a few picks . . . Left Kentucky after his sophomore NCAA title season . . . Can play either forward spot and probably guard some twos . . . Needs to polish the jumper. And add upper bulk . . . Some called him one of, if not the, most versatile players in draft . . . Extremely gifted, just needs experience . . . He'll make $1.35 million . . . Born Aug. 12, 1976, in Chicago.

STEVE HAMER 22 7-0 245   Center
Huge hole in Boston's middle with departure of Eric Montross . . . Sound offensive game, was Tennessee's first captain since 1979 . . . Steadily improved numbers through four-year career . . . Could be a better shot-blocker for his size . . . Was Celts' second-round pick, the 38th player chosen . . . Born Nov. 13, 1973, in Memphis, Tenn.

COACH M.L. CARR: Why not just suit up? . . . Acts like he's still playing on the sidelines . . . Talks trash with opposing players . . . Shall we say questionable tactics at times? . . . As one Boston scribe put it, "He's unencumbered by a clue." . . . Favors up-tempo offense, pressure defense and signing just about everybody to contracts . . . He's also Executive VP and Director of Basketball Operations. Got that title June 14, 1994 . . . Hired himself as 12th coach in team history June 20, 1995 . . . Brought in Dominique Wilkins, Dana Barros, Pervis Ellison, David Wesley, Greg Minor, Thomas Hamilton, etc., etc. . . . In first preseason game, used 13 players in initial 9:08 . . . Six-year scout with Celtics until 1991 . . . Director of community relations for three years before moving to the VP job . . . Former 6-6, 205-pound player. Did six years with Celtics as hard-working, defensive-minded forward . . . Got a pair of title rings in 1981 and 1984 . . . Towel-waver on the bench as a player. Incited, fired up home crowds . . . Still waves towels as a coach . . . Any firing-up he does has been quickly snuffed by play of guys on the court . . . Averaged 9.7 points over nine-year career that began with Detroit in 1976 . . . Signed with Celtics as free agent July 24, 1979 . . . Pistons got Bob McAdoo as compensation. But Detroit sent Celtics two first-round picks which were instrumental in the Robert Parish-Kevin McHale heist of Golden State . . . Came out of Guilford College (N.C.) in 1973 and was a third-round pick of Kentucky in ABA draft, a fifth-rounder of K.C./Omaha in NBA draft . . . Played in Eastern Basketball Association and Israel and did one ABA season with St. Louis before NBA move . . . Initials stand for Michael Leon . . . Born Jan. 9, 1951, in Walleye, N.C.

BIGGEST BLUNDER

There haven't been too many mistakes over the years in Boston. You don't win 16 championships, eight of them in succession, by goofing up all the time. Oh, there have been some recent personnel decisions that cause double-takes, but over the course of history the Celtics usually did the right thing.

But even the Celtics in their glory years proved nobody's perfect. Back in 1963, the Celtics were all pumped up over a potential draft pick, a big, strong forward from Colorado State named Bill Green. Yep, he would be the choice for the Celtics who, given their perennial success, selected last on the first round.

What the Celtics didn't know about Green was his fear of flying. No how, no way, would he get on an airplane. He never played an NBA game. Now, drafting Green was a mistake in itself, but the bigger crime was taking him and bypassing another forward out of Idaho. While Bill Green slipped away to trivia questions and obscurity, Gus Johnson went on to a Hall of Fame career with the Bullets.

ALL-TIME CELTIC LEADERS

SEASON

Points: John Havlicek, 2,338, 1970–71
Assists: Bob Cousy, 715, 1959–60
Rebounds: Bill Russell, 1,930, 1963–64

GAME

Points: Larry Bird, 60 vs. Atlanta, 3/12/85
Assists: Bob Cousy, 28 vs. Minneapolis, 2/27/59
Rebounds: Bill Russell, 51 vs. Syracuse, 2/5/60

CAREER

Points: John Havlicek, 26,395, 1962–78
Assists: Bob Cousy, 6,945, 1950–63
Rebounds: Bill Russell, 21,620, 1956–69

MIAMI HEAT

TEAM DIRECTORY: Managing Gen. Partner: Mickey Arison; VP-Player Personnel Dir.: Kevin Loughery; Dir. College and International Scouting: Chris Wallace; VP-Communications: Mark Pray; Coach: Pat Riley; Asst. Coaches: Jeff Bzdelik, Tony Fiorentino, Bob McAdoo, Scotty Robertson, Stan Van Gundy. Arena: Miami Arena (15,200). Colors: Orange, red, yellow, black and white.

SCOUTING REPORT

SHOOTING: Everything was new and everything changed when the Heat acquired Juwan Howard as a seven-year, $98-million free agent. But he made a round trip back to Washington. They had the league's second-best field-goal percentage man in Chris Gatling. But he's gone. They had a trio of guards in Tim Hardaway, Rex Chapman (also gone) and Sasha Danilovic who could shoot out the lights of Miami Arena from Fort Lauderdale. So why were the Heat just 21st in shooting? Simple. Gatling, Hardaway and Danilovic weren't around all year, and even when they were, consistency was sometimes a rare commodity.

For much of the season, and particularly before a massive three-trade team overhaul on the trading deadline night, the Miami offense simply plodded along. Pat Riley finally saw enough when back-to-back games produced the combined total of 136 points. He was on the phone the next day, probably at halftime, seeking help. In the end he didn't get it from Howard—or the NBA cap accountants—but the free-spending Riley did add P.J. Brown from the Nets and Dan Majerle from the Cavaliers. Majerle keeps firing as a three-point shooter (down to .353 last year).

PLAYMAKING: This is not a Miami strong point, despite the presence of Hardaway, who averaged double-figure assists once he put on a Heat uniform. The Heat needs more penetration this season and the thought is to rev up the offense, open up the court and create more opportunities. Hardaway probably was given more freedom than any point guard not named Magic to play under Riley. Still, despite the freedom, despite the double-digit assists from Hardaway, the Heat ranked a woeful 23rd in the league in assists. And the Heat's assist-to-turnover ratio placed them fourth from the bottom in the league, landing them amid NBA wretches Philadelphia, the Los Angeles Clippers and expansionist Toronto and Vancouver.

Alonzo proved a Mourning glory for the Heat.

REBOUNDING: One of the tenets Riley always has lived by is rebounds equal rings. So you know his teams are going to get after it on the boards. And, although undersized at the four and five spots last season, the Heat got after it. The 6-9 Brown will help here. In Alonzo Mourning, the centerpiece of the franchise's future, the Heat boast a ferocious performer off the glass. So what if he's 6-10? He gets after it. So, too, does last season's pleasant rookie surprise, the intense Kurt Thomas. Riley usually demands that everybody gets in the act, but the backcourt didn't always wow 'em off the glass. But they will. They'll have to.

HEAT ROSTER

No.	Veterans	Pos.	Ht.	Wt.	Age	Yrs. Pro	College
2	Keith Askins	F	6-8	224	28	6	Alabama
42	P.J. Brown	F	6-11	240	27	3	Louisiana Tech
5	Predrag Danilovic	G	6-6	200	26	1	Serbia
10	Tim Hardaway	G	6-0	195	30	7	Texas-El Paso
F-22	Voshon Lenard	G	6-4	205	23	1	Minnesota
9	Dan Majerle	G-F	6-10	234	30	8	Memphis State
33	Alonzo Mourning	C	6-10	261	26	4	Georgetown
40	Kurt Thomas	F	6-9	230	24	1	Texas Christian

F-Free agent

Rd.	Rookie	Sel.No.	Pos.	Ht.	Wt.	College
1	Martin Muursepp	25	F	6-9	235	Estonia

DEFENSE: This is a Pat Riley team, right? So naturally, this is a defensive team. Before Riley had even unpacked, he sought defensive commitment from his players. And they gave it as they went on to lead the league in defensive field goal percentage. Not bad for a team that in years past would have had trouble keeping Princeton from rolling it up. The Riley way is relatively simple: defend man-to-man and defend until you drop. Use whatever the law allows—and if it's a big game, what the law doesn't—but get bodies on people, tire them out, wear them down and make sure you're standing at the end with the opponent on the south side of 92 points. There are few double-teams, fewer gimmicks. Just hard-nose play resulting from long, tough practice hours. How good could the Heat defensive frontcourt be? Consider that with Howard, Thomas and Brown at forwards, Mourning may actually be their worst defender upfront. And he'd be the best on most teams.

OUTLOOK: The Heat are not the superpower they would have been with Howard. Depth will be a problem. Going six, seven deep, the Heat are there with any team that doesn't have Michael

Tim Hardaway found new life in the Florida palms.

Jordan. Beyond that . . . hey, some guys have to make the minimum. It's only going to get better. Riley will see to that. When the offense sloughed last season, he went out and transformed the team with a series of trading-deadline deals and tried to continue with the transformation with free-agent signings.

Riley believes in one thing: winning. He brought in Mourning, he brought in Hardaway, he brought in Brown and he brought in Majerle. He lost Gatling, he gave up on Walt Williams and Chapman but he kept Mourning and Hardaway. The Heat are decidely on the rise and will build their hopes around Mourning. This season, they could and should challenge for first place in the Atlantic Division.

HEAT PROFILES

ALONZO MOURNING 26 6-10 261   Center

Pat Riley got his guy . . . The No. 2 pick in the draft out of Georgetown by Charlotte in 1992 came to the Heat Nov. 3, 1995, with Pete Myers and LeRon Ellis for Glen Rice, Matt Geiger, Khalid Reeves and a first-rounder . . . Agreed to trade after late night/early morning phone chat with Riley . . . Made immediate impact and his snarling court presence was a hit in Riley's system . . . But had nasty playoff fizzle in three-game sweep by Bulls . . . Established Heat franchise record for blocked shots in one season (189) . . . Led team in scoring, rebounds, blocks and minutes . . . Also exploded for single-game career-high 50-point game vs. Bullets, March 29. That was second-best game in Heat history . . . Provided critical low-post element in Riley's inside-oriented game . . . Used more in low post than on perimeter, as in days with Charlotte . . . Big-time trouble with turnovers, though: set franchise per-game record (3.7). And he ain't no point guard . . . Still expected to be anchor of franchise through end of decade . . . Born Feb. 8, 1970, in Chesapeake, Va. . . . Was first player named Player of the Year, Defensive Player of the Year and tournament MVP in the same season in Big East (1991-92) . . . Scraped out a living on 4.56 million last season and will have to manage with new seven-year, $105-million pact agreed to in July.

Year	Team	G	FG	FG Pct.	FT	FT Pct.	Reb.	Ast.	TP	Avg.
1992-93	Charlotte.	78	572	.511	495	.781	805	76	1639	21.0
1993-94	Charlotte.	60	427	.505	433	.762	610	86	1287	21.5
1994-95	Charlotte.	77	571	.519	490	.761	761	111	1643	21.3
1995-96	Miami	70	563	.523	488	.685	727	159	1623	23.2
	Totals	285	2133	.515	1906	.745	2903	432	6192	21.7

TIM HARDAWAY 30 6-0 195   Guard

Yo, Tim was like part of the midseason Miami makeover, ya know? . . . Game was reborn after he arrived from Golden State with Chris Gatling for Billy Owens and Kevin Gamble, Feb. 22, 1996 . . . Averaged double figures in assists (10.0) after acquisition . . . Still showed tendency to hold ball too long and seek his own shot first . . . But he upgraded Heat of-

fense and improved team scoring . . . Remember, this was an outfit that scored 70 and 66 points in the two games before the trade
. . . Was reliable on three-pointers over second half of season . . .
Still effective with cross-over dribble, although quickness not
what it once was . . . How could it be? Suffered torn anterior cru-
ciate ligament in October 1993. Missed entire 1993-94 season . . .
Set Heat franchise record with 19 assists at Milwaukee April 19
. . . Entered offseason as free agent and re-signed multi-year deal
estimated at $98 million last summer . . . Renewed defensive com-
mitment under Pat Riley, especially with steals. Averaged more
than two a game with Heat . . . Scored 26 points in first half of
team's first playoff game against Bulls . . . Career-high 22 assists
Dec. 16, 1994, against Magic as a Warrior . . . Golden State stole
him at No. 14 in 1989 out of Texas-El Paso, where he remains
school's all-time scoring leader . . . All-Rookie team . . . Three-
time All-Star . . . Torn wrist ligaments ended his 1994-95 season
early . . . Born Sept. 1, 1966, in Chicago . . . Made $3.728 million.

Year	Team	G	FG	FG Pct.	FT	FT Pct.	Reb.	Ast.	TP	Avg.
1989-90	Golden State	79	464	.471	211	.764	310	689	1162	14.7
1990-91	Golden State	82	739	.476	306	.803	332	793	1881	22.9
1991-92	Golden State	81	734	.461	298	.766	310	807	1893	23.4
1992-93	Golden State	66	522	.447	273	.744	263	699	1419	21.5
1993-94	Golden State					Injured				
1994-95	Golden State	62	430	.427	219	.760	190	578	1247	20.1
1994-95	G.S.-Mia.	80	419	.422	241	.790	229	640	1217	15.2
	Totals	450	3308	.453	1548	.772	1634	4206	8819	19.6

P.J. BROWN 27 6-11 240   Forward

''Collier'' (real name) swears the P.J. doesn't
stand for anything . . . But, as a Nets free agent,
he stood up for a reported seven-year, $36-
million contract with the Heat . . . Lots of
teams in the league like this hard-working, de-
fense-minded guy . . . What's not to like, besides his still-improving shot? . . . Nets always
used him to double-team; consequently by end
of year he'd been run ragged . . . Good one-on-one defender,
strong rebounder who at times can be terrific rebounder . . . He'll
disappear once a month, though . . . Led the team in minutes . . .
Decent shot-blocker . . . Showed strong gains at start of season,
but shooting slipped in second half . . . Plays three and four. Must
improve .444 shooting to be recognized as legit three . . . Wife,
Dee, is former captain of Louisiana Tech women's team. They

analyze game nightly . . . Was sleeper at No. 29 on second round out of Louisiana Tech in '92 by Nets, who sought defensive small forward . . . Knew he wasn't ready for NBA and did Greece for a year . . . Born Oct. 14, 1969, in Detroit but was Louisiana-reared . . . Made $960,000.

Year	Team	G	FG	FG Pct.	FT	FT Pct.	Reb.	Ast.	TP	Avg.
1993-94	New Jersey	79	167	.415	115	.757	493	93	450	5.7
1994-95	New Jersey	80	254	.446	139	.671	487	135	651	8.1
1995-96	New Jersey	81	354	.444	204	.770	560	165	915	11.3
	Totals	240	775	.438	458	.734	1540	393	2016	8.4

DAN MAJERLE 31 6-6 220   Guard-Forward

Cavalier free agent signed three-year Heat deal reportedly worth $8 million . . . This followed a tale of two seasons in one . . . In first 31 games, he played like he didn't want to be in Cleveland (8.0 points, .364 shooting) . . . Made mental adjustment and averaged 12.3 points and .424 shooting the rest of the year . . . Somehow managed to keep a deep tan through a winter in Cleveland . . . Set a club record for three-pointers attempted (414) . . . Hasn't shot better than .425 from field in three seasons . . . Started 15 games . . . Drafted 14th out of Central Michigan by Phoenix in 1988, he made three All-Star appearances with Suns . . . Still a rugged defender . . . Shipped to Cavs with Antonio Lang and a first-round pick (in '97 or '98) for John Williams prior to last season . . . Earned $3.1 million in last year of contract . . . Born Sept. 9, 1965, in Traverse City, Mich.

Year	Team	G	FG	FG Pct.	FT	FT Pct.	Reb.	Ast.	TP	Avg.
1988-89	Phoenix	54	181	.419	78	.614	209	130	467	8.6
1989-90	Phoenix	73	296	.424	198	.762	430	188	809	11.1
1990-91	Phoenix	77	397	.484	227	.762	418	216	1051	13.6
1991-92	Phoenix	82	551	.478	229	.756	483	274	1418	17.3
1992-93	Phoenix	82	509	.464	203	.778	383	311	1388	16.9
1993-94	Phoenix	80	476	.418	176	.739	349	275	1320	16.5
1994-95	Phoenix	82	438	.425	206	.730	375	340	1281	15.6
1995-96	Cleveland	82	303	.405	120	.710	305	214	872	10.6
	Totals	612	3151	.443	1437	.741	2952	1948	8606	14.1

KEITH ASKINS 28 6-8 224   Forward

Born to play for Pat Riley . . . Outstanding defensive player who can hit a three as well as hit an opponent . . . Physical, often brutal (some say thug-like) off bench . . . Riley rated him as one of league's premier defenders . . . Decent rebounder who showed continued potential with three-point shot . . . But he struggled for months with long distance . . . Gets most of his time at small forward, but has drawn shooting guards and occasionally power forwards . . . Perfect seventh or eighth man in Riley rotations . . . Driven, dedicated type who also makes an impact in locker room . . . As per team policy, did little in playoffs vs. Bulls . . . Undrafted out of Alabama in 1990. Signed by Heat as free agent Sept. 7, 1990 . . . Born Dec. 15, 1967, in Athens, Ala. . . . A $550,000 bargain.

Year	Team	G	FG	FG Pct.	FT	FT Pct.	Reb.	Ast.	TP	Avg.
1990-91	Miami	39	34	.420	12	.480	68	19	86	2.2
1991-92	Miami	59	84	.410	26	.703	142	38	219	3.7
1992-93	Miami	69	88	.413	29	.725	198	31	227	3.3
1993-94	Miami	37	36	.409	9	.900	82	13	85	2.3
1994-95	Miami	50	81	.391	46	.807	198	39	229	4.6
1995-96	Miami	75	157	.402	45	.789	324	121	458	6.1
	Totals	329	480	.405	167	.739	1012	261	1304	4.0

PREDRAG DANILOVIC 26 6-6 200   Guard

Don't confuse him with the Southampton Danilovics . . . The 1994-95 European Player of the Year quickly earned a starting berth with Heat but then underwent surgery for a wrist injury that kept him out until final game of the regular season . . . Missed 62 games as a result . . . Suspended one game for altercation with Cavs' Chris Mills . . . Scored 30 points vs. Suns Dec. 9 when he nailed six three-pointers . . . Member of Yugoslavian National Team in last summer's Olympics . . . Showed outstanding range and can score off dribble . . . Figures to begin season as starter . . . Does play defense, unlike many Euro-stars. Doesn't necessarily play it well . . . Like most on Heat, benefited from Alonzo Mourning's shot-blocking presence . . . Second-round pick, No. 43, by Golden State in 1992 . . . Came to Heat Nov. 2,

1994, with Billy Owens for Rony Seikaly . . . Heat signed him June 15, 1995 . . . Made $1.455 million . . . Led Yugoslavia to European Championship in '95 . . . Led Buckler Bologna to three straight Italian League titles . . . A native of Serbia. Born Feb. 26, 1970, in Sarajevo.

Year	Team	G	FG	FG Pct.	FT	FT Pct.	Reb.	Ast.	TP	Avg.
1995-96	Miami	19	83	.451	55	.764	46	47	255	13.4

VOSHON LENARD 23 6-4 205   Guard

He was a rookie under Pat Riley. Guess what? Didn't lead the team in minutes . . . A CBA pickup, signed by Heat as a minimum-wage free agent Dec. 29 . . . He was CBA's leading scorer at the time (30.1 ppg) . . . Considered to have the best true outside shot of anyone on Heat's season-ending roster. Still, he didn't make playoff roster . . . Offensive spark off bench . . . Scored 19 points in the Feb. 23 shocker over Bulls in Miami . . . Doesn't go to the basket nearly enough . . . Despite limited minutes, Heat held interest as he hit free-agent market . . . Drafted on second round by Bucks in 1994, but elected to return to Minnesota for senior season . . . Finished as Minnesota's all-time leader scorer, No. 16 all-time in the Big 10 . . . Cut by Bucks in '95 training camp . . . High-school teammate of Jalen Rose . . . Born May 14, 1973, in Detroit.

Year	Team	G	FG	FG Pct.	FT	FT Pct.	Reb.	Ast.	TP	Avg.
1995-96	Miami	30	53	.376	34	.791	52	31	176	5.9

KURT THOMAS 24 6-9 230   Forward

See? Heat sometimes hold on to guys they draft . . . At season's end, he was only member of roster who was drafted by Miami . . . First-rounder (No. 10) out of Texas Christian averaged more minutes than any first-round Pat Riley pick except James Worthy. That put him ahead of the likes of Byron Scott, A.C. Green, Vlade Divac and Greg Anthony . . . Heat loved his physical, no-backdown style . . . Started season buried on the bench—rookie under Riley, don't forget—but slew of injuries forced his use. No regrets . . . Showed deft touch with low-post moves but tends to shoot more fadeaways than expected from power player . . . Although an undersized inside presence, he succeeded in getting to the boards and averaged 5.9 rebounds . . . Struggled against bigger power forwards, such as Horace Grant and Charles Oakley. And who doesn't? . . . Also struggled against Bulls in the playoffs. They had this guy named Rodman . . . Could remain starting power forward, but apt to see some time at the three . . . Led NCAA Division 1-A in both scoring (28.9) and rebounding (14.6) as a senior, becoming only the third person ever to do so. The late Hank Gathers at Loyola Marymount and Xavier McDaniel at Wichita State were the others . . . Born Oct. 4, 1972, in Dallas . . . Made $1.071 million.

Year	Team	G	FG	FG Pct.	FT	FT Pct.	Reb.	Ast.	TP	Avg.
1995-96	Miami	74	274	.501	118	.663	439	46	666	9.0

THE ROOKIE

MARTIN MUURSEPP 22 6-9 235   **Forward**
Estonian was such an unexpected first-rounder, the NBA did not have a name banner ready to put on board . . . Drafted No. 25 by Utah and promptly traded to Heat for a future first-rounder . . . Played for BC Kalev Tallinn in Estonia after playing for Maccabi Ramat Gan in Israel . . . Also played in Sweden . . . Averaged 18.5 points and 5.0 rebounds in European Cup play . . . Born Sept. 26, 1974 . . . He'll make $489,200 this season.

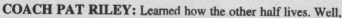

COACH PAT RILEY: Learned how the other half lives. Well, maybe not the other half, but another fifth . . . Kept streak alive for making playoffs as an NBA head coach but his team was eliminated in first round for first time . . . Again, he showed why he is usually the measuring stick for judging coaches. In his first season in south Florida, he directed Heat to 42 victories, tying franchise all-time high . . . And that was probably with the least-talented roster he ever coached . . . Showed commitment to defense early and team latched on. Heat led league in field-goal percentage defense . . . Offense struggled all year. As troubles grew, he gave more free rein to players. Claimed Tim Hardaway had more freedom than any point guard he ever coached . . . Made move to front office with splash, too. Engineered Feb. 22 makeover of team that brought in Tim Hardaway, Chris Gatling and Walt Williams . . . Determined to reverse franchise fortunes . . . Coached four world championship Laker teams (1982, '85, '87, and '88); two-time Coach of the Year . . . Holds record for most playoff games coached (215) and won (137) . . . Needs two victories for 800 in coaching career. Staggering lifetime mark of 798-339 (.702) . . . Made ugly move from Knicks to Miami. Knicks charged tampering. Eventually Heat forked over $1 million and a first-round draft choice. Gave Riley a five-year deal worth $15 million in salary, part ownership. In all, deal was worth estimated $40 million for 10 years . . . Took over Lakers from Paul Westhead 11 games into 1981-82 season . . . Won every division title in his nine Laker seasons . . . After one year on NBC, went back to coaching and directed Knicks for four seasons. Got them to the '94 Finals but lost to Houston in seven games . . . Played nine years after being No. 7 pick by San Diego Rockets in 1967 . . . Helped lead Kentucky to 1967 NCAA title game . . . Drafted by Dallas Cowboys . . . Member of the 1971-72 champion Laker team that won 33 straight games . . . Authored two books, *Showtime* and *The Winner Within* . . . Born March 20, 1945, in Rome, N.Y.

BIGGEST BLUNDER

Blunder? Hardly. More a blooper.

Last summer Pat Riley made an offer Juwan Howard couldn't refuse: $100.8 million over seven years. The Bullet free agent took it.

But that was only the beginning. The NBA said no. It charged the Heat with being over the salary cap. Heated negotiations followed. But to no avail for the Heat. Despite Riley's protestations, the deal was off.

Howard, on the thrust of his third season in the NBA, wound up returning to Washington for $105 million over seven years.

Indeed it was a blooper.

P.J. Brown represents Net loss, Heat gain.

ALL-TIME HEAT LEADERS

SEASON

Points: Glen Rice, 1,831, 1994–95
Assists: Sherman Douglas, 624, 1990–91
Rebounds: Rony Seikaly, 934, 1991–92

GAME

Points: Glen Rice, 56 vs. Orlando, 4/15/95
Assists: Sherman Douglas, 17 vs. Atlanta, 2/26/90
Rebounds: Rony Seikaly, 34 vs. Washington, 3/3/93

CAREER

Points: Glen Rice, 9,248, 1989–95
Assists: Sherman Douglas, 1,243, 1988–91
Rebounds: Rony Seikaly, 4,544, 1988–94

NEW JERSEY NETS

TEAM DIRECTORY: Chairman: Henry Taub; Vice Chairman: David Gerstein; Treasurer: Alan Aufzien; Secretary: Jerry Cohen; Pres./COO: Michael Rowe; Exec. VP-Basketball/Head Coach: John Calipari; GM: John Nash; Dir. Pub. Rel.: John Mertz; Asst. Coaches: Don Casey, Ed Schilling. Arena: Continental Airlines Arena (20,039). Colors: Red, white and blue.

Villanova's Kerry Kittles was No. 7 in the draft.

SCOUTING REPORT

SHOOTING: If ever a team deserved to be shot for its shooting, this was it. Even if the NBA awarded points merely for hitting the backboard, the Nets still couldn't shoot 50 percent. New coach/director of basketball operation John Calipari says he doesn't want to hear about how bad the Net shooting is. Well, you can't help but hear all the bricks clanging off the rim or zipping through the air. The Nets were the second-worst shooting team in the league and posted the second-worst mark in the NBA history of the franchise. And you know there have been some beauts contained in that group. And the already-bad shooting took another hit when Chris Childs, perhaps their best "clutch" shooter, bolted out the free-agent door. The hope—the prayer?— is that David Benoit, an escapee as a free-agent point guard from Utah; first-round pick Kerry Kittles of Villanova and a healthy Kendall Gill will alleviate much of the shooting indigestion.

PLAYMAKING: Offseason free agency held the key. And the key snapped in the lock when Childs rejected the Nets' offer and fled across the Hudson River to the six-year, $24 million deal with the Knicks. Childs, who had assumed the starter's mantle after Kenny Anderson was shipped out to Charlotte, is an above-average playmaker, sometimes iffy in his decisions. But the Nets rebounded nicely by signing free-agent Robert Pack, late of Washington. Pack, who averaged 7.8 assists in 31 games before a leg injury struck, is more explosive than Childs, is quicker than Childs and is stronger than Childs. Unfortunately, he's also more turnover-prone. He can penetrate and dish. But will be asked to do a lot of scoring. So now the Nets are looking at a slew of two guards who they claim can back up the point: Gill, Kittles and Khalid Reeves. Yes, all of them have played the point at one time or another. But all of them also have doodled on envelopes at one time or another. That doesn't make them artists.

REBOUNDING: Here's a Net strength. Or at least, WAS. Of course, with their atrocious shooting, there are always plenty of rebounds to be had. The Nets have size upfront with 7-6 Shawn Bradley, and 6-10 Jayson Williams. But free agency took a ghastly toll: 6-11 stud P.J. Brown, a six-a-night guy, bolted. And the Nets renounced 6-9 Armon Gilliam, who was good for eight

NET ROSTER

No. Veterans	Pos.	Ht.	Wt.	Age	Yrs. Pro	College
22 Vincent Askew	G-F	6-6	235	30	8	Memphis
-- David Benoit	F	6-8	220	28	5	Alabama
45 Shawn Bradley	C	7-6	248	24	3	Brigham Young
33 Yinka Dare	C	7-0	265	24	2	George Washington
21 Kevin Edwards	G	6-3	210	31	8	DePaul
13 Kendall Gill	G	6-5	200	28	6	Illinois
— Robert Pack	G	6-2	190	27	5	USC
13 Ed O'Bannon	F	6-8	220	24	1	UCLA
6 Khalid Reeves	G	6-3	201	24	2	Arizona
55 Jayson Williams	F	6-10	250	28	5	St. John's

Rd. Rookie	Sel.No.	Pos.	Ht.	Wt.	College
1 Kerry Kittles	8	G	6-5	179	Villanova

a game. Williams has an uncanny knack for the ball—he averaged 10 boards in less than 24 minutes last season. Of course, his intent on grabbing every rebound often leaves him torched in defensive transition. But hey, he's trying. And whether the Nets shoot like early rigor-mortis victims again or not, they figure to be among the better boarding teams. Not only do they have it upfront, but they get some in the backcourt. Gill is among the league's best rebounding two guards, especially on the offensive glass.

DEFENSE: Perhaps the saddest part of the Nets' ridiculously inept offensive performance in 1995-96 was that it wasted an otherwise creditable defensive performance. Sadder still is what looms ahead. The Nets were right around the top 10 in points and field goal percentage yielded most of the season. They lost one dead spot in Gilliam. But they also lost two of their leading defenders when Childs and Brown walked out on them. They did make a terrific defensive pickup, getting Vincent Askew from the Sonics in exchange for little-used Greg Graham. Calipari prides himself on his team's defensive performances and he is inheriting a team that already has established itself on the defensive end. Now, one thing the Nets can and should do a lot more of is press. They certainly can afford to with Bradley anchoring the backline to erase any mistakes with his shot-blocking prowess.

Shawn Bradley's blocks per game were No. 2 in NBA.

OUTLOOK: At the start of the free-agency season, things were actually looking up for the Nets. A new coach, a new GM, a nice draft choice in Kittles and a nice nucleus to build around. Then it all changed in a matter of four days when Childs and Brown left and Gilliam was renounced. Once again, the franchise is in familiar waters: desperate ones. Actually, things were looking up even before Pack and Benoit signed, but only on a long-term scale. This season could be horribly grim, even by Net standards. If Calipari can coach and motivate the way he has infused life into the franchise and the faithful populace, then maybe the Nets have a shot at a spot in the playoffs. In two or three years, give them a repeat of last year's defensive effort, toss in some scoring and bingo! You'd have a team that's not bad. Pack, Benoit and Askew will help. But there's just not enough all around for the Nets to realistically be regarded as contenders to escape another lottery pick.

NET PROFILES

SHAWN BRADLEY 24 7-6 248   Center

Can a 7-6 kid from Utah really find happiness in New Jersey? Tune in this year to find out ... Net fans welcomed him with open arms after Nov. 30, 1995, trade with Sixers because, as one observer put it, "He ain't Derrick" ... That would be Derrick Coleman, who wore out his welcome in New Jersey and was sent to Philly along with Sean Higgins and Rex Walters for Bradley, Tim Perry and Greg Graham ... Nets immediately began undoing whatever was done in Philly. Concentrated on Bradley gaining strength, not weight. Paid off ... The manchild with one year of college experience averaged 12.5 points, 7.9 rebounds and 3.73 blocks as a Net ... His 3.65 overall bpg were second in the NBA, behind only Dikembe Mutombo ... Became the first player in NBA history to block 10 or more shots in back-to-back games twice in the same season ... Recorded his first-ever triple-double March 4 vs. Bullets ... Good athlete, runs floor well ... Confidence soared with positive receptions in Jersey. In Philly, he was ripped daily by media and fans ... Did mission for Mormon Church for two years after freshman year at Brigham Young ... Was No. 2 pick by Sixers in '93, between Chris Webber and Penny Hardaway. Signed six-year, $44.2-million deal ... Father was 6-8, mother 6-0 ... Born March 22, 1972, in Landstuhl, Germany, grew up in Castle Dale, Utah.

Year	Team	G	FG	FG Pct.	FT	FT Pct.	Reb.	Ast.	TP	Avg.
1993-94	Philadelphia......	49	201	.409	102	.607	306	98	504	10.3
1994-95	Philadelphia......	82	315	.455	148	.638	659	53	778	9.5
1995-96	Phil.-N.J.	79	387	.443	169	.687	638	63	944	11.9
	Totals	210	903	.439	419	.649	1603	214	2226	10.6

KENDALL GILL 28 6-5 200   Guard

Here was the go-to scorer the Nets longed for. And he showed capabilities of fitting that role until he fractured his left hand guarding Reggie Miller Feb. 14 ... Was part of Nets' second blockbuster trade of season, going from Hornets with Khalid Reeves for Kenny Anderson and Gerald Glass on Jan. 19 ... Burned former Hornet mates for 30 points exactly one week after trade ... Has perimeter range, career 32 percent on three-pointers ... Hey, with Nets that makes him Hall of Fame caliber ... Very talented guy who has picked up bad raps along the way. But tried, really tried, to fit in with Nets and with Hornets on second go-round ... Good size and defensive skills at the two ... Started season as Charlotte's point guard. Could handle position in a pinch ... Exceptionally strong offensive rebounder at his position ... Was the No. 5 pick out of Illinois by Charlotte in 1990 ... Hornets sent him to Seattle for Eddie Johnson, Dana Barros and draft options, Sept. 1, 1993, and then re-acquired him for Hersey Hawkins and David Wingate, June 27, 1995 ... Born May 25, 1968 in Chicago ... All-Rookie team in 1991 ... Made $3.2 million.

Year	Team	G	FG	FG Pct.	FT	FT Pct.	Reb.	Ast.	TP	Avg.
1990-91	Charlotte	82	376	.450	152	.835	263	303	906	11.0
1991-92	Charlotte	79	666	.467	284	.745	402	329	1622	20.5
1992-93	Charlotte	69	463	.449	224	.772	340	268	1167	16.9
1993-94	Seattle	79	429	.443	215	.782	268	275	1111	14.1
1994-95	Seattle	73	392	.457	155	.742	290	192	1002	13.7
1995-96	Char.-N.J.	47	246	.469	138	.784	232	260	656	14.0
	Totals	429	2572	.456	1168	.772	1795	1627	6464	15.1

JAYSON WILLIAMS 28 6-10 250   Forward

A usable quote waiting to happen ... All-Interview team selection. And not a bad rebounder ... Was 10th in the NBA with 10.0 boards a game ... Fanatic off the offensive glass ... In the first two games he started, took 24 and career-high 25 rebounds ... Only averaged 23.2 minutes, too ... Game matured. So did he ... Still the clubhouse free spirit but worked hard and got himself in shape, which was the knock when he played for Chuck Daly ... Offense coming, but it's not there yet ... Can get burned in defensive transition because he goes after EVERY rebound ... Made $2 million after signing three-year, $7-million deal in preseason ... Came to Nets from Philadelphia for future first-rounder, Oct. 8, 1992 ... That trade had clause which limited his time. Free of that restraint last season, he blossomed ... Started just six games and placed third in Sixth Man Award voting ... Averaged an offensive rebound every 5.43 minutes ... Was the 21st pick, by Phoenix, in 1991 after playing at St. John's ... Didn't want to be so far from home—he grew up in lower Manhattan and went to high school at Christ the King in Queens . . . Born Feb. 22,1968, in Ritter, S.C.

Year	Team	G	FG	FG Pct.	FT	FT Pct.	Reb.	Ast.	TP	Avg.
1990-91	Philadelphia......	52	72	.447	37	.661	111	16	182	3.5
1991-92	Philadelphia......	50	75	.364	56	.636	145	12	206	4.1
1992-93	New Jersey......	12	21	.457	7	.389	41	0	49	4.1
1993-94	New Jersey......	70	125	.427	72	.605	263	26	322	4.6
1994-95	New Jersey......	75	149	.461	65	.533	425	35	363	4.8
1995-96	New Jersey......	80	279	.423	161	.592	803	47	721	9.0
	Totals	339	721	.427	398	.590	1788	136	1843	5.4

VINCENT ASKEW 30 6-6 235   Guard-Forward

Sent from Sonics to Nets in offseason trade for Greg Graham . . . Hard-nosed defender and plays two positions . . . Set a career best with 1,725 minutes last season despite spending nine games on injured list . . . So much for journeyman label . . . In addition to three previous NBA stops, he also played in the CBA and Italy . . . All it took for Seattle to get him from Sacramento on Nov. 25, 1992, was a second-round pick . . . Played for George Karl with Albany Patroons . . . Back-to-back league MVP there . . . Born Feb. 28, 1966, in Memphis, Tenn., and played for Memphis State . . . The 76ers drafted him 39th overall in 1987 . . . Made $1.81 million.

Year	Team	G	FG	FG Pct.	FT	FT Pct.	Reb.	Ast.	TP	Avg.
1987-88	Philadelphia......	14	22	.297	8	.727	22	33	52	3.7
1990-91	Golden State.....	7	12	.480	9	.818	11	13	33	4.7
1991-92	Golden State.....	80	193	.509	111	.694	233	188	498	6.2
1992-93	Sac.-Sea.	73	152	.492	105	.705	161	122	411	5.6
1993-94	Seattle	80	273	.481	175	.829	184	194	727	9.1
1994-95	Seattle	71	248	.492	176	.739	181	176	703	9.9
1995-96	Seattle	69	215	.493	125	.767	218	163	584	8.5
	Totals	394	1115	.486	709	.752	1010	889	3008	7.6

ED O'BANNON 24 6-8 220   Forward

Does the name "Kenny Walker" ring a bell? . . . Nets took a postup college player with athleticism and open-court skills. And promptly put him on the perimeter . . . Results were not pretty . . . Unless you find .390 shooting esthetically pleasing . . . Takes forever to get off his shot . . . But don't give up yet . . . Readily admitted he didn't work hard enough after his

College Player of the Year and NCAA championship run at UCLA...Broke his nose, separated his shoulder, sprained his hand. Welcome to the NBA...Can post-up smaller guards. But that's sort of tough to do 18 feet from the basket...Needs work on one-on-one defense, but does anticipate passes well...Very active around the glass...Went No. 9 on first round. Many feared his surgically-repaired knee, which was the least of his worries...Born Aug. 14, 1972, in Los Angeles...Teamed with brother Charles at UCLA...1995 NCAA Tourney MVP...Made $1.133 million.

Year	Team	G	FG	FG Pct.	FT	FT Pct.	Reb.	Ast.	TP	Avg.
1995-96	New Jersey	64	156	.390	77	.713	168	63	399	6.2

YINKA DARE 24 7-0 265   Center

Wouldn't you figure you'd get one assist by accident?...Actually, that almost happened for second-year guy who played just three minutes as a rookie, 626 in second season...Stat crew in Denver gave him unwarranted assist. Later changed...Over-under on that first assist: December, 2007...Sees the court well. Doesn't see the players...Has some defensive and rebounding skills but is still a long way from being a legit starter...Work ethic needs jumper cables...Nets made him No. 14 pick in '94 draft, despite advice of own scouts. Bypassed Wesley Person in the process...Left George Washington after two seasons despite advice of everybody...In two seasons he became GW's all-time blocks leader...Had shown promise. Was named Freshman of the Year and honorable mention All-American...Yep, good college player, bad pro...Was exposed in expansion draft...Still a massive project but has really made gains in his game. Of course, he started at ground zero...Born Oct. 10, 1972, in Kano, Nigeria...Made $1.184 million.

Year	Team	G	FG	FG Pct.	FT	FT Pct.	Reb.	Ast.	TP	Avg.
1994-95	New Jersey	1	0	.000	0	.000	1	0	0	0.0
1995-96	New Jersey	58	63	.438	38	.613	181	0	164	2.8
	Totals	59	63	.434	38	.613	182	0	164	2.8

ROBERT PACK 27 6-2 190 Guard

Not bad. But not great . . . But appealing enough to achieve a five-year deal with the Nets that, with incentives, could exceed $18.5 million . . . With the Bullets, as was the case in his Denver days, there were too many turnovers . . . He's much more effective in short bursts . . . Shoots too much for a point guard. And he only shot .428 . . . But he can make things happen. Not always good things, though . . . Energizer, pushes ball quickly. Loses ball quickly, too . . . Bullets got him from Denver Oct. 30, 1995, for Don MacLean and Doug Overton . . . Undrafted out of USC in 1991 . . . Blazers signed him as a free agent Sept. 16, 1991 . . . Traded to Nuggets for a second-round pick Oct. 23, 1992 . . . Made $1.304 million last year . . . Born Feb. 3, 1969, in New Orleans.

Year	Team	G	FG	FG Pct.	FT	FT Pct.	Reb.	Ast.	TP	Avg.
1991-92	Portland	72	115	.423	102	.803	97	140	332	4.6
1992-93	Denver	77	285	.470	239	.768	160	335	810	10.5
1993-94	Denver	66	223	.443	179	.758	123	356	631	9.6
1994-95	Denver	42	170	.430	137	.783	113	290	507	12.1
1995-96	Washington	31	190	.428	154	.846	132	242	560	18.1
	Totals	288	983	.443	811	.787	625	1363	2840	9.9

KHALID REEVES 24 6-3 201 Guard

Two seasons, three teams . . . Either everybody really likes him or everybody really hates him . . . Would be kind of interesting to see what he can do with playing time and a system he could work in for longer than a week and a half . . . As a rookie, he'd established himself as a sound. offensive-type point guard. In his second year, didn't do much of anything. Was part of the Alonzo Mourning-Glen Rice trade, moving from Miami to Charlotte on Nov. 3, 1995 . . . Came to Nets with Kendall Gill in the deal for Kenny Anderson and Gerald Glass Jan. 19 . . . When he arrived in New Jersey, however, he had a bum ankle that nearly halted the deal . . . Outstanding quickness and does have three-point range . . . Can penetrate . . . Former backcourt mate of Damon Stoudamire at Arizona is considered a question mark, however, because by the time he was healthy to play for Nets, team was about two and a half miles out of playoffs . . .

Born July 15, 1972, in the Bronx, N.Y. . . . Made $1.602 million . . . Heat drafted him No. 12 in 1994.

Year	Team	G	FG	FG Pct.	FT	FT Pct.	Reb.	Ast.	TP	Avg.
1994-95	Miami	67	206	.443	140	.714	186	288	619	9.2
1995-96	Char.-N.J.	51	95	.419	61	.744	79	118	279	5.5
	Totals	118	301	.435	201	.723	265	406	898	7.6

DAVID BENOIT 28 6-8 220   Forward

As free agent, after five seasons with Utah, he signed with Nets in August . . . Starting small forward most of last season, though largely by default . . . Just 8.2 points a game and 43.9 percent from the field . . . Still good enough to get in the opening lineup 63 times . . . Great athlete, but still trying to get a game to go with that . . . Last name pronounced Ben-WA . . . All-Southeastern Conference at Alabama, but undrafted . . . Played a year in Spain before the Jazz signed him as a free agent . . . Born May 9, 1968, in Lafayette, La. . . . Made $1.2 million.

Year	Team	G	FG	FG Pct.	FT	FT Pct.	Reb.	Ast.	TP	Avg.
1991-92	Utah	77	175	.467	81	.810	296	34	434	5.6
1992-93	Utah	82	258	.436	114	.750	392	43	664	8.1
1993-94	Utah	55	139	.385	68	.773	260	23	358	6.5
1994-95	Utah	71	285	.486	132	.841	368	58	740	10.4
1995-96	Utah	81	255	.439	87	.777	383	82	661	8.2
	Totals	366	1112	.446	482	.791	1699	240	2857	7.8

KEVIN EDWARDS 31 6-3 210   Guard

Two seasons down the medical drain . . . After managing just 14 games because of a torn Achilles in 1994-95, the off guard got in just 34 last season with assorted knee injuries that resulted in offseason surgery . . . Had showed promise of comeback in preseason but pain intensified as season wore on . . . Coupled with Kendall Gill injury, Nets were wiped out at off guard . . . In an ideal world, he'll be a strong, solid backup to Gill off bench . . . But Nets worry about what will be there after, basically, two seasons off . . . Adequate defender . . . DePaul, '88 . . . Was college backcourt mate of Rod Strickland . . . Drafted by

Miami as 20th pick ... Signed with Nets as free agent July 8, 1993, ostensibly as backup to the late Drazen Petrovic ... Born Oct. 30, 1965, in Cleveland Heights, Ohio ... Made $1.92 million.

Year	Team	G	FG	FG Pct.	FT	FT Pct.	Reb.	Ast.	TP	Avg.
1988-89	Miami	79	470	.425	144	.746	262	349	1094	13.8
1989-90	Miami	78	395	.412	139	.760	282	252	938	12.0
1990-91	Miami	79	380	.410	171	.803	205	240	955	12.1
1991-92	Miami	81	325	.454	162	.848	211	170	819	10.1
1992-93	Miami	40	216	.468	119	.844	121	120	556	13.9
1993-94	New Jersey	82	471	.458	167	.770	281	232	1144	14.0
1994-95	New Jersey	14	69	.448	40	.952	37	27	196	14.0
1995-96	New Jersey	34	142	.364	68	.810	75	71	394	11.6
	Totals	487	2468	.430	1010	.799	1474	1461	6096	12.5

THE ROOKIE

KERRY KITTLES 22 6-5 179   Guard

If he can put the ball in the ocean, the Nets will love him ... And supposedly, he can ... Good explosiveness, vertical leap. John Calipari's first draft choice can shoot with range and create his own shot ... First team All-American ... First senior drafted, at No. 8 ... Disappeared in big games, though ... Suspended three games as a senior for illegal use of phone credit card. Made sincere, tearful apology and paid the bill ... Born June 12, 1974, in Dayton, Ohio, but reared in New Orleans ... He'll earn $1.129 million.

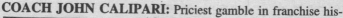

COACH JOHN CALIPARI: Priciest gamble in franchise history ... After twice being snubbed by Rick Pitino, Nets turned to 37-year-old wunderkind of UMass. And turned over $15 million in salary for next five years ... Also made him Director of Basketball Operations. As coach, he'll report to GM, who will report back to Calipari as head of operations. Seems like there's a middleman in there ... Brought UMass from the grave of 10 straight losing seasons to a bid in the Final Four.

UMass lost in semis to eventual champ Kentucky, coached by Pitino . . . It was Pitino, as member of UMass alumni search committee, who recommended Calipari for the job back in '88 . . . Small world, huh? . . . College Coach of the Year . . . Eight-year record, including 35-2 mark last season, at Massachusetts: 193-71. Nets can lose 71 in one year . . . Led UMass to five straight Atlantic 10 regular-season and tourney titles . . . Three-time A-10 Coach of the Year . . . Assistant at Kansas for two years, where he worked under Larry Brown and with Bob Hill . . . Assistant at Pittsburgh before heading to UMass . . . Graduate of Clarion State with a marketing degree . . . Did his first two years at North Carolina-Wilmington. College point guard . . . Born Feb. 10, 1959, in Moon, Pa. . . . Teams known for defense, rebounding and hard work. Offense similar to a Pat Riley or Mike Fratello, rather than Pitino.

BIGGEST BLUNDER

Blunders and the Nets? Is this a trick question or something? Pick a year, any year. You could point to the Harry Weltman regime. You could be safe selecting any of the drug-abuse problems of the '80s. How about being stood up at a press conference by a coach (Rollie Massimino) who was to be introduced to the media? How about offering the job to a coach (Jim Valvano), then swearing you didn't?

But of all the mistakes, gaffes and bonehead moves the franchise ever made, none can compare with the move made on Oct. 20, 1976, the day the Nets sold Julius Erving to the 76ers.

Having won the final ABA championship, the Nets were headed to the NBA through the league merger. Owner Roy Boe was desperate for cash to keep the franchise afloat. Erving was desperate for a deserved raise. Boe solved both problems and sold Dr. J, one of the greatest players ever, to the Sixers for $1 million. Boe eventually sold the team in August 1978. Too late. The "Curse of the Nets" had begun.

ALL-TIME NET LEADERS

SEASON

Points: Rick Barry, 2,518, 1971–72 (ABA)
Bernard King, 1,909, 1977–78
Assists: Kevin Porter, 801, 1977–78
Rebounds: Billy Paultz, 1,035, 1971–72 (ABA)
Buck Williams, 1,027, 1982-83

GAME

Points: Julius Erving, 63 vs. San Diego (4 OT), 2/14/75 (ABA)
Mike Newlin, 52 vs. Boston, 12/16/79
Ray Williams, 52 vs. Detroit, 4/17/82
Assists: Kevin Porter, 29 vs. Houston, 2/24/78
Rebounds: Billy Paultz, 33 vs. Pittsburgh, 2/17/71 (ABA)
Buck Williams, 27 vs. Golden State, 2/1/87

CAREER

Points: Buck Williams, 10,440, 1981–89
Assists: Billy Melchionni, 2,251, 1969–75 (ABA)
Kenny Anderson, 2,116, 1991–95
Rebounds: Buck Williams, 7,576, 1981–89

NEW YORK KNICKS

TEAM DIRECTORY: Pres./GM: Ernie Grunfeld; Dir. Pub. Rel.: Josh Rosenfeld; Dir. Media Services: Lori Hamamoto; Dir. Publications and Inf.: Dennis D'Agostino; Dir. Scouting Services: Dick McGuire; Coach: Jeff Van Gundy; Asst. Coaches: Don Chaney, Brendan Malone, Jeff Nix, Tom Thibodeau.

SCOUTING REPORT

SHOOTING: Water is wet. Sickness is not nice. The Knicks wanted a reliable, consistent big-game perimeter shooter. Some

Patrick Ewing battles Dennis Rodman in playoffs.

things are just universal truths. And finally, the Knicks think they found the truth in free-agent pickup Allan Houston, late of the Pistons. Houston came aboard for $56 million over seven years.

And he wasn't the only one. New York added a reliable point guard in Chris Childs, who will fit perfectly now with an almost embarrassing array of talent that includes Larry Johnson. The Knicks got the former No. 1 pick from Charlotte, shipping out the versatile and talented-but-too-grouchy-for management Anthony Mason. Inside, the Knicks are a force with Patrick Ewing (although coming off a down shooting year), Johnson and the underrated-offensively Charles Oakley.

The Knicks placed 11th in overall shooting percentage. Not bad, not bad at all. And it will get better. Throughout the regular season, the Knicks held their own outside, although John Starks was given to his often erratic displays. The playoffs were another matter. Hubert Davis dipped from 48 to 41 percent and Starks, after a magnificent opening-round series against Cleveland, fizzled in four of five games against the Bulls. And after the off-season moves, it became apparent that either Davis or Starks would be gone. Davis drew the short straw, being shipped to Toronto for a No. 1.

The Knicks scooped up three forwards on the first round in the draft, John Wallace of Syracuse, Walter McCarty of Kentucky and Dontae Jones of Mississippi State, all with the potential to be accomplished scorers. But only Wallace has any range.

PLAYMAKING: Through the whim of Don Nelson, who lasted 59 games, the Knicks went to a point-forward system last year when Mason wound up leading the team in assists at 4.4 a game. While this was terrific for innovation and gave a boost to Mason's pride and ego, it did absolutely nothing for establishing creativity or penetration from the backcourt, something the Knicks sorely need. So they went out and signed Childs, a better-than-average point guard who can make some questionable decisions. But Childs should flourish with the Knicks. He is not a leading offensive character as he was with the scoring-poor Nets. He can sit back and concentrate on setting up others, which he did with 7.0 assists a night with the Nets. The Knicks were decidedly down on the team rung of playmaking in the league (17th) last season. They said goodbye to a class act, Derek Harper, and now have Charlie Ward, a good penetrator, as a backup one.

REBOUNDING: The statistic is shocking: The Knicks, those former lovable maulers who bowled over everything and everybody to get to the glass, finished dead last in offensive rebounding

KNICK ROSTER

No.	Veterans	Pos.	Ht.	Wt.	Age	Yrs. Pro	College
—	Chris Childs	G	6-3	195	28	2	Boise State
33	Patrick Ewing	C	7-0	240	34	11	Georgetown
—	Allan Houston	G	6-6	210	25	3	Tennessee
2	Larry Johnson	F	6-7	253	27	5	UNLV
34	Charles Oakley	F	6-9	245	32	11	Virginia Union
3	John Starks	G	6-5	185	31	7	Oklahoma State
21	Charlie Ward	G	6-2	190	26	2	Florida State
—	Buck Williams	F	6-8	225	36	15	Maryland
F-32	Herb Williams	F-C	6-11	260	38	15	Ohio State

F-Free agent

Rd.	Rookies	Sel.No.	Pos.	Ht.	Wt.	College
1	John Wallace	18	F	6-8	225	Syracuse
1	Walter McCarty	19	F	6-10	230	Kentucky
1	Dontae Jones	21	F	6-7	220	Mississippi State

last season. The Knicks, 29th in a 29-team race? Much of it had to do with Oakley missing a big chunk of the season while various bones healed. And much of it had to do with the fact there were really two separate seasons for the Knicks: with Nelson and without Nelson, the *with* part consuming far more time. The Knicks made a big step toward reclaiming their rebound turf with the free-agent signing of Portland's Buck Williams, one of the league's best all-time boarders. Of course, they'll need a healthy Ewing. If something happens to either one, Williams can step in for extended minutes. In Johnson, the Knicks received a rebounding force, even if old Grandmama is not recognized as a boarder. He'll help. So, too, will Houston and Childs in the backcourt, where the Knicks got much bigger overnight.

DEFENSE: When Jeff Van Gundy took over with 23 games to go, he began getting the Knicks back into their hard-work regimen. And around the Knicks, hard work always means defense. Statistically, the Knicks looked fine: they were fourth in the league in points surrendered. But that didn't reflect the reality of how the Knicks' defense had slipped over the course of the season. The Knicks simply stopped looking like, acting like and playing like the Knicks. In-season trades played a part, as did the absence of Oakley, the squad's best help defender, the guy who last missed a rotation . . . well, we can't remember when he last

Allan Houston drives in from Detroit as a new Knick.

missed a rotation. But by the time the playoffs rolled around, Oakley was back. Like Oakley, Williams is a great interior defender.

They lost something defensively when Mason was traded, but they gained so much more in other areas with Johnson. Childs is a terrific defensive point guard. And Houston can hold his own, but New York may be sorely disappointed when they play the Bulls if Houston resorts to his history against Michael Jordan. His Airness always has his way with shockingly little resistance when matched against Houston.

OUTLOOK: The window of opportunity, long a Knick watchword, slammed shut for the Knicks after last season. And then, boom, it exploded open again. Wide open. It will take an extraordinary effort to get past the Bulls, but the Knicks now may be the second-best team in the league. But Chicago will stand in front of any trip to the Finals. Still, the Knicks always battle Chicago tough, so maybe, just maybe, the Knicks can win it all.

Management went into the offseason eying a major transformation of team personnel and did it. One of the best moves the team made was retaining Van Gundy, who was upgraded from interim to permanent (until he gets fired, of course) head coach.

Van Gundy will employ the Riley-like staples of hard work, defense, rebounding and fundamentals. And now, he has a lot more talent to squeeze.

KNICK PROFILES

PATRICK EWING 34 7-0 240   Center

Wear and tear beginning to show ... Still, had statistical season befitting a franchise player ... Ninth in NBA in scoring, seventh in rebounding and blocks ... All-Star team member for 10th time in 11 years (injured the other) ... Knicks were 1-5 in the six games he sat with nagging injuries ... Is 23rd on the all-time scoring list ... As for Knick career leaders, there's Patrick and then everybody else. First in games played, points, rebounds, blocks, steals and minutes ... Received staggering $18.724-million balloon payment last season. Drops back to earth with $3.3 this season, the final year of his pact ... Recorded the first triple-double of his career in season's final week, nailing 28 points, 11 assists and 15 rebounds against Hornets April 19 ... Those 11 assists say something about how he improved passing over years. Seemed like it took five seasons to get 11 assists ... Jump shot for a big man is near legendary ... Has undergone numerous arthoscopes on knees ... Was first-ever lottery pick in 1985 after sensational career at Georgetown that included '84 NCAA championship and two other title-game appearances ... Got image of nasty, growling cur as Hoya. Nothing could be more distant from the truth. Fine arts major, nice guy ... Native of Kingston, Jamaica, where he was born Aug. 5, 1962 ... Moved to U.S. at age 12 and was high-school All-American at Rindge-Latin in Cambridge, Mass.

Year	Team	G	FG	FG Pct.	FT	FT Pct.	Reb.	Ast.	TP	Avg.
1985-86	New York	50	386	.474	226	.739	451	102	998	20.0
1986-87	New York	63	530	.503	296	.713	555	104	1356	21.5
1987-88	New York	82	656	.555	341	.716	676	125	1653	20.2
1988-89	New York	80	727	.567	361	.746	740	188	1815	22.7
1989-90	New York	82	922	.551	502	.775	893	182	2347	28.6
1990-91	New York	81	845	.514	464	.745	905	244	2154	26.6
1991-92	New York	82	796	.522	377	.738	921	156	1970	24.0
1992-93	New York	81	779	.503	400	.719	980	151	1959	24.2
1993-94	New York	79	745	.496	445	.765	885	179	1939	24.5
1994-95	New York	79	730	.503	420	.750	876	212	1886	23.9
1995-96	New York	76	678	.466	351	.761	806	160	1711	22.5
	Totals	835	7794	.515	4183	.744	8679	1803	19788	23.7

LARRY JOHNSON 27 6-7 253   Forward

Not the same player as before the back injury but still right up there . . . And now he'll do it for the Knicks, who sent Anthony Mason and Brad Lohaus to Charlotte in mammoth summer deal . . . In the process the Knicks took on Johnson's $70-million salary and the final years of his 12-year Hornet contract . . . Scoring average broke 20 for just the second time, mainly because he used his body to draw more fouls than ever before, setting career highs in free throws made (427) and attempted (564) . . . Has missed just two games in two years after back injury knocked him out for 31 in 1993-94 . . . One of the best passing forwards around, he averaged 8.9 assists in eight straight games that point guard Kenny Anderson missed . . . Top pick out of UNLV in the 1991 draft and was 1991-92 Rookie of the Year . . . Was tri-captain of Dream Team II and was first Hornet to start in an All-Star Game . . . Earned $4.295 last season . . . Born March 14, 1969, in Tyler, Tex.

Year	Team	G	FG	FG Pct.	FT	FT Pct.	Reb.	Ast.	TP	Avg.
1991-92	Charlotte.	82	616	.490	339	.829	899	292	1576	19.2
1992-93	Charlotte.	82	728	.526	336	.767	864	353	1810	22.1
1993-94	Charlotte.	51	346	.515	137	.695	448	184	834	16.4
1994-95	Charlotte.	81	585	.480	274	.774	585	369	1525	18.8
1995-96	Charlotte.	81	583	.476	427	.757	683	356	1660	20.5
	Totals	377	2858	.496	1513	.771	3479	1553	7405	19.6

JOHN STARKS 31 6-5 185   Guard

Think they regret that long-term contract? Entering third year of four-year, $13.4-million extension . . . Has trade value of Ebola virus . . . Benched a game in April by coach Jeff Van Gundy for insubordination at practice . . . Had best game in Knicks' shining moment of season, scoring career playoff-high 30 points in Game 3 victory over Bulls in conference semis . . . That came after two pathetic performances. Problem was, all season there were more efforts like Games 1 and 2 and not nearly enough like 3 . . . Had great first-round series vs. Cavs. Averaged 19.7 points, shot .559. Set three-game series record with 14 three-pointers . . . Strange year. Then-coach Don Nelson took away his plays, his confidence, his job. Left him parking space, however.

But just barely . . . Made all-time high 273 three-pointers in 1994-95. Hit 143 last season. Sorta dipped . . . In past, Knicks ran like 15 plays for him a game. They might have run 15 plays total for him in 59 games under Nelson . . . Size remains a big problem as bigger and stronger twos post him . . . Point guard in a pinch . . . Better than average two-guard passer, but had fewest assists in four years . . . Will always be linked with awful 2-of-18 Game 7 shooting in '94 Finals . . . Last of four colleges was Oklahoma State . . . Undrafted in 1988 . . . Signed as free agent and played with Warriors. Eventually cut by—right—Don Nelson, June 16, 1989 . . . Signed as free agent by Knicks, Oct. 1, 1990 . . . Born Aug. 10, 1965, in Tulsa, Okla.

Year	Team	G	FG	FG Pct.	FT	FT Pct.	Reb.	Ast.	TP	Avg.
1988-89	Golden State	36	51	.408	34	.654	41	27	146	4.1
1990-91	New York	61	180	.439	79	.752	131	204	466	7.6
1991-92	New York	82	405	.449	235	.778	191	276	1139	13.9
1992-93	New York	80	513	.428	263	.795	204	404	1397	17.5
1993-94	New York	59	410	.420	187	.754	185	348	1120	19.0
1994-95	New York	80	419	.395	168	.737	219	411	1223	15.3
1995-96	New York	81	375	.443	131	.735	237	315	1024	12.6
	Totals	479	2353	.426	1097	.762	1208	1985	6515	13.6

CHARLIE WARD 26 6-2 190   Guard

See, he can play without shoulder pads and face guards . . . Former Heisman Trophy winner had mediocre regular season, blossomed in playoffs . . . Probably team's best at breaking down defenders. Gets to rim better than anybody else . . . Jumper and defense improving . . . Management needs to know if he really wants it enough . . . Buried on bench by Don Nelson, resurrected by Jeff Van Gundy, who realized team needed to know if he can play before deciding on Derek Harper . . . Likable kid but as thrilling as dry wheat toast with media . . . Team has always been high on his potential . . . At Florida State he only played half-seasons because of football . . . Quarterbacked Seminoles to national championship in 1993 . . . NFL types were wary of his size . . . Knicks picked him 26th on first round in 1994 draft . . . Born Oct. 12, 1970, in Tallahassee, Fla. . . . Made $722,000.

Year	Team	G	FG	FG Pct.	FT	FT Pct.	Reb.	Ast.	TP	Avg.
1994-95	New York	10	4	.211	7	.700	6	4	16	1.6
1995-96	New York	62	87	.399	37	.685	102	132	244	3.9
	Totals	72	91	.384	44	.688	108	136	260	3.6

ALLAN HOUSTON 25 6-6 210   Guard

As Piston free agent, he signed seven-year, $56-million contract with Knicks in July . . . Showed strong finish in 1994-95 (24.8 points over final 24 games) was no fluke, blossoming into one of the most threatening distance shooters in the game . . . Broke his own Pistons' record for three-pointers made (191), attempted (447) and percentage (.427) . . . Learning how to draw contact, he more than doubled his free-throw attempts (from 171 to 362) over the previous season . . . Not one-dimensional, he can get to the rim and finish . . . Tennessee's all-time leading scorer was drafted 11th in 1993 . . . Earned $1.177 million last year . . . Born April 4, 1971, in Louisville, Ky.

Year	Team	G	FG	FG Pct.	FT	FT Pct.	Reb.	Ast.	TP	Avg.
1993-94	Detroit	79	272	.405	89	.824	120	100	668	8.5
1994-95	Detroit	76	398	.463	147	.860	167	164	1101	14.5
1995-96	Detroit	82	564	.453	298	.823	300	250	1617	19.7
	Totals	237	1234	.445	534	.833	587	514	3386	14.3

CHRIS CHILDS 28 6-3 195   Guard

Nets' free agent signed six-year, $23.58-million contract with Knicks in July . . . Was perhaps the NBA's premier backup point guard, then was thrust into starting position when Kenny Anderson was traded . . . So with 30.9 minutes averaged, still passed for 7.0 assists per game, 12th in the NBA . . . Turnovers a bit high (2.9 per). Can play turnover-free one game, rack up six the next . . . Decision-making could improve but overall a super find for Nets, who stole him as a free agent . . . After one-year free-agent deal of $150,000, age deterred Nets from signing him long-term. They screwed up and know it . . . Recovering alcoholic. Did John Lucas' rehab thing . . . He does get everyone involved and is not afraid to shoot it. Decent to good range: .367 on threes . . . Especially tough in the clutch, ice-water-in-veins type . . . Overall shooting needs improvement: his .416 was a big jump from rookie year . . . Born Nov. 20, 1967, in Bakersfield, Cal. . . . Went undrafted out of Boise State in 1990. Felt he should have been a first-rounder. Disappointment led to

booze and almost put life in ashes . . . Wears No. 1, symbolic of
first-round status . . . CBA's Playoff MVP in 1994 for Quad City
. . . Made $35,000 last year

Year	Team	G	FG	FG Pct.	FT	FT Pct.	Reb.	Ast.	TP	Avg.
1994-95	New Jersey	53	106	.380	55	.753	69	219	308	5.8
1995-96	New Jersey	78	324	.416	259	.852	245	548	1002	12.8
	Totals	131	430	.407	314	.833	314	767	1310	10.0

CHARLES OAKLEY 32 6-9 245   Forward

Injuries breaking down warhorse. But these
were fluke jobs, not your typical wear and tear
. . . Broke thumb in February, missed 19 games
. . . Broke orbit bone under right eye, courtesy
of Patrick Ewing elbow. Sources say inadver-
tent. Wore mask during playoffs. Provided
usual nasty edge and diving, hustling play. You
know, Oakley play . . . Has one of the game's
great work ethics . . . Team's best defender on rotations . . . Unheralded jump-shooter. Has quality ability up to about 17 feet . . .
Owns a string of car washes in New York and native Cleveland,
where he was born Dec. 18, 1963 . . . Cavs picked him No. 9 out
of Virginia Union in 1985. Promptly traded him in a major mistake to Bulls for immortals Ennis Whatley and Keith Lee . . .
Came to Knicks June 27, 1988, in trade for Bill Cartwright . . .
Made $2.4 million.

Year	Team	G	FG	FG Pct.	FT	FT Pct.	Reb.	Ast.	TP	Avg.
1985-86	Chicago	77	281	.519	178	.662	664	133	740	9.6
1986-87	Chicago	82	468	.445	245	.686	1074	296	1192	14.5
1987-88	Chicago	82	375	.483	261	.727	1066	248	1014	12.4
1988-89	New York	82	426	.510	197	.773	861	187	1061	12.9
1989-90	New York	61	336	.524	217	.761	727	146	889	14.6
1990-91	New York	76	307	.516	239	.784	920	204	853	11.2
1991-92	New York	82	210	.522	86	.735	700	133	506	6.2
1992-93	New York	82	219	.508	127	.722	708	126	565	6.9
1993-94	New York	82	363	.478	243	.776	965	218	969	11.8
1994-95	New York	50	192	.489	119	.793	445	126	506	10.1
1995-96	New York	53	211	.471	175	.833	460	137	604	11.4
	Totals	809	3388	.493	2087	.746	8590	1954	8899	11.0

BUCK WILLIAMS 36 6-8 225   Forward

Trail Blazer free agent signed two-year contract with Knicks last summer believed to be worth $2.6 million . . . Missed the first 12 games last season with a torn tendon in his left thumb, then played final 70 . . . This after playing at least 80 in each of previous six years after Portland aquired him from New Jersey for Sam Bowie and a first-rounder . . . So he's not exactly breaking down . . . One of eight players in NBA history to get at least 16,000 points and 12,000 rebounds . . . No. 8 all-time in games, No. 9 in minutes . . . Starred at Maryland before Nets picked him third overall in 1981 . . . Rookie of the Year . . . Born March 8, 1960, in Rocky Mount, N.C. . . . Made $3.4 million.

Year	Team	G	FG	FG Pct.	FT	FT Pct.	Reb.	Ast.	TP	Avg.
1981-82	New Jersey	82	513	.582	242	.624	1005	107	1268	15.5
1982-83	New Jersey	82	536	.588	324	.620	1027	125	1396	17.0
1983-84	New Jersey	81	495	.535	284	.570	1000	130	1274	15.7
1984-85	New Jersey	82	577	.530	336	.625	1005	167	1491	18.2
1985-86	New Jersey	82	500	.523	301	.676	986	131	1301	15.9
1986-87	New Jersey	82	521	.557	430	.731	1023	129	1472	18.0
1987-88	New Jersey	70	466	.560	346	.668	834	109	1279	18.3
1988-89	New Jersey	74	373	.531	213	.666	696	78	959	13.0
1989-90	Portland	82	413	.548	288	.706	800	116	1114	13.6
1990-91	Portland	80	358	.602	217	.705	751	97	933	11.7
1991-92	Portland	80	340	.604	221	./54	704	108	901	11.3
1992-93	Portland	82	270	.511	138	.645	690	75	678	8.3
1993-94	Portland	81	291	.555	201	.679	843	80	783	9.7
1994-95	Portland	82	309	.512	138	.673	669	78	757	9.2
1995-96	Portland	70	192	.500	125	.668	404	42	511	7.3
	Totals	1192	6154	.550	3804	.664	12437	1572	16117	13.5

HERB WILLIAMS 38 6-11 260   Center

C'mon, Herb. Tell us again what kind of president Fillmore was . . . Despite long-in-tooth status, still a key guy but more for magnificent locker-room presence. Younger guys (most of them anyway) actually listen to him . . . Started season with Knicks, was traded to Toronto, came back to Knicks . . . Went to Raptors with Doug Christie for Willie Anderson and Victor Alexander on Feb. 18 . . . Played one game for Toronto and had six points and eight rebounds in 31 minutes. He's probably about third on Raptor's all-time rebound list . . . Waived by request by Toronto Feb. 23. Re-signed as free agent by Knicks Feb. 28 and making . . . Minutes were way down. But like a real pro, always stayed prepared . . . Accepts situation, never complains . . . Future coach . . . Became first player at Ohio State to score 2,000 points . . . Was the 14th pick in 1981 by Indiana, where he had some truly outstanding seasons for some truly not outstanding teams . . . Traded to Dallas Feb. 21, 1989, for Detlef Schrempf . . . Originally signed with Knicks as free agent Nov. 15, 1992 . . . Born Feb. 16, 1958, in Columbus, Ohio.

Year	Team	G	FG	FG Pct.	FT	FT Pct.	Reb.	Ast.	TP	Avg.
1981-82	Indiana	82	407	.477	126	.670	605	139	942	11.5
1982-83	Indiana	78	580	.499	155	.705	583	262	1315	16.9
1983-84	Indiana	69	411	.478	207	.702	554	215	1029	14.9
1984-85	Indiana	75	575	.475	224	.657	634	252	1375	18.3
1985-86	Indiana	78	627	.492	294	.730	710	174	1549	19.9
1986-87	Indiana	74	451	.480	199	.740	543	174	1101	14.9
1987-88	Indiana	75	311	.425	126	.737	469	98	748	10.0
1988-89	Ind.-Dal.	76	322	.436	133	.686	593	124	777	10.2
1989-90	Dallas	81	295	.444	108	.679	391	119	700	8.6
1990-91	Dallas	60	332	.507	83	.638	357	95	747	12.5
1991-92	Dallas	75	367	.431	124	.725	454	94	859	11.5
1992-93	New York	55	72	.411	14	.667	146	19	158	2.9
1993-94	New York	70	103	.442	27	.643	182	28	233	3.3
1994-95	New York	56	82	.456	23	.622	132	27	187	3.3
1995-96	N.Y.-Tor.-N.Y.	44	62	.408	13	.650	90	27	138	3.1
	Totals	1048	4997	.468	1856	.697	6443	1847	11858	11.3

THE ROOKIES

JOHN WALLACE 22 6-8 225   Forward
Derrick Lite . . . Made Derrick Coleman his idol at Syracuse . . . Plunged to No. 18, where Knicks couldn't resist . . . Great skills but many teams were scared off by his attitude . . . Second team All-American. First of Knicks' three first-round picks, all from a Final Four team . . . Third all-time leading scorer at Syracuse behind Coleman and Lawrence Moten . . . Added jumper . . . Returned to 'Cuse for senior year and game matured . . . Born Feb. 9, 1974, in Rochester, N.Y. . . . He'll earn $654,500.

WALTER McCARTY 22 6-10 230   Forward
Some say he's P.J. Brown with a shot . . . Hard-working guy, does dirty work. Rebounds, defends. All-around game suited for NBA

three . . . Needs upper bulk . . . One of NCAA champ Kentucky's three first-rounders. Knicks took him at No. 19, which will pay $625,000 . . . Nice touch from midrange . . . Born Feb. 1, 1974, in Evansville, Ind.

DONTAE JONES 21 6-7 220   Forward
Keeps working, keeps improving. Has to keep working for the pros, though . . . Two years of junior college and one year at Mississippi State. Helped Tigers to Final Four . . . JUCO All-American as soph . . . MVP of the Southeast Regional . . . Was the Knicks' third first-rounder, No. 21 overall . . . He'll make $576,000 this season. Surgery to repair a broken pin in his foot will keep him out until December . . . Born June 2, 1975, in Nashville, Tenn.

COACH JEFF VAN GUNDY: Knicks' brass came to his hotel room on March 8 last season and said, "Here's a mess. Perform a miracle." He did . . . Forget the 13-10 regular-season record; what the 34-year-old son of a high school/community college coach did was outstanding in righting the wreck left by Don Nelson . . . Brought back defense, pride and work ethic to team and made most of aging, mismatched talent . . . Directed 3-0 first round sweep of Cavs and then had Knicks competitive in all five games against Chicago with return to sludgeball . . . Demands hard work. Stresses fundamentals of defense and rebounding . . . Learned much from Pat Riley as his assistant for four years . . . Has far better relationship with media and players . . . Was Knick assistant seemingly since Ice Age, serving under Stu Jackson, John MacLeod, Riley and Nelson . . . Started as high-school coach, moved on as assistant under Rick Pitino at Providence . . . High-honors grad of Nazareth College in Rochester, N.Y. . . . Brother, Stan, is Miami assistant under Riley . . . Father, Bill, has coached for over 30 years . . . Born Jan. 19, 1962, in Hemet, Cal. . . . Knicks re-upped him for two years at $1-million per. Great move by team. Unassuming guy celebrated new contract with McDonald's pigout. Didn't learn that from Riley.

Chris Childs crosses river for a career as a Knick.

BIGGEST BLUNDER

Coach Willis Reed was infatuated. Back in 1978, the theory of the ''sleeper'' still was part of the NBA drafting psyche. And

Reed had his sleeper in a frenetic 6-5 guard out of Montana, Micheal Ray Richardson.

There was new leadership at Madison Square Garden that brought pressure to win immediately. Reed was obsessed with Richardson, so much so that at a Memorial Day picnic, he dragged people to view film of Richardson, so much so that he declared Richardson the choice over a fifth-year senior named Larry Bird who, while eligible for the draft, had one year of collegiate eligibility remaining. The Knicks didn't want to wait a year. They drafted Richardson No. 4. Bird went sixth to Boston.

Reed admitted Richardson was raw, but he saw an electricity that would light up the Garden. What he couldn't see was the upcoming NCAA season when Bird and a fellow named Magic Johnson of Michigan State sparked a renewed national interest that forever changed the sport. Bird immediately embarked on a Hall of Fame career. Richardson's career, although brilliant at times, primarily will be remembered for drug abuse.

ALL-TIME KNICK LEADERS

SEASON

Points: Patrick Ewing, 2,347, 1989-90
Assists: Mark Jackson, 868, 1987–88
Rebounds: Willis Reed, 1,191, 1968–69

GAME

Points: Bernard King, 60 vs. New Jersey, 12/25/85
Assists: Richie Guerin, 21 vs. St. Louis, 12/12/58
Rebounds: Harry Gallatin, 33 vs. Ft. Wayne, 3/15/53
　　　　　　Willis Reed, 33 vs. Cincinnati, 2/2/71

CAREER

Points: Patrick Ewing, 19,788, 1985–96
Assists: Walt Frazier, 4,791, 1967–77
Rebounds: Patrick Ewing, 8,679, 1985–96

ORLANDO MAGIC

TEAM DIRECTORY: Chairman: Rich DeVos; Exec. Vice Chairman: Cheri VanderWeide; Pres.: Bob VanderWeide; Sr. Exec. VP: Pat Williams; Exec. VP-Business Oper.: Jack Swope; GM: John Gabriel; Dir. Publicity/Media Rel.: Alex Martins; Coach: Brian Hill; Asst. Coaches: Richie Adubato, Tree Rollins, Tom Sterner. Arena: Orlando Arena (17,248). Colors: Blue, silver, and black.

SCOUTING REPORT

SHOOTING: On paper, it all looked so good: a nearly unstoppable inside force in Shaquille O'Neal; potentially devastating three-point sharpshooters in Dennis Scott, Nick Anderson, Brian Shaw and Penny Hardaway; overall team shooting that ranked third in the league. So what's the catch? Check out films from the conference finals and then get back to us.

The Chicago Bulls exposed the long-distance game of the Magic as one that must be open, wide open to succeed. And now one of the two major components is gone as Shaq left for Tinseltown, So forget the inside force that needs constant double-teams that freed up the perimeter game. Now teams can employ the Chicago strategy at will: keep defenders on Scott and Anderson and the Magic's three-point threat disappears faster than their title hopes. They must get more penetration, more creativity. Well, look at one bright side. Now they'll want Laker O'Neal to shoot a woeful .487 at the line, like last season when the Magic were next-to-last in the league.

The Magic hope ex-Grizzly Gerald Wilkins is back to full health and can add some of his former scoring punch.

PLAYMAKING: When opponents double-team, the Magic can pass them to death. Hardaway drives, picks up the extra coverage and passes out to Scott or Anderson. An extra pass or two and bam, three-pointer. But one key element will be missing in the double-teams: the main guy who drew them, Shaq.

Until Chicago emphasized the importance of staying home on the perimeter guys, the league seemed clueless on how to stop Orlando. The Magic were second overall in assists and tied for first (with the Los Angeles Lakers) for the NBA's finest assist/turnover ratio.

The Magic, while an exceptional passing team, still are searching for that penetrating, creative playmaker, the prototype point

Penny Hardaway soared to new heights in third season.

guard. Hardaway comes close to fitting the role, but some feel he'd be even more effective with receiving, rather than delivering, the ball. And now with O'Neal out of the equation, Penny may have to do more receiving than ever.

DEFENSE: Not what you'd expect of a Conference finalist with All-NBA caliber players. This is one area where O'Neal, despite

MAGIC ROSTER

No.	Veterans	Pos.	Ht.	Wt.	Age	Yrs. Pro	College
25	Nick Anderson	G	6-6	238	28	7	Illinois
F-10	Darrell Armstrong	G	6-1	180	28	3	Fayetteville
54	Horace Grant	F	6-10	235	31	10	Clemson
1	Anfernee Hardaway	G	6-7	200	25	4	Memphis State
45	Jon Koncak	C	7-0	250	33	12	SMU
5	Donald Royal	F	6-8	210	30	7	Notre Dame
3	Dennis Scott	F	6-8	229	28	7	Georgia Tech
20	Brian Shaw	G	6-6	194	30	8	Cal-Santa Barbara
--	Felton Spencer	C	7-0	280	28	6	Louisville
42	David Vaughn	F-C	6-9	240	23	1	Memphis
21	Gerald Wilkins	G-F	6-6	225	1	10	Tenn.-Chattanooga
F-12	Joe Wolf	F-C	6-11	230	31	9	North Carolina

F-Free agent

Rd.	Rookies	Sel.No.	Pos.	Ht.	Wt.	College
1	Brian Evans	27	F	6-8	220	Indiana
2	Amal McCaskill	49	C	6-11	235	Marquette

his Top 10 shot-blocking gifts, will not be missed as much. He was not the dominant force in the middle he should have been in Orlando. Problem for the Magic now is that Shaq still is better than anything else on board.

The hands of Hardaway and Anderson, both of whom placed among the top 20 in the league in steals, are among the Magic's chief defensive weapons in the starting unit. And there's always Horace Grant, the team's premier interior defender whose quickness is utilized effectively in double situations.

REBOUNDING: Average, very average. And with Shaquille in LA-LA land, it's not below average. The Magic still boast rebounder extraordinaire Horace Grant, but injuries curtailed his contributions—as it did with Shaq. So for the first time since Shaq entered the league, the Magic did not have a representative among the top 40 rebounders in the league (they would have, going strictly by average, but no one on the club met the minimum requirements). One area where the Magic are particularly weak in boarding is off the bench. There isn't and hasn't been any noticeable depth on the boards. Orlando hopes that second-year player David Vaughn may step in as a reliable power-forward

Nick Anderson looks to bounce back from playoff misery.

backup to Grant. And they expect 7-foot Felton Spencer, acquired from Utah, to step into the middle for Shaq.

OUTLOOK: They may be one of the more interesting teams around. They will be a far more wide-open team without Shaq. Brian Hill's Magic will have little choice but to turn Hardaway loose on the league and hope for the best. And that should still be pretty darn good because, simply, Penny is that darn good. The Magic don't figure to be the superpower they were before Shaq's lust for the celluloid life and money overwhelmed the franchise. But they won't be awful.

They must overcome a grating wither-and-die habit that was present in the O'Neal era. They would run roughshod over regular-season opponents, achieve near invincible status on their home court, their beloved O-Rena, waylay a playoff opponent or two. And then wither, quit and fold a little deeper in the postseason.

But now, without Shaq, they don't even figure to get too deep in the playoffs. But maybe they will learn the value of mental toughness. There's a huge gap to fill and maybe they'll pull together. In the past, the Magic encountered so few problems in the regular season that they entered the playoffs with the same frame of mind. And for the last three seasons, they've exited the playoffs by being swept in a series.

MAGIC PROFILES

ANFERNEE (PENNY) HARDAWAY 25 6-7 200 Guard

Oh, to be young, gifted and really young and really gifted . . . Needs to work on leadership. After that, the only complaint is which position might he be best at, one or two? . . . When Shaq was out at the start of the season, he became the go-to guy. May have been Magic's best ball of the season . . . Becoming more and more apparent Orlando is his team and he must step forward . . . Probably could lead the league in scoring . . . A 6-7 point guard? Have fun, defenders . . . May be better when ball is brought to him, rather than when he brings the ball to others. Not a prototype penetrator . . . Averaged 21.7 points, team-best 7.1 assists . . . Won three games with final shot . . . All-Star starter for second straight year . . . Third in MVP voting . . . Summer Olympian . . . All-NBA first team two years in a row. All-Rookie team his first year . . . Set career high of 42 points vs. Nets Nov. 8 . . . 11th in scoring, 11th in assists, sixth in steals . . . Grandmother called him "Pretty" and his friends, because of her drawl, translated it as "Penny" . . . Media-friendly. Actually, everybody-on-the-planet friendly . . . Born July 18, 1971, in Memphis, Tenn. . . . Was Tennessee "Mr. Basketball" in high school . . . No. 3 pick by Warriors in 1993 out of Memphis. Immediately sent to Magic along with three first-rounders for Chris Webber. Larceny indictment, strangely, has never followed . . . Made $5.23 million.

Year	Team	G	FG	FG Pct.	FT	FT Pct.	Reb.	Ast.	TP	Avg.
1993-94	Orlando	82	509	.466	245	.742	439	544	1313	16.0
1994-95	Orlando	77	585	.512	356	.769	336	551	1613	20.9
1995-96	Orlando	82	623	.513	445	.767	354	582	1780	21.7
	Totals	241	1717	.498	1046	.762	1129	1677	4706	19.5

NICK ANDERSON 28 6-6 228   Guard

Good perimeter game. When open . . . Aye, there's the rub . . . Like compatriot Dennis Scott, his offense fell through the sub-basement when Bulls did something so crazy in Eastern Finals that it worked: they defended! . . . Had trouble getting off shot. Had more trouble making shot . . . Missed 20 of 29 attempts. Then missed Game 4 with a hand injury . . . Ball-handling liabilities exposed in conference finals when Magic needed FedEx to get the ball upcourt against Chicago pressure . . . Legit concern in Orlando after two straight playoff duds by this powerful off-guard . . . Can post virtually any two guard in the league not named Michael Jordan . . . Solid, all-around regular season . . . Underrated defender. Has real quick hands: placed 20th in the league in steals. He was sixth among two guards . . . Will always be associated with Game 1 of '95 Finals when he missed four free throws in last :10.5 of regulation when Magic blew game and, in essence, the series to Houston . . . Despite disappointments, he has always been a standup guy, shoulders blame, etc. . . . He has known worse. High-school buddy Ben Wilson was shot to death in front of him. Wears No. 25 in his honor . . . He was Magic's first-ever draft pick, selected No. 11 in 1989 . . . Left Illinois after junior season . . . Born Jan. 20, 1968, in Chicago . . . Made $3.2 million.

Year	Team	G	FG	FG Pct.	FT	FT Pct.	Reb.	Ast.	TP	Avg.
1989-90	Orlando	81	372	.494	186	.705	316	124	931	11.5
1990-91	Orlando	70	400	.467	173	.668	386	106	990	14.1
1991-92	Orlando	60	482	.463	202	.667	384	163	1196	19.9
1992-93	Orlando	79	594	.449	298	.741	477	265	1574	19.9
1993-94	Orlando	81	504	.478	168	.672	476	294	1277	15.8
1994-95	Orlando	76	439	.476	143	.704	335	314	1200	15.8
1995-96	Orlando	77	400	.442	166	.692	415	279	1134	14.7
	Totals	524	3191	.465	1336	.695	2789	1545	8302	15.8

HORACE GRANT 31 6-10 235   Forward

Re-signed multi-year pact after season of nagging injuries . . . Missed 18 games with sprains, spasms and tendinitis. Even got suspended for one game . . . Recurring back problems . . . Made $2.763 million last year . . . Remains a magnificent interior defender, superlative offensive rebounder, defensive pressure master, wonderful help defender . . .

Makes double-teams costly by getting to the glass or nailing the open jumper... Remarkably consistent shooter. Shot .513... Magic's hopes for upset of Bulls in Eastern Finals went up in smoke when he injured his shoulder in Game 1... Helped lead Magic to NBA Finals in his first season out of Chicago, 1994-95 ... Part of Bulls' three-ring, pre-Michael-plays-baseball championship run... Hard worker who is showing mileage... Signed with Magic as a free agent, July 29, 1994... Before injury vs. Bulls, shot .649, averaged 15.0 points and 10.4 rebounds in playoffs... Born July 4, 1965, in Augusta, Ga., a few minutes before twin brother Harvey, a forward with Blazers... The No. 10 pick by Bulls out of Clemson in 1987.

Year	Team	G	FG	FG Pct.	FT	FT Pct.	Reb.	Ast.	TP	Avg.
1987-88	Chicago	81	254	.501	114	.626	447	89	622	7.7
1988-89	Chicago	79	405	.519	140	.704	681	168	950	12.0
1989-90	Chicago	80	446	.523	179	.699	629	227	1071	13.4
1990-91	Chicago	78	401	.547	197	.711	659	178	1000	12.8
1991-92	Chicago	81	457	.578	235	.741	807	217	1149	14.2
1992-93	Chicago	77	421	.508	174	.619	729	201	1017	13.2
1993-94	Chicago	70	460	.524	137	.596	769	236	1057	15.1
1994-95	Orlando	74	401	.567	146	.692	715	173	948	12.8
1995-96	Orlando	63	347	.513	152	.734	580	170	847	13.4
	Totals	683	3592	.532	1474	.682	6016	1659	8661	12.7

DENNIS SCOTT 28 6-8 229   Forward

Wait a minute. He might be showing up for the playoffs now... Unbelievably bad conference finals against Bulls. Shot .265... Lives off double-teams. Is a tremendous open shooter with range... But the Bulls covered him. He shot .265... Does the phrase "one-dimensional" mean anything?... Fizzled in '95 Finals against Rockets, too. Shot .310 in that one... Rumored to be on trading block... During regular season, he smashed three-point shooting record, hitting an all-time NBA high 267 triples, shooting .463 in the process. Made at least one three-pointer in 78 straight games—the last three in 1994-95, the first 75 last season... Also established NBA record of 11 triples in one game against Atlanta April 18 . . . Those 11 threes represented two more baskets than he made (of any kind) against Bulls . . . Six games of 30 or more points . . . Has struggled with weight since leaving Georgia Tech in 1990 . . . Magic made him the No. 4 pick in 1990 . . . Calf, heel injuries limited him to 72 combined games in his second and third NBA seasons . . . Tattoos on shoulders in honor of parents . . . Real nice guy . . . Born Sept. 5, 1968, in Hagerstown, Md. . . . Made $3.15 million.

Year	Team	G	FG	FG Pct.	FT	FT Pct.	Reb.	Ast.	TP	Avg.
1990-91	Orlando	82	503	.425	153	.750	235	134	1284	15.7
1991-92	Orlando	18	133	.402	64	.901	66	35	359	19.9
1992-93	Orlando	54	329	.431	92	.786	186	136	858	15.9
1993-94	Orlando	82	384	.405	123	.774	218	216	1046	12.8
1994-95	Orlando	62	283	.439	86	.754	146	131	802	12.9
1995-96	Orlando	82	491	.440	182	.820	309	243	1431	17.5
	Totals	380	2123	.426	700	.789	1160	895	5780	15.2

BRIAN SHAW 30 6-6 194   **Guard**

He experienced 1995-96 before. Like in 1994-95. And 1993-94 . . . You get the picture . . . He still struggled with his shot, shooting under 40 percent for second straight season in central Florida . . . But he has value. His size and speed in the backcourt are invaluable . . . So is his versatility. He can play the one or the two. When teamed with Penny Hardaway, makes the Magic less vulnerable to the press . . . But when he's at the two, that .374 shooting won't cut it . . . Became NBA's first player since Detlef Schrempf in February 1993 to record a triple-double off the bench. Did it in 28 minutes against the Clippers on Dec. 29. Had 11 points, 10 assists and 10 rebounds . . . Signed on Sept. 22, 1994, as a free agent by Magic . . . Received $4.25 million balloon . . . Drafted by Celtics on first round, No. 24, out of UC-Santa Barbara in 1988 . . . Became Celts' first rookie since Kevin McHale in 1980-81 to play in all 82 games . . . Went to Italy for 1989-90 season in contract squabble . . . Traded to Miami for

Sherman Douglas Jan. 10, 1992 . . . Born March 22, 1966, in Oakland.

Year	Team	G	FG	FG Pct.	FT	FT Pct.	Reb.	Ast.	TP	Avg.
1988-89	Boston	82	297	.433	109	.826	376	472	703	8.6
1990-91	Boston	79	442	.469	204	.819	370	602	1091	13.8
1991-92	Bos.-Mia.	63	209	.407	72	.791	204	250	495	7.9
1992-93	Miami	68	197	.393	61	.782	257	235	498	7.3
1993-94	Miami	77	278	.417	64	.719	350	385	693	9.0
1994-95	Orlando	78	192	.389	70	.737	241	406	502	6.4
1995-96	Orlando	75	182	.374	91	.798	224	336	496	6.6
	Totals	522	1797	.419	671	.791	2022	2686	4478	8.6

JON KONCAK 33 7-0 250   Center

Figured he'd have a nice, easy season after signing with Magic as free agent Oct. 3 . . . Then Shaq fractures a thumb in the regular season, Horace Grant dislocates a shoulder in the playoffs . . . Was asked to do too much and forced to play too many minutes . . . But he performed admirably . . . Never has been much of an offensive threat: hasn't averaged better than 5.0 in eight years . . . Started 35 games . . . Nagging injuries. Strained knee in playoffs subbing for Grant . . . Was the No. 5 pick out of SMU by the Hawks in 1985 . . . Had 20-rebound game against Knicks as a rookie . . . Received seven-year, $12.5-million offer sheet from Pistons eight years ago. Remember how outraged folks were back then? That's chicken feed now . . . Got $1 million for last season . . . Born May 17, 1963, in Cedar Rapids, Iowa . . . 1984 Olympic gold medalist.

Year	Team	G	FG	FG Pct.	FT	FT Pct.	Reb.	Ast.	TP	Avg.
1985-86	Atlanta	82	263	.507	156	.607	467	55	682	8.3
1986-87	Atlanta	82	169	.480	125	.654	493	31	463	5.6
1987-88	Atlanta	49	98	.483	83	.610	333	19	279	5.7
1988-89	Atlanta	74	141	.524	63	.553	453	56	345	4.7
1989-90	Atlanta	54	78	.614	42	.532	226	23	198	3.7
1989-90	Atlanta	77	140	.436	32	.593	375	124	313	4.1
1991-92	Atlanta	77	111	.391	19	.655	261	132	241	3.1
1992-93	Atlanta	78	124	.464	24	.480	427	140	275	3.5
1993-94	Atlanta	82	159	.431	24	.667	365	102	342	4.2
1994-95	Atlanta	62	77	.412	13	.542	184	52	179	2.9
1995-96	Orlando	67	84	.480	32	.561	272	51	203	3.0
	Totals	784	1444	.470	613	.597	3856	785	3520	4.5

DONALD ROYAL 30 6-8 210   Forward

Asked Magic for a trade after seeing limited playoff time in seven of 12 games . . . May have a tough job finding the time he wants on a team remotely resembling a winner . . . Has no range to speak of. His strength is, has always been, and always will be, his ability to get to the basket and draw fouls . . . Sound free-throw shooter (.764 career) . . . Scoring dipped to four-year low. But so did his minutes . . . Strictly a role player who started for several seasons in Orlando because there was no one else . . . Adequate defensively, but bulky guys give him trouble . . . A forward 'tweener. Four mentality, three body . . . Born May 22, 1966, in New Orleans . . . Well-traveled. No. 52 pick on the third round by Cavs in 1987, out of Notre Dame . . . Played in CBA for three seasons with an NBA stop in Minnesota and a tour of Israel tossed in . . . Signed and released by Magic and Spurs . . . Got another chance with Magic and signed as free agent Aug. 24, 1992 . . . Made $1.5 million.

Year	Team	G	FG	FG Pct.	FT	FT Pct.	Reb.	Ast.	TP	Avg.
1989-90	Minnesota	66	117	.459	153	.777	137	43	387	5.9
1991-92	San Antonio	60	80	.449	92	.692	124	34	252	4.2
1992-93	Orlando	77	194	.496	318	.815	295	80	706	9.2
1993-94	Orlando	74	174	.501	199	.740	248	61	547	7.4
1994-95	Orlando	70	206	.475	223	.746	279	198	635	9.1
1995-96	Orlando	64	106	.491	125	.762	153	42	337	5.3
	Totals	411	877	.482	1110	.764	1236	458	2864	7.0

GERALD WILKINS 33 6-6 225   Guard

Signed as free agent with the Magic after a season he'd prefer to forget . . . Didn't debut with the Grizzlies until Feb. 25 because of chronic back problems . . . Underwent surgery Nov. 12 . . . This after missing the entire previous season, while with Cavaliers, because of a torn Achilles tendon in his right leg . . . Had played at least 80 games in eight of the nine years before that . . . Did log 30.6 minutes a game in March . . . Highest-paid Grizz in 1995-96 at $2.478 million . . . They got him in the expansion draft . . . Dominique's brother played at Tennes-

see-Chattanooga before Knicks picked him 47th in 1985 . . . Born
Sept. 11, 1963, in Atlanta.

Year	Team	G	FG	FG Pct.	FT	FT Pct.	Reb.	Ast.	TP	Avg.
1985-86	New York	81	437	.468	132	.557	208	161	1013	12.5
1986-87	New York	80	633	.486	235	.701	294	354	1527	19.1
1987-88	New York	81	591	.446	191	.786	270	326	1412	17.4
1988-89	New York	81	462	.451	186	.756	244	274	1161	14.3
1989-90	New York	82	472	.457	208	.803	371	330	1191	14.5
1990-91	New York	68	380	.473	169	.820	207	275	938	13.8
1991-92	New York	82	431	.447	116	.730	206	219	1016	12.4
1992-93	Cleveland	80	361	.453	152	.840	214	183	890	11.1
1993-94	Cleveland	82	446	.457	194	.776	303	255	1170	14.3
1994-95	Cleveland				Injured					
1995-96	Vancouver	28	77	.376	20	.870	65	68	188	6.7
	Totals	745	4290	.458	1603	.749	2382	2445	10506	14.1

JOE WOLF 31 6-11 230   Center-Forward

When Shaq went down, there was an all-points
call for help . . . He got the call and signed as
a free agent for the $225,000 minimum on
Nov. 10 . . . Started season with Charlotte . . .
Played 63 games with Magic . . . Best shooting
season of his career . . . Can hit the 15-footer,
which is his strength . . . But he's still considered soft with inside game . . . And rebound-
ing? He has averaged 3.6 in his career. At 6-11? . . . Picked No.
13 by the Clippers in the 1987 draft after a steady career at North
Carolina . . . Went to Nuggets as a free agent Oct. 5, 1990 . . .
Free-agent signing with Celtics in '92. Lasted a month and a half.
Finished season with Blazers . . . Played in Spain in 1993-94.
signed and waived by Pacers before landing in Charlotte Nov. 3,
1994 . . . Born Dec. 17, 1964, in Kohler, Wis.

Year	Team	G	FG	FG Pct.	FT	FT Pct.	Reb.	Ast.	TP	Avg.
1987-88	L.A. Clippers	42	136	.407	45	.833	187	98	320	7.6
1988-89	L.A. Clippers	66	170	.423	44	.688	271	113	386	5.8
1989-90	L.A. Clippers	77	155	.395	55	.775	232	62	370	4.8
1990-91	Denver	74	234	.451	69	.831	400	107	539	7.3
1991-92	Denver	67	100	.361	53	.803	240	61	254	3.8
1992-93	Bos.-Port.	23	20	.455	13	.813	48	5	53	2.3
1994-95	Charlotte	63	38	.469	12	.750	129	37	90	1.4
1995-96	Char.-Orl.	64	135	.513	21	.724	187	63	291	4.5
	Totals	476	988	.427	312	.782	1694	546	2303	4.8

FELTON SPENCER 28 7-0 280   Center

A starting center in Orlando ... Well, he may be, as a replacement for Shaq O'Neal after being traded from Utah for Brooks Thompson, Kenny Gattison and a first-round pick last summer ... Averaged just 17.8 minutes a game ... By the time the conference finals rolled around, he sat on the bench a lot as Jerry Sloan went with a small lineup ... Missed the first 11 games of the regular season while recovering from an Achilles injury that cost him much of 1994-95, then played the final 71 without an absence ... Jazz got him by sending Mike Brown to the Timberwolves in June 1993 ... Was No. 6 pick by Minnesota in the 1990 draft after a standout career at Louisville ... Born Jan. 15, 1968, in Louisville, Ky. ... Made $2.181 million.

Year	Team	G	FG	FG Pct.	FT	FT Pct.	Reb.	Ast.	TP	Avg.
1990-91	Minnesota.......	81	195	.512	182	.722	641	25	572	7.1
1991-92	Minnesota.......	61	141	.426	123	.691	435	53	405	6.6
1992-93	Minnesota.......	71	105	.465	83	.654	324	17	293	4.1
1993-94	Utah	79	256	.505	165	.607	658	43	677	8.6
1994-95	Utah	34	105	.488	107	.793	260	17	317	9.3
1995-96	Utah	71	146	.520	104	.689	306	11	396	5.6
	Totals	397	948	.488	764	.685	2624	166	2660	6.7

DARRELL ARMSTRONG 28 6-1 180   Guard

Okay, now he's ready. Chalked up 41 valuable minutes of experience to go along with the eight he had in previous season ... But in those 41 minutes, he scored 42 points. Top that, Michael Jordan ... Okay, so Jordan has. Top that, Dennis Rodman ... Magic want to get a closer look. They've been impressed at first glance with his quickness and penetration ... Born June 22, 1968, in Gastonia, N.C. ... Undrafted out of Fayetteville State in 1991 ... Played in CBA, Global Basketball Association (twice), USBL. Also did the obligatory tour of Europe, in Spain. Was a Spanish League All-Star ... Signed by Magic as free agent April 8, 1995, and stuck for last season, when he made $350,000.

Year	Team	G	FG	FG Pct.	FT	FT Pct.	Reb.	Ast.	TP	Avg.
1994-95	Orlando	3	3	.375	2	1.000	1	3	10	3.3
1995-96	Orlando	13	16	.500	4	1.000	2	5	42	3.2
	Totals	16	19	.475	6	1.000	3	8	52	3.3

ANTHONY BONNER 28 6-8 225　　　　　　　Forward

You sort of figured Magic would toss him in during the Bulls series for his rugged defense. But then, you sort of figured the Magic would hold on to the Game 2 18-point second-half lead and avoid a sweep... Signed as minimum-wage free agent April 15, 1996, and pretty much became a bench ornament... Played 16 minutes in the playoffs, nine of them against Bulls... Solid rebounder, especially on offensive glass ... Good athlete who can be used to guard twos... Offensively, range rarely goes beyond arm's length... Played in Italy, averaging 17 points and nine rebounds before hooking on with Magic ... Originally a first-round pick, No. 23, by Sacramento in 1990 out of St. Louis... Did three years with forward-heavy Kings. Signed with Knicks as free agent Oct. 5, 1993... Born June 6, 1968, in St. Louis.

Year	Team	G	FG	FG Pct.	FT	FT Pct.	Reb.	Ast.	TP	Avg.
1990-91	Sacramento	34	103	.448	44	.579	161	49	250	7.4
1991-92	Sacramento	79	294	.447	151	.627	485	125	740	9.4
1992-93	Sacramento	70	229	.461	143	.593	455	96	601	8.6
1993-94	New York	73	162	.563	50	.476	344	88	374	5.1
1994-95	New York	58	88	.456	44	.657	262	80	221	3.8
1995-96	Orlando	4	5	.333	3	.429	19	4	13	3.3
	Totals	318	881	.468	435	.590	1726	442	2199	6.9

DAVID VAUGHN 23 6-10 240　　　　　　　Forward

Has the body, has the skills. Okay, now this is a playbook... Had trouble grasping the NBA game... He can rebound and block shots and that's what important to Magic way of thinking ... Rookie season highs of 10 points, eight rebounds and three blocks vs. Pacers April 12 ... Troubled by strep throat late in season... When playoffs came, he developed 13th man's disease, cleverly disguised as a sprained knee... Played for uncle, former pro Larry Finch, at Memphis. Also Penny Hardaway's alma mater... Torn ACL in left knee knocked him out of 1992-93 season... Checkered medical career in college included fractured foot as senior... No. 2 all-time shot-blocker at Memphis ... Magic took him No. 25 in 1995 draft... Born March 23, 1973, in Tulsa, Okla.... Grew up in Nashville, Tenn.... Made $534,000.

Year	Team	G	FG	FG Pct.	FT	FT Pct.	Reb.	Ast.	TP	Avg.
1995-96	Orlando	33	27	.338	10	.556	80	8	64	1.9

THE ROOKIES

BRIAN EVANS 23 6-8 220   **Forward**
Magic hope he's the scoring forward they need . . . Rick Pitino said this third-team All-American "is as difficult to guard as anybody I've seen in a long time." . . . Bob Knight's first Hoosier to lead the Big 10 in scoring (21.2 ppg) . . . Ninth all-time on Indiana's scoring list . . . Shoulder woes as a soph . . . Magic took him 27th in the first round . . . Born Sept. 13, 1973, in Rockford, Ill. . . . He'll earn $459,400 under rookie cap this year.

AMAL McCASKILL 23 6-11 235   **Center**
Magic backup centers getting a little long in the tooth . . . Strong inside presence off glass and defensively . . . Marquette's No. 11 all-time rebounder, No. 2 shot-blocker . . . In keeping with Magic policy for centers, not good from the line . . . Born Oct. 28, 1973, in Maywood, Ill. . . . Orlando took him on the second round, at No. 49.

COACH BRIAN HILL: Wasn't exactly buddy-buddy with

Shaq any more . . . But he was just being a coach and he has the backing of the owner . . . Has kept it simple, maybe too simple. Offense is predicated on double-teams, so somebody had to come up with plans to get all those open shots . . . But now the next step is devising attack when they don't double. Like what happened in the playoffs . . . Problem is, folks remember the playoffs and forget a 60-victory season . . . Has kept a young and still learning team together . . . But some of these guys aren't that young any more . . . Entering final contract year . . . Stresses defense. Maybe that's why Shaq got miffed . . . Under Hill, Magic have a three-year regular-season record of 167-79 (.679) . . . Ninth-fastest head coach to reach 100 wins . . . Succeeded Matt Guokas as coach June 30, 1993 . . . Served as Magic assistant under Guokas for three years . . . Prior to that, he was under Mike Fratello in Atlanta for four seasons . . . College coaching career covered 14 years, including eight at Lehigh . . . Basketball and track star at Kennedy (Neb.) College . . . His brother, Fred, is Rutgers' baseball coach . . . Born Sept. 19, 1947, in East Orange, N.J.

BIGGEST BLUNDER

Neither a trade nor a draft selection represents the root of the Magic's recurring nightmares. Rather, the final 10.7 seconds of the first NBA Finals game in franchise history will forever have players and fans asking, "What if?"

The Magic had made the finals through an often awesome offense that revolved around the inside might of Shaquille O'Neal, the all-around brilliance of Penny Hardaway, the board prowess of Horace Grant, plus the three-point shooting of Dennis Scott and Nick Anderson. But it was the simplicity of free-throw shooting that doomed Orlando at home that June 7, 1995 night against defending champ Houston.

Orlando already had squandered a 20-point lead. At home. But as regulation ticked down, they needed just one free throw to seal the game. Enter Anderson. Twice, in the final :10.7 of the fourth quarter, he went to the line to shoot two free throws. Four times, he missed. Houston forced overtime and came away a 120-118 winner. The Rockets then went on to sweep the deflated Magic, who only could ask "what if" Game One had belonged to them?

ALL-TIME MAGIC LEADERS

SEASON

Points: Shaquille O'Neal, 2,377, 1993–94
Assists: Scott Skiles, 735, 1992–93
Rebounds: Shaquille O'Neal, 1,122, 1992–93

GAME

Points: Shaquille O'Neal, 53 vs. Minnesota, 4/20/94
Assists: Scott Skiles, 30 vs. Denver, 12/30/90
Rebounds: Shaquille O'Neal, 28 vs. New Jersey, 11/20/93

CAREER

Points: Nick Anderson, 8,302, 1989–96
Assists: Scott Skiles, 2,776, 1989–94
Rebounds: Shaquille O'Neal, 3,691, 1992–96

PHILADELPHIA 76ERS

TEAM DIRECTORY: Owner: Pat Croce; GM/VP Business Oper.: Brad Greenberg; Dir. Player Personnel: Gene Shue: Dir. Scouting: Tony DiLeo; Player Personnel Asst.: Maurice Cheeks; Dir. Pub. Rel.: Jody Silverman; Coach: Johnny Davis; Asst. Coaches: Ed Badger, Bob Ociepka. Arena: The Spectrum (18,168). Colors: Red, white and blue.

Philly hopes for savior in Georgetown's Allen Iverson.

SCOUTING REPORT

SHOOTING: The Sixers took lots of shots. They just didn't have lots of makes. With an offense whose basic concepts were often unfathomable, Philadelphia placed 26th in the league for accuracy last season. There were some highlights, such as the three-point shooting of Vernon Maxwell (now gone) and the steady, regular inside play of Clarence Weatherspoon. But after that, little to nothing. Free-agent pickup Don MacLean will help.

Rookie savior-to-be Jerry Stackhouse looked too often like a rookie, shooting .414. Maybe new coach Johnny Davis would want to take the latest "next Michael Jordan" out of North Carolina and explain to him a good shot from a rancid shot. In transition, the Sixers were awful. Turnovers and bad decisions tend to do that—and keep shooting percentages down.

PLAYMAKING: The Sixers view the arrival of Allen Iverson the way a man dying of thirst in a desert looks upon an oasis. Basically, the Sixers held weekly auditions for the point-guard spot last season and the best they came up with was a shooting guard, Rex Walters, who easily displayed the best handle on the position.

The Sixers were 26th in scoring so obviously, they weren't too high up on the assist chain. Turnovers abounded—the Sixers were comfortably installed as the team with the worst assist/turnover ration in the league—and the offense was a complete and utter mess. Got the ball? Take a shot, who cares? Davis wants uptempo but he doesn't want the craziness that permeated the Philly offense and helped make the Sixers the sorriest team in the East. Davis will have to get Iverson out of his shoot-first mentality. And he's hoping shooting guard Lucious Harris, a free-agent pickup, will help bring depth to the backcourt.

REBOUNDING: They don't have a legitimate center. The one power forward, who'll probably be employed at the three, Weatherspoon, is undersized for the four. The other power forward, Derrick Coleman, has an injury history that has hounded him since he came in the league. Rebounding doesn't appear to be an area where the Sixers will take the league by force. But they signed Michael Cage, the Cavaliers' leading rebounder last year. The glaring gap in the middle has been the problem and the Sixers keep hoping that Coleman will play to his potential.

76ER ROSTER

No.	Veterans	Pos.	Ht.	Wt.	Age	Yrs. Pro	College
21	Derrick Alston	F	6-11	225	24	2	Duquesne
--	Michael Cage	F-C	6-9	248	34	12	San Diego State
44	Derrick Coleman	F	6-10	260	29	6	Syracuse
30	Lucious Harris	G	6-5	190	25	3	Long Beach State
25	Don MacLean	F	6-10	235	26	4	UCLA
42	Jerry Stackhouse	G-F	6-6	218	21	1	North Carolina
23	Rex Walters	G	6-4	190	26	3	Kansas
35	C. Weatherspoon	F	6-7	240	26	4	So. Mississippi
55	Scott Williams	F	6-10	230	28	7	North Carolina

Rd.	Rookies	Sel.No.	Pos.	Ht.	Wt.	College
1	Allen Iverson	1	G	6-4	165	Georgetown
2	Mark Henderson	31	F	6-9	220	Washington State
2	Ryan Minor	32	F	6-7	220	Oklahoma
2	Jamie Feick	48	F-C	6-9	255	Michigan State

DEFENSE: This is where you're supposed to stop the other guys from scoring, right? Just checking. Because obviously no one in Philadelphia has much of a clue as to what it means. The Sixers are coming off a season where they surrendered 104.5 points while allowing opponents to shoot .483. Hey, it wasn't that every opponent got lucky every night. Even expansionist Vancouver had better defensive numbers. And the Grizzlies only won 15 games.

There'll be some help from Cage, who comes off a season with a career-high 79 blocked shots, same as Stackhouse, who was runnerup to Weatherspoon's 108.

A good indicator on how passive the Sixers were defensively came through their personal fouls: only six teams committed less. But all that means is the Sixers weren't too big on getting up on people, rotating to cover or stepping up to clog the lane and maybe—what a novel concept—trying to take a charge.

OUTLOOK: At press time, the Sixers had gotten up to nine veterans under contract: Derrick Alston, Coleman, Williams, Stackhouse, Weatherspoon, MacLean, Harris, Cage and Walters. There is talent in the core nucleus—think there might be a team or two willing to swap its starting backcourt for Stackhouse and Iverson even up? Weatherspoon is quality and Coleman can be

Jerry Stackhouse was highest-scoring rookie last season.

an unstoppable force when the spirit moves him. But how much can his body take after years of being, at best, in borderline shape?

There will be improvement in the record under Davis. It would be pretty hard to regress from 18 victories. Unless, that is, they go the entire season with five players. The Sixers picked up three forwards on the second round and each has a different talent. If they can come up with some legitimate help there, then the franchise will have the makings of a redemption foundation.

SIXER PROFILES

JERRY STACKHOUSE 21 6-6 218 Guard

Last year's Next Michael Jordan . . . Has the explosiveness. Went to North Carolina . . . But like Mike when he came into the league, he needs to work on that perimeter game . . . And his ball-handling isn't quite up to legendary status just yet . . . Missed last eight games of the season with a fractured thumb . . . Did have impressive coming-out party. Led rookie class in scoring at 19.2 ppg and was third in assists at 3.9 . . . He is a potential All-Star . . . Of course in Philadelphia last year, anyone who didn't fall down before crossing midcourt looked like a potential All-Star . . . Scored 30 points five times . . . Season high of 34 points against Sacramento on Nov. 7 was one off Sixers' all-time rookie mark, held by Andrew Toney . . . Will only get better . . . Showed improved shot selection as season wore on. At beginning of year, the only shot he didn't like was the one for tetanus . . . Born Nov. 5, 1974, in Kinston, N.C. . . . Left Tar Heels after sophomore season and was third choice overall in '95 draft by the Sixers . . . Made $1.987 million.

Year	Team	G	FG	FG Pct.	FT	FT Pct.	Reb.	Ast.	IP	Avg.
1995-96	Philadelphia.	72	452	.414	387	.747	265	278	1384	19.2

CLARENCE WEATHERSPOON 26 6-7 240 Forward

Honest, Clarence, there is such a thing as winning . . . In his four years with the Sixers, has never seen the team get out of the 20s in victories . . . To him, a 30-victory season must seem like the Loch Ness Monster. Heard about it, and some even swear it exists. But he's never seen it . . . Think he's frustrated? . . . Has played with more than 50 different teammates . . . Would like some stability . . . Sad part is, this guy comes to play every night . . . Good explosiveness but he is undersized for the power-forward spot . . . Lacks a perimeter touch and a crossover move on rushes from outside . . . Was 14th in the league in rebounding at 9.7 . . . Had back-to-back 20-rebound games Jan. 5

and 10, the first time a Sixer has done that since Charles Barkley in 1990 . . . Career-high 35 points against Raptors April 21 . . . Born Sept. 8, 1970, in Crawford, Miss. . . . Sixers made him ninth pick in 1992 . . . Product of Southern Mississippi . . . Made $4.5 million.

Year	Team	G	FG	FG Pct.	FT	FT Pct.	Reb.	Ast.	TP	Avg.
1992-93	Philadelphia.	82	494	.469	291	.713	589	147	1280	15.6
1993-94	Philadelphia.	82	602	.483	298	.693	832	192	1506	18.4
1994-95	Philadelphia.	76	543	.439	283	.751	528	215	1373	18.1
1995-96	Philadelphia.	78	491	.484	318	.746	753	158	1300	16.7
	Totals	318	2130	.468	1190	.725	2700	712	5459	17.2

DERRICK COLEMAN 29 6-10 260   Forward

Just when you thought it couldn't get any worse in Philadelphia . . . Wanted out of New Jersey, where the Nets won 30. Landed in Philly, where the Sixers won 18 . . . Played 11 games after Nov. 30 trade that brought him, Rex Walters and Sean Higgins to Philly and sent Shawn Bradley, Greg Graham and Tim Perry up the New Jersey Turnpike . . . Not much can be said that hasn't already been said about him. And most of it's bad . . . When in shape and healthy, an astounding talent. Can rebound, shoot, shoot with range, put the ball on the floor and block shots . . . Key words are "when in shape and healthy" . . . No one denies that he plays hard . . . Practice? That's another matter . . . Became Generation X poster child after *Sports Illustrated* cover story two seasons ago . . . Could go down as one of the biggest disappointments in NBA history . . . Yeah, yeah, he was an All-Star. Once . . . Received major scare in preseason when docs discovered irregular heartbeat . . . Laid off practice, ballooned to at least 285 pounds . . . Then, surprise, he was injured . . . Sprained his right ankle Dec. 9 in third game as a Sixer. Missed 27 of 30 games. Returned Feb. 17, aggravated injury Feb. 23 and was lost for season . . . Problem was more severe, involved a leg tendon . . . When Johnny Davis was named coach, he flew to Detroit to meet with testy star . . . Made $5.476 million . . . The No. 1 pick in 1990 by Nets out of Syracuse. Promptly became

Rookie of the Year . . . Born June 21, 1967, in Mobile, Ala., but reared in Detroit.

Year	Team	G	FG	FG Pct.	FT	FT Pct.	Reb.	Ast.	TP	Avg.
1990-91	New Jersey	74	514	.467	323	.731	759	163	1364	18.4
1991-92	New Jersey	65	483	.504	300	.763	618	205	1289	19.8
1992-93	New Jersey	76	564	.460	421	.808	852	276	1572	20.7
1993-94	New Jersey	77	541	.447	439	.774	870	262	1559	20.2
1994-95	New Jersey	56	371	.424	376	.767	591	187	1146	20.5
1995-96	Philadelphia	11	48	.407	20	.625	72	31	123	11.2
	Totals	359	2521	.460	1879	.769	3762	1124	7053	19.6

DERRICK ALSTON 24 6-11 225   Forward-Center

Alston, not Coleman . . . The guy tries . . . And he tries all over the place . . . At 6-11, he can play either forward. And defensively, he can fill in at center for spells . . . Or step out and guard some two guards . . . Offensively, limited at best . . . Range measured by a yardstick. With room to spare . . . But he finished strong. Scored double-figures six times in last 13 games after doing it twice in previous 24 . . . Of course, the Sixers' last 13 games weren't exactly artistic marvels . . . Career-high 30 points against Phoenix March 15 . . . Terrific athleticism . . . A real nice find on the second round, No. 33, in 1994 . . . Born Aug. 20, 1972, in the Bronx, N.Y. . . . High school in Hoboken, N.J. . . . Duquesne product was not a bad bargain for $350,000.

Year	Team	G	FG	FG Pct.	FT	FT Pct.	Reb.	Ast.	TP	Avg.
1994-95	Philadelphia	64	120	.465	59	.492	219	33	299	4.7
1995-96	Philadelphia	73	198	.512	55	.491	302	61	452	6.2
	Totals	137	318	.493	114	.491	521	94	751	5.5

SCOTT WILLIAMS 28 6-10 230   Center-Forward

Somehow you get the feeling the Sixers expected a little more when they signed him as free agent away from the Bulls July 28, 1994 . . . Played in 13 games last season . . . Had hoped to be a Sixer starter but his body keeps breaking down when exposed to long minutes . . . Best in short bursts. Real short bursts . . . Underwent knee surgery in offseason, then needed surgery again in January . . . And even with Bulls, he had chronic shoulder problem ... Four times, he played 20 minutes ... When healthy, he's a strong rebounder, especially off the offensive glass ... But it's tough to rebound when fighting knee, finger, shoulder and quad injuries, which have plagued his career ... Born March 21, 1968, in Hacienda Heights, Cal. ... Came out of North Carolina in 1990 but wasn't drafted ... Bulls stole him as free agent ... A key reserve on Bulls' first three championship teams in 1991, '92 and '93 ... Made $1.95 million in second year with Sixers.

Year	Team	G	FG	FG Pct.	FT	FT Pct.	Reb.	Ast.	TP	Avg.
1990-91	Chicago	51	53	.510	20	.714	98	16	127	2.5
1991-92	Chicago	63	83	.483	48	.649	247	50	214	3.4
1992-93	Chicago	71	166	.466	90	.714	451	68	422	5.9
1993-94	Chicago	38	114	.483	60	.612	181	39	289	7.6
1994-95	Philadelphia	77	206	.475	79	.738	485	59	491	6.4
1995-96	Philadelphia	13	15	.517	10	.833	46	5	40	3.1
	Totals	313	637	.479	307	.690	1508	237	1583	5.1

REX WALTERS 26 6-4 190   Guard

How bad was the Sixer point situation? Here was their best point guard ... Of all the people who auditioned for the job with the Sixers, he showed more knowledge of what the position does and was more effective than anyone else ... And he's a two guard ... Great practice player ... Then, of course, there are the games ... A real workhorse but game simply has not progressed the way it should have since he came out of Kansas as the 16th pick, to New Jersey, in 1993 ... Maybe the point is his future ... Ended season strong: double-doubles for points and assists in his last two games ... Born March 12, 1970, in Omaha, Neb. ... Began college career at Northwestern ... A $1.04-million wage-earner.

Year	Team	G	FG	FG Pct.	FT	FT Pct.	Reb.	Ast.	TP	Avg.
1993-94	New Jersey	48	60	.522	28	.824	38	71	162	3.4
1994-95	New Jersey	80	206	.439	40	.769	93	121	523	6.5
1995-96	N.J-Phil.	44	61	.412	42	.808	55	106	186	4.2
	Totals	172	327	.447	110	.797	186	298	871	5.1

DON MacLEAN 26 6-10 235   Forward

Scoring small forward signed with 76ers after leaving Denver as a free agent... Quick release and soft touch for runners... Property of three teams before playing a single pro game—drafted by Pistons, traded to Clippers, traded to Bullets... Finally debuted for Washington in 1992-93... A season later, was named Most Improved Player... Bullets had a logjam up front and the need for a point guard, so they traded the UCLA product to Denver for Robert Pack on Oct. 30, 1995... Started five times for the Nuggets and took advantage of those opportunities by averaging 22.4 points... No. 1 in Pac-10 Conference scoring history when he left UCLA as No. 19 pick... Only the fourth player ever to lead the Bruins in scoring three straight years. The others are named Lew Alcindor, Bill Walton and Reggie Miller... Born Jan. 16, 1970, in Palo Alto, Cal.... Made $925,000.

Year	Team	G	FG	FG Pct.	FT	FT Pct.	Reb.	Ast.	TP	Avg.
1992-93	Washington	62	157	.435	90	.811	122	39	407	6.6
1993-94	Washington	75	517	.502	328	.824	467	160	1365	18.2
1994-95	Washington	39	158	.438	104	.765	165	51	430	11.0
1995-96	Denver	56	233	.426	145	.732	205	89	625	11.2
	Totals	232	1005	.403	667	.791	959	330	2827	12.2

LUCIOUS HARRIS 25 6-5 190   Guard

Lost the battle for minutes among reserve guards to Tony Dumas... Didn't help that he missed 18 straight games—about five weeks—with a broken left wrist... Has three-point range... Overall shooting percentage has improved all three years since he was drafted 28th out of Cal State-Long Beach... Born Dec. 18, 1970, in Los Angeles... Made $725,000.

Year	Team	G	FG	FG Pct.	FT	FT Pct.	Reb.	Ast.	TP	Avg.
1993-94	Dallas	77	162	.421	87	.731	157	106	418	5.4
1994-95	Dallas	79	280	.459	136	.800	220	132	751	9.5
1995-96	Dallas	61	183	.461	68	.782	122	79	481	7.9
	Totals	217	625	.449	291	.774	499	317	1650	7.6

MICHAEL CAGE 34 6-9 248   Forward-Center

Cavalier free agent signed with 76ers in August . . . He was an island of durability on a team otherwise jinxed by injuries, particularly to big men . . . Hasn't missed a game in the '90s; his streak of 575 in a row is second to Suns' A.C. Green (813) . . . Forced to play out of position at center much of the time, still ranked fifth in the league in offensive rebounds (288) . . . Had a career-high 79 blocked shots as well . . . Drafted 14th out of San Diego State by the Clippers in 1984, he led the league in rebounding in 1987-88 (13.0), then was shipped to Seattle in a three-way deal that also relocated Charles Smith and Hersey Hawkins . . . Cavs picked him up as free agent in '94, and he's played an invaluable support role upfront . . . Earned $2.126 million . . . Born Jan. 28, 1962, in West Memphis, Ark.

Year	Team	G	FG	FG Pct.	FT	FT Pct.	Reb.	Ast.	TP	Avg.
1984-85	L.A. Clippers	75	216	.543	101	.737	392	51	533	7.1
1985-86	L.A. Clippers	78	204	.479	113	.649	417	81	521	6.7
1986-87	L.A. Clippers	80	457	.521	341	.730	922	131	1255	15.7
1987-88	L.A. Clippers	72	360	.470	326	.688	938	110	1046	14.5
1988-89	Seattle	80	314	.498	197	.743	765	126	825	10.3
1989-90	Seattle	82	325	.504	148	.698	821	70	798	9.7
1990-91	Seattle	82	226	.508	70	.625	558	89	522	6.4
1991-92	Seattle	82	307	.566	106	.620	728	92	720	8.8
1992-93	Seattle	82	219	.526	61	.469	659	69	499	6.1
1993-94	Seattle	82	171	.545	36	.486	444	45	378	4.6
1994-95	Cleveland	82	177	.521	53	.602	564	56	407	5.0
1995-96	Cleveland	82	220	.556	50	.543	729	53	490	6.0
	Totals	959	3196	.516	1602	.669	7937	973	7994	8.3

THE ROOKIES

ALLEN IVERSON 21 6-0 165   Guard

Led the '96 kiddie corps . . . The first of a record 17 early-entry candidates . . . The No. 1 pick overall . . . Philadelphia had just one word for its point position: HELP . . . Here it is . . . Frightening quickness and vertical leap . . . Maybe too many turnovers. But who notices? . . . First Georgetown player to leave early under John Thompson . . . Aggressive, heady defender, too . . . Averaged 25.0 points as a soph . . . Born June 7, 1975, in Hampton, Va. . . . He'll make $2.267 million.

MARK HENDRICKSON 22 6-9 220   Forward
Arizona State coach Lute Olson said in preseason this was best all-around player in the Pac 10 . . . Set Washington State record for field-goal percentage at .567 . . . Led team in rebounding all four years. Only Cougar ever to do so . . . Shoots the face-up jumper, has strong moves inside . . . Born June 23, 1974, in Mount Vernon, Wash. . . . Second player picked on second round, No. 31 overall.

RYAN MINOR 22 6-7 220   Forward
Shooting plunged in senior season, from .486 to .417 . . . Still averaged 21.3 points for Oklahoma . . . Led Big Eight in scoring as a junior . . . Drafted out of high school by Baltimore Orioles. Was rated one of nation's top 25 baseball prospects. Led Sooners to NCAA baseball title in '94 . . . Born Jan. 5, 1974, in Hammon, Okla. . . . Sixers grabbed him on second round, No. 32 overall.

JAMIE FEICK 22 6-9 255   Forward-Center
Steady improvement over four years at Michigan State . . . Voted Spartans' Most Improved Player after junior season . . . Powerful rebounder. Took 31 boards in two games at Portsmouth Classic . . . Led Big 10 in rebounds . . . Chosen No. 48 overall on second round . . . Born July 3, 1974, in Lexington, Ohio.

COACH JOHNNY DAVIS: Okay, everyone who has seen him  coach an NBA game step forward . . . Didn't exactly get bowled over in the crush, did you? . . . But he's got as much NBA head-coaching experience as John Calipari. And he came a lot cheaper . . . Spent six years in the league as an assistant doing two years apiece with Atlanta, the Clippers and, most recently, Portland . . . Also served three years in Atlanta as the director of community affairs . . . Named Sixers' coach June 8 after John Lucas was sacked in May . . . Ten-year playing career with Blazers, Pacers, Hawks and Cavs . . . Averaged 12.9 points for career . . . Was 22nd pick overall, taken on second round, by Portland in 1976 after his college days at Dayton . . . Noted during his introductory press conference that he was ''instrumental in taking away [a championship] in 1977'' from the Sixers . . . That

Clarence Witherspoon: Quest for a winning season.

was his rookie season, when he became a starter halfway through the playoffs when Dave Twardzik was injured . . . In the Finals' sixth and deciding game, he grabbed the final rebound with :02 left to preserve a two-point victory for Blazers over Sixers . . . Business and Community Development degree from Georgia State in 1987 . . . Born Oct. 21, 1955, in Detroit.

BIGGEST BLUNDER

The biggest mistake the 76ers' brass ever made was getting out of bed June 16, 1986. On that fateful day, the organization made not one but two of the biggest blunders in its history.

Not only did they trade the No. 1 overall pick in the draft that day, but the Sixers sent future Hall of Famer Moses Malone, serviceable forward Terry Catledge and two first-round draft picks to the Bullets for Jeff Ruland and Cliff Robinson. That's the original Cliff Robinson, not the one in Portland. You know, the Cliff Robinson who played 131 games for the Sixers in three seasons.

Ruland's career was ruined by a knee injury: he played 18 games for the Sixers. Moses hung around for a while, with more than 8,500 points and nearly 5,000 rebounds remaining in his body.

But if that wasn't enough to doom the Sixers, that day they also sent the top pick of the draft to Cleveland—it turned out to be Brad Daugherty, who despite injuries, enjoyed an All-Star career. In return, the Sixers received Roy Hinson and $800,000. Hinson lasted less than two seasons in Philly.

ALL-TIME 76ER LEADERS

SEASON

Points: Wilt Chamberlain, 2,649, 1965–66
Assists: Maurice Cheeks, 753, 1985–86
Rebounds: Wilt Chamberlain, 1,957, 1966–67

GAME

Points: Wilt Chamberlain, 68 vs. Chicago, 12/16/67
Assists: Wilt Chamberlain, 21 vs. Detroit, 2/2/68
           Maurice Cheeks, 21 vs. New Jersey, 10/30/82
Rebounds: Wilt Chamberlain, 43 vs. Boston, 3/6/65

CAREER

Points: Hal Greer, 21,586, 1958–73
Assists: Maurice Cheeks, 6,212, 1978–89
Rebounds: Dolph Schayes, 11,256, 1948–64

BULLET PROFILES

TEAM DIRECTORY: Chairman: Abe Pollin; Pres.: Susan O'Malley; Exec. VP/GM: Wes Unseld; VP-Communications: Matt Williams; Dir. Pub. Rel.: Maureen Lewis; Coach: Jim Lynam; Asst. Coaches: Buzz Braman, Bob Staak. Arena: USAir Arena (18,756). Colors: Red, white and blue.

SCOUTING REPORT

SHOOTING: From three-point range, there was nobody better. Ever. The 1995-96 Bullets established an all-time mark with their triple-threats, led by Tim Legler, the long-distance shootout champion at All-Star Weekend and the NBA's regular-season leader. Inside, the Bullets' game goes beyond potent. Chris Webber has added to his game (and he's not adverse to stepping out to the arc, either). Juwan Howard (22.1) is back after a wild and wooly adventure in Miami. Harvey Grant, after a .462 season, returns from Portland with one of the game's most gifted and explosive point guards, Rod Strickland, who breaks down defenders with ease and can step out for the jumper. Gigantic Gheorghe Muresan doesn't miss too many dunks.

The problem for the Bullets is getting consistent play at the two-guard spot, beyond Legler's home-run touch. They may not be as good as last season, when they were second in the league in field-goal percentage, but the Bullets figure again to be one of the NBA's better shooting outfits.

PLAYMAKING: Bad decisions. Lots of turnovers. Finishing capabilities of cadavers. Mark Price was supposed to change all that. Unfortunately, Price spent all but seven games with his foot in a cast or on crutches. And now he's gone to Golden State. But the Bullets finally answered this need, acquiring Strickland from Portland, where he was fouth in the NBA in assists with 9.6 a game, trailing only John Stockton, Jason Kidd and Avery Johnson. The Bullets have been desperate for a stabilizing playmaker, seemingly since voters liked Ike. Washington received sound, if unspectacular, play from Brent Price, Mark's younger brother, who headed to Houston amid the free-agent frenzy. They got sometimes special, sometimes awful play from trade acquisiton Robert Pack, who was released last summer and signed with the Nets.

The Bullet's biggest shortcomings came on the break, not a good thing if you're trying to be uptempo. In their sets, they were

To Miami and back: Juwan Howard will make capital.

fine. Actually, pretty good. And now the break should improve with the high-octane Strickland. No slouch on the feed, either, Howard was runnerup to Brent Price in team assists last year.

REBOUNDING: You would think that with Muresan and Howard leading the way, the Bullets would have been a premier boarding outfit. Well, you'd think wrong. Washington was disappointingly down in the rebounding stats last year, much of that due to Webber being disappointingly down and out for all but 15 games. In the backcourt, the Bullets guards can snare maybe two or three rebounds a week, which certainly doesn't help matters. And the lack of boarding is critical off the offensive glass. Opponents tend to rebound and run, easily beating the pon-

BULLET ROSTER

No.	Veterans	Pos.	Ht.	Wt.	Age	Yrs. Pro	College
40	Gilbert Cheaney	G-F	6-7	209	25	3	Indiana
44	Harvey Grant	F	6-9	225	31	8	Oklahoma
5	Juwan Howard	F	6-9	250	23	2	Michigan
23	Tim Legler	G	6-4	210	29	6	LaSalle
77	Gheorghe Muresan	C	7-7	303	25	3	Cluj (Romania)
35	Tracy Murray	F	6-7	228	25	4	UCLA
1	Rod Strickland	G	6-3	185	30	8	DePaul
4	Chris Webber	F	6-10	250	23	3	Michigan
12	Chris Whitney	25	6-0	170	25	3	Clemson

Rd.	Rookies	Sel. No.	Pos.	Ht.	Wt.	College
2	Ronnie Henderson	55	G	6-4	206	LSU

derously slow Muresan back. Strickland will get his share of boards as a point guard.

DEFENSE: In sets, good, very good. In transition, bad, very bad. As has been noted, most centers can roll back up court faster than Muresan runs. And the guards are not especially adept defenders. Add it up and get lots of problems. But in the halfcourt, the Bullets are tough, thanks mainly to their shot-blocking, which ranked fifth in the league last season.

Gheorghe the Giant and reserve defensive stud Jim McIlvaine (now gone to Seattle) made Washington the only team with two Top 10 shot-blockers. Muresan, Howard and Webber (when healthy) would seem to make the Bullets a prime candidate to be a pressing team. Unfortunately, the big guys block shots. They don't press. That's up to the guards, usually guards with quickness and quicker hands. So much for pressing.

OUTLOOK: Like so many teams in the NBA, the Bullets' immediate future relied heavily upon the free-agent activity over the summer. They took a big hit in the departure of Jim McIlvaine. But Howard and happy days are here again. As in recent years, the Bullets are sound to powerful upfront. Unlike recent years, they feel a little better about the backcourt. And given the overall shape of the Atlantic Division, the Bullets are primed to make some noise and land a playoff bid.

BULLET PROFILES

CHRIS WEBBER 23 6-10 250   Forward

 It's getting so, even Lloyd's of London won't touch this guy . . . Has got to stay healthy. Period . . . Improved his game around the basket. Too bad points scored in hospital wastebaskets don't count . . . Had shoulder surgery Feb. 1 and played just 15 games all season after just 54 in 1994-95 . . . He and Mark Price, who were to lead Bullets into playoffs, managed just two games together . . . Showed range after working with shooting guru Buzz Braman . . . Hit 15 of 34 attempted three-pointers . . . But his chronic left shoulder problem wiped out the campaign . . . Bullets were 9-6 when he played, so they keep fingers crossed shoulder will stay put . . . Showed so much promise as a rookie in 1993-94. With Warriors, he became first rookie ever to amass 1,000 points, 500 rebounds, 250 assists, 150 blocks and 75 steals . . . Then he and Don Nelson grew sort of distant . . . Forced trade to Bullets for Tom Gugliotta and three first-rounders Nov. 17, 1994 . . . Physically gifted. Great passer, good leaper, quick . . . Was the No. 1 pick by Orlando in 1993 after his Fab Five tour at Michigan. Traded on draft night to Warriors for rights to Penny Hardaway and three first-round picks . . . Made two trips to NCAA championship game. Lost both times, including 1993 when he called non-existent time-out against North Carolina. Oops . . . Rookie of the Year in '94 . . . Paid $7.0 million after huge extension . . . Born March 1, 1973, in Detroit . . . Full name: Mayce Edward Christopher Webber III.

Year	Team	G	FG	FG Pct.	FT	FT Pct.	Reb.	Ast.	TP	Avg.
1993-94	Golden State	76	572	.552	189	.532	694	272	1333	17.5
1994-95	Washington.	54	464	.495	117	.502	518	256	1085	20.1
1995-96	Washington.	15	150	.543	41	.594	114	75	345	23.7
	Totals	145	1186	.527	347	.528	1326	603	2774	19.1

JUWAN HOWARD 23 6-9 250   Forward

Much ado about something . . . As free agent, he signed seven-year, $100.8-million deal with Heat. NBA voided it on grounds it put Heat over salary cap. So he came back to Washington for $105 million over seven years . . . Made $1.702 million last year . . . Outstanding talent. A complete package . . . Terrific low-post game. Good, soft shooting touch with range. An animal rebounder. Can put the ball on the floor. A model work ethic. Does public-service announcements to get kids to read. Visits hospitals . . . Sources say he slurps his soup, though . . . Never did Bullets figure he'd be this good this fast when they drafted him No. 5 in 1994 . . . An All-Star in his second season . . . Had Bullets' season-high game of 42 points at Toronto on April 19 . . . "He's already one of the best at his position," praised no less an authority than Michael Jordan . . . Tenth in the NBA in scoring . . . Third among forwards in assists, behind only Grant Hill and Scottie Pippen. And he got 8.1 rebounds, too . . . Another Michigan Fab Five guy who played in two NCAA championship games . . . On April 29, 1995, he became the first NBA player to leave school early and then go back and graduate on time . . . Born Feb. 7, 1973, in Chicago.

Year	Team	G	FG	FG Pct.	FT	FT Pct.	Reb.	Ast.	TP	Avg.
1994-95	Washington.	65	455	.489	194	.664	545	165	1104	17.0
1995-96	Washington.	81	733	.489	319	.749	660	360	1789	22.1
	Totals	146	1188	.489	513	.714	1205	525	2893	19.8

GHEORGHE MURESAN 25 7-7 303   Center

C'mon, wasn't he one of the villains in the "Dick Tracy" movie? . . . Of course, he's become a real bad guy to opposing centers trying to shoot over him. Take the escalator to the balcony, then try from there . . . Voted the NBA's Most Improved Player . . . Doesn't seem to be much more room for improvement, though, unless he can get jet packs in his socks . . . He averaged 14.5 points, 9.6 rebounds, led the league in field-goal percentage and was eighth in blocks. Go ahead, find another second-round pick with those numbers. Dare ya. Double-dare ya . . . Was picked No. 30 in the 1993 draft . . . Slow, plodding type but he clogs the lane as well as anyone . . . Jumping ability of a brick. And almost as swift . . . His game is as pretty as sludge, but it is effective and productive . . . Added nice little soft-touch shot . . . Scored over 20 points 17 times . . . Blocked nine shots in a game three times . . . Strained knee ligaments knocked him out of last six games. Bullets went 2-4, finished out of playoffs by three games . . . Had career highs of 31 points and 21 rebounds . . . Born Feb. 14, 1971, in Triteni, Romania. That's in Transylvania. A stone's throw from Drac's castle . . . Attended Cluj University . . . Played for Romanian National Team and later played in French League . . . Size 20 shoe . . . Parents were both under six feet . . . Probably had a 9-foot grandparent, though . . . Tallest player ever to play in the NBA . . . Signed through 1998 for an average of $1.93 million.

Year	Team	G	FG	FG Pct.	FT	FT Pct.	Reb.	Ast.	TP	Avg.
1993-94	Washington......	54	128	.545	48	.676	192	18	304	5.6
1994-95	Washington......	73	303	.560	124	.709	488	38	730	10.0
1995-96	Washington......	76	466	.584	172	.619	728	56	1104	14.5
	Totals	203	897	.570	344	.656	1408	112	2138	10.5

HARVEY GRANT 31 6-9 225   Forward

Back in the frontcourt . . . Maybe . . . After moving to shooting guard late in 1994-95, worth a great size advantage over most counterparts, he returned to familiar spot at small forward last season . . . Of his 75 starts, 66 came there, nine at guard . . . Has enough shooting range to play in the backcourt . . . Twin brother of Magic's Horace . . . Aquired from Washington in the summer of '93 for Kevin Duckworth . . . Bullets picked him 12th overall in 1988 . . . Led Oklahoma to NCAA championship game that year before, losing to underdog Kansas . . . Born July 4, 1965, in Augusta, Ga. . . . Made $3.551 million.

Year	Team	G	FG	FG Pct.	FT	FT Pct.	Reb.	Ast.	TP	Avg.
1988-89	Washington......	71	181	.464	34	.596	163	79	396	5.6
1989-90	Washington......	81	284	.473	96	.701	342	131	664	8.2
1990-91	Washington......	77	609	.498	185	.743	557	204	1405	18.2
1991-92	Washington......	64	489	.478	176	.800	432	170	1155	18.0
1992-93	Washington......	72	560	.487	218	.727	412	205	1339	18.6
1993-94	Portland........	77	356	.460	84	.641	351	107	798	10.4
1994-95	Portland........	75	286	.461	103	.705	284	82	683	9.1
1995-96	Portland........	76	314	.462	60	.545	361	111	709	9.3
	Totals	593	3079	.477	956	.708	2902	1089	7149	12.1

CALBERT CHEANEY 25 6-7 209   Guard-Forward

Becoming the Rip Van Winkle of the league. You know, falls asleep for long stretches... When he plays well, he's good. Very good... When he doesn't, he's, well, like asleep... Can't shake the too-nice image. Even on his best nights, he's a bad rebounder... Inconsistency, thy name is Calbert... Three years in the league and they still talk of "potential"...

Shooting was at a career best, but he dropped in virtually every other category... Ankle sprain knocked him out of 11 games... Was the No. 6 pick in the 1993 draft after his College Player of the Year season at Indiana... Indy native; born July 17, 1971, in Evansville... Made $2.8 million.

Year	Team	G	FG	FG Pct.	FT	FT Pct.	Reb.	Ast.	TP	Avg.
1993-94	Washington......	65	327	.470	124	.770	190	126	779	12.0
1994-95	Washington......	78	512	.453	173	.812	321	177	1293	16.6
1995-96	Washington......	70	426	.471	151	.706	239	154	1055	15.1
	Totals	213	1265	.463	448	.762	750	457	3127	14.7

TIM LEGLER 29 6-4 210   Guard

Knows travel agents, flight attendants by first name... Adept at packing for long or short stays... In past seven years, has been with six pro teams. And toss in near-annual visit to the CBA. And don't forget his four tours of the USBL and his stop in the WBL. About the only league he missed was the WWF... Became something of a national hero by winning the three-point shootout at All-Star Weekend, beating Dennis Scott in the finals and establishing a record for points... Led league in three-point shooting, hitting 128-of-246 for a remarkable .522... That's the second-best mark ever. Steve Kerr was .5235 in 1994-95... For second straight season, shot 50 percent from the floor, 80 percent from the line. Only Bullet to do so... By gum, the Bullets will actually run some plays for him this year. Or so they promise... Mainly, he's gotten opportunity shots... When defenses took the three away, he showed he can put the ball on the floor and take it to the basket... Simply better than they hoped for... Born Dec. 26, 1966, in Washington, D.C. ... Another who came out and went undrafted... LaSalle, Class of '88... Signed as free agent Sept. 27, 1995. Got two years, his first ever multi-year contract... Made $250,000 last season...

NBA tryouts and stops included Phoenix, Minnesota, Denver, Washington (the first time), Utah, Dallas and Golden State . . . Has never fouled out.

Year	Team	G	FG	FG Pct.	FT	FT Pct.	Reb.	Ast.	TP	Avg.
1989-90	Phoenix	11	11	.379	6	1.000	8	6	28	2.5
1990-91	Denver	10	25	.347	5	.833	18	12	58	5.8
1992-93	Utah-Dal.	33	105	.436	57	.803	59	46	289	8.8
1993-94	Dallas	79	231	.438	142	.840	128	120	656	8.3
1994-95	Golden State	24	60	.522	30	.882	40	27	176	7.3
1995-96	Washington	77	233	.507	132	.863	140	136	726	9.4
	Totals	234	665	.460	372	.847	393	347	1933	8.3

TRACY MURRAY 25 6-7 228   Forward-Guard

This is why we have expansion teams . . . Maybe he couldn't play defense well enough to help a top team, but maybe that was the wrong way to look at the guy . . . Raptors set him free and, voila, he bumped scoring average from 4.8 to 16.2, the league's largest increase . . . Was best shooter on the team . . . One of the top 20 in the league . . . So, as a free agent last summer, he signed multi-year contract with Bullets . . . Highest-scoring high-school player in California history had prolific career at UCLA . . . After that, follow the paper trail . . . Drafted 18th by San Antonio in 1992, subsequently traded to Milwaukee, then Portland, then Houston . . . Raptors got him as a free agent . . . Made $250,000 . . . Born July 25, 1971, in Los Angeles.

Year	Team	G	FG	FG Pct.	FT	FT Pct.	Reb.	Ast.	TP	Avg.
1992-93	Portland	48	108	.415	35	.875	83	11	272	5.7
1993-94	Portland	66	167	.470	50	.694	111	31	434	6.6
1994-95	Port.-Hou.	54	95	.408	33	.786	59	19	258	4.8
1995-96	Toronto	82	496	.454	182	.831	352	131	1325	16.2
	Totals	250	866	.446	300	.804	605	192	2289	9.2

CHRIS WHITNEY 25 6-0 170   Guard

Some surprises are nice surprises . . . Brendan Malone tried to convince Isiah Thomas in Toronto this guy should have stayed. Whitney didn't stay. Neither did Malone when year was out . . . Showed he belongs in league . . . Real quick, plays defense. Excellent at the line. Decent shooter . . . In limited minutes, better than 2-to-1 assists/turnovers . . . Two years of junior college before finishing at Clemson . . . Drafted by Spurs, 47th on second round, in '93 . . . Didn't do much with Spurs, waived Feb. 23, 1995. Hit the CBA. Tried to latch on with Toronto. Cut, hit the CBA. Bullets signed him to two 10-day pacts, then for remainder of season March 23, 1996 . . . Born Oct. 5, 1971, in Hopkinsville, K.Y.

Year	Team	G	FG	FG Pct.	FT	FT Pct.	Reb.	Ast.	TP	Avg.
1993-94	San Antonio	40	25	.305	12	.800	29	53	72	1.8
1994-95	San Antonio	25	14	.298	11	1.000	13	28	42	1.7
1995-96	Washington.	21	45	.455	41	.932	33	51	150	7.1
	Totals	86	84	.368	64	.914	75	132	264	3.1

ROD STRICKLAND 30 6-3 185   Guard

Kept his bags packed all last season . . . Then didn't go anywhere except AWOL . . . Has to have a new address this season . . . Doesn't he? . . . Terrific player, and at a position where those are at an especially high premium, but the icy relationship with coach P.J. Carlesimo is such a distraction . . . It earned him a six-game suspension in 1995-96 when he walked out on the team . . . All this overshadows the talent . . . No. 4 in the league in assists through it all . . . The 9.6 a game was second on the all-time Trail Blazer list, behind only Terry Porter's 10.1 in 1987-88 . . . Great penetrator, maybe the best in the business . . . Arrived in Portland as an unrestricted free agent . . . Born July 11, 1986, in the Bronx, N.Y., then to DePaul, then back home when the Knicks picked him 19th in 1988 . . . Made $2.28 million.

Year	Team	G	FG	FG Pct.	FT	FT Pct.	Reb.	Ast.	TP	Avg.
1988-89	New York	81	265	.467	172	.745	160	319	721	8.9
1989-90	N.Y.-S.A.	82	343	.454	174	.626	259	468	868	10.6
1990-91	San Antonio	58	314	.482	161	.763	219	463	800	13.8
1991-92	San Antonio	57	300	.455	182	.687	265	491	787	13.8
1992-93	Portland	78	396	.485	273	.717	337	559	1069	13.7
1993-94	Portland	82	528	.483	353	.749	370	740	1411	17.2
1994-95	Portland	64	441	.466	283	.745	317	562	1211	18.9
1995-96	Portland	67	471	.460	276	.652	297	640	1256	18.7
	Totals	569	3058	.470	1874	.710	2224	4242	8123	14.3

THE ROOKIE

RONNIE HENDERSON 22 6-4 206   **Guard**
Bullets have been looking for a shooter since Naismith nailed up the peach basket. Maybe this is the answer ... Early-entry candidate ... Left LSU following 21.6 ppg, .461 shooting junior season ... Two-time SEC scoring champ ... Can create own shot. And likes to. Maybe too much ... Born March 29, 1974, in Gulfport, Miss. ... The 55th pick.

COACH JIM LYNAM: It's starting to come together ... Still needs some guards to push the ball. Desperately. One year after a 21-61 record which equaled franchise record for defeats, Bullets did an 18-game turnaround ... Only Chicago had a better jump ... Vastly improved team defense ... Pushing the tempo, too ... Greatest strength considered to be his communication skills. Gets through to players. Also a good motivator ... Down-to-earth kind of guy, no pretenses ... Stresses positives. Tell him what a guy can, rather than can't, do ... Rides refs too much, though ... Signed on for three more seasons ... Did lose a big supporter, however, in general manager John Nash, who "resigned" with a pistol to his noggin ... Worked with Nash in Philadelphia and followed his friend to Bullets ... Head coach with Clippers, Sixers and Bullets. Career record of 306-368 (.454) ... Best season came with Sixers in 1989-90: 53-29 and the Atlantic Division title ... Assistant coach with Blazers in 1981-82. Served under his former college coach, Jack Ramsey ... A 158-118 record as a 10-year college coach at Fairfield, American and St. Joseph's (Pa.), his alma mater. He's also a member of the school's Hall of Fame ... Born Sept. 15, 1941, in Philadelphia.

BIGGEST BLUNDER

In 1964, the Bullets were enamored of a guard out of Evansville named Jerry Sloan. So they drafted him on the second round—which was after they spent their first-rounder on Gary Bradds, bypassing the likes of Willis Reed, Luke Jackson and

Paul Silas. Sloan stayed in school and came out in 1965. Still, the Bullets wanted him and again they used a second-round pick.

The Bullets' love affair with Sloan, however, diminished after he played just one season in Baltimore. So the Bullets exposed him to the expansion draft, where Chicago's new head coach, Johnny Kerr, a Bullet teammate of Sloan's, quickly gobbled up the guard.

Sloan went on to become synonymous with backcourt defense, earning first-team All-Defensive honors four times and second-team honors twice in his 10 years with the Bulls. Sloan and Norm Van Lier comprised one of the most feared defensive backcourts in league history during the early '70s. So for drafting the same guy twice, all the Bullets got were 59 games. And a decidedly red face.

ALL-TIME BULLET LEADERS

SEASON

Points: Walt Bellamy, 2,495, 1961–62
Assists: Kevin Porter, 734, 1980–81
Rebounds: Walt Bellamy, 1,500, 1961–62

GAME

Points: Earl Monroe, 56 vs. Los Angeles, 2/3/68
Assists: Kevin Porter, 24 vs. Detroit, 3/23/80
Rebounds: Walt Bellamy, 37 vs. St. Louis, 12/4/64

CAREER

Points: Elvin Hayes, 15,551, 1972–81
Assists: Wes Unseld, 3,822, 1968–81
Rebounds: Wes Unseld, 13,769, 1968–81

ATLANTA HAWKS

TEAM DIRECTORY: Pres.: Stan Kasten; GM: Pete Babcock; Dir. Pub. Rel.: Arthur Triche; Coach: Lenny Wilkens; Asst. Coaches: Dick Helm, Bill Hanzlik. Arena: The Omni (16,378). Colors: Red, white, gold, black and yellow.

Mookie Blaylock was born to steal.

SCOUTING REPORT

SHOOTING: The two who shoot the most, guards Steve Smith and Mookie Blaylock, shoot the worst (Smith shot .432 last season, Blaylock .405). In fact, only one regular, Sean Rooks—and he was with the team just 16 games—shot better than 50 percent as the team ranked 25th in the league.

Power forward Christian Laettner may be the most consistent 15-foot shooter on a team overloaded with slashers. Newcomer Dikembe Mutombo isn't known for his scoring ability, averaging less than eight shots a game his final three seasons in Denver. Look for the Hawks to dump the ball inside more frequently in hopes of establishing Mutombo as a player who needs to be double-teamed.

PLAYMAKING: Lenny Wilkens' Cleveland teams were noted for their intelligent, precise ball movement. It's been far different in Atlanta. The Hawks were dead last in assists last season, their halfcourt offense often a shambles.

Laettner, one of the better passers among big men, should help the problem, but he won't solve it. Blaylock can create, and Smith is effective with the ball. That's about all.

If this team isn't generating baskets with turnovers or offensive rebounds, it tends to look lost.

REBOUNDING: The numbers say the Hawks are one of the best offensive rebounding teams in the league. The fact behind the numbers is that the team shoots so poorly it gets more opportunities off the glass than most.

Adding Mutombo solved several problems. Not only do the Hawks get a solid board man at center, it allows Laettner to shift to his natural position, power forward, and gives the team a dramatically stonger look inside. It also takes pressure off huge rookie Priest Lauderdale to step in and provid immediate help, and gives him time to develop.

It's also possible fast-rising forward Alan Henderson could be paired with Laettner and Mutombo, giving the team the kind of strength upfront it has lacked since the days of Truck Robinson.

DEFENSE: Few can terrorize in the open floor like Blaylock, the point man on a high-pressure unit that has a knack for stealing

HAWKS ROSTER

No.	Veterans	Pos.	Ht.	Wt.	Age	Yrs. Pro	College
--	Jon Barry	G	6-5	203	27	4	Georgia Tech
10	Mookie Blaylock	G	6-1	185	29	7	Oklahoma
24	Donnie Boyce	G	6-5	195	23	1	Colorado
44	Alan Henderson	F	6-9	235	23	1	Indiana
F-22	Reggie Jordan	G	6-4	195	27	1	New Mexico State
32	Christian Laettner	F-C	6-11	235	27	3	Duke
55	Dikembe Mutombo	C	7-2	250	30	5	Georgetown
5	Ken Norman	F	6-8	228	32	8	Illinois
8	Steve Smith	G	6-8	215	27	4	Michigan State

F-Free agent

Rd.	Rookies	Sel. No.	Pos.	Ht.	Wt.	College
1	Priest Lauderdale	28	C	7-2	343	Central State

possessions for an offense that needs as many as it can get. Second to Gary Payton in steals (2.62), Blaylock has established himself as The Glove of the East.

Combine that with the shot-blocking, elbow-throwing, presence of Mutumbo inside, and this will be a very difficult team to score against. Always tough in the 90-foot game, the Hawks now should be much better in the half-court, where it all revolves around the front line. Only two teams blocked fewer shots last season. That, too, shall change.

OUTLOOK: That 57-win season of two years ago is starting to look like nothing more than an aberration. But for that, the Hawks have been masters of mediocrity over the past seven years, able to contend for a playoff berth, but not taken as a serious threat.

They started to shake up the roster last season and finished 32-19 but offseason rumblings about deteriorating relationships between Wilkens and several of his key players did not bode well for this team's immediate future. Though they added a much-needed center in Mutombo, the Hawks had to give Stacey Augmon and Grant Long to the Pistons in order to clear salary-cap room. If the Hawks felt they were a center away from contention, they got their man. Odds are, they'll still suffer for their inability to hit consistently from the perimeter.

HAWK PROFILES

STEVE SMITH 27 6-8 215   Guard

Hawks decided to pin their postseason hopes on Smith, telling him to be more aggressive with his shot . . . It worked in the first round (22.8 points, .513 shooting, 5 of 25 three-pointers) against Indiana, but not in the second (20.6 points, .374 shooting, 10 of 36 threes) against Orlando . . . Let his personality emerge, a la Reggie Miller, in the playoffs . . . Had best scoring season of his career (18.1) but shot just .432, including a poor .331 from three-point range . . . Bad knees make him stiff-legged, thus a huge defensive liability . . . Miami invested the fifth pick in 1991 on the Michigan State star, but found he was not another Magic Johnson . . . Never cut it as a point guard, so Heat sent him with Grant Long to the Hawks in 1994 for Kevin Willis . . . Though selected to Dream Team II, he played more like an in-your-dreams teamer . . . Earned $2.568 million in final year of his contract . . . Born March 31, 1969, in Highland Park, Mich.

Year	Team	G	FG	FG Pct.	FT	FT Pct.	Reb.	Ast.	TP	Avg.
1991-92	Miami	61	297	.454	95	.748	188	278	729	12.0
1992-93	Miami	48	279	.451	155	.787	197	267	766	16.0
1993-94	Miami	78	491	.456	273	.835	352	394	1346	17.3
1994-95	Mia.-Atl.	80	428	.426	312	.841	276	274	1305	16.3
1995-96	Atlanta	80	494	.432	318	.826	326	224	1446	18.1
	Totals	347	1989	.442	1153	.819	1339	1437	5592	16.1

MOOKIE BLAYLOCK 29 6-1 185   Guard

Best defensive point guard in the East, second in the league only to Gary Payton . . . Ranked second in steals (2.62) for the second straight year and had his fourth straight season of at least 200 . . . Offensively, it's another story . . . Hasn't shot better than .432 in his career, and last season's .405 was the lowest since his rookie season . . . More than half his shots were three-pointers . . . When Hawks won, he averaged 17.7 points, 6.5 assists and shot .435. When they lost, he averaged 12.3 points, 4.7 assists and shot .372 . . . Hawks' all-time leader in three-pointers (662) and attempts (1,834) . . . Has been at his worst in the playoffs, shooting .368 . . . New Jersey drafted him 12th, out of Oklahoma, in 1989, then were stripped of him by the Hawks in 1992 for Rumeal Robinson . . . Earned $2.5 million last season . . . Born March 20, 1967, in Garland, Tex.

Year	Team	G	FG	FG Pct.	FT	FT Pct.	Reb.	Ast.	TP	Avg.
1989-90	New Jersey	50	212	.371	63	.778	140	210	505	10.1
1990-91	New Jersey	72	432	.416	139	.790	249	441	1017	14.1
1991-92	New Jersey	72	429	.432	126	.712	269	492	996	13.8
1992-93	Atlanta	80	414	.429	123	.728	280	671	1069	13.4
1993-94	Atlanta	81	444	.411	116	.730	424	789	1118	13.8
1994-95	Atlanta	80	509	.425	156	.729	393	616	1373	17.2
1995-96	Atlanta	81	455	.405	127	.747	332	478	1268	15.7
	Totals	516	2895	.416	850	.742	2087	3697	7346	14.2

CHRISTIAN LAETTNER 27 6-11 235   Center-Forward

Rescued from Siberia when the Hawks sent Andrew Lang and Spud Webb to Minnesota for Laettner and Sean Rooks on Feb. 22 . . . Finally reached the postseason, where he was forced to play out of position at center, giving up considerable size and weight against Indiana's Rik Smits and Orlando's Shaquille O'Neal, but didn't back down . . . Averaged 15.7 points and 6.9 rebounds (not to mention 4.1 fouls) in the playoffs . . . The knock on him as a power forward was that he was relatively soft and did his best work on the perimeter . . . Averaged 14.2 points and 7.9 rebounds after the trade . . . Minnesota made him the third pick, out of Duke, in the storied '92 draft (behind O'Neal and Alonzo Mourning) . . . Earned $3.91 million last season . . . Counts horror novelist Stephen King among his circle of friends. No doubt all those years in Minnesota provided some material . . . Born Aug. 17, 1969, in Angola, N.Y.

Year	Team	G	FG	FG Pct.	FT	FT Pct.	Reb.	Ast.	TP	Avg.
1992-93	Minnesota	81	503	.474	462	.835	708	223	1472	18.2
1993-94	Minnesota	70	396	.448	375	.783	602	307	1173	16.8
1994-95	Minnesota	81	450	.489	409	.818	613	234	1322	16.3
1995-96	Minn.-Atl.	74	442	.487	324	.818	538	197	1217	16.4
	Totals	306	1791	.475	1570	.814	2461	961	5184	16.9

DIKEMBE MUTOMBO 30 7-2 250   Center

The first player in NBA history to lead the league in blocked shots for three straight seasons ... Let's not confuse that with being a superstar ... Still, Hawks opened the vault to the tune of a reported $50 million for five years ... There's no debating he can make an impact inside ... His 4.49 blocks last season was the best average in the league since David Robinson in 1991-92 ... Had as many or more swats than the opposition 38 times last season ... Three-time All-Star also a big-time rebounder ... No. 3 in 1995-96 ... Defensive Player of the Year in 1994-95 ... Went fourth in the 1991 draft after starring at Georgetown ... Dikembe Mutumbo Mpolondo Mukamba Jean Jacque Wamutombo was born June 25, 1966, in Kinshasa, Zaire ... Made $3.25 million.

Year	Team	G	FG	FG Pct.	FT	FT Pct.	Reb.	Ast.	TP	Avg.
1991-92	Denver	71	428	.493	321	.642	870	156	1177	16.6
1992-93	Denver	82	398	.510	335	.681	1070	147	1131	13.8
1993-94	Denver	82	365	.569	256	.583	971	127	986	12.0
1994-95	Denver	82	349	.556	248	.654	1029	113	946	11.5
1995-96	Denver	74	284	.499	246	.695	871	108	814	11.0
	Totals	391	1824	.523	1406	.650	4811	651	5054	12.9

ALAN HENDERSON 23 6-9 235   Forward

His rapid progress hastened the departure of veteran power forward Grant Long ... Averaged 9.7 points in season's final 12 games, then followed that up with a solid postseason ... Added 10 pounds of muscle prior to season, enabling him to bang more effectively ... Fundamentally sound low-post player, though he lacks fluidity ... Despite relatively limited minutes, he was second on the team in blocks and third in offensive rebounds ... When he played 20 or more minutes, team was 19-11 ... Wasn't thrilled with finishing second to Glenn Robinson as Indiana's high school Mr. Basketball, but has gotten over it ... Graduated from Indiana University with a degree in biology and has been accepted to medical school ... His father is a cardiologist ... An excellent pick at 16th in 1995 ... Earned $791,000 ... Born Dec. 12, 1972, in Indianapolis.

Year	Team	G	FG	FG Pct.	FT	FT Pct.	Reb.	Ast.	TP	Avg.
1995-96	Atlanta	79	192	.442	119	.595	356	51	503	6.4

KEN NORMAN 32 6-8 228   Forward

Racked up more DNP-CDs last season (44) than in his other eight years combined ... Started first 28 games and averaged 10.2 points but, with team 13-15, he was benched for Stacey Augmon and that was that ... Appeared in just six games the rest of the season, then burned bridges by ripping coach Lenny Wilkens when it was over ... If he isn't traded, it'll be a bigger upset than Princeton over UCLA ... A good jump-shooter who inexplicably has deteriorated at the line, he hit a career-low .354 last season ... Clippers made him the 19th pick out of Illinois in 1987 ... After six seasons in L.A. and one with Bucks, he was dealt to the Hawks in exchange for the salary-cap slot known as Roy Hinson in 1994 ... Born Sept. 5, 1964, in Chicago.

Year	Team	G	FG	FG Pct.	FT	FT Pct.	Reb.	Ast.	TP	Avg.
1987-88	L.A. Clippers	66	241	.482	87	.512	263	78	569	8.6
1988-89	L.A. Clippers	80	638	.502	170	.630	667	277	1450	18.1
1989-90	L.A. Clippers	70	484	.510	153	.632	470	160	1128	16.1
1990-91	L.A. Clippers	70	520	.501	173	.629	497	159	1219	17.4
1991-92	L.A. Clippers	77	402	.490	121	.535	448	125	929	12.1
1992-93	L.A. Clippers	76	498	.511	131	.595	571	165	1137	15.0
1993-94	Milwaukee	82	412	.448	92	.503	500	222	979	11.9
1994-95	Atlanta	74	388	.453	64	.457	362	94	938	12.7
1995-96	Atlanta	34	127	.465	17	.354	132	63	304	8.9
	Totals	629	3710	.488	1008	.568	3910	1343	8653	13.8

DONNIE BOYCE 23 6-5 195   Guard

Rookie season never got off the ground as he missed first 60 games while rehabilitating a broken leg suffered in the 1995 Big Eight tournament ... If not for that injury, he might've been a first-round pick as Colorado's all-time leading scorer (18.6) ... Hawks took him 42nd, knowing they'd have to wait till this year to see if he could help ... Earned $250,000, which isn't bad for a guy who was the third-best player on his high-school team ... Teammates at Chicago's Proviso East included 1995 first-rounders Sherell Ford (Seattle) and Michael Finley (Phoenix) ... Born Sept. 2, 1973, in Chicago.

Year	Team	G	FG	FG Pct.	FT	FT Pct.	Reb.	Ast.	TP	Avg.
1995-96	Atlanta	8	9	.391	2	.500	10	3	24	3.0

Stan Smith led Hawks in scoring and free-throw pct.

JON BARRY 27 6-5 203 Guard

Former Warriors ballboy became Warriors reserve guard and now is a Hawk after signing one-year contract as free agent . . . Had signed with Warriors last year for the $275,000 minimum just four years after being 21st pick in the 1992 draft. Celtics traded him to Bucks early in his rookie season . . . Reputation in Milwaukee was as someone who couldn't shoot and then sulked when he didn't play, but Warriors liked what they saw . . . Had a big jump in his shooting percentage . . . Most notable was that he seemed to find some three-point range, going from 33.3, 27.8 and 33.3 percent the first three seasons to 47.3 in 1995-96 . . . Set team record with eight straight makes from behind the arc ... Son of Hall of Famer Rick and brother of Clippers' Brent was born July 25, 1969, in Oakland and attended Georgia Tech.

Year	Team	G	FG	FG Pct.	FT	FT Pct.	Reb.	Ast.	TP	Avg.
1992-93	Milwaukee	47	76	.369	33	.673	43	68	206	4.4
1993-94	Milwaukee	72	158	.414	97	.795	146	168	445	6.2
1994-95	Milwaukee	52	57	.425	61	.763	49	85	191	3.7
1995-96	Golden State	68	91	.492	31	.838	63	85	257	3.8
	Totals	239	382	.421	222	.771	301	406	1099	4.6

THE ROOKIE

PRIEST LAUDERDALE 23 7-2 343   Center
Hawks swapped two second-rounders to Seattle to move into the first round and take this biggest of big men with the 28th pick ... Averaged 16.1 points and 11.2 rebounds with Peristeri Nikas in Greece ... Native of Chicago's tough south side couldn't find a college home—playing 13 games at Central State before heading overseas ... Very strong, not particularly athletic ... Born Aug. 31, 1973, in Chicago.

COACH LENNY WILKENS: Dream Team III coach had little  summer vacation ... Same gripes—lack of communication, lack of discipline, lack of enthusiasm—that led to his departure from Cleveland in 1993 surfaced again in his third season with Hawks ... Has won more NBA games than anyone (1,014, with 850 losses), but just one championship ring ... Has only been as far as the conference finals once since taking Seattle to the title in 1979 ... Has seven 50-win seasons with three different teams (Seattle, Cleveland and Atlanta) ... Averaged 16.5 points and 6.7 assists in a 15-year playing career that began when the Hawks (then in St. Louis) made him a first-round pick out of Providence College in 1960 ... He also played for Seattle, Cleveland and Portland before ending his playing career after the 1974-75 season ... Is in the Hall of Fame and has been president of the NBA Coaches Association ... Born Oct. 28, 1937, in Brooklyn, N.Y.

BIGGEST BLUNDER

The day before the 1956 draft, the then-St. Louis Hawks made a trade that would bring the franchise its only championship the following season.

Why was this a mistake? Because it kept the Hawks from having a shot at 10 more.

Acquiring proven scorer Ed Macauley (a former St. Louis University star) and promising youngster Cliff Hagan from Boston gave the Hawks an imposing frontline, and they won the title in 1958—beating the Celtics in six games.

But, led by the man whose draft rights the Hawks traded away, future Hall of famer Bill Russell, the Celtics would begin their unrivaled run of eight consecutive championships, and 10 in 11 years, in 1959.

While that deal may have established the genius of Boston's Red Auerbach, it didn't exactly kill the career of the St. Louis general manager Marty Blake, who now is the NBA's director of scouting.

ALL-TIME HAWK LEADERS

SEASON

Points: Bob Pettit, 2,429, 1961–62
Assists: Glenn Rivers, 823, 1986–87
Rebounds: Bob Pettit, 1,540, 1960–61

GAME

Points: Dominique Wilkins, 57 vs. Chicago, 11/10/86
　　　　　Dominique Wilkins, 57 vs. New Jersey, 4/10/86
　　　　　Lou Hudson, 57 vs. Chicago, 11/10/69
　　　　　Bob Pettit, 57 vs. Detroit, 2/18/61
Assists: Mookie Blaylock, 23 vs. Utah, 3/6/93
Rebounds: Bob Pettit, 35 vs. Cincinnati, 3/2/58
　　　　　　Bob Pettit, 35 vs. New York, 1/6/56

CAREER

Points: Dominique Wilkins, 23,292, 1982–94
Assists: Glenn Rivers, 3,866, 1983–91
Rebounds: Bob Pettit, 12,851, 1954–65

CHARLOTTE HORNETS

TEAM DIRECTORY: Owner: George Shinn; VP-Basketball Oper.: Bob Bass; VP-Communications: Harold Kaufman; Dir. Pub. Rel.: Marilynn Bowler; Coach: Dave Cowens; Asst. Coaches: T.R. Dunn, Lee Rose. Arena: Charlotte Coliseum (24,042). Colors: Teal, purple and white.

As a new Hornet, Glen Rice topped team in scoring.

SCOUTING REPORT

SHOOTING: In this franchise's brief history, this never has been a problem. Though the Hornets picked up notorious mason Kenny Anderson, they more than offset that by acquiring Glen Rice from Miami in the Alonzo Mourning trade.

Rice, Dell Curry and Scott Burrell (provided he ever gets healthy) provide a deadly trio of three-point shooters. First-round pick Tony Delk (No. 16) was a deadly long-range shooter at Kentucky, and will only add to the arsenal. Ex-Laker Vlade Divac replaces the low-post scoring that has been missing since Mourning was dealt. Ex-Knick Anthony Mason, while not as proflific a scorer as the traded Larry Johnson, is more efficient and he, too, commands double-teams in the post.

Once the ball goes inside, the problems start. Matt Geiger and George Zidek both played better than expected, but neither scares anyone from the post.

PLAYMAKING: By the end of the season, the reason for acquiring Anderson was startlingly clear: getting rid of Kendall Gill. Though Anderson played well (he even shot 45 percent) with Charlotte, he did little to raise the level of play of his teammates, the basic measuring stick of a point guard.

Anderson left for Portland and Muggsy Bogues is coming off knee problems, so Delk was drafted to provide some insurance at the point. Not really a distributor in college, he'll need to think pass first to score with the Hornets.

What used to be a high-scoring team has slowed down considerably but, then again, so has the rest of the league.

Though they have excellent shooters, the Hornets lack two key complements: slashers to break down the defense, and post players to draw double-teams.

REBOUNDING: Even with Mourning, this was a mediocre team on the boards, at best. Without him, they were outrebounded for the eighth consecutive season, though major strides were made on the defensive glass, thanks largely to newcomers Rice and Geiger.

They don't lack size, but they don't overwhelm anyone, and aren't particularly athletic across the front. Geiger is a tenacious head-banger and Mason uses his broad body well. Divac gives them another rebounder.

HORNET ROSTER

No.	Veterans	Pos.	Ht.	Wt.	Age	Yrs. Pro	College
7	Rafael Addison	F	6-8	241	32	5	Syracuse
1	Tyrone Bogues	G	5-3	141	31	9	Wake Forest
24	Scott Burrell	G-F	6-7	218	25	3	Connecticut
30	Dell Curry	G	6-5	200	32	10	Virginia Tech
12	Vlade Divac	C	7-1	250	28	7	Partizan BC
52	Matt Geiger	C	7-0	245	27	4	Georgia Tech
5	Anthony Goldwire	G	6-2	177	25	1	Houston
4	Darrin Hancock	G-F	6-7	212	24	2	Kansas
54	Brad Lohaus	F	6-11	235	32	9	Iowa
14	Anthony Mason	F	6-7	250	29	7	Tennessee State
20	Pete Myers	G-F	6-6	180	33	8	Arkansas-Little Rock
41	Glen Rice	G-F	6-8	214	29	7	Michigan
25	George Zidek	C	7-0	266	23	1	UCLA

Rd.	Rookies	Sel.No.	Pos.	Ht.	Wt.	College
1	Tony Delk	16	G	6-2	193	Kentucky
2	Malik Rose	44	F	6-7	250	Drexel

DEFENSE: What would you expect from a team dressed in teal uniforms designed by Alexander Julian? Rudeness?

The perpetual politeness of this team was at the top of the agenda for new coach Dave Cowens, who promised to deliver "a little nastier" team this season. That bodes well for Geiger, who already possesses that certain disheveled quality, but it is an idea many of his teammates may find in bad taste.

A group that never quite seemed to grasp the concept of rotation, except as it applied to a jump shot, the Hornets must develop the sense of responsibility to one another, that every basket allowed is an affront to the entire unit. Mason takes defense very personally and should help in this area.

OUTLOOK: This is a team that has begun to change not only its faces, but its personality. Mason and Divac are tough-minded and highly skilled big men who fill Cowens' needs. With Anderson gone, the point remains an unanswered question. The Hornets appear to be headed in the right direction, but much remains to be done.

Hornets hope Vlade Divac will respond in new uniform.

HORNET PROFILES

GLEN RICE 29 6-8 214   Guard-Forward

Like Reggie Miller, he's a long-shooting guard with longer shooting range. Unlike Miller, he has never broken through in the playoffs (15.2 points, .379 shooting in eight games) . . . That appears to be all that's holding him back from becoming a major star . . . Ranked 12th in NBA in scoring (21.6) and 14th (.424) in three-point percentage . . . Rebounds well for a perimeter player (career 4.9) . . . Can surprise you with his hops . . . Not strong off the dribble but virtually unguardable on the perimeter . . . Miami made the Michigan star the fourth pick in 1989 . . . After six seasons as an untouchable, he was dealt with Khalid Rheeves and Matt Geiger to Hornets for Alonzo Mourning, Pete Myers and LeRon Ellis on opening day, 1995 . . . Earned $3.302 million . . . Born May 28, 1967, in Flint, Mich.

Year	Team	G	FG	FG Pct.	FT	FT Pct.	Reb.	Ast.	TP	Avg.
1989-90	Miami	77	470	.439	91	.734	352	138	1048	13.6
1990-91	Miami	77	550	.461	171	.818	381	189	1342	17.4
1991-92	Miami	79	672	.469	266	.836	394	184	1765	22.3
1992-93	Miami	82	582	.440	242	.820	424	180	1554	19.0
1993-94	Miami	81	663	.467	250	.880	434	184	1708	21.1
1994-95	Miami	82	667	.475	312	.855	378	192	1831	22.3
1995-96	Charlotte	79	610	.471	319	.837	378	232	1710	21.6
	Totals	557	4214	.461	1651	.836	2741	1299	10958	19.7

ANTHONY MASON 29 6-7 250   Forward

Wind him up, watch him go. And go. And now the five-year Knick is gone—to Charlotte in the trade with Brad Lohaus for Larry Johnson last summer . . . NBA's iron man. Led the league by averaging 42.2 minutes. Also set a team record with 3,457 minutes . . . After-hours incidents, allegations seemingly were as frequent as his starts . . . Brute underneath whose thin-skinned attitude is often difficult to accept . . . Responds as well to criticism as cats to swimming pools . . . Still, a well-above-average talent . . . Went bonkers when Patrick Ewing suggested Knicks get a forward who could shoot with range . . . A good defender who made his name in the league at that end. Still good, but emphasis on offense has caused defense to dip . . . Versatility may be his best asset. Handles ball like a guard, rebounds like a forward, etc. . . . Shot .563, fourth-best in NBA. Has mastered hook, baseline spin . . . And he led the team in assists . . . Sixth Man of the Year one year ago, he was moved into the starting lineup by Don Nelson . . . Had Knicks over a free-agent barrel and signed six-year megabucks contract that paid him $3.472 million last season . . . Crowd favorite. Has various messages razor-cut into head. Hasn't dyed hair yet, though . . . Rags-to-riches story. Cameos with Blazers, Nuggets and Nets. Bounced around CBA, USBL and Turkey. Signed by Knicks as a free agent July 30, 1991 . . . Improved free-throw shooting back to .720 with unorthodox one-handed style . . . Blazers took him No. 53, out of Tennessee State, in 1988 . . . Born Dec. 14, 1966, in Miami, but grew up in Queens, N.Y.

Year	Team	G	FG	FG Pct.	FT	FT Pct.	Reb.	Ast.	TP	Avg.
1989-90	New Jersey	21	14	.350	9	.600	34	7	37	1.8
1990-91	Denver	3	2	.500	6	.750	5	0	10	3.3
1991-92	New York	82	203	.509	167	.642	573	106	573	7.0
1992-93	New York	81	316	.502	199	.682	640	170	831	10.3
1993-94	New York	73	206	.476	116	.720	427	151	528	7.2
1994-95	New York	77	287	.566	191	.641	650	240	765	9.9
1995-96	New York	82	449	.563	298	.720	764	363	1196	14.6
	Totals	419	1477	.526	986	.681	3093	1037	3940	9.4

SCOTT BURRELL 25 6-7 218   Forward

Captain of the Hornets' MASH unit . . . Hasn't lasted a full season since his junior year at UConn . . . Has missed an average of 37 games in three pro seasons . . . Last year he was twice-bitten . . . Dislocated his right shoulder on Dec. 30 after scoring at least 20 points in three previous games . . . After missing two months, he aggravated same injury in practice trying to come back in February . . . Had surgery to repair the problem . . . When healthy, a solid contributor who works both ends . . . The only athlete ever selected in the first rounds of two sports, he was Seattle's top pick in the 1989 baseball draft, but opted to attend UConn to play basketball. Drafted again by Toronto in 1990, he has pitched in the Jays' minor-league system . . . Hornets took him 20th in 1993 . . . Earned $1.04 million . . . Born Jan. 12, 1971, in Hamden, Conn.

Year	Team	G	FG	FG Pct.	FT	FT Pct.	Reb.	Ast.	TP	Avg.
1993-94	Charlotte.	51	98	.419	46	.657	132	62	244	4.8
1994-95	Charlotte.	65	277	.467	100	.694	368	161	750	11.5
1995-96	Charlotte.	20	92	.447	42	.750	98	47	263	13.2
	Totals	136	467	.452	188	.696	598	270	1257	9.2

DELL CURRY 32 6-5 200   Guard

For those of you who've always wondered, "Gee, how would this guy do if he ever started?" the answer came last season . . . Started (something he hadn't done at all since 1991) 27 straight games from January to March and averaged 17.6 points . . . Wound up with career highs in minutes played (28.9 per game), three-pointers made (164) and attempted (406), and steals (108) . . . Relatively low shooting percentage (.453 last season) belies his talent as one of the fastest, and most accurate, guns in the league . . . Virginia Tech two-sport standout (the school retired his baseball jersey) was drafted 15th by Utah in 1986, then spent a season at Cleveland before Hornets plucked him from expansion pool in '88 . . . Earned $1.57 million . . . Born June 25, 1964, in Harrisonburg, Va.

Year	Team	G	FG	FG Pct.	FT	FT Pct.	Reb.	Ast.	TP	Avg.
1986-87	Utah	67	139	.426	30	.789	78	58	325	4.9
1987-88	Cleveland	79	340	.458	79	.782	166	149	787	10.0
1988-89	Charlotte.	48	256	.491	40	.870	104	50	571	11.9
1989-90	Charlotte.	67	461	.466	96	.923	168	159	1070	16.0
1990-91	Charlotte.	76	337	.471	96	.842	199	166	802	10.6
1991-92	Charlotte.	77	504	.486	127	.836	259	177	1209	15.7
1992-93	Charlotte.	80	498	.452	136	.866	206	180	1227	15.3
1993-94	Charlotte.	82	533	.455	117	.873	262	221	1335	16.3
1994-95	Charlotte.	69	343	.441	95	.856	168	113	935	13.6
1995-96	Charlotte.	82	441	.453	146	.854	264	176	1192	14.5
	Totals	727	3852	.461	962	.853	1954	1449	9453	13.0

RAFAEL ADDISON 32 6-8 241   Forward

Decent defensive player who has played with four NBA teams in parts of five seasons dating back a decade . . . Keep him away from the three-point line (.271 career mark) . . . Drafted 39th out of Syracuse by Phoenix in 1986, he headed to Italy after his rookie season for four huge years in which he averaged 26.9 points and 6.2 rebounds . . . Went back in 1993-94 after two seasons with Nets . . . Earned $360,000 . . . Born July 22, 1964, in Jersey City, N.J.

Year	Team	G	FG	FG Pct.	FT	FT Pct.	Reb.	Ast.	TP	Avg.
1986-87	Phoenix	62	146	.441	51	.797	106	45	359	5.8
1991-92	New Jersey	76	187	.433	56	.737	165	68	444	5.8
1992-93	New Jersey	68	182	.443	57	.814	132	53	428	6.3
1994-95	Detroit	79	279	.476	74	.747	242	109	656	8.3
1995-96	Charlotte	53	77	.467	17	.773	90	30	171	3.2
	Totals	338	871	.452	255	.770	735	305	2058	6.1

MATT GEIGER 27 7-0 245   Center

Doesn't have Alonzo Mourning's skills, but has few peers when it comes to intensity . . . While still with Miami, he incurred league's wrath for hacking, and hurting, Shaquille O'Neal early in the season . . . Part of the monster trade that sent Mourning to Miami, he was thought to be a throw-in . . . Thrown into the starting lineup on Jan. 6, he couldn't be thrown out, averaging 12.9 points and 9.6 rebounds in the final 47 games . . . A clear case of reverse Samson syndrome . . . Miami drafted the former Georgia Tech afterthought 42nd in 1992 . . . Earned $1.532 million . . . Born Sept. 10, 1969, in Salem, Mass.

Year	Team	G	FG	FG Pct.	FT	FT Pct.	Reb.	Ast.	TP	Avg.
1992-93	Miami	48	76	.524	62	.674	120	14	214	4.5
1993-94	Miami	72	202	.574	116	.779	303	32	521	7.2
1994-95	Miami	74	260	.536	93	.650	413	55	617	8.3
1995-96	Charlotte	77	357	.536	149	.727	649	60	866	11.2
	Totals	271	895	.543	420	.713	1485	161	2218	8.2

MUGGSY BOGUES 31 5-3 141   Guard

Had never been on the injured list before, but knee problems kept him out of all but six games . . . Had the left knee scoped, tried to come back twice but wound up back on the injured list both times . . . He and Dell Curry are the lone remaining original Hornets . . . Team was searching for another point guard long before he got hurt . . . As good as he is in the open floor—and he's among the best—his poor jumper is a fatal halfcourt flaw . . . Teammates at Baltimore's Dunbar High included Reggie Williams, the late Reggie Lewis and David Wingate . . . Drafted 12th by Washington out of Wake Forest in 1987, he was taken by the Hornets in the expansion draft the following year . . . Earned $1.35 million . . . Born Jan. 9, 1965, in Baltimore.

Year	Team	G	FG	FG Pct.	FT	FT Pct.	Reb.	Ast.	TP	Avg.
1987-88	Washington	79	166	.390	58	.784	136	404	393	5.0
1988-89	Charlotte	79	178	.426	66	.750	165	620	423	5.4
1989-90	Charlotte	81	326	.491	106	.791	207	867	763	9.4
1990-91	Charlotte	81	241	.460	86	.796	216	669	568	7.0
1991-92	Charlotte	82	317	.472	94	.783	235	743	730	8.9
1992-93	Charlotte	81	331	.453	140	.833	298	711	808	10.0
1993-94	Charlotte	77	354	.471	125	.806	313	780	835	10.8
1994-95	Charlotte	78	348	.477	160	.889	257	675	862	11.1
995-96	Charlotte	6	6	.375	2	1.000	7	19	14	2.3
	Totals	644	2267	.460	837	.813	1834	5488	5396	8.4

BRAD LOHAUS 32 6-11 235   Center-Forward

Quick. What's nearly 7-0 and invisible under the backboards? . . . He came to the Hornets from the Knicks as the minor player with Anthony Mason for Larry Johnson last July . . . Remains one of NBA's most bizarre packages: a 6-11, three-point shooter . . . Perimeter game is his best asset. May be his only asset . . . Can't rebound. Can't defend. Makes a mean latte, though . . . Can pass a bit. But he'd rather shoot the three. Made 24 of 57 (.421) as a Knick . . . Didn't get much time after Feb. 8, 1995, trade from Spurs with J.R. Reid and a first-rounder for Charles Smith and Monty Williams . . . Has one year left on his contract that will pay $550,000, up from $485,000 . . . Born

Sept. 29, 1964, in New Ulm, Minn. . . . Well-traveled since Boston picked him 45th on second round, out of Iowa, in 1987 . . . Sent to Kings with Danny Ainge for Joe Kleine and Ed Pinckney Jan 4, 1990 . . . Minnesota took him in 1989 expansion draft and traded him to Milwaukee for Randy Breuer Jan. 4, 1990 . . . Did a year in Miami as a free agent in 1994-95. Then on to Spurs, again as a free agent.

Year	Team	G	FG	FG Pct.	FT	FT Pct.	Reb.	Ast.	TP	Avg.
1987-88	Boston	70	122	.496	50	.806	138	49	297	4.2
1988-89	Bos.-Sac.	77	210	.432	81	.786	256	66	502	6.5
1989-90	Minn.-Mil.	80	305	.460	75	.728	398	168	732	9.2
1990-91	Milwaukee	81	179	.431	37	.685	217	75	428	5.3
1991-92	Milwaukee	70	162	.450	27	.659	249	74	408	5.8
1992-93	Milwaukee	80	283	.461	73	.723	276	127	724	9.1
1993-94	Milwaukee	67	102	.363	20	.690	150	62	270	4.0
1994-95	Miami	61	97	.420	10	.667	102	43	267	4.4
1995-96	S.A.-N.Y.	55	71	.406	4	.800	64	44	197	3.6
	Totals	641	1531	.441	377	.735	1850	708	3825	6.0

ANTHONY GOLDWIRE 25 6-2 177   Guard

Had season highs in points (20) and assists (15) in one spectacular game against Dallas on March 7 . . . Other than that, looked pretty much like your basic CBA fill-in . . . Did average 11.5 points and 5.3 assists in eight straight emergency starts . . . Drafted 52nd out of Houston by Phoenix in 1994 . . . Earned the minimum . . . Born Sept. 6, 1971, in West Palm Beach, Fla.

Year	Team	G	FG	FG Pct.	FT	FT Pct.	Reb.	Ast.	TP	Avg.
1995-96	Charlotte	42	76	.402	46	.767	43	112	231	5.5

PETE MYERS 33 6-6 180   Guard/Forward

Has lived in more NBA cities than Larry Brown . . . Made Hornets his seventh team when he signed free-agent contract in February . . . Actually, Hornets signed him in October, then sent him to Miami in the Alonzo Mourning trade. After the Heat released him, he returned to Charlotte . . . Better known as the guy who kept Michael Jordan's seat warm for two seasons in Chicago when he played admirably . . . A battler who will find a home as soon as he finds a shot . . . A sixth-round pick out of Arkansas-Little Rock by Chicago in 1986, he also has played for San Antonio, Philadelphia, New York and New Jersey . . . Teams like him so much, three have had him back twice . . . Earned $600,000 . . . Born Sept. 15, 1963, in Mobile, Ala.

Year	Team	G	FG	FG Pct.	FT	FT Pct.	Reb.	Ast.	TP	Avg.
1986-87	Chicago	29	19	.365	28	.651	17	21	66	2.3
1987-88	San Antonio	22	43	.453	26	.667	37	48	112	5.1
1988-89	Phil.-N.Y.	33	31	.425	33	.688	33	48	95	2.9
1989-90	N.Y.-N.J.	52	89	.396	66	.660	96	135	244	4.7
1990-91	San Antonio	8	10	.435	9	.818	18	14	29	3.6
1993-94	Chicago	82	253	.455	136	.701	181	245	650	7.9
1994-95	Chicago	71	119	.415	70	.614	139	148	318	4.5
1995-96	Mia.-Char.	71	91	.368	80	.656	140	145	276	3.9
	Totals	368	655	.420	448	.668	661	804	1790	4.9

VLADE DIVAC 28 7-1 250   Center

New Hornet took a step back last season . . . From two years of consistent play to the Vlade of old, the one that shows some nights and doesn't others . . . No. 14 in the NBA in blocks, but only 24th in rebounding at 8.6 . . . That was still good enough to lead the Lakers for the fourth season in a row . . . George Mikan, Elgin Baylor, Kareem Abdul-Jabbar and A.C. Green are the only other Lakers to do that . . . Good passer, especially from the post, but tends to force plays . . . Hook shot never looks the same twice in a row . . . Came to L.A. from Yugoslavia as the No. 26 pick in 1986 . . . Made $3.333 million . . . Born Feb. 3, 1968, in Prijepolje, Yugoslavia . . . Came to Charlotte in July trade for Kobe Bryant.

Year	Team	G	FG	FG Pct.	FT	FT Pct.	Reb.	Ast.	TP	Avg.
1989-90	L.A. Lakers	82	274	.499	153	.708	512	75	701	8.5
1990-91	L.A. Lakers	82	360	.565	196	.703	666	92	921	11.2
1991-92	L.A. Lakers	36	157	.495	86	.768	247	60	405	11.3
1992-93	L.A. Lakers	82	397	.485	235	.689	729	232	1050	12.8
1993-94	L.A. Lakers	79	453	.506	208	.686	851	307	1123	14.2
1994-95	L.A. Lakers	80	485	.507	297	.777	829	329	1277	16.0
1995-96	L.A. Lakers	79	414	.513	189	.641	679	261	1020	12.9
	Totals	520	2540	.510	1364	.707	4513	1356	6497	12.5

DARRIN HANCOCK 24 6-7 212   Forward

Unpolished, but interesting . . . Superior athlete who didn't start playing basketball till the eighth grade . . . After inconsequential rookie season, was forced to play consistent minutes off the bench last season and continued to progress . . . Former national JUCO Player of the Year turned pro after one season at Kansas, heading to France in 1993-94 . . . Hornets drafted him 38th in 1994 . . . Earned $225,000 . . . Born Nov. 3, 1971, in Birmingham, Ala.

Year	Team	G	FG	FG Pct.	FT	FT Pct.	Reb.	Ast.	TP	Avg.
1994-95	Charlotte........	46	68	.562	16	.410	53	30	153	3.3
1995-96	Charlotte........	63	112	.523	47	.644	98	47	272	4.3
	Totals ....:	109	180	.537	63	.563	151	77	425	3.9

GEORGE ZIDEK 23 7-0 266   Center

Started well, averaging 7.2 points and 17.9 minutes in November, but hit the wall quickly . . . Did start 21 games . . . After he played an unheralded role in leading UCLA to its first national championship since '75, Hornets made him the 22nd pick in 1995 . . . Son of the greatest Czech player ever (Jiri) . . . An Academic All-American in college whose GPA (3.77) was more than half his career scoring average (7.1) . . . Earned $603,000 . . . Born Aug. 2, 1973, in Alin, Czechoslovakia.

Year	Team	G	FG	FG Pct.	FT	FT Pct.	Reb.	Ast.	TP	Avg.
1995-96	Charlotte........	71	105	.423	71	.763	183	16	281	4.0

THE ROOKIES

TONY DELK 22 6-1 193   Guard

With Kenny Anderson gone and Muggsy Bogues' health uncertain, Hornets spent 16th pick on the guard who led Kentucky to NCAA championship . . . But is he a point guard? . . . More of a scorer than a distributor . . . Scored 24 points and hit 7 of 12 three-pointers in the title win over Syracuse . . . Led Wildcats in scoring his final three seasons, including 17.8 as a senior . . . Born Jan. 28, 1974, in Covington, Tenn.

MALIK ROSE 21 6-7 250   **Forward**
Rugged Drexel big man was taken with 44th pick . . . Second to Derrick Coleman on NCAA's modern era rebounding list with 1,514 . . . Averaged 20.2 points and 13.2 boards as a senior . . . Played mostly center in college, will have to make shift to power forward in pros . . . Went to same Philadelphia high school (Overbrook) as Wilt Chamberlain . . . Born Nov. 23, 1974, in Philadelphia.

COACH DAVE COWENS: As a player, he battled his way into the Hall of Fame thanks largely to his defense, rebounding and passion. And he was a solid scorer as well . . . Hornets hope he can transfer those qualities to a team that lacked them under Allan Bristow . . . Spent the last two seasons as Bob Hill's top assistant in San Antonio . . . The fourth pick by the Celtics, out of Florida State, in the 1970 draft, he was NBA Rookie of the Year and, in 1972-73, MVP, when he averaged 20.5 points and 16.2 rebounds . . . After 10 years in Boston, during which he was player-coach in 1978-79, he finished his playing career with less than a season at Milwaukee in 1982-83 . . . Despite being small for a center at 6-9, he averaged 17.6 points and 13.6 rebounds . . . He appeared in six All-Star Games and was named to the All-Defense team three times . . . Born Oct. 25, 1948, in Newport, Ky.

BIGGEST BLUNDER

The mistake wasn't in drafting Larry Johnson of Nevada-Las Vegas with the top pick in 1991. In his first two seasons, Johnson quickly established himself as one of the rising stars of the NBA, averaging better than 20 points and 10 rebounds and shooting well above 50 percent from the field.

But signing Johnson to a 12-year, $84-million contract in 1993 turned out to be a colossal mistake. Back problems that cropped up in the 1993-94 season drastically reduced Johnson's effectiveness, making this once-great talent a virtually untradeable property whose massive long-term contract would affect the franchise's salary structure for years to come.

The domino effect of that deal ultimately cost the Hornets Alonzo Mourning, who was traded to Miami just prior to the start of last season strictly to avoid losing the talented—and expensive—young center to free agency.

ALL-TIME HORNET LEADERS

SEASON

Points: Larry Johnson, 1,810, 1992–93
Assists: Muggsy Bogues, 867, 1989–90
Rebounds: Larry Johnson, 899, 1991–92

GAME

Points: Larry Johnson, 44 vs. Boston, 11/22/95
Assists: Muggsy Bogues, 19 vs. Boston, 4/23/89
      Muggsy Bogues, 19 vs. L.A. Lakers, 11/24/93
      Muggsy Bogues, 19 vs. Milwaukee, 2/18/94
Rebounds: Larry Johnson, 23 vs. Minnesota, 3/10/92

CAREER

Points: Dell Curry, 8,341, 1988–96
Assists: Muggsy Bogues, 5,084, 1988–96
Rebounds: Larry Johnson, 3,479, 1991–96

CHICAGO BULLS

TEAM DIRECTORY: Chairman: Jerry Reinsdorf; VP-Operations: Jerry Krause; Dir. Media Services: Tim Hallam; Coach: Phil Jackson; Asst. Coaches: Jim Rodgers, Tex Winter. Arena: United Center (21,711). Colors: Red, white and black.

Scottie Pippen rounds out a decade as a bountiful Bull.

SCOUTING REPORT

SHOOTING: When Dennis Rodman's Bad Boys were in their prime, those Motor City thugs were decried for their slow pace and lack of scoring talent. In 1988-89, the year of their first championship, they averaged a paltry 106.6 points per game, 17th in the league.

For those who want to make an argument for this as the greatest team ever, consider the Bulls led the NBA in scoring last season—with an average of 105.2. Certainly, they are the best team of the '90s, but the NBA has gone on such a steady diet of expansion it is on the verge of an eating disorder. It simply is too thin.

Not to belittle the Bulls, or their primary offensive catalysts, Michael Jordan and Scottie Pippen. Those two would star on any team in any era. And Toni Kukoc is the best backup in the game. But, when it comes to offense, the rest of the team is strictly offensive.

PLAYMAKING: The greatest shooting guard ever became, by necessity, one of the most devastating point guards ever last season. Such is the brilliance of Jordan. Put him on the floor, give him a ball, and he will beat you. Position designations are far too limiting. He possesses every skill.

Considering Jordan and Pippen dominate the ball, and they combined to average 10.2 assists last season, there really isn't much need, or room, for a conventional point guard.

And don't forget that Kukoc, Rodman and Luc Longley are some of the most deft passers among big men in the game.

REBOUNDING: Caught up in the year-long frenzy, a usually credible national magazine forwarded the idea that Rodman might be the best rebounder ever.

This was consistent; there simply is no fair way to compare eras and the numbers. Rodman is the best of his time, and that should be good enough.

Jordan might well be the second-best rebounding guard ever (behind Oscar Robertson). Pippen has annually been among the leaders at his position.

BULL ROSTER

No. Veterans	Pos.	Ht.	Wt.	Age	Yrs. Pro	College
0 Randy Brown	G	6-2	191	28	5	New Mexico State
F-30 Jud Buechler	G-F	6-6	228	28	6	Arizona
35 Jason Caffey	F	6-8	255	23	1	Alabama
F-53 James Edwards	C	7-0	277	40	19	Washington
9 Ron Harper	G	6-6	216	32	10	Miami (Ohio)
23 Michael Jordan	G	6-6	216	33	11	North Carolina
25 Steve Kerr	G	6-3	181	31	8	Arizona
7 Toni Kukoc	F-G	6-11	232	28	3	Croatia
13 Luc Longley	C	7-2	292	27	5	New Mexico
33 Scottie Pippen	G-F	6-7	228	31	9	Central Arkansas
91 Dennis Rodman	F	6-8	220	35	10	SE Oklahoma State
F-22 John Salley	F-C	6-11	255	32	10	Georgia Tech
8 Dickey Simpkins	F	6-9	248	24	2	Providence
34 Bill Wennington	C	7-0	277	33	9	St. John's

F-Free agent

Given these realities, who needs a center? They did pick one in the draft, Connecticut's Travis Knight, but relinquished their rights to him and he signed with the Lakers.

DEFENSE: With all due respect to Gary Payton, Jordan is not only the best defensive player in the league, he is the best the backcourt ever has seen. The team defense, the true heart of this team, always has started with Jordan. He has the hands, the feet, the eyes and the strength to stop anyone.

Pippen and Rodman aren't far behind. All three were named to the NBA's All-Defensive team, one of the few awards decided by a vote of coaches.

Any questions about Rodman's ability to do his thing in the low post were answered when he embarrassed Shaquille O'Neal in the conference finals by holding his own despite giving up six inches and 100 pounds.

OUTLOOK: Phil Jackson's team might not win 72 again but who's counting?

The biggest problem facing this franchise is time. They are

the oldest team in the league, and there isn't much young talent waiting in line to defend the throne.

As long as Jordan and Pippen are around, this will be the team to beat.

BULL PROFILES

MICHAEL JORDAN 33 6-6 216   Guard

You can take Michael out of baseball, but you can't take the baseball out of Michael . . . To wit, his newfound affinity for the home run . . . A guy who hit .202 (on three-pointers) his first five seasons suddenly became Frank Thomas, knocking them out at will . . . Ranked 11th in the NBA at .427, ahead of guys like Glen Rice, Dennis Scott, Dale Ellis and, yes, even Reggie Miller . . . Which just goes to show there's nothing this man can't do, if he wants . . . Then again, the NBA did bring the fences in . . . Won an unprecedented eighth scoring title, breaking tie with Wilt Chamberlain . . . Passed 24,000 points and 2,000 steals, and became the Bulls' all-time leader in games played, passing Jerry Sloan . . . Obligatory criticism: had lowest assist average (4.3) since his second season . . . The only member of the winningest team in NBA history GM Jerry Krause did not acquire, he was drafted third out of North Carolina by the Bulls in 1984 . . . Exponentially underpaid at $3.85 million, he became a celebrated free agent in July, with a reported asking price of $36 million for two years . . . And re-signed for one year at $25 million . . . Too bad he'll never be fully recognized for his defensive brilliance . . . Born Feb. 17, 1963, in Brooklyn, N.Y., which ought to be enough to make the Big Apple green.

Year	Team	G	FG	FG Pct.	FT	FT Pct.	Reb.	Ast.	TP	Avg.
1984-85	Chicago	82	837	.515	630	.845	534	481	2313	28.2
1985-86	Chicago	18	150	.457	105	.840	64	53	408	22.7
1986-87	Chicago	82	1098	.482	833	.857	430	377	3041	37.1
1987-88	Chicago	82	1069	.535	723	.841	449	485	2868	35.0
1988-89	Chicago	81	966	.538	674	.850	652	650	2633	32.5
1989-90	Chicago	82	1034	.526	593	.848	565	519	2753	33.6
1990-91	Chicago	82	990	.539	571	.851	492	453	2580	31.5
1991-92	Chicago	80	943	.519	491	.832	511	489	2404	30.1
1992-93	Chicago	78	992	.495	476	.837	522	428	2541	32.6
1994-95	Chicago	17	166	.411	109	.801	117	90	457	26.9
1995-96	Chicago	82	916	.495	548	.834	543	352	2491	30.4
	Totals	766	9161	.512	5753	.844	4879	4377	24489	32.0

SCOTTIE PIPPEN 31 6-7 228   Forward

An intern at Dr. J's practice . . . Those who thought he was underrated enjoyed this season, those who thought he was overrated remember 1994-95 . . . Was off to a great start until a variety of minor, yet nagging, injuries, dampened his wick . . . Like Michael Jordan, he has taken full advantage of the shorter three-point line to lengthen his effectiveness, shooting a career-best .374 from the arc . . . Seattle's worst nightmare, on many levels. Sonics drafted him fifth out of tiny Central Arkansas in '87, then immediately shipped him to the Bulls for, well, Olden Polynice and some other stuff . . . Sonics then spent five years trying to figure out how to trade for him . . . Bulls said no, won four titles in six years . . . Earned $2.925 million, which makes him the biggest bargain since Manhattan . . . Born Sept. 25, 1965, in Hamburg, Ark.

Year	Team	G	FG	FG Pct.	FT	FT Pct.	Reb.	Ast.	TP	Avg.
1987-88	Chicago	79	261	.463	99	.576	298	169	625	7.9
1988-89	Chicago	73	413	.476	201	.668	445	256	1048	14.4
1989-90	Chicago	82	562	.489	199	.675	547	444	1351	16.5
1990-91	Chicago	82	600	.520	240	.706	595	511	1461	17.8
1991-92	Chicago	82	687	.506	330	.760	630	572	1720	21.0
1992-93	Chicago	81	628	.473	232	.663	621	507	1510	18.6
1993-94	Chicago	72	627	.491	270	.660	629	403	1587	22.0
1994-95	Chicago	79	634	.480	315	.716	639	409	1692	21.4
1995-96	Chicago	77	563	.463	220	.679	496	452	1496	19.4
	Totals	707	4975	.486	2106	.687	4900	3723	12490	17.7

DENNIS RODMAN 35 6-8 220   Forward

Two words: Glamour Don't . . . Cut through all the extraneous, impertinent self-promotion, and you have one fine basketball player . . . Won fifth straight rebounding title (14.9), no mean feat these days . . . Wrote a book, scared the suburbs, won another ring . . . Living proof that it doesn't necessarily have to play in Peoria . . . Turned his head into a billboard for the disenfranchised during the Finals . . . Bill Laimbeer never could have pulled this off . . . A walking distraction, but only if you look his way . . . The only way to beat him is to ignore him . . . Pistons took him 27th out of Southeast Oklahoma State in 1986 . . . Dealt to San Antonio in '93 and his hair has been on fire ever since . . . Spurs were so eager to get rid of him, they accepted Will Perdue in return prior to last season . . . Bulls re-signed him in July to a one-year contract significantly more than the $6 million offered but less than the $10 million he sought . . . Born May 13, 1961, in Trenton, N.J.

Year	Team	G	FG	FG Pct.	FT	FT Pct.	Reb.	Ast.	TP	Avg.
1986-87	Detroit	77	213	.545	74	.587	332	56	500	6.5
1987-88	Detroit	82	398	.561	152	.535	715	110	953	11.6
1988-89	Detroit	82	316	.595	97	.626	772	99	735	9.0
1989-90	Detroit	82	288	.581	142	.654	792	72	719	8.8
1990-91	Detroit	82	276	.493	111	.631	1026	85	669	8.2
1991-92	Detroit	82	342	.539	84	.600	1530	191	800	9.8
1992-93	Detroit	62	183	.427	87	.534	1132	102	468	7.5
1993-94	San Antonio	79	156	.534	53	.520	1367	184	370	4.7
1994-95	San Antonio	49	137	.571	75	.676	823	97	349	7.1
1995-96	Chicago	64	146	.480	56	.528	952	160	351	5.5
	Totals	741	2455	.535	931	.589	9441	1156	5914	8.0

TONI KUKOC 28 6-11 232   Forward

Won Sixth Man Award, then scoffed at the honor because he thinks he should start . . . Problem is, his defense is softer than France in 1939 . . . Offensively, storms the beach with the best . . . Had fewer opportunities with Michael Jordan back, but became more efficient . . . Jacked three-point percentage up 90 points (to .403) . . . Is at his best with the ball on the move, particularly in the halfcourt . . . GM Jerry Krause still gloats about getting him with the 29th pick in 1990, even though it meant three years of recruiting that would make UNLV blush . . . No. 2 on the team's salary scale at $3.56 million last year . . . Born Sept. 18, 1968, in Split, Croatia.

Year	Team	G	FG	FG Pct.	FT	FT Pct.	Reb.	Ast.	TP	Avg.
1993-94	Chicago	75	313	.431	156	.743	297	252	814	10.9
1994-95	Chicago	81	487	.504	235	.748	440	372	1271	15.7
1995-96	Chicago	81	386	.490	206	.772	323	287	1065	13.1
	Totals	237	1186	.478	597	.755	1060	911	3150	13.3

LUC LONGLEY 27 7-2 292   Center

Like Rik Smits, he has great touch and many moves . . . Like Smits, soft as a spring shower on defense . . . Like Smits, is not allowed to guard anyone in the low post, as NBA officials tend to regard foreign centers as foul magnets . . . Unlike Smits, has never hit a big shot . . . Finally started earning some of that money ($2.3 million last season) with career-best scoring average of 9.1 . . . Fouls out as frequently as Michael Jordan goes for 40 (nine times in two injury-abbreviated seasons) . . . Drafted seventh out of New Mexico by Minnesota in 1991, he didn't live down to the Wolves' standards and was dealt to the Bulls for Stacey King, who obviously did, at the 1994 trade deadline . . . Born Jan. 19, 1969, in Melbourne, Australia.

Year	Team	G	FG	FG Pct.	FT	FT Pct.	Reb.	Ast.	TP	Avg.
1991-92	Minnesota	66	114	.458	53	.663	257	53	281	4.3
1992-93	Minnesota	55	133	.455	53	.716	240	51	319	5.8
1993-94	Minn.-Chi.	76	219	.471	90	.720	433	109	528	6.9
1994-95	Chicago	55	135	.447	88	.822	263	73	358	6.5
1995-96	Chicago	62	242	.482	80	.777	318	119	564	9.1
	Totals	314	843	.466	364	.744	1511	405	2050	6.5

RON HARPER 32 6-6 216   Guard

Who would've ever thought he'd remain in the lineup after Michael Jordan returned? . . . Has made transition from star (20.1 points, 6.1 rebounds, 4.6 assists with Clippers in 1992-93) to role player (7.4, 2.7, 2.7 last season) . . . Has been involved in two huge mistakes for different franchises . . . Cleveland took him eighth out of Miami (Ohio) in 1986, then sent him in package to Clippers for Danny Ferry . . . After five solid seasons in L.A., was given a lucrative six-year contract by Bulls GM Jerry Krause, ostensibly to fill Jordan's void . . . Jordan's back, but Harper's contract lives on . . . Earned $3.19 million, more than all teammates except Jordan and Toni Kukoč . . . Born Jan. 20, 1964, in Dayton, Ohio.

Year	Team	G	FG	FG Pct.	FT	FT Pct.	Reb.	Ast.	TP	Avg.
1986-87	Cleveland	82	734	.455	386	.684	392	394	1874	22.9
1987-88	Cleveland	57	340	.464	196	.705	223	281	879	15.4
1988-89	Cleveland	82	587	.511	323	.751	409	434	1526	18.6
1989-90	Clev.-LAC	35	301	.473	182	.788	206	182	798	22.8
1990-91	L.A. Clippers	39	285	.391	145	.668	188	209	763	19.6
1991-92	L.A. Clippers	82	569	.440	293	.736	447	417	1495	18.2
1992-93	L.A. Clippers	80	542	.451	307	.769	425	360	1443	18.0
1993-94	L.A. Clippers	75	569	.426	299	.715	460	344	1508	20.1
1994-95	Chicago	77	209	.426	81	.618	180	157	530	6.9
1995-96	Chicago	80	234	.467	98	.705	213	208	594	7.4
	Totals	689	4370	.451	2310	.721	3143	2986	11410	16.6

STEVE KERR 31 6-3 181   Guard

The anti-Jordan . . . A guy who stands out at the three-point line and waits for an open shot . . . Knows what to do with it when he gets one, as his .480 career three-point percentage, the best in league history, attests . . . Until he wins a big game out there, he won't be remembered as fondly as John Paxson . . . In football parlance, he's an east-west ball-handler . . . In baseball parlance, he's a no-glove defender . . . Suns took him 50th out of Arizona in 1988 . . . Bounced to Cleveland and Orlando before settling into his comfortable eight-point groove in Chicago . . . Earned $800,000 . . . Born Sept. 27, 1965, in Beirut, Lebanon.

Year	Team	G	FG	FG Pct.	FT	FT Pct.	Reb.	Ast.	TP	Avg.
1988-89	Phoenix	26	20	.435	6	.667	17	24	54	2.1
1989-90	Cleveland	78	192	.444	63	.863	98	248	520	6.7
1990-91	Cleveland	57	99	.444	45	.849	37	131	271	4.8
1991-92	Cleveland	48	121	.511	45	.833	78	110	319	6.6
1992-93	Clev.-Orl.	52	53	.434	22	.917	45	70	134	2.6
1993-94	Chicago	82	287	.497	83	.856	131	210	709	8.6
1994-95	Chicago	82	261	.527	63	.778	119	151	674	8.2
1995-96	Chicago	82	244	.506	78	.929	110	192	688	8.4
	Totals	507	1277	.489	405	.853	635	1136	3369	6.6

RANDY BROWN 28 6-2 191   Guard

Nice defender, but . . . The career percentages tell it all: field goals .443, free throws .672, three-pointers .230 . . . In other words, hasn't found a shot he can make . . . Drafted 31st out of New Mexico State (otherwise known as the Land of the Lost Jumper) by Sacramento in 1991 . . . Earned $900,000 . . . Born May 22, 1968, in Chicago, he went on to star locally at Collins High.

Year	Team	G	FG	FG Pct.	FT	FT Pct.	Reb.	Ast.	TP	Avg.
1991-92	Sacramento	56	77	.456	38	.655	69	59	192	3.4
1992-93	Sacramento	75	225	.463	115	.732	212	196	567	7.6
1993-94	Sacramento	61	110	.438	53	.609	112	133	273	4.5
1994-95	Sacramento	67	124	.432	55	.671	108	133	317	4.7
1995-96	Chicago	68	78	.406	28	.609	66	73	185	2.7
	Totals	327	614	.443	289	.672	567	594	1534	4.7

JUD BUECHLER 28 6-6 228   Forward

This Jud's for you . . . An endorsement waiting to happen, if he ever played more than 10 minutes a game . . . Has been a valuable member of the bench with his three-point shooting, a career-best .444 last season . . . Drafted 38th out of Arizona by Seattle in 1990, he was then sent to New Jersey in return for the Nets' promise not to select Dennis Scott. One question: Why? . . . Also played for the Spurs and Warriors . . . Became free agent after earning $300,000 . . . Born June 19, 1968, in Poway, Cal.

Year	Team	G	FG	FG Pct.	FT	FT Pct.	Reb.	Ast.	TP	Avg.
1990-91	New Jersey	74	94	.416	43	.652	141	51	232	3.1
1991-92	N.J.-S.A.-G.S.	28	29	.408	12	.571	52	23	70	2.5
1992-93	Golden State	70	176	.437	65	.747	195	94	437	6.2
1993-94	Golden State	36	42	.500	10	.500	32	16	106	2.9
1994-95	Chicago	57	90	.492	22	.564	98	50	217	3.8
1995-96	Chicago	74	112	.463	14	.636	111	56	278	3.8
	Totals	339	543	.449	166	.651	629	290	1340	4.0

BILL WENNINGTON 33 7-0 277   Center

Best Canadian backup center of this generation . . . Solid veteran unafraid to take a shot in a big moment . . . From 17 feet in, with no one guarding him, deadly . . . It may not sound like much, but it's more than tomorrow's underclassmen can claim . . . A little tougher than Luc Longley, for what it's worth . . . Maybe it's the beard . . . Left St. John's for Dallas with the 16th pick in 1985 . . . Spent one year in Sacramento before coming to Bulls as a free agent in 1993 . . . Made $1 million . . . Born April 26, 1963, in Montreal.

Year	Team	G	FG	FG Pct.	FT	FT Pct.	Reb.	Ast.	TP	Avg.
1985-86	Dallas	56	72	.471	45	.726	132	21	189	3.4
1986-87	Dallas	58	56	.424	45	.750	129	24	157	2.7
1987-88	Dallas	30	25	.510	12	.632	39	4	63	2.1
1988-89	Dallas	65	119	.433	61	.744	286	46	300	4.6
1989-90	Dallas	60	105	.449	60	.800	198	41	270	4.5
1990-91	Sacramento	77	181	.436	74	.787	340	69	437	5.7
1993-94	Chicago	76	235	.488	72	.818	353	70	542	7.1
1994-95	Chicago	73	156	.492	51	.810	190	40	363	5.0
1995-96	Chicago	71	169	.493	37	.860	174	46	376	5.3
	Totals	566	1118	.466	457	.780	1841	361	2697	4.8

JASON CAFFEY 23 6-8 255   Forward

This year's Dickie Simpkins . . . Not bad as a rookie, but not good enough to be included on the playoff roster . . . More aggressive than your typical Alabama forward . . . Didn't rebound or block shots up to advertised standards . . . Drafted 20th by the Bulls in 1995 . . . In college, was selected to the Otis Spunkmeyer Basketball Classic All-Tournament team . . . It says so, right there in the Bulls' media guide, which kind of tells you there's not a whole lot to say about this guy . . . Earned $627,000 . . . Born June 12, 1973, in Mobile, Ala.

Year	Team	G	FG	FG Pct.	FT	FT Pct.	Reb.	Ast.	TP	Avg.
1995-96	Chicago	57	71	.438	40	.588	111	24	182	3.2

JOHN SALLEY 32 6-11 255   Forward-Center

It's not often an athletic big man with two championship rings becomes available via the 10-day contract . . . They don't call him Spider for nothing . . . Long arms, long legs, long wit . . . Once said the notion of practicing anything other than safe sex would be like playing Russian roulette . . . Pistons took him 11th out of Georgia Tech in 1986 . . . Ever since then, he's been given away, to Miami for the draft rights to Isiah Morris, to Toronto in the expansion draft, to the Bulls for nothing . . . Well, not quite; he earned $2.402 million . . . Born June 16, 1964, in Brooklyn, N.Y.

Year	Team	G	FG	FG Pct.	FT	FT Pct.	Reb.	Ast.	TP	Avg.
1986-87	Detroit	82	163	.562	105	.614	296	54	431	5.3
1987-88	Detroit	82	258	.566	185	.709	402	113	701	8.5
1988-89	Detroit	67	166	.498	135	.692	335	75	467	7.0
1989-90	Detroit	82	209	.512	174	.713	439	67	593	7.2
1990-91	Detroit	74	179	.475	186	.727	327	70	544	7.4
1991-92	Detroit	72	249	.512	186	.715	296	116	684	9.5
1992-93	Miami	51	154	.502	115	.799	313	83	423	8.3
1993-94	Miami	76	208	.477	164	.729	407	135	582	7.7
1994-95	Miami	75	197	.499	153	.739	336	123	547	7.3
1995-96	Tor.-Chi.	42	63	.450	59	.694	140	54	185	4.4
	Totals	703	1846	.509	1462	.714	3291	890	5157	7.3

JAMES EDWARDS 40 7-1 252   Center

Like his patented shot, his career is fading away . . . Was picked up as free agent to provide depth in the middle, but totaled just 274 minutes and 28 appearances . . . Has scored fewer points in the last two seasons combined (173) than he did in the 1989 Finals with Detroit (286) . . . One of three former Bad Boys on the Bulls, along with Dennis Rodman and John Salley . . . For a 46th pick (out of Washington to the Lakers in 1977), he has enjoyed a prolific career . . . Bulls are his eighth, and probably last, team . . . Has scored nearly 15,000 points despite never averaging close to 20 in any season . . . Earned $225,000 on one-year deal . . . Born Nov. 22, 1955, in Seattle.

Year	Team	G	FG	FG Pct.	FT	FT Pct.	Reb.	Ast.	TP	Avg.
1977-78	L.A.-Ind.........	83	495	.453	272	.646	615	85	1252	15.2
1978-79	Indiana.........	82	534	.501	298	.676	693	92	1366	16.7
1979-80	Indiana.........	82	528	.512	231	.681	578	127	1287	15.7
1980-81	Indiana.........	81	511	.509	244	.703	571	212	1266	15.6
1981-82	Cleveland	77	528	.511	232	.684	581	123	1288	16.7
1982-83	Clev.-Phoe.......	31	128	.487	69	.639	155	40	325	10.5
1983-84	Phoenix	72	438	.536	183	.720	348	184	1059	14.7
1984-85	Phoenix	70	384	.501	276	.746	387	153	1044	14.9
1985-86	Phoenix	52	310	.542	212	.702	301	74	848	16.3
1986-87	Phoenix	14	57	.518	54	.771	60	19	168	12.0
1987-88	Phoe.-Det.......	69	302	.470	210	.654	412	78	814	11.8
1988-89	Detroit	76	211	.500	133	.686	231	49	555	7.3
1989-90	Detroit	82	462	.498	265	.749	345	63	1189	14.5
1990-91	Detroit	72	383	.484	215	.729	277	65	982	13.6
1991-92	L.A. Clippers	72	250	.465	198	.731	202	53	698	9.7
1992-93	L.A. Lakers	52	122	.452	84	.712	100	41	328	6.3
1993-94	L.A. Lakers	45	78	.464	54	.684	65	22	210	4.7
1994-95	Portland	28	32	.386	11	.647	43	8	75	2.7
1995-96	Chicago	28	41	.373	16	.615	40	11	98	3.5
	Totals	1168	5802	.495	3257	.698	6004	1499	14862	12.7

DICKEY SIMPKINS 24 6-9 248   Forward

Last year's Jason Caffey . . . If Jerry Krause is so smart, why do his first-round picks keep getting left off the playoff roster? . . . Didn't progress one whit from his rookie season, and might've regressed . . . Actually started 12 games, which is all you need to know about today's watered-down NBA . . . Drafted 21st in 1994, out of Providence . . . Paid $845,000 . . .

Born April 6, 1972, in Washington, D.C.

Year	Team	G	FG	FG Pct.	FT	FT Pct.	Reb.	Ast.	TP	Avg.
1994-95	Chicago	59	78	.424	50	.694	151	37	206	3.5
1995-96	Chicago	60	77	.481	61	.629	156	38	216	3.6
	Totals	119	155	.451	111	.657	307	75	422	3.5

THE ROOKIE

TRAVIS KNIGHT 22 7-0 235 **Center**
Jerry Krause keeps reaching for big men, this time using the 29th pick on the Connecticut center . . . Fairly effective rebounder and shot-blocker who still is growing into his frame . . . Averaged 9.1 points and 9.3 rebounds as a senior, then boosted his stock with strong showing in the Desert Classic . . . Born Sept. 13, 1974, in Salt Lake City, Utah.

COACH PHIL JACKSON Forget the zen, this offseason was about yen . . . His contract expired after he directed the Bulls to their fourth championship in his seven seasons at the helm . . . He made it clear that if the price wasn't right, he'd sit out the new season . . . And the Bulls responded with a one-year contract with a base salary estimated at $2.25 million, with additional incentives that could raise the package to $2.7 million . . . Last year he made $900,000 . . . He had the credentials to name his price . . . Winning percentages in regular season: .721, playoffs: .730 . . . Tied for third all-time with 81 playoff wins, behind only Pat Riley and Red Auerbach . . . Has averaged 59 victories per season . . . Only man to coach championship teams in the NBA and CBA (with Albany) . . . One of nine to win NBA titles as player (in '73 with Knicks) and coach . . . Was a two-time All-American at North Dakota, where he played for Bill Fitch and became a Knicks' second-round pick in

'67 . . . Played 13 seasons (the last two with the Nets) despite back problems . . . Took over Bulls in '89 after serving as an assistant under Doug Collins . . . Born Sept. 17, 1945, in Deer Lodge, Mont.

BIGGEST BLUNDER

But for a fateful day in 1979, Showtime would've opened in the Second City. The Bulls had the second-worst record in the NBA and would call the coin flip with the Lakers—who had acquired the rights to this pick three years prior from the New Orleans Jazz for Gail Goodrich.

The Bulls called heads. The coin landed tails.

The Lakers wound up with Magic Johnson. The Bulls compounded their frustration by drafting David Greenwood over Bill Cartwright and Sidney Moncrief with the No. 2 pick. It launched an era of futility in which Chicago would finish below .500 in seven of the next eight seasons.

Of course, had the Bulls won the flip and taken Johnson, they probably never would've had the chance to draft Michael Jordan with the third pick in 1984. So, in retrospect, it turned out to be a heads-up call, after all.

ALL-TIME BULL LEADERS

SEASON

Points: Michael Jordan, 3,041, 1986–87
Assists: Guy Rodgers, 908, 1966–67
Rebounds: Tom Boerwinkle, 1,133, 1970–71

GAME

Points: Michael Jordan, 69 vs. Cleveland, 3/28/90
Assists: Ennis Whatley, 22 vs. New York, 1/14/84
        Ennis Whatley, 22 vs. Atlanta, 3/3/84
Rebounds: Tom Boerwinkle, 37 vs. Phoenix, 1/8/70

CAREER

Points: Michael Jordan, 24,489, 1984–96
Assists: Michael Jordan, 4,377, 1984–96
Rebounds: Tom Boerwinkle, 5,745, 1968–78

CLEVELAND CAVALIERS

TEAM DIRECTORY: Chairman: Gordon Gund; Pres./Team Division: Wayne Embry; Dir. Player Personnel: Gary Fitzsimmons; Sr. Dir. Pub. Rel.: Bob Price; Dir. Media Rel.: Bob Zink; Coach: Mike Fratello; Asst. Coaches: Ron Rothstein, Jim Boylan, Sidney Lowe. Arena: Gund Arena (20,562). Colors: Blue, black and orange.

SCOUTING REPORT

SHOOTING: When they get around to it, the Cavs actually are fairly proficient. In the backcourt, Terrell Brandon, Bobby Phills, Dan Majerle and Bobby Sura all must be guarded from 20 feet and beyond. Forward Chris Mills is an emerging force and Danny Ferry finally found the basket, and his niche, last season.

Once the ball goes inside, however, the problems begin. None of their little big men command anything other than the routine double-teams. The highest-scoring inside player was Michael Cage, who averaged 6.0 points.

Of the two centers taken in the first round, Lithuanian Zydrunas Ilgauskas has the better offensive potential, but he'll need time to build strength. Vitaly Potapenko is more of a banger.

PLAYMAKING: Do not blame Mike Fratello for the crawlball style his team employs. He doesn't have a thoroughbred in the stable, so he keeps his horses reined. And, like it or not, it works.

The Cavs won 47 games, which was about 40 more than the skeptics projected after taking a look at this team on paper.

Brandon is a gifted point guard who can beat defense inside or out. He sets the tone for this conservative offense that doesn't fill it up, but doesn't make mistakes. The Cavs committed just 13.1 turnovers per game last season, the fewest in the league, and had assists on two-thirds of their baskets.

REBOUNDING: Brad Daugherty hadn't played in two years and was released. John Williams was traded away for a shooting guard. Tyrone Hill's season was a car wreck. John Amaechi, not even the best center in a doughnut conference (the Big Ten), actually started some games in the middle. He's been waived.

Get the picture?

The Cavs took big steps toward solving their size problems by

What a year it was for the emerging Terrell Brandon!

drafting the 6-11 Potapenko and 7-1 Ilgauskas in the first round. They also signed 6-10 Mark West, a 35-year-old veteran last with the Pistons. Those additions should open the door for Hill to return to the starting lineup at power forward.

CAVALIER ROSTER

No.	Veterans	Pos.	Ht.	Wt.	Age	Yrs. Pro	College
1	Terrell Brandon	G	5-11	180	26	5	Oregon
35	Danny Ferry	F	6-10	235	30	6	Duke
32	Tyrone Hill	F	6-9	245	28	6	Xavier
F-30	Darryl Johnson	G	6-1	185	31	1	Michigan State
21	Antonio Lang	F	6-8	230	24	2	Duke
F-33	Donny Marshall	F	6-7	230	24	1	Connecticut
24	Chris Mills	F	6-6	216	26	3	Arizona
14	Bobby Phills	G	6-5	220	26	5	Southern
3	Bob Sura	G	6-5	200	23	1	Florida State
--	Mark West	C	6-10	246	35	13	Old Dominion

F-Free agent

Rd.	Rookies	Sel.No.	Pos.	Ht.	Wt.	College
1	Vitaly Potapenko	12	C-F	6-10	280	Wright State
1	Zydrunas Ilgauskas	20	C	7-1	238	Lithuania
2	Reggie Geary	56	G	6-2	197	Arizona

DEFENSE: In the old days, before scoring was outlawed, critics joked about the lack of defense played in places like Denver and Los Angeles. The coaches would fire back by arguing that, because they score so often, there simply were more possessions for opponents, which drove up the numbers.

Could the reverse be true here? The statistics (88.5 points per game allowed) say the Cavs were one of the best defensive teams in league history. But those numbers are more reflective of the slowdown style than any great defensive presence.

They did a masterful job of camouflaging the interior by making the perimeter so active. Brandon and Phills are excellent defenders both on and off the ball, and Hill can hold his ground. Potapenko, a thick-bodied specimen, surely will help.

OUTLOOK: The problem with being lovable overachievers is that it actually can be counterproductive. Sure, the Cavs can reach the playoffs but they won't be serious contenders. And drafting in the middle of the first round year after year doesn't offer a lot of opportunity for advancement.

If Potapenko and Ilgauskas pan out, the Cavs would make strides toward legitimate contention—if they can stay healthy, always a big question in Cleveland.

CAVALIER PROFILES

TERRELL BRANDON 26 5-11 180   Guard

A star is born ... Entered season with career scoring average of 9.3, but more than doubled it ... Had career highs in scoring (19.3), assists (6.5), steals (1.76) and free-throw percentage (.887, third in the league) ... Earned first All-Star berth ... Only the eighth sub-6-footer so honored ... Surprisingly effective rebounder for a little guy ... Rarely makes a mistake ... Had nearly as many steals (132) as turnovers (149) ... Has worked to become an effective three-point shooter ... Drafted 11th out of Oregon in 1991 ... Earned $1.155 million ... Born May 20, 1970, in Portland.

Year	Team	G	FG	FG Pct.	FT	FT Pct.	Reb.	Ast.	TP	Avg.
1991-92	Cleveland	82	252	.419	100	.806	162	316	605	7.4
1992-93	Cleveland	82	297	.478	118	.825	179	302	725	8.8
1993-94	Cleveland	73	230	.420	139	.858	159	277	606	8.3
1994-95	Cleveland	67	341	.448	159	.855	186	363	889	13.3
1995-96	Cleveland	75	510	.465	338	.887	248	487	1449	19.3
	Totals	379	1630	.449	854	.857	934	1745	4274	11.3

CHRIS MILLS 26 6-6 216   Forward

Has improved every season ... Had career highs in every major statistical category except three-point percentage (a solid .376) ... If he keeps it up, he will be a star very soon ... Loves to take the big shot ... For mysterious reasons, his stock dropped like a rock during the 1993 draft and he slid all the way to 22nd, where the Cavs were happy to snap him up ... When he scored at least 20 points, Cavs were 16-4 ... Durable, too. Missed two games: one for a suspension, one for surgery on a fractured nose ... Began career at Kentucky but transferred to Arizona, where he became the Pac-10 Player of the Year ... Earned $1.04 million ... Born Jan. 25, 1970, in Los Angeles.

Year	Team	G	FG	FG Pct.	FT	FT Pct.	Reb.	Ast.	TP	Avg.
1993-94	Cleveland	79	.284	.419	137	.778	401	128	743	9.4
1994-95	Cleveland	80	359	.420	174	.817	366	154	986	12.3
1995-96	Cleveland	80	454	.468	218	.829	443	188	1205	15.1
	Totals	239	1097	.438	529	.811	1210	470	2934	12.3

BOBBY PHILLS 26 6-5 220   Guard-Forward

Showed last year he can Phills it up . . . Always strong with the ball inside the defense, he developed the ability to shoot over it . . . Was seventh in the NBA in three-point percentage (.441) after hitting .297 in his first four seasons . . . As a result, he added more than three points to his scoring average, also a career best . . . Excellent defender, passer, ball-handler and rebounder . . . Bucks took him 45th out of Southern U. in 1991, but didn't keep him . . . Cavs rescued him from the CBA with a 10-day contract on March 19, 1992, and he's never looked back . . . Earned $1.658 million . . . Born Dec. 20, 1969, in Baton Rouge, La.

Year	Team	G	FG	FG Pct.	FT	FT Pct.	Reb.	Ast.	TP	Avg.
1991-92	Cleveland	10	12	.429	7	.636	8	4	31	3.1
1992-93	Cleveland	31	38	.463	15	.600	17	10	93	3.0
1993-94	Cleveland	72	242	.471	113	.720	212	133	598	8.3
1994-95	Cleveland	80	338	.414	183	.779	265	180	878	11.0
1995-96	Cleveland	72	386	.467	186	.775	261	271	1051	14.6
	Totals	265	1016	.448	504	.754	763	598	2651	10.0

TYRONE HILL 28 6-9 245   Forward

Don't think the Cavs are hexed? . . . Coming off an All-Star season, he was rear-ended on his way to the third game of the year, suffered a bruised spinal cord and missed half the season . . . Cavs brought him back slowly, keeping minutes down (21.1), hence his numbers dropped off . . . Hill, who didn't start after returning, wasn't entirely thrilled with the notion . . . When healthy, one of the best defenders and rebounders at the position, and he can score on occasion . . . Drafted 11th out of Xavier by Golden State in 1990, Cavs picked him up in '93 for a first-round pick that turned into Clifford Rozier . . . Earned $3.425 million . . . Born March 19, 1968, in Cincinnati.

Year	Team	G	FG	FG Pct.	FT	FT Pct.	Reb.	Ast.	TP	Avg.
1990-91	Golden State	74	147	.492	96	.632	383	19	390	5.3
1991-92	Golden State	82	254	.522	163	.694	593	47	671	8.2
1992-93	Golden State	74	251	.508	138	.624	754	68	640	8.6
1993-94	Cleveland	57	216	.543	171	.668	499	46	603	10.6
1994-95	Cleveland	70	350	.504	263	.662	765	55	963	13.8
1995-96	Cleveland	44	130	.512	81	.600	244	33	341	7.8
	Totals	401	1348	.513	912	.653	3238	268	3608	9.0

Now Danny Ferry has to prove his revival was no fluke.

DANNY FERRY 30 6-10 235   Forward

Carved something of a niche, at last . . . Started 79 games, mostly at power forward, and had career bests in scoring and rebounding . . . His three-pointers attempted (363) and made (143) were third-most in club history . . . Still a powerless forward on the boards (3.0 career), but a good passer, ball-handler and shooter who can draw bigger defenders outside to make space for cutters . . . Lit Knicks up for 32 points late in the season, then totaled 29 in three playoff games . . . Earned $4.63 million last season . . . Has $24 million more coming over next four seasons . . . Former Duke star was drafted second in 1989 by the Clippers. He chose Italy over L.A., forcing Clips to deal his rights . . . Cavs sent Ron Harper and two first-round picks for Ferry and

Reggie Williams . . . Son of former Bullets GM Bob Ferry was born Oct. 17, 1966, in Baltimore.

Year	Team	G	FG	FG Pct.	FT	FT Pct.	Reb.	Ast.	TP	Avg.
1990-91	Cleveland	81	275	.428	124	.816	286	142	697	8.6
1991-92	Cleveland	68	134	.409	61	.836	213	75	346	5.1
1992-93	Cleveland	76	220	.479	99	.876	279	137	573	7.5
1993-94	Cleveland	70	149	.446	38	.884	141	74	350	5.0
1994-95	Cleveland	82	223	.446	74	.881	143	96	614	7.5
1995-96	Cleveland	82	422	.459	103	.769	309	191	1090	13.3
	Totals	459	1423	.447	499	.833	1371	715	3670	8.0

MARK WEST 35 6-10 246   Center

Returned to Cleveland as a Detroit free agent last summer . . . Had upbeat playoffs when he started all three games and averaged 9.3 points and 5.3 rebounds against Orlando . . . Racked up 35 DNP-CDs during the regular season . . . The 47 games played was the fewest since his rookie season with Dallas in 1983-84 . . . And yet, he started 21 times . . . Entered the season with the NBA's top active career field-goal percentage (.589), but worst mark since rookie season dropped it to .585 . . . Dallas took him 30th out of Old Dominion in 1983 . . . Had best seasons with Phoenix from 1988-94 . . . Averaged 10.5 points, 8.9 rebounds and 2.24 blocks in 1989-90 . . . Earned $1.5 million . . . Born Nov. 5, 1960, in Ft. Campbell, Ky.

Year	Team	G	FG	FG Pct.	FT	FT Pct.	Reb.	Ast.	TP	Avg.
1983-84	Dallas	34	15	.357	7	.318	46	13	37	1.1
1984-85	Mil.-Clev.	66	106	.546	43	.494	251	15	255	3.9
1985-86	Cleveland	67	113	.541	54	.524	322	20	280	4.2
1986-87	Cleveland	78	209	.543	89	.514	339	41	507	6.5
1987-88	Clev.-Phoe.	83	316	.551	170	.596	523	74	802	9.7
1988-89	Phoenix	82	243	.653	108	.535	551	39	594	7.2
1989-90	Phoenix	82	331	.625	199	.691	728	45	861	10.5
1990-91	Phoenix	82	247	.647	135	.655	564	37	629	7.7
1991-92	Phoenix	82	196	.632	109	.637	372	22	501	6.1
1992-93	Phoenix	82	175	.614	86	.518	458	29	436	5.3
1993-94	Phoenix	82	162	.566	58	.500	295	33	382	4.7
1994-95	Detroit	67	217	.556	66	.478	408	18	500	7.5
1995-96	Detroit	47	61	.484	28	.622	133	6	150	3.2
	Totals	934	2391	.585	1152	.575	4990	392	5934	6.4

BOB SURA 23 6-5 200   Guard

Looks like another savvy pick from late in the first round, No. 17, in last year's draft, following prolific college career at Florida State ... Came on strong in second half of season, playing both guard spots ... In three starts, he averaged 13.7 points, 6.7 assists, 5.0 rebounds and 1.33 steals ... Plays with a lot of energy, but can get out of control ... Should become a solid shooter ... First player in ACC history to rack up 2,000 points, 700 rebounds, 400 assists and 200 steals ... He's FSU's all-time leading scorer ... Earned $752,000 ... Born March 25, 1973, in Wilkes-Barre, Pa.

Year	Team	G	FG	FG Pct.	FT	FT Pct.	Reb.	Ast.	TP	Avg.
1995-96	Cleveland	79	148	.411	99	.702	135	233	422	5.3

ANTONIO LANG 24 6-8 230   Forward

Spent first 32 games on the injured list recovering from scope of left knee ... Played semi-regularly thereafter, appearing in 41 of a possible 50 games ... Hit 15 of first 18 shots after coming back, but 44 percent thereafter ... Drafted 29th by Phoenix out of Duke in 1994, he played just 12 games as a rookie, then came to Cavs with Dan Majerle in the John Williams deal ... Earned $423,000 ... Born May 15, 1972, in Columbia, S.C.

Year	Team	G	FG	FG Pct.	FT	FT Pct.	Reb.	Ast.	TP	Avg.
1994-95	Phoenix	12	4	.400	3	.750	4	1	11	0.9
1995-96	Cleveland	41	41	.532	34	.723	53	12	116	2.8
	Totals	53	45	.517	37	.725	57	13	127	2.4

DONNY MARSHALL 24 6-7 230   Forward

Same alma mater (UConn) and same last name as lottery pick Donyell, but there's no relation ... Played sparingly after being drafted 39th by Cavs last year ... Averaged an even six fouls per 48 minutes played ... A battler who impressed the coaches with his work in practice, he could find a role, if he finds his shot ... Highlight of his college career was averaging 22.3 points in UConn's four 1995 NCAA Tournament games ... Earned $200,000 ... Born July 17, 1972, in Detroit.

Year	Team	G	FG	FG Pct.	FT	FT Pct.	Reb.	Ast.	TP	Avg.
1995-96	Cleveland	34	24	.353	22	.629	26	7	77	2.3

THE ROOKIES

VITALY POTAPENKO 21 6-10 280   Center
"The Ukraine Train" was taken out of Wright State with the 12th pick ... Native of Kiev averaged 20.2 points and 6.8 rebounds and shot .607 over two years ... Big, strong, aggressive player who reminds some of Jeff Ruland ... Shed some weight and added muscle and became the hit of the postseason camps ... Born March 21, 1975, in Kiev, Ukraine.

ZYDRUNAS ILGAUSKAS 21 7-1 238   Center
One of a record six foreign-born players taken in first round, the Lithuanian went 20th ... May be a little bit of a project because he needs to add muscle, but his offensive skills are worth the wait ... Averaged 20.3 points, 12.8 rebounds and 2.8 blocked shots for Lithuanian team ... In an exhibition against Kentucky in 1994, he posted 26 points, 19 rebounds and four blocks ... Declared for draft in 1995 but withdrew due to a broken foot ... Born June 5, 1975, in Kaunas, Lithuania.

REGGIE GEARY 23 6-2 197   Guard
Point guard from Arizona was taken 56th ... Played shooting guard and small forward while Khalid Reeves and Damon Stoudamire were around but moved to the point last season and ranked eighth in the country in assists (7.0) ... Tough defender who broke Kenny Lofton's Arizona record for steals in a career (200) ... More than half his shots were three-pointers last season, and he hit a respectable .385 ... Born Aug. 31, 1973, in Trenton, N.J.

Bob Sura proved a wise choice in '95 draft.

COACH MIKE FRATELLO: Due for a break . . . Team has been ravaged by injuries, yet they've remained highly competitive . . . Out of necessity, he had to slow tempo and play a defensive style . . . In each of his three seasons, they've lowered the club record for points allowed to a modern-era NBA best of 88.5 last season . . . Is 137-109 with Cavs, 461-359 overall . . . Coached Atlanta to four straight 50-win seasons in late 1980s . . . Was Coach of the Year in 1986-87 . . . Hasn't enjoyed much playoff success, with a 19-31 record, 1-9 with the Cavs . . . One of Hubie Brown's many proteges to advance through the ranks . . . Three years away from coaching with NBC (1990-93) gave him a fresh perspective and, as a result, he has toned down his intensity—slightly, but noticeable . . . Big baseball fan, he's a close friend of ex-Dodger manager Tom Lasorda . . . Montclair State grad . . . Born Feb. 24, 1947, in Hackensack, N.J.

BIGGEST BLUNDER

This comes with an asterisk, since it was made during the Ted Stepien era, when virtually every move the volatile owner made turned out to be a mistake. So many first-round picks were traded away, the league eventually had to step in and begin voiding deals.

When new owners George and Gordon Gund purchased the team, in fact, the NBA gave them bonus first-round picks to sweeten the deal. One of those played a part in what turned out to be the biggest of this franchise's miscues.

In the 1985 draft, the Cavs swapped first-round picks with Chicago, sending their bonus pick (ninth overall) to the Bulls for the 11th pick and guard Ennis Whatley. The Bulls wound up with Charles Oakley. At No. 11, the Cavs bypassed Karl Malone and took Keith Lee.

Lee was a complete bust, while either Oakley or Malone would've given the Cavs the physical power forward that might've pushed them over the top in the contending years that followed.

Chris Mills hit all sorts of career highs.

ALL-TIME CAVALIER LEADERS

SEASON

Points: Mike Mitchell, 2,012, 1980–81
Assists: John Bagley, 735, 1985–86
Rebounds: Jim Brewer, 891, 1975–76

GAME

Points: Walt Wesley, 50 vs. Cincinnati, 2/19/71
Asissts: Geoff Huston, 27 vs. Golden State, 1/27/82
Rebounds: Rick Roberson, 25 vs. Houston, 3/4/72

CAREER

Points: Brad Daugherty, 10,389, 1986–95
Assists: Mark Price, 4,206, 1986–95
Rebounds: Brad Daugherty, 5,227, 1986–95

DETROIT PISTONS

TEAM DIRECTORY: Managing Partner: Bill Davidson; Pres.: Tom Wilson; VP-Player Personnel: Rick Sund; Dir. Pub. Rel.: Matt Dobek; Dir. Media Rel.: Bill Wickett; Coach: Doug Collins; Asst. Coaches: Alvin Gentry, Brian James, Johnny Bach. Arena: The Palace of Auburn Hills (21,454). Colors: Red, white and blue.

Grant Hill must lead way without Allan Houston.

SCOUTING REPORT

SHOOTING: The good news was Allan Houston continued his rise toward the top of the two-guard charts. The bad news was the free agent parlayed his new-found market value into a fat contract with the Knicks, leaving a gaping hole in what already was an anemic offense.

Stacey Augmon is nothing like Houston. He isn't a shooter, isn't a particularly aggressive offensive player, but is one of the better defenders in the league at the position. The other Atlanta import, Grant Long, will pair with Terry Mills to give the Pistons two of the best-shooting power forwards in the game. The problem is, neither one is much of a threat from the post.

Joe Dumars, Lindsey Hunter and midseason pickup Michael Curry augment the crew. The Pistons—second in three-point percentage (.404)—won't approach that again without Houston.

Veteran Otis Thorpe was basically it from the post and he's back with a three-year contract. Grant Hill wasn't going anywhere, except back to the gym for another summer of work on his jumper. Consistency from the perimeter is the only chink in his armor.

PLAYMAKING: Had Dumars come into the league with a team that needed it, he might've become one of the best point guards in the league. With the Hunter experiment a bust, Dumars ran the club the second half of the season and did so admirably.

The offense will continue to run through Hill, who led the team in assists (6.9), among other things. He is by far the most creative player on a team otherwise lacking. The Pistons were next-to-last in assists last season, a trend that shows no sign of changing.

REBOUNDING: The search for help in the middle turned up Don Reid, Mark West (now a Cavalier) and Eric Leckner (now a free agent). Those three combined to start 75 games and none averaged more than 2.9 boards.

Still, the Pistons did improve with help from Thorpe and athletic rookie Theo Ratliff, who energized an otherwise tired front line and enabled the team to compete on the boards. Hill and Dumars all are among the best rebounders at their positions.

Like many of their Central Division brethren, the Pistons consider themselves one more big man away from serious contention. That player could be rookie Jerome Williams, an athletic but slender power forward from Georgetown who has drawn comparisons

PISTON ROSTER

No.	Veterans	Pos.	Ht.	Wt.	Age	Yrs. Pro	College
2	Stacey Augmon	G-F	6-8	205	28	5	UNLV
12	Michael Curry	G	6-5	210	28	2	Georgia Southern
4	Joe Dumars	G	6-3	195	33	11	McNeese State
33	Grant Hill	F	6-8	225	24	2	Duke
1	Lindsey Hunter	G	6-2	195	25	3	Jackson State
43	Grant Long	F	6-9	248	30	8	Eastern Michigan
--	Rick Mahorn	F-C	6-10	260	38	15	Hampton Institute
6	Terry Mills	F	6-10	250	28	6	Michigan
42	Theo Ratliff	F-C	6-10	225	23	1	Wyoming
52	Don Reid	F	6-8	250	22	1	Georgetown
50	Otis Thorpe	F	6-10	246	34	12	Providence

Rd.	Rookies	Sel.No.	Pos.	Ht.	Wt.	College
1	Jerome Williams	26	F	6-9	206	Georgetown
2	Ron Riley	47	G	6-5	205	Arizona State

to Dennis Rodman for his work ethic. The Pistons brought back 6-10 Rick Mahorn, a Nets free agent, but, at 38, his value may be in helping Williams.

DEFENSE: This is where coach Doug Collins had the greatest impact, selling his philosophy well. The Pistons carved 13 points per game from the previous season's average of over 105 and wound up the second-best in the league. That, more than anything else, was responsible for the team's 18-win improvement.

Ratliff gives them the shot-blocker they've lacked since the early days of John Salley's career. Hill is improving his man-to-man skills and Dumars long has been one of the most tortuous guards in the league for opponents.

If Mills wants to see his minutes rise, he'll need to give the team what it needs inside, a banger on the post. At 225, Ratliff simply isn't strong enough.

OUTLOOK: Just when it looked like the Pistons might be a young team on the verge of breaking through, Houston bolted for the bright lights (which bring intense heat) of the Big Apple. They still have one of the game's brightest young stars in Hill, a proud champion in Dumars and a fiery, aggressive coach in Collins. In the Central Division, however, you need much, much more.

PISTON PROFILES

GRANT HILL 24 6-8 225   Forward

There's almost nothing he can't do... Led team in scoring (20.2), rebounds (9.8) and assists (6.9)... Also topped Pistons in minutes (40.8) and steals (1.25)... Led NBA with 10 triple-doubles... Started in his second All-Star Game and was once again the leading vote-getter... Played with Dream Team III in the Atlanta Olympics... Needs to spend more time extending his range. In two seasons, he's nine of 53 (.170) from the three-point line... So there's one thing he can't do... Could stand to be a little more dominating; he has averaged 15.2 shot attempts in each of his first two seasons... Won two national championships at Duke... Was drafted third in 1994... Son of Calvin Hill, former star running back in the NFL for Dallas and Washington... Earned $4.05 million... Born Oct. 5, 1972, in Reston, Va.

Year	Team	G	FG	FG Pct.	FT	FT Pct.	Reb.	Ast.	TP	Avg.
1994-95	Detroit	70	508	.477	374	.732	445	353	1394	19.9
1995-96	Detroit	80	564	.462	485	.751	783	548	1618	20.2
	Totals	150	1072	.469	859	.742	1228	901	3012	20.1

JOE DUMARS 33 6-3 195   Guard

Last of the Bad Boys, but still pretty good... Took over at point when the Lindsey Hunter experiment failed (again) and finished season strong, averaging 13.9 points in the final 25 games... Started 40 games... Has missed at least 13 games in each of the last three seasons... Sore left hamstring was his only real problem last year... Fourth on Pistons' all-time scoring list (13,872), also third in assists (3,907) and steals (778)... Drafted 18th out of McNeese State in 1985... MVP of the 1989 NBA Finals when he averaged 27.3 points to lead the Pistons' four-game sweep of the Lakers ... Earned $6.681 million ... Born May 24, 1963, in Natchitoches, La.

Year	Team	G	FG	FG Pct.	FT	FT Pct.	Reb.	Ast.	TP	Avg.
1985-86	Detroit	82	287	.481	190	.798	119	390	769	9.4
1986-87	Detroit	79	369	.493	184	.748	167	352	931	11.8
1987-88	Detroit	82	453	.472	251	.815	200	387	1161	14.2
1988-89	Detroit	69	456	.505	260	.850	172	390	1186	17.2
1989-90	Detroit	75	508	.480	297	.900	212	368	1335	17.8
1990-91	Detroit	80	622	.481	371	.890	187	443	1629	20.4
1991-92	Detroit	82	587	.448	412	.867	188	375	1635	19.9
1992-93	Detroit	77	677	.466	343	.864	148	308	1809	23.5
1993-94	Detroit	69	505	.452	276	.836	151	261	1410	20.4
1994-95	Detroit	67	417	.430	277	.805	158	368	1214	18.1
1995-96	Detroit	67	255	.426	162	.822	138	265	793	11.8
	Totals	829	5136	.466	3023	.843	1840	3907	13872	16.7

OTIS THORPE 34 6-10 246   Forward

One of two Pistons with a championship ring (the other is Joe Dumars) ... Played in all 82 games for the ninth time in 12 seasons ... Career field-goal percentage of .553 one of best in NBA history ... Hit 12 straight shots in a 27-point game against Charlotte in April ... Kansas City Kings drafted him ninth out of Providence in 1984 ... Sent from Kings to Houston in '88, then from Rockets to Portland in '95 ... Blazers shipped him to Pistons in exchange for Bill Curley and draft rights to Randolph Childress ... Became free agent after earning $2.607 million, then re-signed three-year contract worth between $15 and $20 million ... Born Aug. 5, 1962, in Boynton Beach, Fla.

Year	Team	G	FG	FG Pct.	FT	FT Pct.	Reb.	Ast.	TP	Avg.
1984-85	Kansas City	82	411	.600	230	.620	556	111	1052	12.8
1985-86	Sacramento	75	289	.587	164	.661	420	84	742	9.9
1986-87	Sacramento	82	567	.540	413	.761	819	201	1547	18.9
1987-88	Sacramento	82	622	.507	460	.755	837	266	1704	20.8
1988-89	Houston	82	521	.542	328	.729	787	202	1370	16.7
1989-90	Houston	82	547	.548	307	.688	734	261	1401	17.1
1990-91	Houston	82	549	.556	334	.696	846	197	1435	17.5
1991-92	Houston	82	558	.592	304	.657	862	250	1420	17.3
1992-93	Houston	72	385	.558	153	.598	589	181	923	12.8
1993-94	Houston	82	449	.561	251	.657	870	189	1149	14.0
1994-95	Hou.-Port.	70	385	.565	167	.594	558	112	937	13.4
1995-96	Detroit	82	452	.530	257	.710	688	158	1161	14.2
	Totals	955	5735	.553	3368	.689	8566	2212	14841	15.5

THEO RATLIFF 23 6-10 225   Forward

Pistons surprised many by using 18th pick on the slender forward from Wyoming, but he proved them right . . . Blocked team-high 116 shots despite averaging just 17.4 minutes . . . Averaged nearly six fouls per 48 minutes played . . . Played just four minutes in first-round playoff loss to Orlando . . . If he continues to grow into his frame, he could be a major force inside . . . Has grown three inches and added 55 pounds since freshman days at college . . . Went for 21 points and 15 rebounds against Seattle in November . . . Earned $714,000 . . . Born April 17, 1973, in Demopolis, Ala.

Year	Team	G	FG	FG Pct.	FT	FT Pct.	Reb.	Ast.	TP	Avg.
1995-96	Detroit	75	128	.557	85	.708	297	13	341	4.5

STACEY AUGMON 28 6-8 205   Guard-Forward

Pistons got him and Grant Long from Hawks in summer trade for four conditional draft picks . . . Spent the first two months on the bench and the team struggled . . . Ken Norman was benched and the team went 31-18 in Augmon's starts . . . Team allowed 101.1 points when he didn't start, 95.0 when he did . . . More comfortable, offensively, as a small forward, where his poor perimeter game isn't as glaring . . . Had lowest scoring average of his career (12.7) . . . Excellent slasher, strong with the ball, finishes well . . . Good hands and anticipation in the open floor defensively . . . Hawks traded away Doc Rivers to obtain the rights to draft Augmon, out of UNLV, with the ninth pick in 1991 . . . Nicknamed "Plastic Man" . . . Earned $2.16 million last season . . . Born Aug. 1, 1968, in Pasadena, Cal.

Year	Team	G	FG	FG Pct.	FT	FT Pct.	Reb.	Ast.	TP	Avg.
1991-92	Atlanta	82	440	.489	213	.666	420	201	1094	13.3
1992-93	Atlanta	73	397	.501	227	.739	287	170	1021	14.0
1993-94	Atlanta	82	439	.510	333	.764	394	187	1212	14.8
1994-95	Atlanta	76	397	.453	252	.728	368	197	1053	13.9
1995-96	Atlanta	77	362	.491	251	.792	304	137	976	12.7
	Totals	390	2035	.488	1276	.739	1773	892	5356	13.7

TERRY MILLS 28 6-10 250   Forward-Center

Minutes, shooting percentage, scoring average and role all diminished for second straight season . . . Has dropped from peaks of 17.3 points and .511 shooting in 1993-94 to 9.4 points and .419 last season . . . Excellent perimeter shooter but guys his size need to make their living inside . . . Relatively soft defense didn't mesh with new team philosophy . . . Bucks drafted him 16th out of Michigan in 1990, then traded him to Denver for Danny Schayes . . . Nuggets subsequently dealt him to Nets, who declined to match the Pistons' offer sheet in '92 . . . Earned $2.177 million . . . Born Dec. 21, 1967, in Detroit.

Year	Team	G	FG	FG Pct.	FT	FT Pct.	Reb.	Ast.	TP	Avg.
1990-91	Den.-N.J.	55	134	.465	47	.712	229	33	315	5.7
1991-92	New Jersey	82	310	.463	114	.750	453	84	742	9.0
1992-93	Detroit	81	494	.461	201	.791	472	111	1199	14.8
1993-94	Detroit	80	588	.511	181	.797	672	177	1381	17.3
1994-95	Detroit	72	417	.447	175	.799	558	160	1118	15.5
1995-96	Detroit	82	283	.419	121	.771	352	98	769	9.4
	Totals	452	2226	.465	839	.780	2736	663	5524	12.2

RICK MAHORN 38 6-10 260   Forward-Center

One more time . . . Nets' free agent signed one-year contract in August with team with which he won a championship ring (1988-89) . . . Was big part in the development of Shawn Bradley . . . Spirit is definitely willing, body definitely not what it once was . . . Will bang and taunt and do anything to gain edge on opponent . . . Terrific guy off court. Nothing like on-court presence . . . Born Sept. 2, 1958, in Hartford, Conn. . . . Washington made him the No. 35 pick on second round out of Hampton Institute (Va.) . . . Had wanted to go to UConn . . . Traded to Detroit with Mike Gibson for Dan Roundfield, June 17, 1985, and became part of the original Bad Boys . . . Minnesota grabbed him in expansion draft Oct. 27, 1989. All things considered, he would rather have been in Philadelphia, which is where he landed as part of a draft package trade, Oct. 27, 1989. Had refused to report to Minnesota . . . Did two years in Italy. Signed with Nets as a free agent Nov. 9, 1992 . . . Re-signed last preseason for $400,000.

Year	Team	G	FG	FG Pct.	FT	FT Pct.	Reb.	Ast.	TP	Avg.
1980-81	Washington	52	111	.507	27	.675	215	25	249	4.8
1981-82	Washington	80	414	.507	148	.632	704	150	976	12.2
1982-83	Washington	82	376	.490	146	.575	779	115	898	11.0
1983-84	Washington	82	307	.507	125	.651	738	131	739	9.0
1984-85	Washington	77	206	.499	71	.683	608	121	483	6.3
1985-86	Detroit	80	157	.455	81	.681	412	64	395	4.9
1986-87	Detroit	63	144	.447	96	.821	375	38	384	6.1
1987-88	Detroit	67	276	.574	164	.756	565	60	717	10.7
1988-89	Detroit	72	203	.517	116	.748	496	59	522	7.3
1989-90	Philadelphia	75	313	.497	183	.715	568	98	811	10.8
1990-91	Philadelphia	80	261	.467	189	.788	621	118	711	8.9
1992-93	New Jersey	74	101	.472	88	.800	279	33	291	3.9
1993-94	New Jersey	28	23	.489	13	.650	54	5	59	2.1
1994-95	New Jersey	58	79	.523	39	.796	162	26	198	3.4
1995-96	New Jersey	50	43	.352	34	.723	110	16	120	2.4
	Totals	1020	3014	.495	1520	.706	6686	1059	7553	7.4

DON REID 22 6-8 250   Center-Forward

Patrick Ewing, Dikembe Mutombo, Alonzo Mourning, Don Reid . . . In his own way, he continued the legacy of Georgetown big men . . . Last pick (58th) in the 1995 draft wound up starting 46 games at center, with the Pistons going 30-16 . . . Didn't produce any flashy numbers—he never scored more than 12 points—but displayed toughness and willingness to do the dirty work underneath . . . Kind of like his college career, in which he averaged 4.5 points and 4.0 rebounds . . . Earned $200,000 . . . Born Dec. 30, 1973, in Washington, D.C.

Year	Team	G	FG	FG Pct.	FT	FT Pct.	Reb.	Ast.	TP	Avg.
1995-96	Detroit	69	106	.567	51	.662	203	11	263	3.8

GRANT LONG 30 6-9 248   Forward

Gets the most out of his skills and now will put them to work for the Pistons after being traded from Hawks with Stacey Augmon for four conditional draft choices . . . Put his attitude in Christian Laettner's body, and you've got a tougher Alonzo Mourning . . . Averaged a career-high 9.6 rebounds to rank 15th in league . . . Doesn't have a signature skill, other than his work ethic ... Has good NBA pedigree, as his uncle is former long-time guard John Long and his cousin is new teammate Terry Mills ... Only Hawk to play in all 82 games ... Miami took him 33rd out of Eastern Michigan in 1988, then traded him with Steve Smith to the Hawks for Kevin Willis and a '95 second-round pick on Nov. 7, 1994 ... The deal was a steal for the Hawks ... Earned $1.86 million ... Born March 12, 1966, in Wayne, Mich.

Year	Team	G	FG	FG Pct.	FT	FT Pct.	Reb.	Ast.	TP	Avg.
1988-89	Miami	82	336	.486	304	.749	546	149	976	11.9
1989-90	Miami	81	257	.483	172	.714	402	96	686	8.5
1990-91	Miami	80	276	.492	181	.787	568	176	734	9.2
1991-92	Miami	82	440	.494	326	.807	691	225	1212	14.8
1992-93	Miami	76	397	.469	261	.765	568	182	1061	14.0
1993-94	Miami	69	300	.446	187	.786	495	170	788	11.4
1994-95	Mia.-Atl.	81	342	.478	244	.751	606	131	939	11.6
1995-96	Atlanta	82	395	.471	257	.763	788	183	1078	13.1
	Totals	633	2743	.477	1932	.766	4664	1312	7474	11.8

LINDSEY HUNTER 25 6-2 195   Guard

Not the next Isiah Thomas ... Maybe not even the next Carl Thomas ... Started the first 43 games and averaged 10.5 points but was sent to the bench thereafter ... Did improve three-point shooting to a career best .405, but actually shot worse (.372) inside the arc ... Did have more steals (84) than turnovers (80) ... Had those turnovers in 2,138 minutes, a dramatic improvement from the previous season (79 TOs in 944 minutes) ... Drafted 10th in 1993 out of Jackson State ... Earned $1.44 million ... Born Dec. 3, 1970, in Utica, Miss.

Year	Team	G	FG	FG Pct.	FT	FT Pct.	Reb.	Ast.	TP	Avg.
1993-94	Detroit	82	335	.375	104	.732	189	390	843	10.3
1994-95	Detroit	42	119	.374	40	.727	75	159	314	7.5
1995-96	Detroit	80	239	.381	84	.700	194	188	679	8.5
	Totals	204	693	.377	228	.719	458	737	1836	9.0

MICHAEL CURRY 28 6-5 210   Guard-Forward

After playing in four countries, the CBA, USBL and GBL, he may finally have found a home ... Impressed coaching staff with his work ethic, not to mention his 40 percent three-point shooting ... Unlike college teammate and former first-round pick Jeff Sanders, he was undrafted out of Georgia Southern in 1990, and wound up playing in Germany, Belgium, Italy and Spain . . . Had brief stints with Sixers and Bullets before catching on with Pistons last February . . . Averaged 4.9 points in 41 games with Detroit . . . Earned $220,000 . . . Born Aug. 22, 1968, in Anniston, Ala.

Year	Team	G	FG	FG Pct.	FT	FT Pct.	Reb.	Ast.	TP	Avg.
1993-94	Philadelphia	10	3	.214	3	.750	1	1	0	0.9
1995-96	Wash.-Det.	46	73	.453	45	.726	85	27	211	4.6
	Totals	56	76	.434	48	.727	86	28	220	3.9

THE ROOKIES

JEROME WILLIAMS 23 6-9 206   Forward
Georgetown power forward likened to Dennis Rodman (without the mascara) was grabbed by Pistons at No. 26 . . . Good athlete, relentless rebounder (9.3 average in two seasons with Hoyas), can't shoot . . . Can handle the ball well for a big man . . . His stock rose after being named MVP of the Desert Classic . . . Born May 10, 1973, in Germantown, Md.

RON RILEY 22 6-5 205   Guard
Perimeter player, but a streaky shooter . . . Good athlete . . . Left Arizona State as the all-time leading scorer . . . His 20.1 points as a senior was the most by a Sun Devil since Byron Scott in 1982-83 . . . Never missed a game in four years, playing in 116 . . . Sonics got him at No. 47 and traded him to Detroit . . . Born Dec. 27, 1973, in Las Vegas.

COACH DOUG COLLINS: Aggression, energy and passion helped fuel an 18-game improvement to 46-36 in his first season with Pistons, tying the biggest turnaround in franchise history . . . Has reached the playoffs in all four seasons as a head coach, the first three with the Bulls . . . Was fired after directing Chicago to the conference finals in 1989 . . . Overall record is 183-145 (.558) . . . Only two other coaches, Ray Scott and Chuck Daly, took Pistons to winning records in their first seasons . . . First pick in the 1973 draft out of Illinois State, Collins went on to make All-Star team four times in eight seasons, the final three of which were shortened by injuries . . . Career averages of 17.9 points, 3.3 assists and 3.2 rebounds . . . Won silver medal with 1972 Olympic team . . . Born July 28, 1951, in Christopher, Ill. . . . Son, Chris, plays at Duke.

BIGGEST BLUNDER

This one's easy: Hiring Dick Vitale. For ESPN, it was a gold mine. For the Pistons, it was the shaft. For in less than two years at the Pistons' helm, Vitale did a decade's worth of damage.

In 1979, he pulled off a memorable faux pas, trading up to select a lesser player. The Pistons traded their pick (No. 5) and cash to Milwaukee for the No. 4 pick, which they used on local hero Greg Kelser, better known as the other guy on Michigan State's 1979 title team. The Bucks then pocketed the cash and took the player they wanted all along, guard Sidney Moncrief.

Later in the first round, Vitale grabbed UCLA's Roy Hamilton ahead of USC's Cliff Robinson and Dayton's Jim Paxson.

It got even worse the following year, when two 1980 first-round picks were traded to Boston for a declining Bob McAdoo. One of those picks (No. 3 overall) turned into Kevin McHale; the other was packaged in the trade that brought Robert Parish to the Celtics from Golden State.

Which just goes to prove the old saying: those who can, do; those who can't, go into broadcasting.

ALL-TIME PISTON LEADERS

SEASON

Points: Dave Bing, 2,213, 1970–71
Assists: Isiah Thomas, 1,123, 1984–85
Rebounds: Bob Lanier, 1,205, 1972–73

GAME

Points: Kelly Tripucka, 56 vs. Chicago, 1/29/83
Assists: Kevin Porter, 25 vs. Phoenix, 4/1/79
       Kevin Porter, 25 vs. Boston, 3/9/79
       Isiah Thomas, 25 vs. Dallas, 2/13/85
Rebounds: Dennis Rodman, 34 vs. Indiana, 3/4/92

CAREER

Points: Isiah Thomas, 18,822, 1981–94
Assists: Isiah Thomas, 9,061, 1981–94
Rebounds: Bill Laimbeer, 9,330, 1982–94

INDIANA PACERS

TEAM DIRECTORY: Owners: Herb Simon, Melvin Simon; Pres.: Donnie Walsh; VP-Basketball: Billy Knight; Media Rel. Dir.: David Benner; Coach: Larry Brown; Asst. Coaches: Gar Heard, Billy King, Bill Blair, Herb Brown. Arena: Market Square Arena (16,530). Colors: Blue and yellow.

SCOUTING REPORT

SHOOTING: Any team with Reggie Miller planted at the three-point line has a garden of verses for opposing defenders to read. And he just loves to talk fertilizer. Miller can hit from anywhere.

Without Miller, or a reasonable facsimile thereof, the Pacers become any team—opponents will double the post and dare someone to be fundamentally pure from the perimeter. With Miller, they are among the best shooting teams, which isn't quite like being one of the highest-scoring teams in the old AFL, but it'll do.

Newcomers Jalen Rose and Reggie Williams are more scorers than shooters. Both are streaky from the perimeter, but command attention. And, unlike many of their new teammates, they know how to take the orange into the grove.

PLAYMAKING: There was much consternation over the trade of Mark Jackson to Denver, but perhaps it was misplaced. Rose virtually duplicated Jackson's scoring and assist numbers in far fewer minutes. He makes more mistakes, but he's younger (and quicker, and taller . . . you get the picture).

And he won't start, unless he beats out Travis Best in training camp. For the least-noticed former Georgia Tech point guard, well, the best is yet to come. This is a little guy with three-point range and plenty of SportsCenter stuff. He does have to learn to create more shots for others and less for himself, no small task for a point guard.

Don't forget, should both Rose and Best fail, there's always Haywoode Workman. The last time he started at the point on a consistent basis, the Pacers went 31-12 to finish the 1993-94 season.

The point is, the position may well be in more hands, but they're good hands.

After all, Reggie Miller begins 10th year in Indiana.

REBOUNDING: With both Davises back, close the book: Dale is overdue, Antonio is a work in progress. Dale is perhaps the best vertical rebounder in the game, with long arms attached to a pair of pogos. Antonio's work tends to be more of the soaring-into-traffic, get-out-of-the-way, variety. Ask any scout in the league about his one-handed cup rebounds, and you'll start a conversation.

When it comes to center Rik Smits, the tone shifts. The knee-jerk assumption is that a guy 7-4 ought to own the boards. This is why knee-jerk reactions produce embarrassing bruises 98.6 percent of the time. Smits doesn't have particularly long arms or much jumping ability. Those that come to him, he gets.

The draft yielded an unexpected bounty with 6-11 Erick Dam-

PACER ROSTER

No.	Veterans	Pos.	Ht.	Wt.	Age	Yrs. Pro	College
4	Travis Best	G	5-11	172	24	1	Georgia Tech
F-50	Adrian Caldwell	F-C	6-9	265	30	4	Lamar
33	Antonio Davis	F-C	6-9	230	28	3	Texas-El Paso
32	Dale Davis	F	6-11	230	27	5	Clemson
27	Duane Ferrell	F	6-7	215	31	8	Georgia Tech
44	Scott Haskin	F	6-11	250	26	2	Oregon State
F-20	Fred Hoiberg	G	6-4	203	24	1	Iowa State
8	Eddie Johnson	F	6-7	215	37	14	Illinois
9	Derrick McKey	F	6-10	225	30	9	Alabama
F-31	Reggie Miller	G	6-7	185	31	9	UCLA
5	Jalen Rose	G	6-8	210	23	3	Michigan
F-55	Dwayne Schintzius	C	7-2	265	28	6	Florida
45	Rik Smits	C	7-4	265	30	8	Marist
7	Reggie Williams	F-G	6-7	195	32	10	Georgetown
3	Haywoode Workman	G	6-3	180	30	5	Oral Roberts

F-Free agent

Rd.	Rookies	Sel.No.	Pos.	Ht.	Wt.	College
1	Erick Dampier	10	C	6-11	265	Mississippi State
2	Mark Pope	52	F-C	6-10	235	Kentucky

pier of Mississippi State, a legitimate force inside.

The team occasionally got into trouble when the guards didn't rebound, but the additions of the 6-8 Rose and the 6-7 Williams should remedy that.

DEFENSE: The Denver trade underscored Larry Brown's philosophy. He wants this to be a 94-foot team, forcing turnovers to feed what has been a woeful transition offense.

Rose and Williams both fit this mold perfectly. Their additions, at the very least, give Brown the power to dictate matchups. Think you're going to post up the 5-10 Best? Send in Rose. Derrick McKey isn't running the wing? Send in Williams. When Rose plays the point, the Pacers could regularly field a lineup in which the shortest player is the 6-7 Miller.

They are among the league's most tenacious units in the half-court, primarily because of the Davises and McKey, the latter among the best defenders at small forward.

Though they are among the tallest teams in the league, they don't block many shots (tied for 18th last season), an area that

In his eighth season, Rik Smits shot a career high.

begs improvement, particularly from Smits and Dale Davis. This, too, is an area where Dampier should help.

OUTLOOK: In three years under Brown, the Pacers have averaged 50 victories—a level they hadn't reached since their ABA days—so there was a natural reluctance to think about rebuilding.

That didn't stop Donnie Walsh from pulling the trigger on a trade that accomplished a series of objectives. They got younger, more athletic and more versatile.

But did they get better? It's Walsh's gamble, and he rarely bluffs.

PACER PROFILES

REGGIE MILLER 31 6-7 185   Guard

Though he returned earlier than expected after surgery to repair a blowout fracture of his right eye socket, scoring 29 points in Game 5 of the first-round series with Atlanta, the Pacers were eliminated at home . . . Reversed his usual regular-season pattern by starting off hot but cooling toward the end . . . Has settled into a comfort zone over the last five seasons, averaging between 19.6 and 21.2 points, but bumping it to 25.4 in the playoffs . . . Has hit at least 100 three-pointers for an NBA-record seven straight seasons . . . Passed the 14,000-point mark and made his club-record third All-Star appearance . . . Earned $4 million last season and was expected to re-sign for a barrel more . . . Drafted 11th out of UCLA in 1987 . . . Born Aug. 24, 1965, in Riverside, Cal.

Year	Team	G	FG	FG Pct.	FT	FT Pct.	Reb.	Ast.	TP	Avg.
1987-88	Indiana	82	306	.488	149	.801	190	132	822	10.0
1988-89	Indiana	74	398	.479	287	.844	292	227	1181	16.0
1989-90	Indiana	82	661	.514	544	.868	295	311	2016	24.6
1990-91	Indiana	82	596	.512	551	.918	281	331	1855	22.6
1991-92	Indiana	82	562	.501	442	.858	318	314	1695	20.7
1992-93	Indiana	82	571	.479	427	.880	258	262	1736	21.2
1993-94	Indiana	79	524	.503	403	.908	212	248	1574	19.9
1994-95	Indiana	81	505	.462	383	.897	210	242	1588	19.6
1995-96	Indiana	76	504	.473	430	.863	214	253	1606	21.1
	Totals	720	4627	.491	3616	.877	2270	2320	14073	19.5

RIK SMITS 30 7-4 265   Center

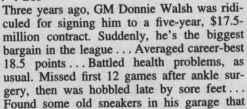

Three years ago, GM Donnie Walsh was ridiculed for signing him to a five-year, $17.5-million contract. Suddenly, he's the biggest bargain in the league . . . Averaged career-best 18.5 points . . . Battled health problems, as usual. Missed first 12 games after ankle surgery, then was hobbled late by sore feet . . . Found some old sneakers in his garage that seemed to solve the problem and he averaged 19 points and shot .545 in the playoffs despite the absence of a perimeter game to take pressure off him . . . Still telegraphs his passes out of the post when double-teamed . . . At 7-4, why pass at all? He can shoot over everyone but Shawn Bradley and Gheorghe Muresan . . . Drafted No. 2 out of Marist in 1988 . . . He earned $3.75 million last season . . . Born Aug. 23, 1966, in Eindhoven, Holland.

Year	Team	G	FG	FG Pct.	FT	FT Pct.	Reb.	Ast.	TP	Avg.
1988-89	Indiana.........	82	386	.517	184	.722	500	70	956	11.7
1989-90	Indiana.........	82	515	.533	241	.811	512	142	1271	15.5
1990-91	Indiana.........	76	342	.485	144	.762	357	84	828	10.9
1991-92	Indiana.........	74	436	.510	152	.788	417	116	1024	13.8
1992-93	Indiana.........	81	494	.486	167	.732	432	121	1155	14.3
1993-94	Indiana.........	78	493	.534	238	.793	483	156	1224	15.7
1994-95	Indiana.........	78	558	.526	284	.753	601	111	1400	17.9
1995-96	Indiana.........	63	466	.521	231	.788	433	110	1164	18.5
	Totals	614	3690	.515	1641	.770	3735	910	9022	14.7

DALE DAVIS 27 6-11 230   Forward

A keg of untapped potential, or at least the Pacers hope so . . . His most healthy of seasons as a starter was his least productive, with three-year lows in scoring (10.3), rebounds (9.1) and blocked shots (1.44) . . . Shot a paltry .467 from the line, a drop of more than 100 points from his rookie season and a major cause for concern . . . Has had operations on both shoulders and had a problem with a disc in his neck that hindered his mobility late last season . . . Normally cool-headed player snapped on Nov. 10, grabbing Sacramento's Michael Smith in a choke-hold to start the most penalized brawl in NBA history (10 suspensions, including his two-gamer). Cameras also caught him taking a swipe at an official . . . When they used the 13th pick in the 1991 draft on the Clemson forward, Pacers throught they were getting a more athletic Buck Williams, but it hasn't quite worked out that way . . . Highest-paid player on team at $4.05 million last year . . . Signed seven-year, $42-million contract last summer . . . Born March 25, 1969, in Toccoa, Ga.

Year	Team	G	FG	FG Pct.	FT	FT Pct.	Reb.	Ast.	TP	Avg.
1991-92	Indiana.........	64	154	.552	87	.572	410	30	395	6.2
1992-93	Indiana.........	82	304	.568	119	.529	723	69	727	8.9
1993-94	Indiana.........	66	308	.529	87	.529	718	100	771	11.7
1994-95	Indiana.........	74	324	.563	138	.533	696	58	786	10.6
1995-96	Indiana.........	78	334	.558	135	.467	709	76	803	10.3
	Totals	364	1424	.554	634	.520	3256	333	3482	9.6

DERRICK McKEY 30 6-10 225   Forward

Sometimes, looks like a poor man's Scottie Pippen. More often, looks like a rich man's Buck Johnson . . . He can do it all, but only does it when so inspired . . . Had lowest averages in scoring (11.7), rebounding (4.8) and assists (3.5) of his three seasons with the Pacers . . . Scoring average was the lowest since his rookie season . . . At the other end, good enough to earn second-team All-Defense honors . . . Uses quick hands, long frame, sound fundamentals and quick thinking to frustrate opponents, particularly in the post . . . Uses passive offensive nature to frustrate coaches . . . Came to the Pacers in 1993 for Detlef Schrempf, one of those rare deals that actually did help both teams . . . Signed a five-year contract extension that doesn't take effect until the 1997-98 season . . . Seattle drafted him ninth in 1987 . . . Earned $2.8 million last season . . . Born Oct. 10, 1966, in Meridian, Miss.

Year	Team	G	FG	FG Pct.	FT	FT Pct.	Reb.	Ast.	TP	Avg.
1987-88	Seattle	82	255	.491	173	.772	328	107	694	8.5
1988-89	Seattle	82	487	.502	301	.803	464	219	1305	15.9
1989-90	Seattle	80	468	.493	315	.782	489	187	1254	15.7
1990-91	Seattle	73	438	.517	235	.845	423	169	1115	15.3
1991-92	Seattle	52	285	.472	188	.847	268	120	777	14.9
1992-93	Seattle	77	387	.496	220	.741	327	197	1034	13.4
1993-94	Indiana	76	355	.500	192	.756	402	327	911	12.0
1994-95	Indiana	81	411	.493	221	.744	394	276	1075	13.3
1995-96	Indiana	75	346	.486	170	.769	361	262	879	11.7
	Totals	678	3432	.496	2015	.784	3456	1864	9044	13.3

ANTONIO DAVIS 28 6-9 230   Forward-Center

Could start at power forward for a lot of NBA teams, including this one . . . Came back from an injury-shortened season in 1994-95 to post career highs in scoring (8.8) and free throw percentage (.713) . . . A better offensive player than starter Dale Davis, he has a decent face-up jumper and is developing some post moves . . . Explosive leaper . . . Forced to split minutes at center, where he's often overmatched, but never outworked . . . Soft-spoken off the court, but a deep thinker . . . Drafted out of Texas-El Paso with 45th pick in 1990, he spent three years developing game, and physique, in Europe before signing as a free agent in 1993 . . . Proved to be a steal at $800,000 last season, but free-agent status got him a seven-year contract estimated at more than triple that annual figure . . . Born Oct. 31, 1968, in Oakland.

Year	Team	G	FG	FG Pct.	FT	FT Pct.	Reb.	Ast.	TP	Avg.
1993-94	Indiana.........	81	216	.508	194	.642	505	55	626	7.7
1994-95	Indiana.........	44	109	.445	117	.672	280	25	335	7.6
1995-96	Indiana.........	82	236	.490	246	.713	501	43	719	8.8
	Totals	207	561	.487	557	.678	1286	123	1680	8.1

TRAVIS BEST 24 5-11 172   Guard

Trade of Mark Jackson to Denver makes the starter's job his to lose . . . A non-factor early, he learned quietly, then assumed the backup role in time for the playoffs, averaging 16.8 minutes, 5.8 points and 1.8 assists in the first-round loss to Atlanta . . . Has fullcourt quickness, three-point range and a calm, confident demeanor . . . Used to being the best scorer on every other team he's been on, but like many young point guards, needs to adopt the mentality that it's better to give than receive . . . Looking like a draft coup, considering he was the 23rd pick out of Georgia Tech last year . . . Born July 12, 1972, in Springfield, Mass., where an 82-point game in high school earned him the nickname "The Springfield Rifle." . . . Made $580,000 last season.

Year	Team	G	FG	FG Pct.	FT	FT Pct.	Reb.	Ast.	TP	Avg.
1995-96	Indiana.........	59	69	.423	75	.833	44	97	221	3.7

JALEN ROSE 23 6-8 210   Guard-Forward

Packed his droopy drawers for Indiana in June trade that also brought Reggie Williams and the 10th pick in exchange for Mark Jackson, Ricky Pierce and the 23rd pick . . . Could combine with Reggie Miller for an all-talk, all-the-time backcourt . . . Didn't do anything wrong in Denver other than fail to become Magic Johnson . . . Started first five games, team went 0-5, then was benched . . . Finally returned to lineup when Mahmoud Abdul-Rauf sat out the national anthem, not to mention the rest of the season . . . As a starter, averaged 10.6 points and 7.6 assists . . . His 495 assists were the most by a Nugget since Michael Adams had 693 in 1990-91 . . . Needs to show he can hit the three consistently (.306 over two seasons) . . . Earned $1.268 million . . . Drafted ninth out of Michigan in 1994 . . . Emotional leader of storied Fab Five . . . Born Jan. 30, 1973, in Detroit.

Year	Team	G	FG	FG Pct.	FT	FT Pct.	Reb.	Ast.	TP	Avg.
1994-95	Denver	81	227	.454	173	.739	217	389	663	8.2
1995-96	Denver	80	290	.480	191	.690	260	495	803	10.0
	Totals	161	517	.468	364	.712	477	884	1466	9.1

HAYWOODE WORKMAN 30 6-3 180   Guard

Lost his backup job to rookie Travis Best late in the season and became expendable . . . A Tasmanian devil on defense . . . Still can't hit the jumper consistently (.390 last season) and tends to play out of control, with head-down drives into traffic . . . Then again, it's only natural for the former Charlotte player of the year in football and basketball . . . Pacers' all-time leader in playoff assists with 161 . . . Hasn't been the same player since losing his job to Mark Jackson after the 1993-94 season . . . Former Oral Roberts star was signed as a free agent in 1993 . . . Earned $900,000 in first year of new contract last season . . . Hawks drafted him 49th in 1989 . . . Born Jan. 23, 1966, in Charlotte.

Year	Team	G	FG	FG Pct.	FT	FT Pct.	Reb.	Ast.	TP	Avg.
1989-90	Atlanta	6	2	.667	2	1.000	3	2	6	1.0
1990-91	Washington	73	234	.454	101	.759	242	353	581	8.0
1993-94	Indiana	65	195	.424	93	.802	204	404	501	7.7
1994-95	Indiana	69	101	.375	55	.743	111	194	292	4.2
1995-96	Indiana	77	101	.390	54	.740	124	213	279	3.6
	Totals	290	633	.420	305	.766	684	1166	1659	5.7

REGGIE WILLIAMS 32 6-7 195   Guard-Forward

Some throw-in . . . Was packaged with Jalen Rose and the 10th pick in the trade that sent Mark Jackson, Ricky Pierce and the 23rd pick to Denver in mid-June . . . Skeptics scoffed his value was simply in balancing the salaries to make the trade possible . . . If he can get his head back in the game, could play invaluable role . . . Has a lot of skills Pacers don't, mainly that he can slash on offense and defense . . . Last season was a wash. He missed 16 games with a stress fracture in his leg, five more due to a death in the family, and wound up with the worst stats of his career ... Shoots the three like he can make it, which is bad thinking (.299 career) ... The first Reggie drafted in 1987, this Georgetown star went fourth to the Clippers. Reggie Miller went seven spots later ... After stops in Cleveland and San Antonio, he found his game in Denver ... Earned $1.853 million ... Born March 5, 1964, in Baltimore.

Year	Team	G	FG	FG Pct.	FT	FT Pct.	Reb.	Ast.	TP	Avg.
1987-88	L.A.Clippers	35	152	.356	48	.727	118	58	365	10.4
1988-89	L.A.Clippers	63	260	.438	92	.754	179	103	642	10.2
1989-90	LAC-Clev.-S.A.	47	131	.388	52	.765	83	53	320	6.8
1990-91	S.A.-Den.	73	384	.449	166	.843	306	133	991	13.6
1991-92	Denver	81	601	.471	216	.803	405	235	1474	18.2
1992-93	Denver	79	535	.458	238	.804	428	295	1341	17.0
1993-94	Denver	82	418	.412	165	.733	392	300	1065	13.0
1994-95	Denver	74	388	.459	132	.759	329	231	993	13.4
1995-96	Denver	52	94	.370	33	.846	122	74	241	4.6
	Totals	586	2963	.438	1142	.784	2362	1482	7432	12.7

FRED HOIBERG 24 6-4 203   Guard

The Damon Bailey of Iowa had slightly more success. At least he made the team ... Appeared in just 15 games but did impress coaching staff in practice ... Good shooter, hard worker, could become another Craig Ehlo type ... A second-round draft pick (52nd) from Iowa State (where he was nicknamed "The Mayor") in 1995, he earned $200,000 last season ... Born Oct. 15, 1972, in Lincoln, Neb.

Year	Team	G	FG	FG Pct.	FT	FT Pct.	Reb.	Ast.	TP	Avg.
1995-96	Indiana	15	8	.421	15	.833	9	8	32	2.1

EDDIE JOHNSON 37 6-7 215   Forward

Started the season like a player 10 years younger but wore down, was bothered by injuries and, ultimately, was phased out ... How far out? Played nine minutes of Game 1 of playoffs, missed all five shots, and didn't play again ... Shot a career-low .413 overall, but showed he still could hit the three ... When he isn't hitting, he isn't helping, as his defense is a liability ... Passed two career milestones: 18,000 points and 30,000 minutes ... Former Sixth Man Award winner was signed to a two-year free agent contract by the Pacers after one season in Greece... One of the most prolific second-round picks ever, he was taken by Kansas City 29th, out of Illinois, in 1981... Earned $1 million last season... Born May 1, 1959, in Chicago, Ill.

Year	Team	G	FG	FG Pct.	FT	FT Pct.	Reb.	Ast.	TP	Avg.
1981-82	Kansas City	74	295	.459	99	.664	322	109	690	9.3
1982-83	Kansas City	82	677	.494	247	.779	501	216	1621	19.8
1983-84	Kansas City	82	753	.485	268	.810	455	296	1794	21.9
1984-85	Kansas City	82	769	.491	325	.871	407	273	1876	22.9
1985-86	Sacramento	82	623	.475	280	.816	419	214	1530	18.7
1986-87	Sacramento	81	606	.463	267	.829	353	251	1516	18.7
1987-88	Phoenix	73	533	.480	204	.850	318	180	1294	17.7
1988-89	Phoenix	70	608	.497	217	.868	306	162	1504	21.5
1989-90	Phoenix	64	411	.453	188	.917	246	107	1080	16.9
1990-91	Phoe.-Sea.	81	543	.484	229	.891	271	111	1354	16.7
1991-92	Seattle	81	534	.459	291	.861	292	161	1386	17.1
1992-93	Seattle	82	463	.467	234	.911	272	135	1177	14.4
1993-94	Charlotte	73	339	.459	99	.780	224	125	836	11.5
1995-96	Indiana	62	180	.413	70	.886	153	69	475	7.7
	Totals	1069	7334	.475	3018	.841	4539	2409	18133	17.0

DUANE FERRELL 31 6-7 215   Forward

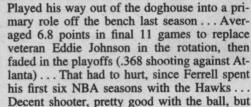

Played his way out of the doghouse into a primary role off the bench last season... Averaged 6.8 points in final 11 games to replace veteran Eddie Johnson in the rotation, then faded in the playoffs (.368 shooting against Atlanta)... That had to hurt, since Ferrell spent his first six NBA seasons with the Hawks... Decent shooter, pretty good with the ball, but is prone to losing it on his way to the basket... Undrafted out of Georgia Tech in 1988... Earned $845,000 last season, and didn't exercise his option to become a free agent... Born Feb. 28, 1965, in Baltimore.

Year	Team	G	FG	FG Pct.	FT	FT Pct.	Reb.	Ast.	TP	Avg.
1988-89	Atlanta	41	35	.422	30	.682	41	10	100	2.4
1989-90	Atlanta	14	5	.357	2	.333	7	2	12	0.9
1990-91	Atlanta	78	174	.489	125	.801	179	55	475	6.1
1991-92	Atlanta	66	331	.524	166	.761	210	92	839	12.7
1992-93	Atlanta	82	327	.470	176	.779	191	132	839	10.2
1993-94	Atlanta	72	184	.485	144	.783	129	65	513	7.1
1994-95	Indiana	56	83	.480	64	.753	88	31	231	4.1
1995-96	Indiana	54	80	.482	42	.737	93	30	202	3.7
	Totals	463	1219	.488	749	.767	938	417	3211	6.9

DWAYNE SCHINTZIUS 28 7-2 265   Center

Vowed to put his career back on track but wound up getting most of his meaningful minutes in the movie *Eddie*, in which he played a Soviet center for the Knicks . . . Larry Brown's annual reclamation project did lose weight and hair, but didn't gain much . . . Still too soft . . . Has nice touch and good hands, so likely will find work for a while . . . Great sense of humor, intelligent guy . . . Earned $225,000 on one-year free-agent deal . . . Pacers were his fourth team in six seasons . . . A first-round pick (24th), out of San Antonio, in 1990 . . . Born Oct. 14, 1968, in Brandon, Fla.

Year	Team	G	FG	FG Pct.	FT	FT Pct.	Reb.	Ast.	TP	Avg.
1990-91	San Antonio	42	68	.439	22	.550	121	17	158	3.8
1991-92	Sacramento	33	50	.427	10	.833	118	20	110	3.3
1992-93	New Jersey	5	2	.286	3	1.000	8	2	7	1.4
1993-94	New Jersey	30	29	.345	10	.588	89	13	68	2.3
1994-95	New Jersey	43	41	.380	6	.545	81	15	88	2.0
1995-96	Indiana	33	49	.445	13	.619	78	14	111	3.4
	Totals	186	239	.411	64	.615	495	81	542	2.9

ADRIAN CALDWELL 30 6-9 265   Forward-Center

After spending parts of three seasons as a 12th man in Houston, filled the same role with the Pacers . . . A prototypical banger . . . Not a bad offensive player, once he catches the ball . . . Has battled weight problems much of his career, but kept it off with Indiana . . . Had his only career double-double (10 points, 11 rebounds) in final regular-season game against Cleveland . . . Undrafted Lamar product signed a one-year, $250,000 contract prior to last season . . . Born July 4, 1966, in Corpus Christi, Tex.

Year	Team	G	FG	FG Pct.	FT	FT Pct.	Reb.	Ast.	TP	Avg.
1989-90	Houston	51	42	.553	13	.464	109	7	97	1.9
1990-91	Houston	42	35	.422	7	.412	100	8	77	1.8
1994-95	Houston	7	1	.250	3	.500	10	0	5	0.7
1995-96	Indiana	51	46	.554	18	.500	110	6	110	2.2
	Totals	151	124	.504	41	.471	329	21	289	1.9

SCOTT HASKIN 26 6-11 250   Forward-Center

This could be the end of the road . . . Missed all of last two seasons after tearing an ACL in Orlando on Feb. 26, 1994 . . . While rehabbing the knee, he popped a disc in his back, which killed a nerve in his leg, which led to muscle atrophy . . . If he isn't ready for training camp, he may retire . . . Pacers bypassed Chris Mills and Scott Burrell, among others, to select the easy-going big man from Oregon State with the 14th pick in the 1993 draft, and they've been searching for punch at small forward ever since . . . Earned $1.3 million last season . . . Born Sept. 19, 1970, in Riverside, Cal.

Year	Team	G	FG	FG Pct.	FT	FT Pct.	Reb.	Ast.	TP	Avg.
1993-94	Indiana.	27	21	.467	13	.684	55	6	55	2.0
1994-95	Indiana.					Injured				
1995-96	Indiana.					Injured				
	Totals	27	21	.467	13	.684	55	6	55	2.0

THE ROOKIES

ERICK DAMPIER 22 6-11 265   Center

Pacers were delighted the Mississippi State center slipped to the 10th pick . . . Will add depth, defense, rebounding and shot-blocking to frontline . . . Doesn't have much of an offensive game, but did average 13.2 points on .587 shooting in three seasons . . . Imposing physical specimen with remarkably little body fat . . . Will be given time to develop, rather than forced to bear the burden of great expectations . . . Born July 14, 1974, in Jackson, Miss.

MARK POPE 24 6-10 235   Forward-Center

Kentucky backup was taken No. 52 . . . Traded opportunity for stardom at Washington (11.2 points, 8.1 rebounds as freshman and sophomore) for a shot at a championship when he transferred to Kentucky in 1993 . . . Got his title, but hurt his draft prospects in the process . . . Averaged 7.9 points and 5.7 rebounds with 'Cats . . . Has athletic skills, can shoot the face-up jumper, can play multiple positions . . . Born Sept. 11, 1972, in Omaha, Neb.

COACH LARRY BROWN: If he's really only happy when he's unhappy, shouldn't he be happy all the time? . . . May be in the most enjoyable stop of his career . . . Since re-marrying just before moving here, and the birth of his first son two years ago, Brown has showed signs of settling down . . . Every time an NBA vacancy opens, his name comes up, but he swears his next job will either be at the college or high-school level . . . John Calipari's biggest fan. Big contract for Nets' coach activated a clause in Brown's contract that bumps his salary $500,000 per over the next three years . . . In three years here, he has averaged 50 wins, no mean feat for a team that never had won more than 44 in its prior NBA history . . . Coming off most disappointing season with Pacers, a first-round elimination after consecutive trips to the conference finals . . . Is nine wins away from 1,000 in his career (college, ABA and NBA) . . . ABA-NBA record is 814-544 . . . Has never coached a pro team in a championship series . . . Took UCLA to NCAA title game, took Kansas to NCAA championship . . . Played five years in ABA after leaving North Carolina . . . 1964 Olympic gold medalist . . . Born Sept. 14, 1940, in Brooklyn, N.Y.

BIGGEST BLUNDER

Trying to choose between the mistakes made by this franchise in the pre-Donnie Walsh years is akin to picking the worst Rocky sequel. But there are two of such magnitude, they must share the stage.

In the 1978 draft, holding the third pick overall, the Pacers could've taken a flyer on a skinny junior 75 miles down the road: Indiana State's Larry Bird. But management wasn't convinced of Bird's future greatness and went instead for immediate help, drafting Kentucky bruiser Rick Robey. Midway through his rookie season, Robey was shipped to Boston, where Bird, taken sixth by the Celtics, would later become his teammate.

The Pacers were even more short-sighted three years later. On June 5, 1981, the Pacers—who had lost center James Edwards to free agency and were desperate for a big man—traded their 1984 first-round pick to Portland for journeyman center Tom Owens. That pick would be the second overall. Michael Jordan went third.

ALL-TIME PACER LEADERS

SEASON

Points: George McGinnis, 2,353, 1974–75 (ABA)
      Billy Knight, 2,075, 1976–77
Assists: Don Buse, 689, 1975–76 (ABA)
      Don Buse, 685, 1976–77
Rebounds: Mel Daniels, 1,475, 1970–71 (ABA)
      Clark Kellogg, 860, 1982–83

GAME

Points: George McGinnis, 58 vs. Dallas, 11/28/72 (ABA)
      Reggie Miller, 57 vs. Charlotte, 11/28/92
Assists: Don Buse, 20 vs. Denver, 3/26/76 (ABA)
      Vern Fleming, 18 vs. Houston, 11/23/90
      Micheal Williams, 18 vs. New York 11/13/91
Rebounds: George McGinnis, 37 vs. Carolina, 1/12/71 (ABA)
      Herb Williams, 29 vs. Denver, 1/23/89

CAREER

Points: Billy Knight, 10,780, 1974–83 (ABA and NBA)
      Reggie Miller, 14,073, 1987–96
Assists: Vern Fleming, 4,038, 1984–95
      Don Buse, 2,747, 1972–77, 1980–82 (ABA)
Rebounds: Mel Daniels, 7,622, 1968–74 (ABA)
      Herb Williams, 4,494, 1981–89

MILWAUKEE BUCKS

TEAM DIRECTORY: Pres.: Herb Kohl; VP-Bus. Oper.: John Steinmiller; VP-Basketball Oper./GM: Mike Dunleavy; Dir. Pub. Rel.: Bill King II; Coach: Chris Ford; Asst. Coaches: TBA. Arena: Bradley Center (18,633). Colors: Hunter green, purple and silver.

Vin Baker capped fine season with a 41-point game.

SCOUTING REPORT

SHOOTING: No other team in the league has two 20-point scorers starting at forward, so why is this offense so miserable? Glenn Robinson has all the skills but has yet to reach the level expected of a No. 1 pick. Vin Baker is the team's offensive focal point, a sometimes awkward looking post player who nevertheless gets it done. And now add Armon Gilliam (18.3 with the Nets last year) to the arsenal

The problems lie in the backcourt. Sherman Douglas and Johnny Newman are simply too erratic, and Shawn Respert didn't provide much help during his rookie season.

To that end, the Bucks made a draft-day trade to acquire UConn shooting guard Ray Allen, a smooth, athletic scorer who could step right into the lineup.

The Bucks set an all-time franchise low for scoring (95.6 per game) last season, while hitting a dismal .338 from the three-point line. Allen could help improve those numbers.

PLAYMAKING: The only point guard in the league who'd lose a footrace with Mark Jackson, Douglas gets the most out of his skills, but he doesn't have that many. Lee Mayberry, now in Vancouver, was more gifted but was either too laid-back, or perhaps shell-shocked, to assert himself in the offense. To fill the need, the Bucks were reportedly wrapping up a deal for Phoenix point guard Elliot Perry.

Keep an eye on second-round pick Moochie Norris of West Florida, who has the confident swagger at the point. If he is as good as the postseason camps indicated, he could be the Nick Van Exel of this draft.

Baker knows what to do with the ball when he catches it inside, but Robinson has yet to figure it out entirely. For a guy who draws crowds of defenders, he doesn't generate much for anyone other than himself.

REBOUNDING: Despite having some of the biggest big men around, the Bucks couldn't get out of their own way on the boards. Neither Kevin Duckworth nor Benoit Benjamin solved the problem, so now the Bucks have Gilliam (713 boards last season) and ex-Timberwolf Andrew Lang.

Baker is active on both boards, as is Robinson. Veteran Terry Cummings showed he could still lend a hand, as well but, overall, this is a team that lacks physical presence. Even Baker, one of the league's better rebounders, does so more with finesse than brute strength.

BUCK ROSTER

No.	Veterans	Pos.	Ht.	Wt.	Age	Yrs. Pro	College
42	Vin Baker	F	6-11	244	24	3	Hartford
30	Marty Conlon	F	6-10	231	28	5	Providence
F-34	Terry Cummings	F	6-9	250	35	14	DePaul
20	Sherman Douglas	G	6-1	198	30	7	Syracuse
--	Armon Gilliam	C	6-9	245	32	9	UNLV
F-31	Randolph Keys	F	6-7	210	30	5	Southern Mississippi
28	Andrew Lang	C	6-11	250	30	8	Arkansas
22	Johnny Newman	F	6-6	199	32	10	Richmond
F-54	Mike Paplowski	C	6-10	270	26	3	Michigan State
2	Elliot Perry	G	6-0	160	27	4	Memphis State
3	Shawn Respert	G	6-2	195	24	1	Michigan State
13	Glenn Robinson	F	6-7	220	23	2	Purdue

F-Free agent

Rd.	Rookies	Sel.No.	Pos.	Ht.	Wt.	College
1	Ray Allen	5	G	6-5	205	Connecticut
2	Moochie Norris	33	G	6-1	175	West Florida
2	Jeff Nordgaard	53	F	6-7	226	Wisconsin-Green Bay

DEFENSE: They improved from the previous season but this remains a trouble spot. Opponents shot 48 percent against them overall, 40 percent from the three-point line, the latter an indicator of a team unable, or unwilling, to effectively rotate after double-teaming inside.

The team lacks quickness on the perimeter (24th in steals) and strength inside (28th in blocked shots), bringing a whole new meaning to the term "help defense." Lang figures to contribute in this sector.

OUTLOOK: After four seasons heading in no particular direction, Mike Dunleavy was bounced off the bench and into the general manager's role, the problem there being he probably was a better coach than GM. He hasn't done particularly well in the draft with Robinson—currently the fourth-best player in his draft class—and his trades have been head-scratchers.

Last season, for example, he packed off the promise of youth (Todd Day, Eric Murdock and Eric Mobley) for unwanted veterans (Douglas and Benjamin).

It took Dunleavy forever to decide on a head coach. He didn't hire ex-Celtic boss Chris Ford until mid-June. Ford had some success in Boston, riding out the end of the Bird-McHale-Parish era, and brings a strong defensive background to a team that needs one.

BUCK PROFILES

VIN BAKER 24 6-10 244   Forward

Has quietly emerged as one of the best in the league at power forward ... Was 12 rebounds shy of a 20-10 season ... As it was, he finished at 21.1 points and 9.9 rebounds ... Scoring has increased each year in the league ... Curiously, blocked shots dropped by 25 last season ... Went for career-high 41 against Portland, the Bucks' first 40-point game since '89 (Ricky Pierce) ... Had more turnovers (216) than assists (212) ... Lone bright light shining among otherwise dim bulbs on Bucks' draft tree ... Signed a 10-year contract after being drafted eighth out of Hartford in 1993 ... Original deal would've made him a free agent after last season, but he agreed to move the opt-out back to the summer of '99 ... Oops ... Earned $3.765 million ... Born Nov. 23, 1971, in Lake Wales, Fla. ... Father, James, is a rare combination, a Baptist minister and an auto mechanic.

Year	Team	G	FG	FG Pct.	FT	FT Pct.	Reb.	Ast.	TP	Avg.
1993-94	Milwaukee	82	435	.501	234	.569	621	163	1105	13.5
1994-95	Milwaukee	82	594	.483	256	.593	846	296	1451	17.7
1995-96	Milwaukee	82	699	.489	321	.670	808	212	1729	21.1
	Totals	246	1728	.490	811	.613	2275	671	4285	17.4

GLENN ROBINSON 23 6-7 220   Forward

Was his selection at No. 1 overall in '94 a mistake? ... Thus far, he's been no better than the fourth-best player in that draft, behind Grant Hill, Jason Kidd and Juwan Howard ... Two-year averages (21.1 points, 6.3 rebounds, 3.0 assists) are solid, but not the kind of numbers expected from a guy signed to a celebrated 10-year, $68-million contract out of Purdue ... Has piled up nearly 600 turnovers (3.7 per game) in two years ... Absolutely no truth to the rumor he picked up the nickname "Big Dog" based on his defense ... Likes the three a little too much (.331 career) ... Needs to use his strength more inside ... But he's still very young. In the old days, this would be his rookie season ... The third No. 1 pick in Bucks' history. First two (Lew Alcindor in '69 and Kent Benson in '77) brought mixed results, which makes him the tie-breaker . . . Earned $3.770 million in the second of his 10 installments . . . Born Jan. 10, 1973, in Gary, Ind.

Year	Team	G	FG	FG Pct.	FT	FT Pct.	Reb.	Ast.	TP	Avg.
1994-95	Milwaukee.......	80	636	.451	397	.796	513	197	1755	21.9
1995-96	Milwaukee.......	82	627	.454	316	.812	504	293	1660	20.2
	Totals	162	1263	.452	713	.803	1017	490	3415	21.1

JOHNNY NEWMAN 32 6-6 199   Guard-Forward

Has skills to be excellent sixth man . . . Unfortunately, he had to start all 82 games for the Bucks, the most of his career . . . Demonstrated he's a solid 10-12-point scorer whether he plays 22 minutes a game or 32 . . . His consistency made it easier for the Bucks to give up on Todd Day . . . Drafted 29th out of Richmond by Cleveland in '89, he's with his fifth team . . . Bucks signed him to a three-year contract prior to last season . . . Made $1.1 million . . . Born Nov. 28, 1963, in Danville, Va. . . . Has a degree in sociology and criminal justice.

Year	Team	G	FG	FG Pct.	FT	FT Pct.	Reb.	Ast.	TP	Avg.
1986-87	Cleveland	59	113	.411	66	.868	70	27	293	5.0
1987-88	New York.......	77	270	.435	207	.841	159	62	773	10.0
1988-89	New York.......	81	455	.475	286	.815	206	162	1293	16.0
1989-90	New York.......	80	374	.476	239	.799	191	180	1032	12.9
1990-91	Charlotte........	81	478	.470	385	.809	254	188	1371	16.9
1991-92	Charlotte........	55	295	.477	236	.766	179	146	839	15.3
1992-93	Charlotte........	64	279	.522	194	.808	143	117	764	11.9
1993-94	Char.-N.J........	81	313	.471	182	.809	180	72	832	10.3
1994-95	Milwaukee.......	82	226	.463	137	.801	173	91	634	7.7
1995-96	Milwaukee.......	82	321	.495	186	.802	200	154	889	10.8
	Totals	742	3124	.473	2118	.807	1755	1199	8720	11.8

SHERMAN DOUGLAS 30 6-1 198   Guard

Another curious pickup who made the Bucks older but not necessarily better . . . They sent Todd Day and Alton Lister to Celtics for him in November . . . Averaged 11.5 points and 5.8 assists with Bucks . . . Had first career triple-double (15 points, 10 rebounds, 11 assists) Jan. 5 against Portland . . . Had best season of career from the line (.731) . . . On a team with two forwards who need the ball, his skills wouldn't seem to mesh

... Not known as a great halfcourt passer, or for drive-and-dish skills ... Can create a shot for himself ... Drafted 28th by Miami out of Syracuse in 1989 ... Two worst years of his career, statistically (1991-92 and 1992-93 in Boston), were his only two on a winning team ... Now reunited with the coach, Chris Ford, from those wonder years ... Earned $3.163 million ... Born Sept. 15, 1966, in Washington, D.C.

Year	Team	G	FG	FG Pct.	FT	FT Pct.	Reb.	Ast.	TP	Avg.
1989-90	Miami	81	463	.494	224	.687	206	619	1155	14.3
1990-91	Miami	73	532	.504	284	.686	209	624	1352	18.5
1991-92	Mia.-Bos.	42	117	.462	73	.682	63	172	308	7.3
1992-93	Boston	79	264	.498	84	.560	162	508	618	7.8
1993-94	Boston	78	425	.462	177	.641	193	683	1040	13.3
1994-95	Boston	65	365	.475	204	.689	170	446	954	14.7
1995-96	Bos.-Mil.	79	345	.504	160	.731	180	436	890	11.3
	Totals	497	2511	.488	1206	.674	1183	3488	6317	12.7

ANDREW LANG 30 6-11 250   Center

One of the game's more underrated shot-blockers and durable centers came to Bucks for No.1 pick in July ... Finished 13th in league last season at 1.77 blocks per game ... Averaged 2.05 in his 20 games with Timberwolves ... Missed 11 others with a slightly torn left-calf muscle ... Sidelined by injuries only 10 games the previous five seasons ... Tied career high with eight blocks March 3, the second-highest total in club history ... Arrived in Minnesota with Spud Webb from Atlanta in exchange for Christian Laettner and Sean Rooks just before trade deadline ... Went from Arkansas to the NBA when Phoenix used the 28th pick to draft him in 1988 ... Born June 28, 1966, in Pine Bluff, ark. ... Made $1.964 million.

Year	Team	G	FG	FG Pct.	FT	FT Pct.	Reb.	Ast.	TP	Avg.
1988-89	Phoenix	62	60	.513	39	.650	147	9	159	2.6
1989-90	Phoenix	74	97	.557	64	.653	271	21	258	3.5
1990-91	Phoenix	63	109	.577	93	.715	303	27	311	4.9
1991-92	Phoenix	81	248	.522	126	.768	546	43	622	7.7
1992-93	Philadelphia	73	149	.425	87	.763	436	79	386	5.3
1993-94	Atlanta	82	215	.469	73	.689	313	51	504	6.1
1994-95	Atlanta	82	320	.473	152	.809	456	72	794	9.7
1995-96	Atl.-Minn.	71	353	.447	125	.801	455	65	832	11.7
	Totals	588	1551	.480	759	.747	2927	367	3866	6.6

TERRY CUMMINGS 35 6-9 250   Forward

Veteran of some of the Bucks' salad days (1984-89) was brought back . . . They could've used a little more dressing . . . Proud, intense competitor didn't fit in with this bunch . . . Had best season in last four with averages of 8.0 points, 5.5 rebounds and 21.9 minutes . . . Also a Pentecostal minister, musician and screenwriter . . . Second player picked out of DePaul by the San Diego Clippers in 1982, he has put together an exceptional career despite a heart problem diagnosed in his early years . . . Spurs paid $1.1 million buyout to make him a free agent after 1994-95 season, and the Bucks picked him up for $650,000 . . . Averaged at least 20 points in seven of first eight seasons . . . Born March 15, 1961, in Chicago.

Year	Team	G	FG	FG Pct.	FT	FT Pct.	Reb.	Ast.	TP	Avg.
1982-83	San Diego	70	684	.523	292	.709	744	177	1660	23.7
1983-84	San Diego	81	737	.494	380	.720	777	139	1854	22.9
1984-85	Milwaukee	79	759	.495	343	.741	716	228	1861	23.6
1985-86	Milwaukee	82	681	.474	265	.656	694	193	1627	19.8
1986-87	Milwaukee	82	729	.511	249	.662	700	229	1707	20.8
1987-88	Milwaukee	76	675	.485	270	.665	553	181	1621	21.3
1988-89	Milwaukee	80	730	.467	362	.787	650	198	1829	22.9
1989-90	San Antonio	81	728	.475	343	.780	677	219	1818	22.4
1990-91	San Antonio	67	503	.484	164	.683	521	157	1177	17.6
1991-92	San Antonio	70	514	.488	177	.711	631	102	1210	17.3
1992-93	San Antonio	8	11	.379	5	.500	19	4	27	3.4
1993-94	San Antonio	59	183	.428	63	.589	297	50	429	7.3
1994-95	San Antonio	76	224	.483	72	.585	378	59	520	6.8
1995-96	Milwaukee	81	270	.462	104	.650	445	89	645	8.0
	Totals	992	7428	.486	3089	.706	7802	2025	17985	18.1

ARMON GILLIAM 32 6-9 245   Forward

Nets' free agent signed four-year contract with Bucks in August. Had career high in minutes. So, by end of ninth NBA season, career high in oxygen and Gatorade needed . . . Was Nets' only consistent scorer and had best statistical season of his career . . . May be NBA's best at scoring with either hand in low post . . . Learned to use left hand by tying his right behind back while eating . . . Must have been really bored at dinner table . . . Decent range on jumper but top weapon is the jump hook . . . Played 235 straight games before run was ended with sprained ankle . . . Good, strong positional rebounder, averaged double-figure boards most of season before staggering through last weeks. Finished 19th in the league with 9.1 per . . . Named Net of the Year . . . Won team's first NBA Player of the Week honor in five seasons . . . Real nice guy, devout, clean-living type. You know, boring . . . Defensively? Not exactly Michael Jordan, okay? Gets burned in rotations . . . Passed 10,000 points and 5,000 rebounds. Too bad for Nets he didn't have them all last year . . . Phoenix picked him No. 2 in '87 out of UNLV . . . Sent to Charlotte with draft picks for Kurt Rambis Dec. 13, 1989 . . . On to Sixers with Dave Hoppen for Mike Gminski Jan, 4, 1991. Sixers waived him and he signed as a free agent with Nets Aug. 11, 1993 . . . Born May 28, 1964, in Pittsburgh . . . Made $1.92 million. Had buyout clause for the final year of contract, allowing him to become a free agent.

Year	Team	G	FG	FG Pct.	FT	FT Pct.	Reb.	Ast.	TP	Avg.
1987-88	Phoenix	55	342	.475	131	.679	434	72	815	14.8
1988-89	Phoenix	74	468	.503	240	.743	541	52	1176	15.9
1989-90	Phoe.-Char.	76	484	.515	303	.723	599	99	1271	16.7
1990-91	Char.-Phil.	75	487	.487	268	.815	598	105	1242	16.6
1991-92	Philadelphia	81	512	.511	343	.807	660	118	1367	16.9
1992-93	Philadelphia	80	359	.464	274	.843	472	116	992	12.4
1993-94	New Jersey	82	348	.510	274	.759	500	69	970	11.8
1994-95	New Jersey	82	455	.503	302	.770	613	99	1212	14.8
1995-96	New Jersey	78	576	.474	277	.791	713	140	1429	18.3
	Totals	683	4031	.493	2412	.774	5130	870	10474	15.3

SHAWN RESPERT 24 6-2 195   Guard

Jury's still out, but the opening argument wasn't very convincing . . . Bucks risked two first-round picks (Gary Trent in '95 and a conditional pick in '96) to acquire Respert, who Portland took eighth in 1995 . . . Must've figured he'd be the answer to their prayers at shooting guard . . . Still on their knees after the rookie averaged 4.9 points and shot an alarming .387 . . . He did finish strong, averaging 8.6 points and shooting .544 in April . . . Michigan State's all-time leading scorer with 2,351 points . . . Made $1.232 million . . . Born Feb. 6, 1972, in Detroit.

Year	Team	G	FG	FG Pct.	FT	FT Pct.	Reb.	Ast.	TP	Avg.
1995-96	Milwaukee	62	113	.387	35	.833	74	68	303	4.9

RANDOLPH KEYS 30 6-7 210   Forward-Guard

Resurrected career after spending previous four seasons in Italy, France and the CBA ... Lakers picked him up late in 1994-95 season and Bucks then signed him prior to training camp ... May be back to stay because he still can shoot ... Scored 17 against Phoenix in late March ... Should be a better three-point shooter (.310 last year, .272 career) ... Drafted 22nd by Cleveland out of Southern Mississippi in 1988 ... Earned $363,000 ... Born April 19, 1966, in Collins, Miss.

Year	Team	G	FG	FG Pct.	FT	FT Pct.	Reb.	Ast.	TP	Avg.
1988-89	Cleveland	42	74	.430	20	.690	56	19	169	4.0
1989-90	Clev.-Char.	80	293	.432	101	.721	253	88	701	8.8
1990-91	Charlotte	44	59	.407	19	.576	100	18	140	3.2
1994-95	L.A. Lakers	6	9	.346	2	1.000	17	2	20	3.3
1995-96	Milwaukee	69	87	.418	36	.837	125	65	232	3.4
	Totals	241	522	.425	178	.721	551	192	1262	5.2

MARTY CONLON 28 6-10 231   Forward

A poor man's Danny Ferry ... OK, maybe middle-class ... Doesn't have Ferry's range or ball-handling skills but is a better rebounder ... Numbers declined across the board last season, his minutes cut almost in half (to 12.9 from 25.2) due to the acquisition of Terry Cummings ... Is with his fifth NBA team, probably not his last ... Undrafted out of Providence in 1990, he bounced between the NBA and CBA for four seasons before catching on with Bucks ... Had career year in 1994-95 (9.9 points, 5.2 rebounds) ... Would really help himself by extending range to three-point line, where he's just 13 of 64 for his career ... Earned $1.165 million ... Born Jan. 19, 1968, in the Bronx, N.Y.

Year	Team	G	FG	FG Pct.	FT	FT Pct.	Reb.	Ast.	TP	Avg.
1991-92	Seattle	45	48	.475	24	.750	69	12	120	2.7
1992-93	Sacramento	46	81	.474	57	.704	123	37	219	4.8
1993-94	Char.-Wash.	30	95	.576	43	.811	139	34	233	7.8
1994-95	Milwaukee	82	344	.532	119	.613	426	110	815	9.9
1995-96	Milwaukee	74	153	.468	84	.764	177	68	395	5.3
	Totals	277	721	.511	327	.696	934	261	1782	6.4

ELLIOT PERRY 27 6-0 160   Guard

Came to Bucks from Suns in summer trade for a future first-round draft pick . . . Little guy was a big man in Phoenix . . . Usually only got a chance to start when Kevin Johnson was hurt (what's that, three times a week?), but didn't waste the opportunities . . . In 26 such games last season, averaged 14.8 points, 7.7 assists and 2.16 steals and shot 51.3 percent . . . In the last two campaigns, Suns are 51-27 with him in the opening lineup . . . Not bad for a guy they originally got out of the CBA for a 10-day contract . . . Not bad for anybody, come to think of it . . . Runner-up to Dana Barros as Most Improved Player in 1994-95 . . . High school and college (Memphis) teammate of Penny Hardaway . . . Clippers took him 31st in 1991 . . . Born March 28, 1969, in Memphis, Tenn. . . . Gets an average of $2.025 million per year.

Year	Team	G	FG	FG Pct.	FT	FT Pct.	Reb.	Ast.	TP	Avg.
1991-92	LA-Char.	50	49	.380	27	.659	39	78	126	2.5
1993-94	Phoenix	27	42	.372	21	.750	39	125	105	3.9
1994-95	Phoenix	82	306	.520	158	.810	151	394	795	9.7
1995-96	Phoenix	81	261	.475	151	.778	136	353	697	8.6
	Totals	240	658	.477	357	.779	365	950	1723	7.2

THE ROOKIES

RAY ALLEN 21 6-5 205   Guard

So that's what they were up to . . . Bucks traded No. 4 pick Stephon Marbury to Minnesota to obtain UConn's Allen, picked fifth, and a future first-rounder . . . Bucks gambled on Shawn Respert last year, but believe Allen is a sure thing at shooting guard . . . First-team All-American averaged 23.4 points, 6.5 rebounds and 3.3 assists . . . Hit .466 from arc as a senior . . . Good jumper, quick shooter, excellent build for the pros . . . Born July 20, 1975, in Merced, Cal.

MOOCHIE NORRIS 23 6-1 175   Guard

Transfer from Auburn to West Florida was taken 33rd . . . Had monster year at NAIA school (23.6 points, 8.9 assists, 5.8 rebounds, 2.5 steals) . . . Proved he had big-time skills in the Portsmouth and Phoenix pre-draft camps . . . Has all the moves . . .

Streaky shooter . . . Has a take-charge personality that should fit in well with Bucks . . . Born July 7, 1973, in Washington, D.C.

JEFF NORDGAARD 23 6-7 226   **Forward-Guard**
Popular pick in Milwaukee, the Wisconsin-Green Bay iron man was taken 53rd . . . Did not miss a game in four college seasons, averaged 39.8 minutes as a senior . . . Fundamentally sound player, not a great athlete . . . Good shooter who needs to extend range . . . Went for 29 points against Kentucky . . . Born Feb. 23, 1973, in Dawson, Minn.

COACH CHRIS FORD: Interviewed for most every NBA opening, he wound up with this . . . Would another year off been a less desirable alternative? . . . Reunited with his former part-time point guard in Boston, Sherman Douglas . . . Won two Atlantic Division titles in five years with Celtics but failed to advance past the second round of the playoffs . . . Overall record of 222-188 . . . Was 67-97 his last two years with Celtics but few hold him even remotely responsible . . . Solid tactician, good defensive mind . . . Needs to find a way to motivate this remarkably uninspired bunch . . . A second-round pick (No. 17) of the Pistons out of Villanova in 1972, he went on to play 10 solid but unspectacular seasons with the Pistons and Celtics . . . Member of Boston's 1980-81 champs . . . On Oct. 17, 1989, he made the first three-point shot in NBA history. The day was more notable in that one of his teammates, making his NBA debut, was Larry Bird . . . Born Jan. 11, 1949, in Atlantic City, N.J.

BIGGEST BLUNDER

Any time a team trades away a franchise player without getting one in return, as the Bucks did when they granted Kareem Abdul-Jabbar's wish to return to to the West Coast by trading him to the Los Angeles Lakers in 1975 (for a cast of thousands headed by Brian Winters and Junior Bridgeman), it runs a great risk.

Though the Bucks took a while to recover from the trade that launched the Lakers into their golden era, that wasn't the franchise's worst judgment. In the 1977 draft, the Bucks had three of the top 11 picks, all acquired in trades. With the first pick overall, they selected center Kent Benson from Indiana University's national championship team, who averaged 9.1 points and 5.7 rebounds in a remarkably undistinguished career. They did well with the third pick, taking UCLA's Marques Johnson, who would be a productive scorer for years. But at No. 11, they missed again, taking Tennessee forward Ernie Grunfeld ahead of Cedric Maxwell, Tree Rollins, Brad Davis, Rickey Green and Norm Nixon.

Despite holding three high picks, the Bucks managed to get none of the top players in the draft. Walter Davis, Bernard King and Jack Sikma all went in the top 10.

ALL-TIME BUCK LEADERS

SEASON

Points: Kareem Abdul-Jabbar, 2,822, 1971–72
Assists: Oscar Robertson, 668, 1970–71
Rebounds: Kareem Abdul-Jabbar, 1,346, 1971–72

GAME

Points: Kareem Abdul-Jabbar, 55 vs. Boston, 12/10/71
Assists: Guy Rodgers, 22 vs. Detroit, 10/31/68
Rebounds: Swen Nater, 33 vs. Atlanta, 12/19/76

CAREER

Points: Kareem Abdul-Jabbar, 14,211, 1969–75
Assists: Paul Pressey, 3,272, 1982–90
Rebounds: Kareem Abdul-Jabbar, 7,161, 1969–75

TORONTO RAPTORS

TEAM DIRECTORY: Pres.: John Bitove; Exec. VP-Basketball: Isiah Thomas; Exec. Dir. Communications: John Lashway; Communications Mgr.: Rick Kaplan; Coach: Darrell Walker; Asst. Coaches: John Shumate, Jim Thomas, Bob Zuffelato. Arena: SkyDome (22,911). Colors: Red, purple, black and silver.

SCOUTING REPORT

SHOOTING: Typically, this is a huge problem for an expansion team but not so for the Raptors. Damon Stoudamire is a serious

Raptors prize Rookie of the Year Damon Stoudamire.

three-point threat and late-season pickup Doug Christie should only help. Stoudamire needs to work on his shot selection (.426 overall) but, in his defense, he was the best option most of the time.

They have promise inside, as well. Sharone Wright has a nice touch. And don't forget the surprising Zan Tabak. There isn't a lot of offensive depth, but there are some promising pieces in place. And they have great expectations for Massachusetts' Marcus Camby, No. 2 in the draft.

PLAYMAKING: A point guard in Isiah Thomas' image, Stoudamire dominates the ball and has the freedom to run the team, a rare role for a player so young. Not a pure point man in college, he remains somewhat fast and loose with his dribble (3.8 turnovers per game). But, like Thomas, he can be impossible to defend.

The problem was in finding a capable backup to take some pressure off Stoudamire. Until someone steps forward to share the burden, the Raptors will run the risk of burning out their most prized commodity.

A big man who knows what to do with the ball when doubleteamed is needed to replace the departed Oliver Miller.

REBOUNDING: Stealing Wright late in the season could go a long way toward settling the frontcourt. A wide-body with good hands, the former Philadelphia lottery pick can bang.

Camby provides some flexibility, not to mention talent. He is is expected to play both forward spots and should be very active on the boards. The acquisition of Popeye Jones (10.8 rebounds per game) from Dallas will be a big boost.

Christie and Carlos Rogers represent unfulfilled athletic potential but could thrive, while Stoudamire and Alvin Robertson regularly sneak in from the backcourt to give help on the boards.

DEFENSE: As it should be for an expansion team, it can only get better. If the roster ever stabilizes, coach Darrell Walker—known primarily for his defense in his playing days—should be able to develop the chemistry and unity necessary.

RAPTOR ROSTER

No.	Veterans	Pos.	Ht.	Wt.	Age	Yrs. Pro	College
13	Doug Christie	G-F	6-6	205	26	4	Pepperdine
—	Hubert Davis	G	6-5	183	26	4	North Carolina
55	Acie Earl	C	6-10	240	26	4	Iowa
—	Popeye Jones	F	6-8	250	26	3	Murray State
F-32	Martin Lewis	G	6-6	225	21	1	Seward County CC
F-7	Alvin Robertson	G	6-4	208	34	11	Arkansas
34	Carlos Rogers	F-C	6-11	220	25	2	Tennessee State
20	Damon Stoudamire	G	5-10	171	23	1	Arizona
3	Zan Tabak	C	7-0	245	26	2	Croatia
1	B.J. Tyler	G	6-1	185	25	2	Texas
F-10	Dwayne Whitfield	F	6-9	240	24	1	Jackson State
4	Sharone Wright	C-F	6-11	260	23	2	Clemson

F-Free agent

Rd.	Rookie	Sel.No.	Pos.	Ht.	Wt.	College
1	Marcus Camby	2	C-F	6-11	220	Massachusetts

Many of the elements are in place. They ranked third in the league in steals, led by Robertson, Stoudamire and Miller, and sixth in blocked shots. Camby gives them another set of long arms inside.

Nonetheless, they allowed 105 points and .475 shooting; even at the Canadian exchange rate, that's giving up far too much.

OUTLOOK: Walker has fire, energy and youth on his side but he's painfully inexperienced. He does have some talent to work with. The Raptors managed to beat the three top teams in the league (Chicago, Orlando and Seattle) and were consistently competitive. In all but 20 games, they were within six points during the fourth quarter and lost nine games by three points or less.

Thomas did a masterful job of assembling youth, starting with the drafting of Stoudamire and followed by the acquisitions of talents like Wright, Christie and Rogers in exchange for tired veterans.

Drafting Camby, the College Player of the Year, could turn out to be the master stroke.

RAPTOR PROFILES

DAMON STOUDAMIRE 23 5-10 171   Guard

Baby Zeke ... Fabulous numbers ... Led all rookies in assists, steals, free-throw percentage and minutes ... Led team in scoring, assists and minutes ... Then again, hit half his shots (or more) in just 18 of 70 games ... Is that any way to run a team? ... Broke down late in the year because he was forced to play too much, due to the lack of a competent backup ... Never met a shot, or play, he didn't think he could make ... Must learn to become more selective ... Raptors chief Isiah Thomas surprised many by naming him the seventh pick in 1996 draft ... Made $1.345 million ... Born Sept. 3, 1973, in Portland ... Father, Willie, played at Portland State, cousin Antoine at Oregon, uncle Anthony was drafted by the NFL's Detroit Lions.

Year	Team	G	FG	FG Pct.	FT	FT Pct.	Reb.	Ast.	TP	Avg.
1995-96	Toronto	70	481	.426	236	.797	281	653	1331	19.0

HUBERT DAVIS 26 6-5 183   Guard

Traded by Knicks to Raptors last summer for 1997 first-round draft pick ... Biggest improvement last year came on defensive end. Of course, considering he couldn't guard a locked door with a Uzi his first three seasons, anything was an improvement ... Actually became competent defensively ... Outstanding free-throw shooter ... Deadly perimeter type who has added some driving moves in past two seasons ... Was third in NBA in three-point shooting at .476. In past two seasons, has connected on 258 triples with .465 accuracy ... Had terrific first-round playoff shooting series: .714. Okay, he only took 14 shots ... But past penchant of struggling as playoffs grew deeper continued. Shot .412 in conference semis ... A super nice guy. His idea of a wild time is calling liquor store and asking if they have Old Granddad in a bottle. Real hell-raiser, you know? ... Devout, religious type ... His dad taught him to shoot. Must be a heckuva teacher because uncle is former NBA great Walter Davis ...

Came to Knicks from North Carolina as the No. 20 pick in 1992
... Carolina kid all the way: Born May 17, 1970, in Winston-
Salem ... Made $1.116 million.

Year	Team	G	FG	FG Pct.	FT	FT Pct.	Reb.	Ast.	TP	Avg.
1992-93	New York	50	110	.438	43	.796	56	83	269	5.4
1993-94	New York	56	238	.471	85	.825	67	165	614	11.0
1994-95	New York	82	296	.480	97	.808	110	150	820	10.0
1995-96	New York	74	275	.486	112	.868	123	103	789	10.7
	Totals	262	919	.474	337	.830	356	501	2492	9.5

SHARONE WRIGHT 23 6-11 260   Center-Forward

What was Philadelphia thinking? ... Sixers of-
fered this young, high-lottery pick (No. 6 in
1994) for disposable veterans Ed Pinckney and
Tony Massenburg ... Raptors said gimme ...
Averaged 16.5 points and 5.2 rebounds in 11
games with Toronto before back spasms ended
season early ... Scored at least 20 in five of
his last seven games ... Needs to rebound bet-
ter, but a good shot-blocker ... Might want to move his feet on
defense once in a while ... Ranks behind only Tree Rollins, Dale
Davis and Horace Grant on Clemson's rebound list ... Better
touch than all but Grant ... Loves hockey ... Made $2.5 million
... Born Jan. 30, 1973, in Macon, Ga.

Year	Team	G	FG	FG Pct.	FT	FT Pct.	Reb.	Ast.	TP	Avg.
1994-95	Philadelphia	79	361	.465	182	.645	472	48	904	11.4
1995-96	Phi.-Tor.	57	248	.484	167	.645	356	38	664	11.6
	Totals	136	609	.473	349	.645	828	86	1568	11.5

RON (POPEYE) JONES 26 6-8 250   Forward

Raptors acquired him and 1997 first-round
draft pick from Dallas for Jimmy King and
second-round picks in 1997 and '98 ... One of
the league's most underrated players rolled in
1995-96, finishing with the fourth-highest rebounding average in Maverick history ... The
10.8 would have been good for No. 7 in the
league but fell two games shy of the qualifying
minimum ... No. 4 in offensive rebounds per game ... One of

just 10 players to finish with a scoring-rebounding double-double . . . He and Loy Vaught of the Clippers were the only two of the 10 not to make the All-Star Game . . . Missed 14 consecutive games because of tendinitis in the right knee . . . Houston picked Murray State product 41st in 1992, but he didn't make NBA debut until Rockets traded him to Dallas in the summer of '93 for Eric Riley . . . Born June 17, 1970, in Martin, Tenn. . . . Made $1.425 million.

Year	Team	G	FG	FG Pct.	FT	FT Pct.	Reb.	Ast.	TP	Avg.
1993-94	Dallas	81	195	.479	78	.729	605	99	468	5.8
1994-95	Dallas	80	372	.443	80	.645	844	163	825	10.3
1995-96	Dallas	68	327	.446	102	.767	737	132	770	11.3
	Totals	229	894	.452	260	.714	2186	394	2063	9.0

ALVIN ROBERTSON 34 6-4 208   Guard

On court, no problem . . . Off court, in court too much . . . After two-year absence, he came back to show he could still play (9.3 points, 4.4 rebounds, 4.2 assists, 2.16 steals) . . . That's never been the question . . . One of many Raptors to turn in huge game against former team, went for 25 points, 10 rebounds, six assists and six steals against Bucks . . . Per-game average of 2.71 steals tops in NBA history . . . Third in total steals at 2,112 . . . Holds one-season steals record of 301 . . . Four-time All-Star . . . Became free agent after making $225,000 . . . Originally drafted sixth by San Antonio in 1984, he spent most of his years with Spurs and Bucks . . . Born July 22, 1962, in Barberton, Ohio.

Year	Team	G	FG	FG Pct.	FT	FT Pct.	Reb.	Ast.	TP	Avg.
1984-85	San Antonio	79	299	.498	124	.734	265	275	726	9.2
1985-86	San Antonio	82	562	.514	260	.795	516	448	1392	17.0
1986-87	San Antonio	81	589	.466	244	.753	424	421	1435	17.7
1987-88	San Antonio	82	655	.465	273	.748	498	557	1610	19.6
1988-89	San Antonio	65	465	.483	183	.723	384	393	1122	17.3
1989-90	Milwaukee	81	476	.503	197	.741	559	445	1153	14.2
1990-91	Milwaukee	81	438	.485	199	.757	459	444	1098	13.6
1991-92	Milwaukee	82	396	.430	151	.763	350	360	1010	12.3
1992-93	Mil.-Det.	69	247	.458	84	.656	269	107	618	9.0
1993-94	Det.-Den.					Injured				
1995-96	Toronto	77	285	.470	107	.677	342	323	718	9.3
	Totals	779	4412	.477	1822	.743	4066	3773	10882	14.0

DOUG CHRISTIE 26 6-6 205   Guard-Forward

Hello, career . . . Just when you thought it was over, he escaped from New York . . . Averaged 10.1 points, 3.8 rebounds, 2.9 assists, 1.89 steals in 32 games with Raptors, which kind of makes you wonder why he totaled a paltry 35 games in 1½ seasons in New York . . . It wasn't like the Knicks were overloaded with youthful athleticism . . . If he can remain healthy—the left ankle keeps cropping up in injury reports—he could make something of himself . . . Born May 9, 1970, in Seattle, he played high school ball in Seattle, keeps offseason home in Seattle but, when Sonics took him 17th out of Pepperdine in 1992, he held out and forced trade to Lakers . . . Averaged 14.5 points and 4.7 rebounds in 34 starts with Lakers in 1993-94, prompting his trade to Knicks for nothing (otherwise disguised as two future second-round picks) . . . Knicks sent him to Raptors for nothing (otherwise disguised as Willie Anderson and Victor Alexander) in February . . . Made $1.466 million.

Year	Team	G	FG	FG Pct.	FT	FT Pct.	Reb.	Ast.	TP	Avg.
1992-93	L.A. Lakers	23	45	.425	50	.758	51	53	142	6.2
1993-94	L.A. Lakers	65	244	.434	145	.697	235	136	672	10.3
1994-95	New York	12	5	.227	4	.800	13	8	15	1.3
1995-96	N.Y.-Tor..	55	150	.445	69	.742	154	117	415	7.5
	Totals	155	444	.432	268	.720	453	314	1244	8.0

ZAN TABAK 26 7-0 245   Center-Forward

Two of his three 20-plus games came against Houston and Chicago . . . Much better than anticipated, averaging 7.7 points, 4.8 rebounds and 19.9 minutes in 67 games . . . Surprisingly invaluable . . . Shot team-high .543 from field . . . Rockets took the Croatian 51st in 1991, didn't sign him for three years . . . Didn't play him, even then . . . Raptors snatched him in expansion draft . . . Went for 20 points and 15 rebounds against his former team in November . . . Spent nine years in European leagues, most with Yugoslavia in his hometown of Split . . . Made $650,000 . . . Born June 15, 1970, in Split, Croatia.

Year	Team	G	FG	FG Pct.	FT	FT Pct.	Reb.	Ast.	TP	Avg.
1994-95	Houston	37	24	.453	27	.614	57	4	75	2.0
1995-96	Toronto	67	225	.543	64	.561	320	62	514	7.7
	Totals	104	249	.533	91	.576	377	66	589	5.7

ACIE EARL 26 6-10 240   Center-Forward

Pervis Ellison did his hair . . . Dale Davis taught him how to shoot . . . Kevin Duckworth showed him how to run . . . Then, all of a sudden, he goes for 40 points and 12 rebounds against the Boston team that dumped him, and the Raptors say, eh? . . . An afterthought most of the season, he was thrown into the lineup late and did this: 21.0 points per game in April, including four straight of at least 25 . . . Celts took him 19th out of Iowa in 1993 . . . After Acie-deucey seasons, he was exposed to Raptors in expansion draft . . . Made $1.04 million . . . Born June 23, 1970, in Peoria, Ill.

Year	Team	G	FG	FG Pct.	FT	FT Pct.	Reb.	Ast.	TP	Avg.
1993-94	Boston	74	151	.406	108	.675	247	12	410	5.5
1994-95	Boston	30	26	.382	14	.483	45	2	66	2.2
1995-96	Toronto	42	117	.424	82	.719	129	27	316	7.5
	Totals	146	294	.411	204	.673	421	41	792	5.4

CARLOS ROGERS 25 6-11 220   Forward-Center

Drafted high, traded twice in two seasons . . . Which indicates talent isn't the problem . . . Can't he just get along? . . . Has a chance with youthful Raptors . . . One of many thrown into the fray late, he averaged 14.7 points, 5.7 rebounds and 2.1 blocks in 11 games before a neck sprain preempted his comeback . . . Leading scorer on 1993 U.S. World University Games team that included current teammates Damon Stoudamire and Sharone Wright . . . Seattle took him 11th out of Tennessee State in '94 . . . Came to Raptors from Golden State in huge, yet meaningless, package in September 1995 . . . Made $930,000 . . . Born Feb. 6, 1971, in Detroit.

Year	Team	G	FG	FG Pct.	FT	FT Pct.	Reb.	Ast.	TP	Avg.
1994-95	Golden State	49	180	.529	76	.521	278	37	438	8.9
1995-96	Toronto	56	178	.517	71	.546	170	35	430	7.7
	Totals	105	358	.523	147	.533	448	72	868	8.3

Massachusetts' Marcus Camby: No. 2 in the draft.

THE ROOKIE

MARCUS CAMBY 22 6-11 220   **Forward**

Isiah Thomas toyed with the idea of taking Cal's Shareef Abdur-Rahim with the second pick but stuck with the more proven Massachusetts big man ... Consensus Player of the Year led UMass to its first-ever berth in Final Four ... Averaged 20.5 points, 8.2 rebounds and 3.9 blocks ... Could play either forward position ... Needs to add 10-15 pounds ... Collapsed before a game midway through his senior season but no medical problem was found ... Admitted accepting gifts from a would-be agent while in school, bringing NCAA scrutiny to UMass ... Born March 22, 1974, in Hartford, Conn.

COACH DARRELL WALKER:  Brings one season as an assistant coach with a team that won 21 games to the table ... That, and he's Isiah Thomas' buddy ... Prior to serving on Brendan Malone's staff last year, he had never coached at any level ... What a way to break in ... Played with the Knicks, Nuggets, Bullets, Pistons and Bulls, establishing reputation as a defensive specialist who wasn't afraid of anyone ... Was Knicks' 12th pick, out of Arkansas, in 1983 ... Worked with NBA Players Association after retiring, counseling players in HIV prevention, drug and alcohol awareness, career development, degree completion and financial planning ... But can he coach? ... Stay tuned.

BIGGEST BLUNDER

In his first year running the expansion franchise, Isiah Thomas generally proved a shrewd evaluator of talent and skillful dredger of the scrap heap. But his one major failure snowballed into a problem that cost him his head coach and a sizable chunk of his reputation.

With the seventh pick in the 1995 draft, Thomas stole the show by selecting Arizona's Damon Stoudamire. That was the good news. The bad news was Thomas failed to acquire a suitable backup for the young point guard, who was forced to endure remarkably heavy minutes for a rookie. As a result, his production slipped late in the year.

Trying to cover his own mistakes, Thomas encouraged coach Brendan Malone to try unproven players, like rookie shooting guard Jimmy King, at the point. When Malone balked, it led to a rift between coach and general manager. After Thomas went public with his criticism of Malone, the point of no return had been breached and, ultimately, Malone was fired.

ALL-TIME RAPTOR LEADERS

SEASON

Points: Damon Stoudamire, 1,331, 1995–96
Assists: Damon Stoudamire, 653, 1995–96
Rebounds: Oliver Miller, 562, 1995–96

GAME

Points: Tracy Murray, 40 vs. Denver, 3/18/96
　　　　Acie Earl, 40 vs. Boston, 4/12/96
Assists: Damon Stoudamire, 19 vs. Houston, 2/27/96
Rebounds: Oliver Miller, 17 vs. Washington, 4/14/96

CAREER

Points: Damon Stoudamire, 1,331, 1995–96
Assists: Damon Stoudamire, 653, 1995–96
Rebounds: Oliver Miller, 562, 1995–96

DALLAS MAVERICKS

TEAM DIRECTORY: Owners: Ross Perot Jr., David McDavid, David Zaccanelli; VP-Player Personnel: Keith Grant; VP-Business Oper.: Jim Livingston; VP-Communications: Kevin Sullivan; Media Services Mgr.: Tony Fay; Coach: Jim Cleamons; Asst. Coach: Butch Beard. Arena: Reunion Arena (18,042). Colors: Blue and green.

SCOUTING REPORT

SHOOTING: The Mavericks took 529 more shots than anybody in the league last season and had 1,433 more attempts than Cleveland, the latter of which comes out to an amazing 17.5 additional scoring opportunities a game. We would congratulate them for such an accomplishment if it wasn't such a sham.

By the end of the year, opponents had come to realize the Mavericks *weren't* running an offense so much as just firing away, looking to a lot of people like they were just mailing it in. They finished with NBA records for three-pointers made (735) and attempted (2,039), but the 36-percent accuracy rate was below the league average. So they weren't good from long range so much as just exhaustive.

Then again, they usually struggle from everywhere. Jamal Mashburn was at 37.9 percent when his season was ended by injury after 18 games. Jim Jackson finished 43.5. Jason Kidd has gone 38.1 and 38.5 his first two years as a pro. George McCloud, the beneficiary of Mashburn's injury, filled the void by averaging 18.9 points in a huge surprise, but also by shooting 41.4. Some help should come with the arrival of first-round pick Samaki Walker, who while at Louisville showed a nice ability to score around the basket. He might not fit in with those high-percentage shots, though.

PLAYMAKING: Where Kidd makes up for his poor trigger finger. He finished second in the league in assists and began to take on more of a leadership role, even if it meant speaking out against Jackson.

The problem is the lack of depth. The Mavericks only had Scott Brooks and Lucious Harris, and both of them are gone.

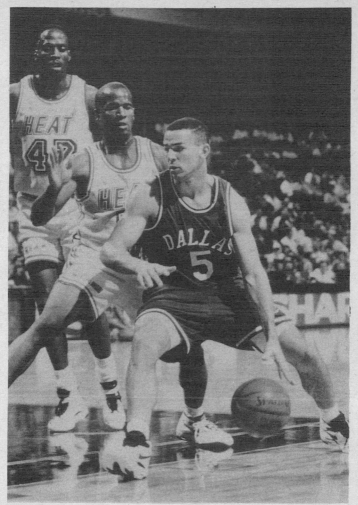

Jason Kidd leads the way without being a marksman.

REBOUNDING: Surprise. They started Lorenzo Williams at center and unheralded Popeye Jones at power forward, then finished sixth in the league by percentage. Walker will now get the

MAVERICK ROSTER

No.	Veterans	Pos.	Ht.	Wt.	Age	Yrs. Pro	College
43	Terry Davis	F-C	6-10	250	29	7	Virginia Union
7	Tony Dumas	G	6-6	190	24	2	Missouri-KC
25	Chris Gatling	F-C	6-10	230	29	5	Old Dominion
12	Derek Harper	G	6-4	206	35	13	Illinois
24	Jim Jackson	G	6-6	215	26	4	Ohio State
5	Jason Kidd	G	6-4	208	23	2	California
23	Jimmy King	G	6-5	210	23	1	Michigan
32	Jamal Mashburn	F	6-8	240	23	3	Kentucky
21	George McCloud	F-G	6-8	215	29	6	Florida State
40	Loren Meyer	C	6-10	260	23	1	Iowa State
00	Eric Montross	C	7-0	270	25	2	North Carolina

Rd.	Rookies	Sel.No.	Pos.	Ht.	Wt.	College
1	Samaki Walker	9	F	6-9	240	Louisville
2	Shawn Harvey	34	G	6-4	180	West Virginia State
2	Darnell Robinson	58	C	6-11	270	Arkansas

playing time of Jones, who was traded to Toronto. But the loss of Jones, a demon on the offensive boards, will be felt.

DEFENSE: Jim Cleamons, the new coach, can bring the approach that made the Bulls so successful. Now to just find a way to bring the Bulls' players. OK, we'll start slow: any players committed to defense.

Williams does his best to provide a shot-blocking presence at 6-9, finishing 11th, and Kidd is a good defender at the point, but that only gets the Mavericks so far. They not only landed at the bottom in points allowed (107.5) because of their run-and-gun offense, but were also 29th in shooting defense.

OUTLOOK: The Mavericks either have a ton of potential or a ton of problems. Either way, it comes from within—the three Js make this a team that could be feared or torn apart from within. Their decision. Unless management makes it for them and subtracts one of the letters. It's a crossroads for the team, that's all.

MAVERICK PROFILES

JASON KIDD 23 6-4 212   Guard

An All-Star and a star, period . . . Last season became the first Maverick ever to start in the midseason classic . . . Says Bob Cousy: "His instincts are unbelievable and he has a natural feel for the game that you can't teach. It's refreshing that a guy isn't seven feet tall, shoots less than 40 percent and hardly ever dunks and can still dominate a game." . . . When he got 21 points, 16 rebounds and 16 assists last season, it was the first time a player had a triple-double of at least 20-15-15 since Magic Johnson on April 18, 1989 . . . Only the sixth player in NBA history to record at least 700 assists and 500 rebounds . . . And he did it in what would have been his senior season at Cal . . . Grew up in Oakland with a friend named Gary Payton . . . Already tied for 10th all-time in triple-doubles . . . No. 2 pick in 1994 . . . Born March 23, 1973, in San Francisco . . . Made $3.588 million.

Year	Team	G	FG	FG Pct.	FT	FT Pct.	Reb.	Ast.	TP	Avg.
1994-95	Dallas	79	330	.385	192	.698	430	607	922	11.7
1995-96	Dallas	81	493	.381	229	.092	550	783	1348	16.6
	Totals	160	823	.383	421	.695	983	1390	2270	14.2

JIM JACKSON 26 6-6 215   Guard

Part of the problem or the solution? . . . Through all the offcourt friction, he was the only Maverick to play all 82 games last season . . . No. 1 on the team in scoring and tied for No. 22 in the league . . . Still needs to become a more consistent shooter, but dangerous enough that defenses have to stay close on the perimeter . . . Strong enough to cause most shooting guards problems inside . . . Had 11 consecutive starts at small forward in 1995-96 as Mavericks tried a small lineup after injury to Jamal Mashburn . . . Is No. 7 on the franchise's all-time scoring list since arriving as the fourth pick, out of Ohio State, in 1992 . . . Born Oct. 14, 1970, in Toledo, Ohio . . . Made $3.2 million.

Year	Team	G	FG	FG Pct.	FT	FT Pct.	Reb.	Ast.	TP	Avg.
1992-93	Dallas	28	184	.395	68	.739	122	131	457	16.3
1993-94	Dallas	82	637	.445	285	.821	388	374	1576	19.2
1994-95	Dallas	51	484	.472	306	.805	260	191	1309	25.7
1995-96	Dallas	82	569	.435	345	.825	410	235	1604	19.6
	Totals	243	1874	.443	1004	.812	1180	931	4946	20.4

JAMAL MASHBURN 23 6-8 240   Forward

Coming off serious knee injury, but expected to be ready for training camp . . . Lasted 18 games before being sidelined with a sore left knee . . . Final game was Dec. 9 . . . Officially done for the season after undergoing surgery Feb. 13 . . . No guarantee that the condition will not return . . . Career scoring average of 21.8 is second only to Mark Aguirre (24.6) in team history . . . Can shoot from the outside or put the ball on the floor with success . . . Or at least he could before the injury . . . Can handle the ball . . . Kentucky product was the fourth pick in the 1993 draft . . . Born Nov. 29, 1972, in New York . . . Made $3.233 million.

Year	Team	G	FG	FG Pct.	FT	FT Pct.	Reb.	Ast.	TP	Avg.
1993-94	Dallas	79	561	.406	306	.699	353	266	1513	19.2
1994-95	Dallas	80	683	.436	447	.739	331	298	1926	24.1
1995-96	Dallas	18	145	.379	97	.729	97	50	422	23.4
	Totals	177	1389	.417	850	.723	781	614	3861	21.8

ERIC MONTROSS 25 7-0 270   Center

Left the problems of Boston behind just in time to right smack into the problems of Dallas . . . Sent to Mavs a week before '96 draft. Got there just in time for all the Jim Jackson-Jason Kidd fun . . . Celtics gave up their '94 lottery pick, No. 9 overall, to Dallas for Mavs' 1997 first-rounder and a swap of the '96 firsts. Mavs went from six to nine in the draft . . . Celtics feared losing former North Carolina center to free agency after this season ... Gee, why wouldn't anyone want to stay a Celtic these days? ... After impressive rookie season, he regressed in the green and white ... Blame him, in part. His instincts offensively are not the best. But also blame the Celtic offense, which ran virtually nothing his way ... Was he supposed to pop that 7-foot frame out to the perimeter for opportunity jumpers? ... Did not score 20 points in a game all year ... Had a good percentage from the floor: .566. At the line, he made Shaq look like Bird: .376 ... Missed a fourth of the season with calf and ankle injuries ... Born Sept. 23, 1971, in Indianapolis, Ind. ... Grandson of Johnny Townsend, NBA star in the '30s and '40s ... Helped North Carolina to '93 NCAA title ... Made $1.04 million.

Year	Team	G	FG	FG Pct.	FT	FT Pct.	Reb.	Ast.	TP	Avg.
1994-95	Boston	78	307	.534	167	.635	566	36	781	10.0
1995-96	Boston	61	196	.566	50	.376	352	43	442	7.2
	Totals	139	503	.546	217	.548	918	79	1223	8.8

GEORGE McCLOUD 29 6-8 215   Forward

Look what showed up. A career ... Former first-round bust with the Pacers is coming off a breakthrough season ... Finished second to Gheorge Muresan in the balloting for Most Improved Player ... Participated in three-point contest at All-Star Weekend ... Not a bad passer for someone regarded strictly as a shooter ... Indiana tried using him at point guard after drafting him seventh in 1989 out of Florida State ... His time in Indy was a series of injuries, missed shots and abuse from fans ... Spent a season in Italy, then Rapid City ... Mavericks invited him in on a 10-day contract in 1994-95 and he didn't waste the chance ... Moved into the starting lineup last season when Jamal Mashburn went down, and he flourished ... Broke nearly every team record for three-point shooting ... In 63 starts, averaged 20.9 points ... Born May 27, 1967, in Daytona Beach, Fla. ... Made $950,000.

Year	Team	G	FG	FG Pct.	FT	FT Pct.	Reb.	Ast.	TP	Avg.
1989-90	Indiana	44	45	.313	15	.789	42	45	118	2.7
1990-91	Indiana	74	131	.373	38	.776	118	150	343	4.6
1991-92	Indiana	51	128	.409	60	.781	132	116	338	6.6
1992-93	Indiana	78	216	.411	75	.735	205	192	565	7.2
1994-95	Dallas	42	144	.439	80	.833	147	53	402	9.6
1995-96	Dallas	79	530	.414	180	.804	379	212	1497	18.9
	Totals	368	1194	.406	438	.791	1023	768	3263	8.9

DEREK HARPER 35 6-4 206 Guard

Seemed like every week, there was a story about Knicks being on verge of extending contract of 13th-season veteran. Yeah, and there were lots of stories about Elvis sightings, too ... So he wound up returning to his original team for a final fling ... Classy vet started all 82 games and played most minutes since 1989-90 ... But the extra duty took toll and he struggled in playoffs as offensive numbers dipped dramatically ... May not have the legs to be full-time starter, but has something left ... Defended Michael Jordan as well as could be expected in playoffs ... Class act all the way. Superb locker-room influence ... Remains quality defender, with great hands and anticipation ... Still tops the Dallas all-time list for assists and steals ... Spent 10½ seasons with Mavs and teamed with Rolando Blackman to give Dallas one of most lethal backcourts in game ... Knicks stole him on Jan. 6, 1994 for Tony Campbell and a first-rounder ... Went to Dallas as 11th pick in 1983 after his junior year at Illinois ... Born Oct. 13, 1961, in Elberton, Ga. ... Last season's salary: $2.837 million.

Year	Team	G	FG	FG Pct.	FT	FT Pct.	Reb.	Ast.	TP	Avg.
1983-84	Dallas	82	200	.443	66	.673	172	239	469	5.7
1984-85	Dallas	82	329	.520	111	.721	199	360	790	9.6
1985-86	Dallas	79	390	.534	171	.747	226	416	963	12.2
1986-87	Dallas	77	497	.501	160	.684	199	609	1230	16.0
1987-88	Dallas	82	536	.459	261	.759	246	634	1393	17.0
1988-89	Dallas	81	538	.477	229	.806	228	570	1404	17.3
1989-90	Dallas	82	567	.488	250	.794	244	609	1473	18.0
1990-91	Dallas	77	572	.467	286	.731	233	548	1519	19.7
1991-92	Dallas	65	448	.443	198	.759	170	373	1152	17.7
1992-93	Dallas	62	393	.419	239	.756	123	334	1126	18.2
1993-94	Dal.-N.Y.	82	303	.407	112	.687	141	334	791	9.6
1994-95	New York	80	337	.446	139	.724	194	458	919	11.5
1995-96	New York	82	436	.464	156	.757	202	352	1149	14.0
	Totals	1013	5546	.467	2378	.746	2577	5836	14378	14.2

CHRIS GATLING 29 6-10 230 Center-Forward

Most figured he was good. But this good? ... Finished second in NBA in shooting. That was a comedown. He led league in 1994-95 ... Flourished in Miami's low-post offense with his wide assortment of moves ... Also has ability to hit the short-to-midrange jumper ... Could use some bulk for under the boards but managed over seven rebounds per game for

Heat off bench . . . Numbers indicate he could be potential starter. But he has stated preference for coming off bench. What's this guy, unselfish? Trying to give others a bad name? . . . Went into offseason as free agent and signed with the Mavericks . . . Born Sept. 3, 1967, in Elizabeth, N.J., and thanks powers that be his folks didn't name him after birthplace . . . Serious teenage accident: fell off a van he was working on with father and suffered head injury that caused paralysis, slurred speech. Two years and two operations, which included a plate implant in his head, brought recovery . . . Transferred to Old Dominion after one year at Pitt. Golden State took him No. 16 in 1991. Traded with Tim Hardaway to Heat for Kevin Willis and Bimbo Coles Feb. 22, 1996 . . . Made $1.54 million.

Year	Team	G	FG	FG Pct.	FT	FT Pct.	Reb.	Ast.	TP	Avg.
1991-92	Golden State	54	117	.568	72	.661	182	16	306	5.7
1992-93	Golden State	70	249	.539	150	.725	320	40	648	9.3
1993-94	Golden State	82	271	.588	129	.620	397	41	671	8.2
1994-95	Golden State	58	324	.633	148	.592	443	51	796	13.7
1994-95	G.S.-Mia.	71	326	.575	139	.671	417	43	791	11.1
	Totals	335	1287	.583	638	.650	1759	191	3212	9.6

LOREN MEYER 23 6-10 260   Center

At least Mavs knew going in he wasn't going to be an instant star . . . Shot just 43.9 percent as a rookie, but has promising offensive skills, especially a soft touch as far as 15 feet out . . . Soft hands . . . Grew up in tiny Ruthven, Iowa (population: 700), a town with one grocery store and no stoplights . . . Entire community filed into the fire station to watch him become the 24th pick in the draft . . . Wears uniform No. 40 as a tribute to close friend Chris Street, the former player at Iowa who was killed in an auto accident . . . Starred at Iowa State . . . Born Dec. 30, 1972, in Emmetsburg, Iowa . . . Made $556,000.

Year	Team	G	FG	FG Pct.	FT	FT Pct.	Reb.	Ast.	TP	Avg.
1995-96	Dallas	72	145	.439	70	.686	319	57	363	5.0

TONY DUMAS 24 6-6 190   Guard

Scoring potential off the bench ... Satisfied with his minutes—19.2 last season ... The 11.6 points in that time was the highest-scoring average in the league for players who averaged less then 20 minutes ... Scored at least 12 points in a period 17 times, including nine fourth-quarter outbursts of 13 points or more ... His 39 points Jan. 12 at Phoenix, highlighted by 20 in the second period, was the most by any Maverick in 1995-96, a club record for scoring by a reserve and the best output off the bench in the league last season ... Very good first step ... No. 19 pick out of Missouri-Kansas City in 1994 ... Born Aug. 25, 1972, in Chicago ... Made $910,000.

Year	Team	G	FG	FG Pct.	FT	FT Pct.	Reb.	Ast.	TP	Avg.
1994-95	Dallas	58	96	.384	50	.649	62	57	264	4.6
1995-96	Dallas	67	274	.418	154	.599	115	99	776	11.6
	Totals	125	370	.409	204	.611	177	156	1040	8.3

JIMMY KING 23 6-5 210   Guard-Forward

Acquired by Dallas with two future first-round draft picks from Toronto for Popeye Jones and a 1997 first-rounder. Played the role of The Solid Guy at Michigan, which projects to The Future Assistant Coach in the pros ... Could be useful as a backup two or three if he develops some semblance of a jumper along the way ... Did finish well, averaging 9.0 points in the final nine games ... Fourth (and last) of the Fab Five to be drafted, following Chris Webber, Juwan Howard and Jalen Rose ... Taken 35th by Toronto in '95 ... Made $300,000 ... Born Aug. 9, 1973, in South Bend, Ind.

Year	Team	G	FG	FG Pct.	FT	FT Pct.	Reb.	Ast.	TP	Avg.
1995-96	Toronto	62	110	.431	54	.701	110	88	279	4.5

TERRY DAVIS 29 6-10 250   Forward-Center

A remember when . . . As in, remember when he played . . . Once the starting power forward who averaged 9.9 and 9.3 rebounds in back-to-back seasons . . . Now, after a serious elbow injury caused by an auto accident derailed his career, trying to get a regular role in the rotation behind Popeye Jones and the kids . . . Averaged 17.9 minutes last season, a decent amount, but missed the final 27 games after undergoing arthroscopic surgery to remove torn cartilage from his left knee . . . Only Maverick left from the 1991-92 team . . . Undrafted out of Virginia Union in 1989 . . . Dallas got him as a free agent in 1991 . . . Born June 17, 1967, in South Boston, Va. . . . Made $1.92 million.

Year	Team	G	FG	FG Pct.	FT	FT Pct.	Reb.	Ast.	TP	Avg.
1989-90	Miami	63	122	.466	54	.621	229	25	298	4.7
1990-91	Miami	55	115	.487	69	.556	266	39	300	5.5
1991-92	Dallas	68	256	.482	181	.635	672	57	693	10.2
1992-93	Dallas	75	393	.455	167	.594	701	68	955	12.7
1993-94	Dallas	15	24	.407	8	.667	74	6	56	3.7
1994-95	Dallas	46	49	.434	42	.636	156	10	140	3.0
1995-96	Dallas	28	55	.509	27	.574	117	21	137	4.9
	Totals	350	1014	.467	548	.608	2215	226	2579	7.4

THE ROOKIES

SAMAKI WALKER 20 6-9 240   Forward

The incumbent at power forward, Popeye Jones, had better come ready to defend his turf . . . Louisville product can score around the basket and averaged 2.42 blocked shots a game . . . In other words, he has potential to be a very good low-post player . . . Left school after sophomore season . . . Mavericks took him ninth . . . Born Feb. 25, 1976, in Columbus, Ohio.

SHAWN HARVEY 22 6-4 180   Guard

Wiry guard went 34th . . . Second-team NAIA All-American at West Virginia State . . . Helped his cause even more by making all-tournament at Portsmouth predraft camp . . . Big-time scorer in college, averaging 27.5, 25.3 and 23.1 points . . . Began at Essex County College in Newark, N.J. . . . Born Dec. 31, 1973, in Philadelphia.

DARNELL ROBINSON 22 6-11 270   **Center**

Last pick in the draft, No. 58 . . . Left Arkansas after junior season, having played just 20 games because of a broken foot . . . Also hampered by injuries as a freshman . . . Razorback teammate of Corliss Williamson of the Kings . . . Born May 30, 1974, in Oakland.

COACH JIM CLEAMONS: About time . . . Had been described as one of the league's most promising coaching prospects for the last several years . . . Had spent the last seven seasons as an assistant with the Bulls, winning four championship rings . . . Finally gets a chance on the hot seat with the Mavericks . . . Named coach in Dallas during the playoffs, then he finished out the postseason with Chicago . . . Only previous experiences as a head coach was at Youngstown State, before the Bulls hired him . . . Was an assistant at Furman and Ohio State, his alma mater . . . Averaged 18.5 points and 7.3 rebounds in four seasons as a Buckeye . . . Lakers picked him in the first round from there, 13th overall . . . Earned championship in Los Angeles as a rookie on the 1971-72 team that won 69 games, the most in league history before Bulls of last season . . . Best pro season was with Cleveland in 1975-76, when he averaged 12.2 points, 5.2 assists and 4.3 rebounds . . . Also second-team All-Defense that year . . . Teammate of Phil Jackson on the 1977-78 Knicks . . . Finished nine-year career with Bullets in 1980 . . . Born Sept. 13, 1949, in Lincolnton, N.C.

BIGGEST BLUNDER

En route to becoming one of the greatest players in team history, Derek Harper would become responsible for the biggest goof.

It was Game 4 of the 1984 Western Conference semifinals against the Lakers. The Mavericks, playing at home, were down 2-1 in the series, but now had the ball in a tied game with about 12 seconds left and a great opportunity for the last shot to even the series. That's when Harper did the strangest thing: thinking

Dallas was ahead by a point, he stood inside midcourt and just dribbled the clock out.

The Lakers won in overtime. Propelled by the unexpected gift, they wound up taking the series in five games.

ALL-TIME MAVERICK LEADERS

SEASON

Points: Mark Aguirre, 2,330, 1983–84
Assists: Jason Kidd, 783, 1995–96
Rebounds: James Donaldson, 973, 1986–87

GAME

Points: Jamal Mashburn, 50 vs. Chicago, 11/12/94
          Jim Jackson, 50 vs. Denver, 11/26/94
Assists: Jason Kidd, 25 vs. Utah, 2/8/96
Rebounds: Popeye Jones, 28 vs. Indiana, 1/9/96

CAREER

Points: Rolando Blackman, 16,643, 1981–92
Assists: Derek Harper, 4,790, 1983–84
Rebounds: James Donaldson, 4,589, 1985–92

DENVER NUGGETS

TEAM DIRECTORY: Owner: Comsat; Pres./Head Coach: Bernie Bickerstaff; Dir. Player Personnel: Mike Evans; Dir. Media Services: Tommy Sheppard; Asst. Coaches: Gene Littles, Tom Nissalke, Dick Motta, Jim Bovelli. Arena: McNichols Sports Arena (17,171). Colors: Gold, blue and red.

Antonio McDyess made the All-Rookie team.

SCOUTING REPORT

SHOOTING: Gone is Mahmoud-Abdul-Rauf, who finished second on the team in attempts last season, four behind Dale Ellis. Four behind, that is, despite playing about 600 fewer minutes. No one steps in to fill the void because a reserve, Sarunas Marciulionis, came in exchange for Abdul-Rauf, an assist-first point guard, Mark Jackson, takes over there and the first-round pick went to a center, Efthimios Retzias.

The Nuggets already took fewer shots than their opponents last season and may fall even farther behind in 1996-97. At least they still have a long-range weapon like Ellis, and there should be more chances for Antonio McDyess, who posted an encouraging 48.5 percent as a rookie. Now to do something about the shooting guard who can't shoot—Bryant Stith. Ricky Pierce and Marciulionis will be ready behind him to supply the offense.

PLAYMAKING: The Nuggets traded Reggie Williams and Jalen Rose to Indiana to get Jackson and Pierce. What could they have been thinking? A prototype point guard in Denver? Is that allowed? Jackson is no star, this being his fourth team in five seasons, but he's also no Robert Pack (now with the Nets), Abdul-Rauf or Rose.

Bernie Bickerstaff, who has been trying to bring some leadership skills into the backcourt for years, should be happy. He should also be concerned. As of late July, there was no other Nugget who had any pro experience at the point. Second-round pick Jeff McInnis, who at least has experience in big games since he played four years at North Carolina, may get a chance to play big minutes as a rookie.

REBOUNDING: No longer a rookie, McDyess will also no longer be brought along slowly. He must produce on the boards and on defense to compensate for Dikembe Mutombo's departure as a free agent. The 7.5 rebounds of 1995-96 won't come close to doing the job, though it sure helps to have a backup like LaPhonso Ellis and even someone who can make a contribution from the backcourt like Stith.

We don't know what to expect here from Mutombo's succes-

NUGGET ROSTER

No.	Veterans	Pos.	Ht.	Wt.	Age	Yrs. Pro	College
8	Rastko Cvetkovic	C	7-1	260	26	1	Yugoslavia
3	Dale Ellis	G-F	6-7	215	36	13	Tennessee
20	LaPhonso Ellis	F	6-8	240	26	4	Notre Dame
9	Greg Grant	G	5-7	140	30	6	Trenton State
21	Tom Hammonds	F	6-9	223	29	7	Georgia Tech
13	Mark Jackson	G	6-1	180	31	9	St. John's
—	Ervin Johnson	C	6-11	245	28	3	New Orleans
8	Sarunas Marciulionis	G	6-5	215	32	7	Lithuania
24	Antonio McDyess	F	6-9	220	22	1	Alabama
22	Ricky Pierce	G	6-4	215	37	14	Rice
23	Bryant Stith	G	6-5	208	25	4	Virginia

Rd.	Rookies	Sel.No.	Pos.	Ht.	Wt.	College
1	Efthimios Rentzias	23	C-F	6-11	243	PAOK (Greece)
2	Jeff McInnis	37	G	6-4	190	North Carolina

sor, Ervin Johnson, because Johnson has never really carried the load as a starter with starter's playing time; he averaged just 18.8 minutes at Seattle last season despite being a regular in the opening lineup, though the 5.3 rebounds in that time isn't bad. And the impact of Retzias is even more of an unknown, seeing as he's never even played in the NBA.

DEFENSE: See above. Johnson can be a shot-blocker, but he's no Mutombo. McDyess should be better. It's not just about interior defense, though. The Nuggets need to start forcing turnovers, or at least turning up the pressure on opposing guards. What a novel concept—Denver was last in the league last season in turnovers. Now there's no Mutombo back there as a safety net.

OUTLOOK: They have made an obvious move away from youth by trading away Abdul-Rauf, Rose and a lottery pick in one offseason to get Jackson, Marciulionis and Pierce. That's OK. The Nuggets will have another lottery pick this summer.

NUGGET PROFILES

ANTONIO McDYESS 22 6-9 220   Forward

Why the Clippers are the Clippers . . . They draft this guy with great potential second overall, then immediately trade him for a couple of good players (Brian Williams and Rodney Rogers) and a 15th pick (Brent Barry) . . . McDyess shows flashes of being the real deal . . . Explosive leaper . . . Doesn't just get up, but gets up super quick . . . That's how a guy becomes a factor as a shot-blocker one day at 6-9 . . . Named by league's coaches to the All-Rookie team . . . Played in the same frontcourt at Alabama as Chicago's Jason Caffey, also a '95 first-round pick . . . Born Sept. 7, 1974, in Quitman, Miss. . . . Made $2.213 million.

Year	Team	G	FG	FG Pct.	FT	FT Pct.	Reb.	Ast.	TP	Avg.
1995-96	Denver.........	76	427	.485	166	.683	572	75	1020	13.4

LaPHONSO ELLIS 26 6-8 240   Forward

On the road to recovery . . . After missing 107 of a possible 113 games because of degenerative knees, he returned last season to play 45 times and start the final 28 . . . Problem is, doctors aren't sure what caused the problems, so they can't say it won't happen again . . . Nice prospect before being hobbled . . . Had good post moves when he arrived from Notre Dame in 1992 as No. 5 pick . . . Seventh in the nation in rebounding as a senior . . . First-team All-Rookie from there and the first Nugget rookie to start all 82 . . . Born May 5, 1970, in East St. Louis, Ill. . . . Made $3.039 million.

Year	Team	G	FG	FG Pct.	FT	FT Pct.	Reb.	Ast.	TP	Avg.
1992-93	Denver..........	82	483	.504	237	.748	744	151	1205	14.7
1993-94	Denver..........	79	483	.502	242	.674	682	167	1215	15.4
1994-95	Denver..........	6	9	.360	6	1.000	17	4	24	4.0
1995-96	Denver..........	45	189	.438	89	.601	322	74	471	10.5
	Totals	212	1164	.489	574	.692	1765	396	2915	13.8

MARK JACKSON 31 6-1 180   **Guard**

Nuggets finally get a true point guard . . . No dragster who can keep up with the Rod Stricklands/Nick Van Exels/Stephon Marburys, but should at least bring veteran stability to a team that has sorely needed it . . . In the clubhouse and on the court . . . Came to Denver this summer along with Ricky Pierce from Indiana for Jalen Rose and Reggie Williams . . . Wears his wedding ring tied to a loop in his shoelaces during games . . . Rookie of the Year with the Knicks in 1987-88, after lasting all the way to No. 18 in the draft . . . Standout at St. John's before that . . . Born April 1, 1965, in Brooklyn, N.Y. . . . Made $2.6 million.

Year	Team	G	FG	FG Pct.	FT	FT Pct.	Reb.	Ast.	TP	Avg.
1987-88	New York	82	438	.432	206	.774	396	868	1114	13.6
1988-89	New York	72	479	.467	180	.698	341	619	1219	16.9
1989-90	New York	82	327	.437	120	.727	318	604	809	9.9
1990-91	New York	72	250	.492	117	.731	197	452	630	8.8
1991-92	New York	81	367	.491	171	.770	305	694	916	11.3
1992-93	L.A. Clippers	82	459	.486	241	.803	388	724	1181	14.4
1993-94	L.A. Clippers	79	331	.452	167	.791	348	678	865	10.9
1994-95	Indiana	82	239	.422	119	.778	306	616	624	7.6
1995-96	Indiana	81	296	.473	150	.785	307	635	806	10.0
	Totals	713	3186	.461	1471	.764	2906	5890	8164	11.5

BRYANT STITH 25 6-5 208   **Guard**

The only Nugget to play all 82 last season . . . Of course, that only gave him more chances to miss more shots than anybody . . . He usually didn't disappoint . . . A starting shooting guard going 41.6 percent is a joke . . . The 13.6 points a game was a career best, though . . . Good defender because of size, but not that good . . . No three-point range . . . Has missed just one game the last three seasons . . . Team captain . . . Nuggets got him with the No. 13 pick in 1992 after a career at Virginia . . . Senior season capped when he led Cavaliers to the NIT title with a win in the championship game over LaPhonso Ellis and

Notre Dame ... Born Dec. 10, 1970, in Emporia, Va.... Made $1.55 million.

Year	Team	G	FG	FG Pct.	FT	FT Pct.	Reb.	Ast.	TP	Avg.
1992-93	Denver	39	124	.446	99	.832	124	49	347	8.9
1993-94	Denver	82	365	.450	291	.829	349	199	1023	12.5
1994-95	Denver	81	312	.472	267	.824	268	153	911	11.2
1995-96	Denver	82	379	.416	320	.844	400	241	1119	13.6
	Totals	284	1180	.443	977	.833	1141	642	3400	12.0

ERVIN JOHNSON 28 6-11 245   Center

When things really got good last season, he got the Sonic bench ... Was replaced by Frank Brickowski after a lackluster start in the Finals against the Bulls, then was all but left out of the Sonics' comeback ... The closest thing Seattle had to a defensive presence inside went into the summer as a free agent and signed a seven-year pact with the Nuggets ... Always has been something of a project ... Didn't play high-school ball and worked at a supermarket for 2½ years before beginning college ... Developed at New Orleans and became Sun Belt Conference Player of the Year and third-team All-American by UPI as a senior ... Was older before making pro debut than teammate Shawn Kemp was after five years in the NBA ... Born Dec. 21, 1967, in New Orleans ... Made $767,000.

Year	Team	G	FG	FG Pct.	FT	FT Pct.	Reb.	Ast.	TP	Avg.
1993-94	Seattle	45	44	.415	29	.630	118	7	117	2.6
1994-95	Seattle	64	85	.443	29	.630	289	16	199	3.1
1995-96	Seattle	81	180	.511	85	.669	433	48	446	5.5
	Totals	190	309	.475	143	.653	840	71	762	4.0

RICKY PIERCE 37 6-4 215   Guard

Dale Ellis isn't the only hired gun in town ... Competition for post-practice shooting contests came in the offseason along with Mark Jackson when Jalen Rose and Reggie Williams were shipped to Indiana ... Originally No. 18 pick by Detroit in 1982 ... Came out of Rice ... Coach there was current Timberwolves' assistant Mike Schuler ... Hasn't stopped knocking down three-pointers since ... Probably won't stop now, either ...

All-Star in 1991 while playing for the Bucks ... Sixth Man of the Year in 1986-87 and 1989-90, both also with Milwaukee ... Born Aug. 14, 1959, in Dallas ... Made $1 million.

Year	Team	G	FG	FG Pct.	FT	FT Pct.	Reb.	Ast.	TP	Avg.
1982-83	Detroit	39	33	.375	18	.563	35	14	85	2.2
1983-84	San Diego	69	268	.470	149	.861	135	60	685	9.9
1984-85	Milwaukee	44	165	.537	102	.823	117	94	433	9.8
1985-86	Milwaukee	81	429	.538	266	.858	231	177	1127	13.9
1986-87	Milwaukee	79	575	.534	387	.880	266	144	1540	19.5
1987-88	Milwaukee	37	248	.510	107	.877	83	73	606	16.4
1988-89	Milwaukee	75	527	.518	255	.859	197	156	1317	17.6
1989-90	Milwaukee	59	503	.510	307	.839	167	133	1359	23.0
1990-91	Mil.-Sea.	78	561	.485	430	.913	191	168	1598	20.5
1991-92	Seattle	78	620	.475	417	.916	233	241	1690	21.7
1992-93	Seattle	77	524	.489	313	.889	192	220	1403	18.2
1993-94	Seattle	51	272	.471	189	.896	83	91	739	14.5
1994-95	Golden State	27	111	.437	93	.877	64	40	338	12.5
1995-96	Indiana	76	264	.447	174	.849	136	101	737	9.7
	Totals	870	5100	.496	3207	.875	2130	1712	13657	15.7

SARUNAS MARCIULIONIS 32 6-5 215 Guard

How do you say "journeyman" in Lithuanian? ... More importantly, does he stand for the national anthem? ... Wonder if the Nuggets double-checked that before finalizing the offseason deal that brought him from Sacramento to Denver for Mahmoud Abdul-Rauf ... Known for aggressive drives to the basket, but was also developing into a nice three-point shooter ... Doesn't take a ton of shots from back there, but was better than 40 percent each of the last two seasons ... Has played in the Olympics for the Soviet Union and, after the breakup, his native Lithuania ... Warriors brought him to the NBA, and the USA, as a free agent in 1989-90 ... Born June 13, 1964, in Launas, Lithuania ... Made $2.4 million.

Year	Team	G	FG	FG Pct.	FT	FT Pct.	Reb.	Ast.	TP	Avg.
1989-90	Golden State	75	289	.519	317	.787	221	121	905	12.1
1990-91	Golden State	50	183	.501	178	.724	118	85	545	10.9
1991-92	Golden State	72	491	.538	376	.788	208	243	1361	18.9
1992-93	Golden State	30	178	.543	162	.761	97	105	521	17.4
1993-94	Golden State					Injured				
1994-95	Seattle	66	216	.473	145	.732	68	110	612	9.3
1995-96	Sacramento	53	176	.452	155	.775	77	118	571	10.8
	Totals	346	1533	.510	1333	.767	789	782	4515	13.0

DALE ELLIS 36 6-7 215   Guard-Forward

No rust on those crosshairs . . . Finished last season as Nuggets' second-leading scorer . . . Started 52 times . . . The 150 three-pointers marked the second-highest single-season output of his illustrious career and the most by a Denver player since Michael Adams got 167 in 1990-91 . . . All-time leader in NBA with 1,269 makes . . . Pro career started in 1983, when the Mavericks used the No. 9 pick to get him out of Tennessee . . . Most Improved Player in 1986-87, an All-Star in 1989 . . . Played league-record 69 minutes Nov. 9, 1989, against Milwaukee . . . The Nuggets got him with a free-agent contract on Oct. 4, 1994 . . . Born Aug. 6, 1960, in Marietta, Ga. . . . Made $1.31 million.

Year	Team	G	FG	FG Pct.	FT	FT Pct.	Reb.	Ast.	TP	Avg.
1983-84	Dallas	67	225	.456	87	.719	250	56	549	8.2
1984-85	Dallas	72	274	.454	77	.740	238	56	667	9.3
1985-86	Dallas	72	193	.411	59	.720	168	37	508	7.1
1986-87	Seattle	82	785	.516	385	.787	447	238	2041	24.9
1987-88	Seattle	75	764	.503	303	.767	340	197	1938	25.8
1988-89	Seattle	82	857	.501	377	.816	342	164	2253	27.5
1989-90	Seattle	55	502	.497	193	.818	238	110	1293	23.5
1990-91	Sea.-Mil.	51	340	.474	120	.723	173	95	857	16.8
1991-92	Milwaukee	81	485	.469	164	.774	253	104	1272	15.7
1992-93	San Antonio	82	545	.499	157	.797	312	107	1366	16.7
1993-94	San Antonio	77	478	.494	83	.776	255	80	1170	15.2
1994-95	Denver	81	351	.453	110	.866	222	57	918	11.3
1995-96	Denver	81	459	.479	136	.760	315	139	1204	14.9
	Totals	958	6258	.486	2251	.782	3553	1440	16036	16.7

TOM HAMMONDS 29 6-9 223   Forward

Got the most minutes of his three-plus season run as a Nugget during 1995-96 . . . That's not saying much, though . . . Averaged 14.7 minutes . . . But they keep finding a place for him, with at least 70 appearances each campaign since he was signed as a free agent Feb. 4, 1993 . . . Eight of his 10 best scoring nights came after the All-Star break . . . Disappointment as the ninth pick overall by the Bullets in 1989 out of Georgia Tech . . . Yellowjackets retired his jersey No. 20 . . . Finalist for the Wooden Award as a senior ... Born March 27, 1967, in Crestview, Fla. ... Made $970,000.

Year	Team	G	FG	FG Pct.	FT	FT Pct.	Reb.	Ast.	TP	Avg.
1989-90	Washington......	61	129	.437	63	.643	168	51	321	5.3
1990-91	Washington......	70	155	.461	57	.722	206	43	367	5.2
1991-92	Washington......	37	195	.488	50	.610	185	36	440	11.9
1992-93	Char.-Den.	54	105	.475	38	.613	127	24	248	4.6
1993-94	Denver.........	74	115	.500	71	.683	199	34	301	4.1
1994-95	Denver.........	70	139	.535	132	.746	222	36	410	5.9
1995-96	Denver.........	71	127	.474	88	.765	223	23	342	4.8
	Totals	437	965	.480	499	.696	1330	247	2429	5.6

RASTKO CVETKOVIC 26 7-1 260 Center

Pronounced ROSS-co SVET-ko-vich ... On second thought, don't bother ... Just 48 minutes last season, his first in the NBA, after Nuggets signed him to a free-agent deal Sept. 29, 1996 ... Very raw ... Roomed with Vlade Divac years ago in the former Yugoslavia ... Played professionally for Red Star there before coming to the U.S. ... Was to have been a member of Yugoslavia's 1992 Olympic team, but they were banned by United Nations sanction ... Selected to play in the Atlanta Games ... Father, Vladimir, represented the country in the 1964 and '68 Olympics in basketball ... Older sister, Zorana, played at Rhode Island ... Born June 22, 1970, in Belgrade, Yugoslavia ... Made $200,000.

Year	Team	G	FG	FG Pct.	FT	FT Pct.	Reb.	Ast.	TP	Avg.
1995-96	Denver.........	14	5	.313	0	.000	11	3	10	0.7

THE ROOKIES

EFTHIMIS RETZIAS 20 6-11 243 Center-Forward

More size for the Nuggets to replace Dikembe Mutombo ... No. 23 pick has been a member of the Greek national team since age 16 ... Helped them to a fourth-place finish at the 1994 World Championships in Toronto ... Spent last two seasons with PAOK, a major team there ... Was teammate of Sacramento pick Predrag Stojakovic ... Born Jan. 11, 1976, in Trikala, Greece.

Mark Jackson hopes to get sky-high in Denver.

JEFF McINNIS 22 6-4 190   **Guard**
Could challenge for time as backup point guard . . . Nuggets got
him at No. 37 . . . Left North Carolina after his junior season No.
9 all-time in assists . . . One of six Tar Heels to record at least
1,000 points and 400 assists . . . Second-team All-ACC in 1995-
96 . . . Born Oct. 22, 1974, in Charlotte, N.C.

No Nugget ever scored as many points as Alex English.

COACH BERNIE BICKERSTAFF: May have bit off more than he can chew this time . . . Dual role as coach and president has proven especially difficult while trying to find a new course for the Nuggets . . . Before, they were loaded with youngsters. Now, he re-tools by getting Mark Jackson, Ricky Pierce and Sarunas Marciulionis . . . Returned to the sidelines Feb. 20, 1995, and directed a dramatic turnaround that got the once-flailing Nuggets into the playoffs for the second straight year . . . They were 21-29 and eight games out of the final postseason spot when he replaced interim coach Gene Littles, who had moved into the job when Dan Issel quit . . . Under Bickerstaff, Denver went 20-12, the seventh-best mark in the league for those final 32 games . . . Followed that up in 1995-96 with a disappointing 35-47 . . . Career: 257-267 . . . Previously head coach for five years with Sonics, from 1985-90 . . . NBA Coach of the Year in 1986-87 . . . Also No. 1 assistant with Washington from 1974-85, during which time the Bullets were in the Finals three times and won the championship in 1978 . . . Quit there largely because of the stress that caused health concerns . . . Came to Denver to run the show from the front office, not the sidelines . . . Starred at the University of San Diego . . . Member of the USA Basketball committee that selected the coaching staff and players for the 1996 Olympics . . . Has a street dedicated in his honor—Bernard Bickerstaff Boulevard—in hometown of Benham, Ky. . . . Born Feb. 11, 1944, in Benham.

BIGGEST BLUNDER

Let's just say Flag Day will be a bit touchy around the Nuggets.

Mahmoud Abdul-Rauf would not be considered at fault for following his heart and his religious beliefs, especially since he meant no disrespect. The organization was not wrong for trying to resolve the matter in a private way, even if that part went on way too long. And the NBA did not err in taking a stand in favor of patriotism, even if no one is quite sure when they got into the morality business.

It's just that when the controversy over Abdul-Rauf refusing to stand for the national anthem, or choosing to stay back in the hallway or locker room during its playing, turned into a mess that dug at the Nuggets' 1995-96 season and will probably follow him through the rest of his career, which begins anew in Sacramento this season.

ALL-TIME NUGGET LEADERS

SEASON

Points: Spencer Haywood, 2,519, 1969–70 (ABA)
       Alex English, 2,414, 1985–86
Assists: Michael Adams, 693, 1990–91
Rebounds: Spencer Haywood, 1,637, 1969–70 (ABA)
        Dikembe Mutombo, 1,070, 1992–93

GAME

Points: David Thompson, 73 vs. Detroit, 4/9/78
Assists: Larry Brown, 23 vs. Pittsburgh, 2/20/72 (ABA)
      Lafayette Lever, 23 vs. Golden State, 4/21/89
Rebounds: Spencer Haywood, 31 vs. Kentucky, 11/13/69 (ABA)
        Jerome Lane, 25 vs. Houston, 4/21/91

CAREER

Points: Alex English, 21,645, 1979–90
Assists: Alex English, 3,679, 1979–90
Rebounds: Dan Issel, 6,630, 1975–85

HOUSTON ROCKETS

TEAM DIRECTORY: Owner: Les Alexander; VP-Basketball Oper.: Bob Weinhauer; VP-Bus. Oper.: John Thomas; Dir. Pub. Rel.: Kathy Frietsch; Coach: Rudy Tomjanovich; Asst. Coaches: Bill Berry, Jim Boylen; Larry Smith. Arena: The Summit (16,279). Colors: Blue, silver and red.

Hakeem Olajuwon passed 20,000-point mark in 12th year.

SCOUTING REPORT

SHOOTING: They didn't shoot the ball particularly well last season—Hakeem Olajuwon was at 51.4 percent, but Clyde Drexler went 43.3, Robert Horry 41.0, Sam Cassell 43.9. But the Rockets still averaged 102.5 points a game, tied for 11th-best in the league, helped largely by making the second-most three-pointers.

That has long been a weapon. Just not as long as Olajuwon, who turns 34 in January but shows no sign of slowing down. His signature spin moves inside are still impossible to defend, his fallaways from the high post still graceful and deadly, his medium-range jumpers a very reliable option. Oh, and he runs the court like a 24-year-old, combining with Drexler and newcomer Charles Barkley to give the Rockets a very good transition game even with their bigger players.

PLAYMAKING: A seven-year contract for Brent Price? The Rockets obviously saw something they liked while he was averaging 5.1 assists and 10 points last season with the Bullets. Or they just really, really, really needed to be able to replace Kenny Smith.

Smith was renounced as a free agent, which everyone figured would happen. After Cassell was traded to the Suns, that left Price as the lone point guard with any NBA experience.

The Rockets picked up Randy Livingston through the draft. Healthy, he had the skills to be a first-rounder. But with bad knees that seriously hampered his career at Louisiana State, Livingston fell to No. 42 and this fall fights to make the NBA.

REBOUNDING: Bad. Still. Even with Olajuwon getting 10.9 boards a game and Drexler adding 7.2 from the backcourt, the Rockets finished 28th on the offensive boards by percentage and 27th overall, better than only a pair of last-place teams, Vancouver and Philadelphia.

ROCKET ROSTER

No.	Veterans	Pos.	Ht.	Wt.	Age	Yrs. Pro	College
—	Charles Barkley	F	6-5	252	33	12	Auburn
—	Emanual Davis	G	6-5	195	28	0	Delaware State
22	Clyde Drexler	G	6-7	222	34	13	Houston
17	Mario Elie	F-G	6-5	210	32	6	American Int'l
F-27	Charles Jones	C	6-9	215	39	13	Albany State
F-4	Sam Mack	F	6-7	220	26	2	Houston
F-20	Tracy Moore	G	6-4	200	30	4	Tulsa
34	Hakeem Olajuwon	C	7-0	255	33	12	Houston
—	Brent Price	G	6-1	185	27	4	Oklahoma
—	Kevin Willis	F-C	7-0	245	34	12	Michigan State

F-Free agent

Rd.	Rookies	Sel.No.	Pos.	Ht.	Wt.	College
2	Othella Harrington	30	F-C	6-9	235	Georgetown
2	Randy Livingston	42	G	6-4	209	LSU
2	Terrell Bell	50	C	6-10	240	Georgia

But it's a minor problem at best. Remember that they were also near the bottom of the league while winning back-to-back championships. The addition of Barkley, No. 6 in the league in his final campaign in Phoenix, will obviously help, as will the arrival of Kevin Willis from Golden State. Also, the Rockets' top pick in the draft went to 6-9 Othello Harrington of Georgetown.

DEFENSE: Having Olajuwon in the paint, waiting for guards to try and penetrate, means they are feared. In truth, though, the Rockets were just average in shooting percentage-against last season and do a poor job forcing turnovers. They're a group that has been known to play good team defense, so the potential is there.

OUTLOOK: Any team that has Olajuwon, Drexler and Barkley will be feared, and no club pulls it together and becomes more focused in the playoffs than Rudy Tomjanovich's Rockets. They may be old, but they may also win the West.

ROCKET PROFILES

HAKEEM OLAJUWON 33 7-0 255   Center

Really slowing down at age 33, isn't he? . . . All he did last season was go for 26.9 points, 10.9 rebounds and 2.90 blocks while shooting 51.4 percent . . . Had three triple-doubles . . . Made his 11th straight All-Star appearance . . . Became NBA's all-time leader in blocked shots at 3,190 when he swatted away an attempt by A.C. Green on April 21 at Phoenix . . . One of only nine players ever to collect 20,000 points and 11,000 rebounds . . . Spent summer vacation as a member of Dream Team III, an especially big deal because he renounced Nigerian citizenship to become a U.S. citizen April 2, 1993 . . . MVP and Defensive Player of the Year in 1993-94 . . . Born Jan. 21, 1963, in Lagos, Nigeria . . . From the University of Houston to the Houston Rockets as the No. 1 pick overall in 1984 . . . Made $5.305 million last year and re-signed for five years at $11 million a year . . . Following Islamic custom of pre-arranged marriages, he married 18-year-old Dalia Asafi in August.

Year	Team	G	FG	FG Pct.	FT	FT Pct.	Reb.	Ast.	TP	Avg.
1984-85	Houston	82	677	.538	338	.613	974	111	1692	20.6
1985-86	Houston	68	625	.526	347	.645	781	137	1597	23.5
1986-87	Houston	75	677	.508	400	.702	858	220	1755	23.4
1987-88	Houston	79	712	.514	381	.695	959	163	1805	22.8
1988-89	Houston	82	790	.508	454	.696	1105	149	2034	24.8
1989-90	Houston	82	806	.501	382	.713	1149	234	1995	24.3
1990-91	Houston	56	487	.508	213	.769	770	131	1187	21.2
1991-92	Houston	70	591	.502	328	.766	845	157	1510	21.6
1992-93	Houston	82	848	.529	444	.779	1068	291	2140	26.1
1993-94	Houston	80	894	.528	388	.716	955	287	2184	27.3
1994-95	Houston	72	798	.517	406	.756	775	255	2005	27.8
1995-96	Houston	72	768	.514	397	.724	784	257	1936	26.9
	Totals	900	8673	.516	4478	.711	11023	2392	21840	24.3

CLYDE DREXLER 34 6-7 222   Guard

Clyde the Limp . . . Managed just 52 games last season due to a torn muscle in his right knee and a deep bruise on his right shin . . . Then again, hid it well if he was struggling the rest of the time: 19.3 points, 7.2 rebounds, 5.8 assists . . . An All-Star for ninth time . . . Fifth among active players and 23rd all-time with 19,794 career points . . . Has reached playoffs

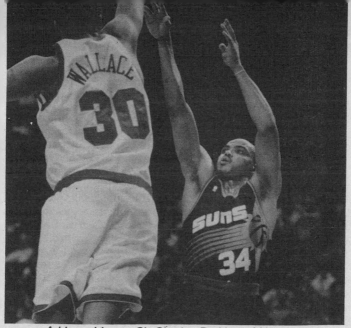

Address him as Sir Charles Barkley of Houston.

every year since he came into league as 14th pick in 1983 by Trail Blazers . . . Spent entire career there before being traded to his hometown in the Feb. 14, 1995, deal that also included Otis Thorpe and Tracy Murray . . . Also teamed with Hakeem Olajuwon at University of Houston . . . Born June 22, 1962, in Houston . . . Made $9.81 million last season as a balloon payment, tops on the team.

Year	Team	G	FG	FG Pct.	FT	FT Pct.	Reb.	Ast.	TP	Avg.
1983-84	Portland	82	252	.451	123	.728	235	153	628	7.7
1984-85	Portland	80	573	.494	223	.759	476	441	1377	17.2
1985-86	Portland	75	542	.475	293	.769	421	600	1389	18.5
1986-87	Portland	82	707	.502	357	.760	518	566	1782	21.7
1987-88	Portland	81	849	.506	476	.811	533	467	2185	27.0
1988-89	Portland	78	829	.496	438	.799	615	450	2123	27.2
1989-90	Portland	73	670	.494	333	.774	507	432	1703	23.3
1990-91	Portland	82	645	.482	416	.794	546	493	1767	21.5
1991-92	Portland	76	694	.470	401	.794	500	512	1903	25.0
1992-93	Portland	49	350	.429	245	.839	309	278	976	19.9
1993-94	Portland	68	473	.428	286	.777	445	333	1303	19.2
1994-95	Port.-Hou.	76	571	.461	364	.824	480	362	1653	21.8
1995-96	Houston	52	331	.433	265	.784	373	302	1005	19.3
	Totals	954	7486	.476	4220	.789	5958	5389	19794	20.7

BRENT PRICE 27 6-1 185   Guard

Okay, he does belong in the league ... But until his vast improvement last season, that was a question about Mark's kid brother ... Bullets received winning play from him. Only they didn't win ... Nuggets signed him as free agent ... Good three-point shooter, decent playmaker ... Can run a team, if not a fast break, on the floor ... Always bothered by pressure ... Had been waived after 1994-95 season. Mark signed on and Bullets re-signed little brother a week later for $250,000. Good thing they did ... In one season, he surpassed his totals for points, assists, rebounds, free throws and three-pointers from his first two combined seasons ... Established NBA record with 13 consecutive three-point shots made ... Originally drafted by Bullets on second round, No. 32, in 1992 after he was All-Big Eight at Oklahoma ... Missed all of 1994-95 season when he tore anterior cruciate in left knee during a summer-league game ... That made last season even more remarkable ... Born Dec. 9, 1968, in Enid, Okla.

Year	Team	G	FG	FG Pct.	FT	FT Pct.	Reb.	Ast.	TP	Avg.
1992-93	Washington	68	100	.358	54	.794	103	154	262	3.9
1993-94	Washington	65	141	.433	68	.782	90	213	400	6.2
1994-95	Washington					Injured				
1995-96	Washington	81	252	.472	167	.874	228	416	810	10.0
	Totals	214	493	.433	289	.835	421	783	1472	6.9

MARIO ELIE 32 6-5 210   Guard-Forward

Last season he was derailed by fractured right arm ... Cost him 35 games and a chance to start regularly since every other Rocket was hurt at the time ... Got 16 trips to opening lineup in 45 appearances ... Playoff participant all six years in the league—three times with Rockets, twice with Warriors and once with Trail Blazers ... Not bad considering he was drafted in the seventh round by Milwaukee in 1985, cut, signed by the Lakers and cut again before his rookie season even started ... Houston stole him from Portland in August 1993 for a second-round pick and he became a key contributor to both NBA titles ... Born Nov. 26, 1963, in New York and attended

American International . . . Making an average of $1.45 million annually . . . Re-signed two-year contract last summer.

Year	Team	G	FG	FG Pct.	FT	FT Pct.	Reb.	Ast.	TP	Avg.
1990-91	Phil.-G.S.	33	79	.497	75	.843	110	45	237	7.2
1991-92	Golden State	79	221	.521	155	.852	227	174	620	7.8
1992-93	Portland	82	240	.458	183	.855	216	177	708	8.6
1993-94	Houston	67	208	.446	154	.860	181	208	626	9.3
1994-95	Houston	81	243	.499	144	.842	196	189	710	8.8
1995-96	Houston	45	180	.504	98	.852	155	138	499	11.1
	Totals	387	1171	.484	809	.852	1085	931	3400	8.8

CHARLES BARKLEY 33 6-5 252   Forward

Wanted Houston and got it via blockbuster trade in August that brought Robert Horry, Sam Cassell, Mark Bryant and Chucky Brown to Phoenix . . . Still running neck and neck: his game, his mouth . . . Years after saying he would be in retirement, all he did was finish eighth in the league in scoring and fifth in rebounding . . . Became the 10th player ever to record 20,000 points and 10,000 rebounds . . . Only two other players active last year were on that plateau: Hakeem Olajuwon and Robert Parish . . . He trashed the organization in offseason . . . . . . Dream Team I & III . . . In the top 10 in scoring for nine consecutive years . . . MVP in 1992-93 . . . Suns gave up Jeff Hornacek, Andrew Lang and Tim Perry to get him from the 76ers in the summer of '92 . . . Born Feb. 20, 1963, in Leeds, Ala. . . . Fifth pick in '84 draft, out of Auburn . . . Made $4.76 million.

Year	Team	G	FG	FG Pct.	FT	FT Pct.	Reb.	Ast.	TP	Avg.
1984-85	Philadelphia.	82	427	.545	293	.733	703	155	1148	14.0
1985-86	Philadelphia.	80	595	.572	396	.685	1026	312	1603	20.0
1986-87	Philadelphia.	68	557	.594	429	.761	994	331	1564	23.0
1987-88	Philadelphia.	80	753	.587	714	.751	951	254	2264	28.3
1988-89	Philadelphia.	79	700	.579	602	.753	986	325	2037	25.8
1989-90	Philadelphia.	79	706	.600	557	.749	909	307	1989	25.2
1990-91	Philadelphia.	67	665	.570	475	.722	680	284	1849	27.6
1991-92	Philadelphia.	75	622	.552	454	.695	830	308	1730	23.1
1992-93	Phoenix	76	716	.520	445	.765	928	385	1944	25.6
1993-94	Phoenix	65	518	.495	318	.704	727	296	1402	21.6
1994-95	Phoenix	68	554	.486	379	.748	756	276	1561	23.0
1995-96	Phoenix	71	580	.500	440	.777	821	262	1649	23.2
	Totals	890	7393	.550	5502	.738	10311	3495	20740	23.3

KEVIN WILLIS 34 7-0 245   Forward-Center

Signed with the Rockets as a Golden State free agent last summer ... Provided Warriors with additional size and inside scoring ... They got him from the Heat just before the trade deadline last season along with Bimbo Coles for Tim Hardaway and Chris Gatling ... Averaged 11.3 points and 7.8 rebounds after the deal, decent numbers for someone averaging 28.5 minutes ... Just not such good numbers for someone making $3.65 million ... Originally No. 11 pick from Michigan State by Atlanta in 1984 ... Has climbed to eighth among active players with 8,590 rebounds ... One of 17 players in league history to get at least 12,000 points, 8,000 rebounds and 500 blocked shots ... Born Sept. 6, 1962, in Los Angeles.

Year	Team	G	FG	FG Pct.	FT	FT Pct.	Reb.	Ast.	TP	Avg.
1984-85	Atlanta	82	322	.467	119	.657	522	36	765	9.3
1985-86	Atlanta	82	419	.517	172	.654	704	45	1010	12.3
1986-87	Atlanta	81	538	.536	227	.709	849	62	1304	16.1
1987-88	Atlanta	75	356	.518	159	.649	547	28	871	11.6
1988-89	Atlanta					Injured				
1989-90	Atlanta	81	418	.519	168	.683	645	57	1006	12.4
1990-91	Atlanta	80	444	.504	159	.668	704	99	1051	13.1
1991-92	Atlanta	81	591	.483	292	.804	1258	173	1480	18.3
1992-93	Atlanta	80	616	.506	196	.653	1028	165	1435	17.9
1993-94	Atlanta	80	627	.499	268	.713	963	150	1531	19.1
1994-95	Atl.-Mia.	67	473	.466	205	.690	732	86	1154	17.2
1995-96	Mia.-G.S.	75	325	.456	143	.708	638	53	794	10.6
	Totals	864	5129	.498	2108	.695	8590	954	12401	14.4

CHARLES JONES 39 6-9 215   Center

So why do you say there's a shortage of big men in the NBA? ... Keeps making the roster ... Rudy Tomjanovich was starting in the All-Star Game a few months before Jones was drafted by the Suns out of Albany State ... That was 1979, as an eighth-round pick ... Has had stints with three teams in the CBA, one in Italy and five in the NBA ... Best known for being with the Bullets for parts of nine seasons ... Came to Rockets on a 10-day contract March 2, 1995, and stuck through the championship drive and then the offseason to get re-upped ... Brothers Caldwell and Major also played for the Rockets and another, Wil, was also in the NBA . . . Born April 3, 1957, in McGehee, Ark. . . . Made $350,000.

Year	Team	G	FG	FG Pct.	FT	FT Pct.	Reb.	Ast.	TP	Avg.
1983-84	Philadelphia......	1	0	.000	1	.250	0	0	1	1.0
1984-85	Chi.-Wash.......	31	67	.528	40	.690	184	26	174	5.6
1985-86	Washington......	81	129	.508	54	.628	321	76	312	3.9
1986-87	Washington......	79	118	.474	48	.632	356	80	284	3.6
1987-88	Washington......	69	72	.407	53	.707	325	59	197	2.9
1988-89	Washington......	53	60	.480	16	.640	257	42	136	2.6
1989-90	Washington......	81	94	.508	68	.648	504	139	256	3.2
1990-91	Washington......	62	67	.540	29	.580	359	48	163	2.6
1991-92	Washington......	75	33	.367	20	.500	317	62	86	1.1
1992-93	Washington......	67	33	.524	22	.579	277	42	88	1.3
1993-94	Detroit.........	42	36	.462	19	.559	235	29	91	2.2
1994-95	Houston........	3	1	.333	1	.500	7	0	3	1.0
1995-96	Houston........	46	6	.316	4	.308	74	12	16	0.3
	Totals.........	690	716	.479	375	.619	3216	615	1807	2.6

SAM MACK 26 6-7 220   Guard

Nice size for a guard . . . Fourth in the CBA in scoring while with Rockford when the Rockets called in mid-February . . . In starting lineup 20 games due to Houston's rash of injuries . . . Took advantage by averaging 10.8 points . . . But what's with the 42.2 percent shooting? . . . Has played for five different CBA teams . . . Had only other NBA stint with Spurs in 1993-94 . . . Graduated from Thornridge High School in suburban Chicago, which also produced Quinn Buckner and Kevin Duckworth . . . Began college career at Iowa State before transferring to a junior college and ending up at Houston . . . Teammate of Clippers' Charles Outlaw with the Cougars . . . Undrafted . . . Born May 26, 1970, in Chicago.

Year	Team	G	FG	FG Pct.	FT	FT Pct.	Reb.	Ast.	TP	Avg.
1992-93	San Antonio.....	40	47	.398	45	.776	48	15	142	3.6
1995-96	Houston........	31	121	.422	39	.848	98	79	335	10.8
	Totals.........	71	168	.415	84	.808	146	94	477	6.7

TRACY MOORE 30 6-4 200   Guard

CBA call-up last season . . . But who wasn't on Rockets? . . . Leading scorer in that league at 26.1 points before coming to NBA with 10-day contract on March 13 . . . Signed for remainder of 1995-96 on April 3 . . . Started two games . . . Has shown three-point range . . . The *Daily Oklahoman* selected him as the High-School Player of the Year as a senior . . . Went to Tulsa from there and became a three-time All-Missouri Valley Conference selection . . . Born Dec. 28, 1965, in Oklahoma City, Okla.

Year	Team	G	FG	FG Pct.	FT	FT Pct.	Reb.	Ast.	TP	Avg.
1991-92	Dallas	42	130	.400	65	.833	82	48	355	8.5
1992-93	Dallas	39	103	.414	53	.869	52	47	282	7.2
1993-94	Detroit	3	2	.667	2	1.000	1	0	6	2.0
1995-96	Houston	8	30	.395	18	.947	22	6	91	11.4
	Totals	92	265	.406	138	.863	157	101	734	8.0

THE ROOKIES

OTHELLA HARRINGTON 22 6-9 235   Forward-Center

Got tons of attention when he arrived at Georgetown as the next great player in the Patrick Ewing-Dikembe Mutombo-Alonzo Mourning line . . . In the end, went in the second round, No. 30 overall . . . No. 4 in school history in rebounds and blocks and No. 5 in points . . . Works hard around the basket, one reason he's considered a good rebounder . . . Intelligent . . . Born Jan. 31, 1974, in Jackson, Miss.

RANDY LIVINGSTON 21 6-4 209   Guard

What could have been . . . Great high-school player had his promising career take a detour after a series of leg injuries . . . Worked to find his game without the same wheels . . . Only played in 29 games at LSU, 16 as a freshman and 13 as a sophomore before going into the draft as No. 42 . . . Born April 2, 1975, in New Orleans.

TERRELL BELL 22 6-10 240   Center

More hope for a backup big man . . . Had a limited role his first three years at Georgia before coming on as a senior . . . Went from two starts those first three seasons to making the opening

ineup all 31 outings in 1995-96 ... Finished 19th in the nation
n blocked shots ... No. 50 ... Johneirio Terrell Bell was born
Dec. 15, 1973, in Athens, Ga.

COACH RUDY TOMJANOVICH: The championship run
ended at two, but the great coaching job continued ... Held the Rockets together last season during a terrible stretch of injuries, then a
first-round playoff win over the Lakers ...
Great guy who gets a tremendous amount of
respect from his players ... "He's just cool,
that's all," Robert Horry said. "Some people
are dictators, some are not. He doesn't try to
ell and get on you. He doesn't feel he has to do that for us to
espond." ... Lifetime: 224-134 (62.6 percent) ... Heads into his
27th consecutive season with the Rockets, the only home he has
ever known since leaving University of Michigan in 1970 as No.
overall pick ... That was with the San Diego Rockets, before
he move to Houston ... Went on to have an 11-year career that
ncluded five All-Star appearances ... Later had jersey No. 45
etired ... Became a scout after retiring in 1981, then an assistant
oach from 1983-92 ... Moved to hot seat on an interim basis for
inal 30 games of 1991-92 after Don Chaney was fired ... Got
ermanent job the next season ... In all, that's 11 seasons as a
layer, two as a scout, nine as an assistant and four as head coach
.. Only Golden State's Al Attles (35 years) and Washington's
Wes Unseld (27) can claim longer continuous service with one
eam ... Has been involved in all four of the Rockets' division
hampionships—as leading scorer and All-Star in 1976-77, assis-
ant coach in 1985-86 and the boss in 1992-93 and 1993-94 ...
Born Nov. 24, 1948, in Hamtramck, Mich.

BIGGEST BLUNDER

No, not changing to their current uniforms. When the Rockets
aded Elvin Hayes in June 1972, it was a shocker all around.
he Big E was, after all, a local hero from the University of
Houston who became a first-round pick with the San Diego Rock-
ts in 1968, then returned home in 1971 when the franchise
oved.

Then he was gone, sent to the Bullets in his prime for Jack

Clyde Drexler endures injuries as he enters 14th season.

Marin, who would last one season in Houston.

Hayes, of course, starred in his new surroundings, spending nine years with the Bullets. He did come back to the Rockets again, in 1981, but by then he was at the end of his distinguished career.

ALL-TIME ROCKET LEADERS

SEASON

Points: Moses Malone, 2,520, 1981–82
Assists: John Lucas, 768, 1977–78
Rebounds: Moses Malone, 1,444, 1978–79

GAME

Points: Calvin Murphy, 57 vs. New Jersey, 3/18/78
Assists: Art Williams, 22 vs. San Francisco, 2/14/70
         Art Williams, 22 vs. Phoenix, 12/28/68
         Allen Leavell, 22 vs. New Jersey, 1/25/83
Rebounds: Moses Malone, 37 vs. New Orleans, 2/9/79

CAREER

Points: Hakeem Olajuwon, 21,840, 1984–96
Assists: Calvin Murphy, 4,402, 1970–83
Rebounds: Hakeem Olajuwon, 11,023, 1984–96

MINNESOTA TIMBERWOLVES

TEAM DIRECTORY: Owner: Glen Taylor; GM/Head Coach: Flip Saunders; VP Basketball Oper.: Kevin McHale; Dir. Media Rel.: Kent Wipf; Asst. Coaches: Mike Schuler, Randy Wittman, Greg Ballard. Arena: Target Center (19,006). Colors: Blue, green and silver.

SCOUTING REPORT

SHOOTING: They struggle to get shots. They struggle to make shots. And don't even get us started about their three-pointers.

On second thought, get us started. No one is suggesting that once they start hitting some bombs, everything will immediately turn around, but there is no doubt the effect it has for any team in stretching the defenses and creating more opportunities. The Timberwolves have finished last in the league in percentage from behind the arc in each of the last two seasons.

Then again, things aren't much better from inside—they were 18th from the field overall and 19th in scoring. Nobody broke 50 percent. Isaiah Rider, talented but misguided in that he continued to mistake himself for having three-point range, took enough shots that he would have led 13 teams in attempts and still didn't average 20 points a game. And now he's gone to Portland. Tom Gugliotta, who does have good range for a power forward, thus extending defenses to an extent, was a respectable 47.1 percent.

There is reason for encouragement, though. Kevin Garnett was 49.1 as a rookie—a 19-year-old rookie at that. James Robinson, acquired in the Rider deal, did not have a great shooting percentage but he displayed occasional flashes from outside the arc for Portland. And the arrival of Stephon Marbury brings a legitimate point guard who should be able to create better scoring opportunities, even while learning on the fly.

PLAYMAKING: Not that the Timberwolves were in need of help here or anything, but Doug West spent some time at point guard last season. That's where Marbury comes in.

This would only be his sophomore year at Georgia Tech, so no one is expecting he play like a superstar now (veteran teammate/close friend Garnett can show the kid the ropes in the meantime). Terry Porter would be a good tutor, but Marbury's maturation process will still come as Micheal Williams tries the recovery process again, having played just 10 games the last two campaigns because of heel problems.

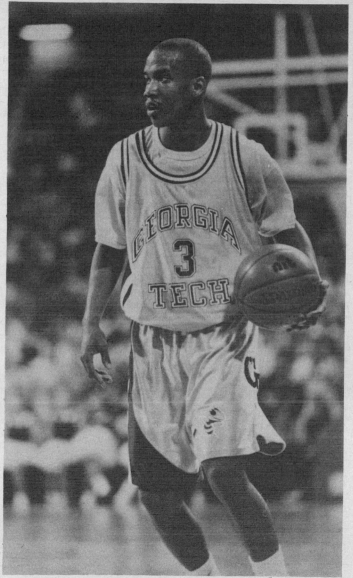

Wolves traded for Georgia Tech's Stephen Marbury.

TIMBERWOLF ROSTER

No. Veterans	Pos.	Ht.	Wt.	Age	Yrs. Pro	College
53 Jerome Allen	G	6-4	184	23	1	Pennsylvania
33 Marques Bragg	F	6-8	230	26	1	Providence
-- Bill Curley	F	6-9	245	24	2	Boston College
7 Mark Davis	F	6-7	210	23	1	Texas Tech
21 Kevin Garnett	F	6-11	220	20	1	Farragut HS
24 Tom Gugliotta	F	6-10	240	26	4	North Carolina State
42 Sam Mitchell	F	6-7	210	33	7	Mercer
44 Cherokee Parks	F-C	6-11	240	24	1	Duke
30 Terry Porter	G	6-3	195	33	11	Wisc.-Stevens Point
40 Eric Riley	C	7-0	245	26	4	Michigan
-- James Robinson	G	6-2	180	26	3	Alabama
5 Doug West	G-F	6-6	220	29	7	Villanova
— Micheal Williams	G	6-2	175	30	8	Baylor

Rd. Rookie	Sel.No.	Pos.	Ht.	Wt.	College
1 Stephon Marbury	4	G	6-2	180	Georgia Tech

REBOUNDING: Not good, but better than you might think for a team that has a revolving door at center and Gugliotta, hardly known as a muscle man, at power forward. But Googs squeezed out 8.8 per outing in his first full season in Minnesota, good enough to set a franchise record. With a point guard in hand, finding someone to smash that becomes a priority. Garnett made a nice contribution at small forward with 6.3 in 28.7 minutes, numbers that should both increase with another year and a few more pounds.

DEFENSE: They should be better, what with all the time spent on this end after the poor shooting and numerous turnovers. Along those lines, the Timberwolves are decent—able to force some turnovers and even block some shots, but in the end stop no one. They 46.9 percent-against was 18th-best, the 103.2 points allowed 23rd.

Gugliotta led all forwards in steals last season, even if the drawback is he can't muscle the true power forwards out of the post.

OUTLOOK: If nothing else, Bill Blair's 'Wolves have earned a new beginning thanks to the new foundation of Garnett and Marbury, the only tandem in the league that can be together for the next eight years and still barely be in their prime.

TIMBERWOLF PROFILES

KEVIN GARNETT 20 6-11 220   Forward

This is no kid ... Doesn't play like it, doesn't act like it ... Upside: Wolves made a great move taking him with fifth pick in 1995, even without so much as a game of college experience ... Downside: half the high-school players who made all-league think they can make the jump, too ... Big mistake ... Special case ... Had already lived away from home for a year, having moved from South Carolina to attend Farragut Academy in Chicago ... His transition from high-school senior to NBA starter was measured in months, not years ... Was 19 years, 9 months old when he cracked the opening lineup for the first time, Jan. 9 against the Lakers. That made him the youngest pro starter since Darryl Dawkins was 19 years, 4 months in 1975-76 ... Born May 19, 1976, in Mauldin, S.C. ... Made $1.622 million.

Year	Team	G	FG	FG Pct.	FT	FT Pct.	Reb.	Ast.	TP	Avg.
1995-96	Minnesota.......	80	361	.491	105	.705	501	145	835	10.4

Kevin Garnett stood tall in first year out of high school.

TOM GUGLIOTTA 26 6-10 240   Forward

People around these parts would appreciate it more if they could just stop laughing . . . Donyell Marshall for Tom Gugliotta? What's the catch? . . . No catch. Wolves ripped off the Warriors to get a forward who can actually play . . . Can't rebound with the other brutes, but does so many other things well . . . Scores from outside and works into the lane . . . Led all forwards in steals last season, finishing 10th overall . . . Behind only Scottie Pippen in that category among forwards the year before . . . The 8.8 rebounds is decent around the league and the best ever for the Timberwolves . . . Former North Carolina State star was born Dec. 19, 1969, in Huntington Station, N.Y. . . . Bullets drafted him as No. 6 in 1992 . . . Made $4.5 million, tops on the team.

Year	Team	G	FG	FG Pct.	FT	FT Pct.	Reb.	Ast.	TP	Avg.
1992-93	Washington	81	484	.426	181	.644	781	306	1187	14.7
1993-94	Washington	78	540	.466	213	.685	728	276	1333	17.1
1994-95	Wash.-G.S.-Minn.	77	371	.443	174	.690	572	279	976	12.7
1995-96	Minnesota	78	473	.471	289	.773	690	238	1261	16.2
	Totals	314	1868	.452	857	.704	2771	1099	4757	15.1

DOUG WEST 29 6-6 200   Guard-Forward

Last season, he played some point guard for the first time as a pro . . . That was more a sign of Minnesota's struggles at that position than his expanding versatility . . . He's a swingman, and a pretty good one at that, even if most fans around the league don't realize it . . . Can expect his role with Timberwolves to be phased out as more time is given to Kevin Garnett at small forward . . . Already lost about 700 minutes during Garnett's rookie season . . . Only holdover from the inaugural season . . . Timberwolves took Villanova standout 38th in 1989 . . . Born

May 27, 1967, in Altoona, Pa. . . . Makes an average of $1.9 million annually.

Year	Team	G	FG	FG Pct.	FT	FT Pct.	Reb.	Ast.	TP	Avg.
1989-90	Minnesota	52	53	.393	26	.813	70	18	135	2.6
1990-91	Minnesota	75	118	.480	58	.690	136	48	294	3.9
1991-92	Minnesota	80	463	.518	186	.805	257	281	1116	14.0
1992-93	Minnesota	80	646	.517	249	.841	247	235	1543	19.3
1993-94	Minnesota	72	434	.487	187	.810	231	172	1056	14.7
1994-95	Minnesota	71	351	.461	206	.837	227	185	919	12.9
1995-96	Minnesota	73	175	.445	114	.792	161	119	465	6.4
	Totals	503	2240	.490	1026	.812	1329	1058	5528	11.0

TERRY PORTER 33 6-3 195   Guard

Signed to become a much-needed clubhouse leader, he also became a floor leader . . . Only player on the team to play all 82 games . . . Started 40 times . . . Moved to backup role when Spud Webb arrived . . . Durability has long been a trademark . . . If Kevin Garnett has any questions about how an NBA player is supposed to act, he should just watch the veteran point guard from Wisconsin-Stevens Point . . . One of only five active players to have 12,000 points and 5,000 assists . . . Most of that, of course, came as a Trail Blazer . . . Portland got him with 24th pick in 1985 . . . After 10 seasons there, including two trips to the All-Star Game and two trips to the Finals, Minnesota signed him as free agent . . . Born April 8, 1963, in Milwaukee . . . Made $1.525 million.

Year	Team	G	FG	FG Pct.	FT	FT Pct.	Reb.	Ast.	TP	Avg.
1985-86	Portland	79	212	.474	125	.806	117	198	562	7.1
1986-87	Portland	80	376	.488	280	.838	337	715	1045	13.1
1987-88	Portland	82	462	.519	274	.846	378	831	1222	14.9
1988-89	Portland	81	540	.471	272	.840	367	770	1431	17.7
1989-90	Portland	80	448	.462	421	.892	272	726	1406	17.6
1990-91	Portland	81	486	.515	279	.823	282	649	1381	17.0
1991-92	Portland	82	521	.461	315	.856	255	477	1485	18.1
1992-93	Portland	81	503	.454	327	.843	316	419	1476	18.2
1993-94	Portland	77	348	.416	204	.872	215	401	1010	13.1
1994-95	Portland	35	105	.393	58	.707	81	133	312	8.9
1995-96	Minnesota	82	269	.442	164	.785	212	452	773	9.4
	Totals	840	4270	.469	2719	.842	2832	5771	12103	14.4

SAM MITCHELL 33 6-7 210   Forward

What, once wasn't enough? ... Spent the first three seasons of his NBA career with the Timberwolves ... It was also their first three seasons ... Shipped to Indiana as part of the Pooh Richardson-Chuck Person deal ... Became a free agent and re-upped in Minnesota ... Suddenly a shooting demon ... Has improved his percentage each of the last four years ... All the way to a career-high 49 from the field and 81.4 from the line in 1995-96 ... No. 1 in team history in offensive rebounds, No. 2 in games behind Doug West ... No. 54 pick by Houston in 1985 out of Mercer, but had a couple of seasons in the CBA and a couple in France before making the NBA ... Born Sept. 2, 1963, in Columbus, Ga. ... Made $1 million.

Year	Team	G	FG	FG Pct.	FT	FT Pct.	Reb.	Ast.	TP	Avg.
1989-90	Minnesota	80	372	.446	268	.768	462	89	1012	12.7
1990-91	Minnesota	82	445	.441	307	.775	520	133	1197	14.6
1991-92	Minnesota	82	307	.423	209	.786	473	94	825	10.1
1992-93	Indiana	81	215	.445	150	.811	248	76	584	7.2
1993-94	Indiana	75	140	.458	82	.745	190	65	362	4.8
1994-95	Indiana	81	201	.487	126	.724	243	61	529	6.5
1995-96	Minnesota	78	303	.490	237	.814	339	74	844	10.8
	Totals	559	1983	.452	1379	.779	2475	592	5353	9.6

JAMES ROBINSON 26 6-2 180   Guard

Came to Wolves from Trail Blazers in summer trade with Bill Curley and future first-rounder for Isaiah Rider..."Hollywood" won two games for Trail Blazers in 1995-96 with last-second three-pointers, Nov. 21 against Lakers and Feb. 5 against Raptors ... Also hit a three-pointer April 14 at Vancouver that tied the game in the final minute to help Portland earn a come-from-behind win ... But relegated to backup duty ... Has shown the range, but shooting percentages still need to come way up ... Led Alabama in scoring three straight years before Trail Blazers grabbed him with 21st pick in 1993 ... Born Aug. 31, 1970, in Jackson, Miss. ... Made $1.04 million.

Year	Team	G	FG	FG Pct.	FT	FT Pct.	Reb.	Ast.	TP	Avg.
1993-94	Portland	58	104	.365	45	.672	78	68	276	4.8
1994-95	Portland	71	255	.409	65	.591	132	180	651	9.2
1995-96	Portland	76	229	.399	89	.659	157	150	649	8.5
	Totals	205	588	.396	199	.638	367	398	1576	7.7

MICHEAL WILLIAMS 30 6-2 175   Guard

What a heel ... Not him. His heel. What a heel it's been the last two seasons ... Managed just one appearance in 1994-95 because of a strained left heel ... Returned last season and lasted all of nine games before the same injury put him on the shelf for final five months ... Last game was Nov. 28 ... Defenses beg him to shoot from the outside ... Timberwolves' starting point guard in 1993-94 ... Minnesota got the Baylor product with Chuck Person from Indiana in September 1992 for Pooh Richardson and Sam Mitchell ... A second-round pick by Pistons in 1988 ... Born July 23, 1966, in Dallas ... Made $2,375 million.

Year	Team	G	FG	FG Pct.	FT	FT Pct.	Reb.	Ast.	TP	Avg.
1988-89	Detroit	49	47	.364	31	.660	27	70	127	2.6
1989-90	Phoe.-Char.	28	60	.504	36	.783	32	81	156	5.6
1990-91	Indiana	73	261	.499	290	.879	176	348	813	11.1
1991-92	Indiana	79	404	.490	372	.871	282	647	1188	15.0
1992-93	Minnesota	76	353	.446	419	.907	273	661	1151	15.1
1993-94	Minnesota	71	314	.457	333	.839	221	512	971	13.7
1994-95	Minnesota	1	1	.250	4	.800	1	3	6	6.0
1995-96	Minnesota	9	13	.325	28	.848	23	31	55	6.1
	Totals	386	1453	.466	1513	.866	1035	2353	4467	11.6

ERIC RILEY 26 7-0 245   Center-Forward

Still big. Still in the league ... If that's what you want to call it ... Bumps from team to team like a pinball ... Got just 12.4 minutes a game in 1995-96 ... Signed as free agent Oct. 14 ... No. 33 pick by Dallas in 1993 after playing at Michigan ... Traded to Houston for Popeye Jones ... Mavericks should be arrested for grand theft ... At least he got a ring out of it from the 1994 NBA title. That's more than the Rockets got out of it ... They cut him, Clippers signed him for the rest of 1994-95 ... Born June 2, 1970, in Cleveland ... Made $300,000.

Year	Team	G	FG	FG Pct.	FT	FT Pct.	Reb.	Ast.	TP	Avg.
1993-94	Houston	47	34	.486	20	.541	59	9	88	1.9
1994-95	L.A. Clippers	40	65	.448	47	.734	112	11	177	4.4
1995-96	Minnesota	25	35	.473	22	.786	76	5	92	3.7
	Totals	112	134	.464	89	.690	247	25	357	3.2

CHEROKEE PARKS 24 6-11 240   Forward

No. 12 pick in the draft in '95 was about No. 12 on the Dallas roster last season . . . Big disappointment . . . No one on the Mavs averaged fewer minutes than his 13.6 and he wound up being traded to the Timberwolves as Minnesota agreed to remove 2-6 lottery protection on the 1997 first-round pick Dallas acquired in the 1994 trade for Sean Rooks . . . No. 2 all-time at Duke in blocked shots . . . Improved his scoring, rebounding and assists in all four seasons in college . . . Member of the U.S. team for the 1994 Goodwill Games . . . Born Oct. 11, 1972, in Huntington Beach, Cal. . . . Made $971,000.

Year	Team	G	FG	FG Pct.	FT	FT Pct.	Reb.	Ast.	TP	Avg.
1995-96	Dallas	64	101	.409	41	.661	216	29	250	3.9

MARQUES BRAGG 26 6-8 230   Forward

Rookie free-agent signee last season averaged the fewest minutes of any permanent member of the Timberwolves . . . The accomplishment was making the team in training camp . . . Spent the previous season with Grand Rapids of the CBA and was named that league's Newcomer of the Year . . . All-CBA and started in their All-Star Game . . . He and Terry Porter were the only Wolves last season who did not miss a game due to injury . . . Of course, there were the 29 games he missed due to coach's decision . . . Providence product was born March 24, 1970, in Newark. N.J. . . . Made $225,000.

Year	Team	G	FG	FG Pct.	FT	FT Pct.	Reb.	Ast.	TP	Avg.
1995-96	Minnesota	53	54	.450	23	.561	79	8	131	2.5

MARK DAVIS 23 6-7 210   Forward

Earned a roster spot as a rookie last season by finishing the preseason schedule as Minnesota's second-leading scorer . . . Should have retired on the spot . . . Shot just 27.7 percent his final 14 appearances . . . Finished at 36.9 for the season . . . Committed seven turnovers March 15 vs. Sacramento, equaling the season high by a Minnesota player . . . On the bright side, at least he got the minutes to be so bad . . . No. 48 pick in the 1995 draft . . . All-Southwest Conference as a senior at Texas Tech . . . Born April 26, 1973, in Thibodaux, La. . . . Made $200,000.

Year	Team	G	FG	FG Pct.	FT	FT Pct.	Reb.	Ast.	TP	Avg.
1995-96	Minnesota	57	55	.369	74	.638	125	47	188	3.3

JEROME ALLEN 23 6-4 184   Guard

Rookie hazing: BMOC in college, drafted by the pros, gets minutes at the start of the season . . . Then falls off the end of the earth . . . Logged 279 minutes the first 27 outings; squeezed out just 83 in the 55 games after Jan. 1 . . . Did cut turnovers down in the second half . . . Two-time Ivy League Player of the Year and three-time all-conference at Penn . . . Timberwolves got him with 49th pick in '95 . . . First Ivy Leaguer drafted since Walter Palmer went to Utah in the second round in 1990 . . . Born Jan. 28, 1973, in Philadelphia . . . Made $200,000.

Year	Team	G	FG	FG Pct.	FT	FT Pct.	Reb.	Ast.	TP	Avg.
1995-96	Minnesota	41	36	.343	26	.722	25	49	108	2.6

THE ROOKIE

STEPHON MARBURY 19 6-2 180   Guard

Kevin Garnett gets a close friend and a big-time point-guard prospect . . . Left Georgia Tech after freshman season . . . First-team All-ACC . . . Milwaukee took him at No. 4, then sent him to Timberwolves for Ray Allen and a future first-rounder . . . Very quick, with a cross-over dribble . . . The latest playground legend to come out of Gotham was born Feb. 20, 1977, in Brooklyn, N.Y.

COACH FLIP SAUNDERS: Kevin McHale's buddy does double duty . . . Already general manager, Philip Saunders moved to the sidelines when Bill Blair was fired Dec. 18 . . . NBA fans didn't know him, but he had seven seasons of experience in the CBA to his credit . . . Second-winningest coach in that league with 253 victories . . . Won championships with the La Crosse Catbirds in 1990 and '92 . . . Also coached Rapid City and Sioux Falls . . . Before that, was an assistant at his alma mater, the University of Minnesota (1981-86), and Tulsa (1986-88) . . . Coaching career began with four seasons at Golden Valley Lutheran College . . . Played four seasons with the Gophers . . . Starter for 101 of his 103 appearances . . . As a senior in 1976-77, he teamed with freshman McHale to lead team to a school-record 24-3 mark . . . Prepped in Cuyahoga Heights, Ohio, and was named the state's Class A Player of the Year in 1973 . . . Born Feb. 23, 1955, in Cleveland.

No forward had more steals than Tom Gugliotta last year.

BIGGEST BLUNDER

The only thing worse than making a bad first-round pick, especially in the lottery, is making two of them. In a row. At the same position.

In 1990, the Timberwolves chose Louisville's Felton Spencer as their center of the future, if not the center of their future. Obviously impressed with what they saw, the pick a year later was New Mexico's Luc Longley.

So what happened? Spencer and Longley were eventually traded, with the Wolves getting nothing of long-term value in return. And last season Longley won a ring with the champion Bulls.

ALL-TIME TIMBERWOLF LEADERS

SEASON

Points: Tony Campbell, 1,903, 1989–90
Assists: Jerome Richardson, 734, 1990–91
Rebounds: Christian Laettner, 708, 1992–93

GAME

Points: Tony Campbell, 44 vs. Boston, 2/2/90
Assists: Sidney Lowe, 17 vs. Golden State, 3/20/90
Pooh Richardson, 17 vs. Washington, 3/13/92
Micheal Williams, 17 vs. L.A. Clippers, 12/10/93
Rebounds: Todd Murphy, 20 vs. L.A. Clippers, 1/2/90
Tom Gugliotta, 20 vs. Dallas, 2/3/96

CAREER

Points: Doug West, 5,528, 1989–96
Assists: Jerome Richardson, 1,973, 1989–92
Rebounds: Christian Laettner, 2,225, 1992–96

SAN ANTONIO SPURS

TEAM DIRECTORY: Chairman: Peter Holt; Pres./CEO: John Diller; Exec.VP Basketball Oper./GM: Gregg Popovich; Exec. VP Business Oper.: Russ Bookbinder; Media Services Dir.: Tom James; Coach: Bob Hill; Asst. Coaches: Hank Egan, Paul Pressey. Arena: Alamodome (20,557/34,215). Colors: Metallic silver and black.

David Robinson launches one vs. Suns in '96 playoffs.

SCOUTING REPORT

SHOOTING: The Spurs haven't been able to find the right emotional pieces to surround David Robinson, a wonderful talent who too often lacks a warrior mentality when it counts, but have done a commendable job in building around him on offense.

There's Chuck Person, still a dangerous three-point shooter after all these years, and Sean Elliott, underrated from long range, making defenses pay for double-teaming in the post, and Charles Smith to draw some of the attention to the other side. This all came last season as the starting backcourt of Vinny Del Negro and Avery Johnson shot 49.7 and 49.4 percent, respectively.

So it comes as no surprise that San Antonio ranks among the leaders in accuracy, finishing fourth two seasons ago and eighth in 1995-96. Their average of 103.4 points a game, sixth overall, would have been even better if this wasn't such a poor team from the line, strangely enough.

Everything revolves around Robinson, of course. He's 31 years old, but still gets out in transition, and remains dependable with medium-range jumpers. What's not to like?

PLAYMAKING: Your NBA assist leaders last season: 1. John Stockton, 11.2; 2. Jason Kidd, 9.7; 3. (tie) Avery Johnson and Rod Strickland, 9.6. Do not adjust your sets. Two stars, one would-be star if not for off-court troubles, and some guy who wasn't drafted and has bounced around so much since that this is his third stint with the Spurs, the most recent coming when they didn't exactly have to outbid the rest of the league to sign him as a free agent a couple of years back.

Yet, there Johnson is, and there they are. With him leading the way, the Spurs were No. 4 in assists and No. 5 in the fewest turnovers. He and Del Negro finished with the best assist-to-turnover ratio among all starting backcourts, and Johnson was No. 2 among all individuals, behind only Chicago Bulls reserve Steve Kerr. It helps that Del Negro is a former starter at the point. Doc Rivers' retirement could provide an opportunity for second-year man Cory Alexander.

REBOUNDING: OK, so they miss Dennis Rodman in one way. Twenty-sixth in the league on the offensive boards last season by percentage? A team with Robinson, No. 2 overall at 12.2 per game, behind only, uh, Rodman? Imagine how many extra points the Spurs would have collected with any competence in this area. C'mon! Draft a soccer player and send him out there to let misses

SPUR ROSTER

No.	Veterans	Pos.	Ht.	Wt.	Age	Yrs. Pro	College
1	Cory Alexander	G	6-1	185	23	1	Virginia
33	Greg Anderson	F-C	6-10	250	32	8	Houston
15	Vinny Del Negro	G	6-4	200	20	6	North Carolina State
5	Dell Demps	G	6-4	210	26	2	Pacific
32	Sean Elliott	F	6-8	215	28	7	Arizona
11	Carl Herrera	F	6-9	225	29	5	Houston
6	Avery Johnson	G	5-11	175	31	8	Southern
41	Will Perdue	C	7-0	250	31	8	Vanderbilt
45	Chuck Person	F	6-8	225	32	10	Auburn
50	David Robinson	C	7-1	235	31	7	Navy
54	Charles Smith	F	6-10	245	31	8	Pittsburgh
3	Monty Williams	F	6-8	225	25	2	Notre Dame

hit off his head and go into the basket if these guys can't do it with their hands.

The problem is at power forward, one reason they had seven starters there last season. One, Will Perdue, at least could do the job in this area, finishing with a better rebound-per-minute average than Robinson. The problem was the other areas—Perdue got 17.5 minutes an outing and lost the job.

DEFENSE: Good riddance to that Rodman. Two years ago, with one of the era's best defenders on board, the Spurs allowed 100.6 points a game and were sixth in shooting percentage-against. In 1995-96, they felt like they had removed a bunion by trading Rodman, then didn't collapse here without him, surrendering 97.1 points while finishing third in shooting defense. Only Miami and Seattle were better.

OUTLOOK: Good . . . still. These remain the same Spurs, capable of losing in the first round or winning the West. Don't be surprised if management makes a bold move to try and push them over the top, whether by trade or coaching change, especially after Bob Hill didn't get the extension he wanted heading into the summer. The time for patience has passed.

SPUR PROFILES

DAVID ROBINSON 31 7-1 235   Center

Great scorer, great rebounder, great shot-blocker, great athlete, great guy . . . So why so many critics? . . . Jealousy, it's not . . . Critics say he's not strong enough, but that's misplaced. No one is consistently in the top five in the league in rebounding without being physically able . . . But he needs to be more emotionally strong in playoff battles . . . Last season he was fifth in the NBA in scoring, second in boards, third in blocks . . . Just 29th in minutes, but still the only player to grab 1,000 rebounds . . . Career average of 3.60 blocks is tops in league history for players with at least 400 appearances . . . Rookie of the Year in 1989-90 and MVP in 1994-95 . . . First male basketball player to compete in three Olympics . . . Out of the Naval Academy in 1987, completed a military obligation before joining NBA . . . Born Aug. 6, 1965, in Key West, Fla. . . . Made $7.7 million.

Year	Team	G	FG	FG Pct.	FT	FT Pct.	Reb.	Ast.	TP	Avg.
1989-90	San Antonio	82	690	.531	613	.732	983	164	1993	24.3
1990-91	San Antonio	82	754	.552	592	.762	1063	208	2101	25.6
1991-92	San Antonio	68	592	.551	393	.701	829	181	1578	23.2
1992-93	San Antonio	82	676	.501	561	.732	956	301	1916	23.4
1993-94	San Antonio	80	840	.507	693	.749	855	381	2383	29.8
1994-95	San Antonio	81	788	.530	656	.774	877	236	2238	27.6
1995-96	San Antonio	82	711	.516	626	.761	1000	247	2051	25.0
	Totals	557	5051	.526	4134	.747	6563	1718	14260	25.6

SEAN ELLIOTT 28 6-8 215   Forward

No longer just a good player . . . A two-time All-Star . . . All the better that the 1996 game was at the Alamodome . . . Went from that to finishing the best season of the career that started when the Spurs took him third overall in 1989 out of Arizona . . . Six of the seven years have been in San Antonio, interrupted only with a cup of coffee in Detroit . . . Returned-to-sender in summer of '95 for Bill Curley and a second-rounder . . . The 20 points a game in 1995-96 was third-best among all small forwards . . . Must be respected from three-point range . . . Also an All-Star in '93 . . . Born Feb. 2, 1968, in Tucson, Ariz. . . . Making an average of $5.333 million annually.

Year	Team	G	FG	FG Pct.	FT	FT Pct.	Reb.	Ast.	TP	Avg.
1989-90	San Antonio	81	311	.481	187	.866	297	154	810	10.0
1990-91	San Antonio	82	478	.490	325	.808	456	238	1301	15.9
1991-92	San Antonio	82	514	.494	285	.861	439	214	1338	16.3
1992-93	San Antonio	70	451	.491	268	.795	322	265	1207	17.2
1993-94	Detroit	73	360	.455	139	.803	263	197	885	12.1
1994-95	San Antonio	81	502	.468	326	.807	287	206	1466	18.1
1995-96	San Antonio	77	525	.466	326	.771	396	211	1537	20.0
	Totals	546	3141	.478	1856	.812	2460	1485	8544	15.6

VINNY DEL NEGRO 30 6-4 200   Guard

Coming off a career year . . . Posted single-season bests in 11 categories . . . Nothing special as a three-point shooter, but makes up for that with his versatility . . . Can play backup point guard . . . Once played starting point guard, but not quick enough to defend there on a regular basis . . . Career took off when Bob Hill moved him to the other spot before 1994-95 . . . Had spent two seasons in Italy before Spurs signed North Carolina State product as free agent July 30, 1992 . . . Teammate of Toni Kukoc on Benetton Treviso . . . No. 29 pick by Sacramento in 1988 . . . Born Aug. 9, 1966, in Springfield, Mass. . . . Made $1.747 million.

Year	Team	G	FG	FG Pct.	FT	FT Pct.	Reb.	Ast.	TP	Avg.
1988-89	Sacramento	80	239	.475	85	.850	171	206	569	7.1
1989-90	Sacramento	76	297	.462	135	.871	198	250	739	9.7
1992-93	San Antonio	73	218	.507	101	.863	163	291	543	7.4
1993-94	San Antonio	77	309	.487	140	.824	161	320	773	10.0
1994-95	San Antonio	75	372	.486	128	.790	192	226	938	12.5
1995-96	San Antonio	82	478	.497	178	.832	272	315	1191	14.5
	Totals	463	1913	.486	767	.836	1157	1608	4753	10.3

AVERY JOHNSON 31 5-11 175   Guard

Not just good, but consistently good . . . One of the more underrated guards in the league . . . Or do you think most people realize he finished third in assists last season, behind only John Stockton and Jason Kidd? . . . How important is he to the Spurs? No one played more total minutes than this free-agent pickup from the summer of 1994 . . . Increased his scoring average in each of his first seven seasons in the NBA before a fraction of a dip in 1995-96 ... One of only five players ever to roll that seven ... Entered the league with Seattle after going undrafted out of Southern University ... Born March 25, 1965, in New Orleans ... A steal at $845,000.

Year	Team	G	FG	FG Pct.	FT	FT Pct.	Reb.	Ast.	TP	Avg.
1988-89	Seattle	43	29	.349	9	.563	24	73	68	1.6
1989-90	Seattle	53	55	.387	29	.725	43	162	140	2.6
1990-91	Den.-S.A.	68	130	.469	59	.678	77	230	320	4.7
1991-92	S.A.-Hou.	69	158	.479	66	.653	80	266	386	5.6
1992-93	San Antonio	75	256	.502	144	.791	146	561	656	8.7
1993-94	Golden State	82	356	.492	178	.704	176	433	890	10.9
1994-95	San Antonio	82	448	.519	202	.685	208	670	1101	13.4
1995-96	San Antonio	82	438	.494	189	.721	206	789	1071	13.1
	Totals	554	1870	.490	876	.709	960	3184	4632	8.4

CHARLES SMITH 31 6-10 245   Forward

Got beat up worse in New York worse than a guy walking through Central Park at midnight with hundreds hanging out of his pocket ... One difference: Smith had to last through 3½ seasons of it ... He was glad to get out of there. Try finding 10 people who were sorry to see him leave ... A new beginning came with Feb. 8 trade that brought him to San Antonio along with Monty Williams for J.R. Reid, Brad Lohaus and a first-round pick ... Played 32 games with the Spurs ... Averaged 9.6 points, 6.3 rebounds and 25.8 minutes ... Plays both forward spots ... Former Pittsburgh star was No. 3 pick in 1988 by Philadelphia and was sent to the Clippers later that night ... Born July 16, 1965, in Bridgeport, Conn. ... Made $3.357 million.

Year	Team	G	FG	FG Pct.	FT	FT Pct.	Reb.	Ast.	TP	Avg.
1988-89	L.A.Clippers	71	435	.495	285	.725	465	103	1155	16.3
1989-90	L.A.Clippers	78	595	.520	454	.794	524	114	1645	21.1
1990-91	L.A.Clippers	74	548	.469	384	.793	608	134	1480	20.0
1991-92	L.A.Clippers	49	251	.466	212	.785	301	56	714	14.6
1992-93	New York	81	358	.469	287	.782	432	142	1003	12.4
1993-94	New York	43	176	.443	87	.719	165	50	447	10.4
1994-95	New York	76	352	.471	255	.792	324	120	966	12.7
1995-96	N.Y.-S.A.	73	244	.422	119	.730	362	65	609	8.3
	Totals	545	2959	.476	2083	.774	3181	784	8019	14.7

WILL PERDUE 31 7-0 250 — Forward-Center

Why he's loved in San Antonio: He's not Dennis Rodman... Why he's hated in San Antonio: He's not Dennis Rodman... The Worm's replacement, in trade and position... They'll never believe this in Chicago, but he made a nice contribution after coming in the Oct. 1995 deal... Averaged 6.1 rebounds in just 17.5 minutes overall and 9.0 boards in 25.8 minutes of 22 starts at power forward... Also played backup center... Won championship rings with Bulls in 1991, '92 and '93... Chicago drafted him out of Vanderbilt with 11th pick in 1988... Born Aug. 29, 1965, in Melbourne, Fla.... Made $1.34 million.

Year	Team	G	FG	FG Pct.	FT	FT Pct.	Reb.	Ast.	TP	Avg.
1988-89	Chicago	30	29	.403	8	.571	45	11	66	2.2
1989-90	Chicago	77	111	.414	72	.692	214	46	294	3.8
1990-91	Chicago	74	116	.494	75	.670	336	47	307	4.1
1991-92	Chicago	77	152	.547	45	.495	312	80	350	4.5
1992-93	Chicago	72	137	.557	67	.604	287	74	341	4.7
1993-94	Chicago	43	47	.420	23	.719	126	34	117	2.7
1994-95	Chicago	78	254	.553	113	.582	522	90	621	8.0
1995-96	San Antonio	80	173	.523	67	.536	485	33	413	5.2
	Totals	531	1019	.509	470	.600	2327	415	2509	4.7

CARL HERRERA 29 6-9 225 — Forward

Didn't work out last season as a free-agent signee... Kind of like the Hindenburg didn't work out as a mode of transportation... From an important member of the Rockets' back-to-back titles to a scrub... Averaged just 8.9 minutes... Left Houston as No. 7 on the all-time list for field-goal percentage... Miami picked him 30th in 1990 draft, but he never played there... Shipped to Houston, where he also played college ball for Cougars... Has played in the Olympics and Pan-American Games for Venezuela... Born Dec. 14, 1966, in Trinidad... Made $1.3 million.

Year	Team	G	FG	FG Pct.	FT	FT Pct.	Reb.	Ast.	TP	Avg.
1991-92	Houston	43	83	.516	25	.568	99	27	191	4.4
1992-93	Houston	81	240	.541	125	.710	454	61	605	7.5
1993-94	Houston	75	142	.458	69	.711	285	37	353	4.7
1994-95	Houston	61	171	.523	73	.624	278	44	415	6.8
1995-96	San Antonio	44	40	.412	5	.294	81	16	85	1.9
	Totals	304	676	.505	297	.659	1197	185	1649	5.4

CHUCK PERSON 32 6-8 225   Forward

At least he doesn't have to spend the entire offseason icing down his shooting elbow anymore ... Attempts have decreased for four straight years now, by about 500 ... Defenses still have to take him seriously, though ... Fifth in the league last season in three-pointers made and 21st in downtown percentage ... The 190 makes was a personal best and a Spurs record ... The 1,046 career hits is third all-time, behind Dale Ellis and Reggie Miller ... Rookie of the Year in 1986 after the Pacers took him fourth ... Older brother of Suns' Wesley ... Born June 27, 1964, in Brantley, Ala., and stayed close to attend Auburn ... Made $1.69 million.

Year	Team	G	FG	FG Pct.	FT	FT Pct.	Reb.	Ast.	TP	Avg.
1986-87	Indiana	82	635	.468	222	.747	677	295	1541	18.8
1987-88	Indiana	79	575	.459	132	.670	536	309	1341	17.0
1988-89	Indiana	80	711	.489	243	.792	516	289	1728	21.6
1989-90	Indiana	77	605	.487	211	.781	445	230	1515	19.7
1990-91	Indiana	80	620	.504	165	.721	417	238	1474	18.4
1991-92	Indiana	81	616	.480	133	.675	426	382	1497	18.5
1992-93	Minnesota	78	541	.433	109	.649	433	343	1309	16.8
1993-94	Minnesota	77	356	.422	82	.759	253	185	894	11.6
1994-95	San Antonio	81	317	.423	66	.647	258	106	872	10.8
1995-96	San Antonio	80	308	.437	67	.644	413	100	873	10.9
	Totals	795	5284	.465	1430	.723	4374	2477	13044	16.4

CORY ALEXANDER 23 6-1 185   Guard

Spurs' lone rookie last season ... So at least he has an excuse for shooting 40.6 percent and getting just 9.3 minutes a game ... Did show potential from three-point range in limited chances ... Last pick of first round—No. 29—in 1995 after standout career at Virginia ... Left following junior season ... Started all 85 games in which he played for Cavaliers ... No. 5 in school history in assists ... Born June 22, 1973, in Waynesboro, Va. ... Made $490,000.

Year	Team	G	FG	FG Pct.	FT	FT Pct.	Reb.	Ast.	TP	Avg.
1995-96	San Antonio	60	63	.406	16	.640	42	121	168	2.8

GREG ANDERSON 32 6-10 250   Forward-Center

Cadillac looks pretty totaled . . . On a team that spent most of the season searching for help at power forward, he averaged just 7.5 minutes a game and had 33 DNP-CDs . . . Got his chance seven times, sort of . . . In seven starts in December, he contributed an average of three rebounds and one point in 11.9 minutes . . . Originally selected by Spurs with 23rd pick in 1987 . . . Lasted two seasons before being traded . . . Made five stops over the years, including a season in Italy, before returning to San Antonio in 1995-96 as a free agent . . . Played college ball at Houston . . . Born June 22, 1964, in Houston . . . Made $485,000.

Year	Team	G	FG	FG Pct.	FT	FT Pct.	Reb.	Ast.	TP	Avg.
1987-88	San Antonio	82	379	.501	198	.604	513	79	957	11.7
1988-89	San Antonio	82	460	.503	207	.514	676	61	1127	13.7
1989-90	Milwaukee	60	219	.507	91	.535	373	24	529	8.8
1990-91	Mil.-N.J.-Den.	68	116	.430	60	.522	318	16	292	4.3
1991-92	Denver	82	389	.456	167	.623	941	78	945	11.5
1993-94	Detroit	77	201	.543	88	.571	571	51	491	6.4
1994-95	Atlanta	51	57	.548	34	.479	188	17	148	2.9
1995-96	San Antonio	46	24	.511	6	.240	100	10	54	1.2
	Totals	548	1845	.492	851	.555	3680	336	4543	8.3

MONTY WILLIAMS 25 6-8 225   Forward

The new beginning looked an awful lot like the old ending . . . Speaking of awful: 39.7 percent from the field with the Spurs . . . Must have been all that rust . . . Had more DNP-CDs (19) than appearances (17) after being traded from the Knicks . . . Averaged just 7.2 minutes in those 17 outings . . . This, after failing to get off the bench in 32 games with New York . . . They packaged him with Charles Smith in return for J.R. Reid, Brad Lohaus and a first-rounder Feb. 8 . . . Had nice career at Notre Dame despite missing two years because of a rare condition in which a muscle thickened between the heart chambers . . . That was one reason he dropped to the Knicks at No. 24 in the '94 draft . . . Born Oct. 8, 1971, in Fredricksburg, Va. . . . Made $845,000.

Year	Team	G	FG	FG Pct.	FT	FT Pct.	Reb.	Ast.	TP	Avg.
1994-95	New York	41	60	.451	17	.447	98	49	137	3.3
1995-96	N.Y.-S.A.	31	27	.397	14	.700	40	8	68	2.2
	Totals	72	87	.433	31	.534	138	57	205	2.8

DELL DEMPS 26 6-4 210   Guard

Talk about going to extremes to come up with a bogus ailment to stash a guy on the injured list . . . The Spurs had their team plane run into horrible turbulence Nov. 3, causing Demps' seat to become untracked . . . Suffered back problems that stayed with him most of last season, mainly recurrent spasms . . . He was on and off the injured list, four times in all . . . All-Big West Conference three straight years at the University of the Pacific . . . A second-round pick by Rapid City of the CBA in 1992 . . . Spurs got him as a free agent Oct. 6, 1995 . . . Born Feb. 12, 1970, in Long Beach, Cal. . . . Made $225,000.

Year	Team	G	FG	FG Pct.	FT	FT Pct.	Reb.	Ast.	TP	Avg.
1993-94	Golden State	2	2	.333	0	.000	0	1	4	2.0
1995-96	San Antonio	16	19	.576	14	.824	9	8	53	3.3
	Totals	18	21	.538	14	.737	9	9	57	3.2

COACH BOB HILL:

Has 121-43 record (73.8 percent) in two seasons with Spurs . . . Which would be great if they brought him in to win regular-season games . . . Hasn't been able to deliver at least a trip to the Finals, so the hoped-for contract extension last spring didn't materialize . . . Has won two straight Midwest Division titles . . . Last season also included directing a franchise-record 17-game winning streak . . . The 16-0 March equaled the 1971-72 Lakers for the best month in league history . . . Lifetime: 254-197 . . . Winning percentage of 56.3 is 20th on the all-time list and seventh among active coaches with at least 400 games . . . Previously coached Knicks and Pacers . . . Played basketball and baseball at Bowling Green and was even drafted by the San Diego Padres . . . Became as assistant at Bowling Green, Pitt and Kansas . . . The NBA was the next stop, first on Hubie Brown's staff in New York. When Brown was fired after a 4-12 start to 1986-87, he took over and went 20-46 the rest of the way. Rick Pitino arrived after the season . . . Became a scout with Hornets, a broadcaster with Nets, coach of Topeka of the CBA and then coach of Vitrus Knorr in Italy . . . Returned to NBA as an assistant with the Pacers. When Dick Versace was fired in December 1990, Hill got the promotion and spent 2½ seasons on the sideline in Indiana . . . Was an assistant with Orlando when the Spurs came calling in summer of '95 . . . Born Nov. 24, 1948, in Columbus, Ohio.

BIGGEST BLUNDER

It seemed like progress at the time: move from HemisFair Arena, their home since the ABA days, to the new, spacious Alamodome down the street.

Could it end up spelling the end of the Spurs in San Antonio? For whatever reasons, they moved into the made-for-football stadium—financial, political, etc.—and it now appears they will probably have to move out to avoid losing big money on a regular basis because arena configurations make selling luxury boxes, the real cash cows in sports these days, difficult.

The city is in no mood, or financial standing, to build another new sports structure while having the Alamodome sit practically empty. That has already sparked the inevitable—rumors that the Spurs may move in the next few years.

ALL-TIME SPUR LEADERS

SEASON

Points: George Gervin, 2,585, 1979–80
Assists: Johnny Moore, 816, 1984–85
Rebounds: Swen Nater, 1,279, 1974–75 (ABA)
          David Robinson, 1,063, 1990–91

GAME

Points: David Robinson, 71 vs. LA Clippers, 4/24/94
Assists: John Lucas, 24 vs. Denver, 4/15/84
Rebounds: Manny Leaks, 35 vs. Kentucky, 11/27/70 (ABA)
          Edgar Jones, 25 vs. Dallas, 3/13/84
          Artis Gilmore, 25 vs. Utah, 1/17/87

CAREER

Points: George Gervin, 23,602, 1974–85
Assists: Johnny Moore, 3,865, 1980–90
Rebounds: David Robinson, 6,563, 1989–96

Couple of 32s: Magic watches Sean Elliott go for it.

UTAH JAZZ

TEAM DIRECTORY: Owner: Larry Miller; Pres.: Frank Layden; GM: R. Tim Howells; Dir. Basketball Oper.: Scott Layden; VP-Pub. Rel.: David Allred; Dir. Media Rel.: Kim Turner; Coach: Jerry Sloan; Asst. Coaches: Phil Johnson, David Fredman, Gordon Chiesa. Arena: Delta Center (19,911). Colors: Purple, blue, green, black, white and copper.

John Stockton passed Maurice Cheeks in all-time steals.

SCOUTING REPORT

SHOOTING: Like marksmen. Only six teams had fewer attempts last season—Seattle was the lone Western Conference club—and still Utah managed 102.5 points with its signature halfcourt, pick-and-roll game. There's no mystery why. The Jazz led the league in shooting. For the second year in a row.

Karl Malone still does the bull-in-a-china-shop from the post and seems better than ever on fallaways and medium-range jumpers, pushing him to fourth in the league in scoring (25.8) despite fewer trips to the line. The starting backcourt of John Stockton and Jeff Hornacek shot 53.8 and 50.2 percent, respectively, and is especially dangerous since they can get down the lane or break defenses from three-point range, Hornacek having finished fifth in the NBA there in 1995-96. Felton Spencer (traded to Orlando) wasn't a threat in the offense, but didn't waste the chances, going 52 percent while also coming back from a serious Achilles injury.

The 28 other teams should just be thankful the Jazz don't have a consistent weapon at small forward, a place most clubs consider a scoring position. If that ever happens, look out.

PLAYMAKING: The other reason the Jazz are an offensive force. Stockton is 34 and continues to control the tempo like a 24-year-old, picking apart defenses because he has such great vision, instincts and passing skills. And that doesn't even begin to touch on his legendary two-man game with Malone.

To think there's more. Stockton the individual and Utah the team both were No. 1 in assists, but credit also belongs to Hornacek, the starter at shooting guard but the kind of backup at the point that most teams can only dream of. He was never better than when the stakes were highest for the Jazz in the Western Conference finals.

REBOUNDING: More bad news, NBA. The team that doesn't make mistakes also crashes the boards, finishing fourth in defensive rebounding, 10th on the offensive end and fifth overall, thanks mainly to Malone, who pulled down 9.8 per. Greg Ostertag, the No. 1 pick of '95, could make a contribution here, but first needs to play well enough to get more than 11.6 minutes.

JAZZ ROSTER

No.	Veterans	Pos.	Ht.	Wt.	Age	Yrs. Pro	College
55	Antoine Carr	F	6-9	255	35	12	Wichita State
10	Howard Eisley	G	6-2	177	23	2	Boston College
44	Greg Foster	C	6-11	240	28	6	Texas-El Paso
--	Kenny Gattison	F	6-8	256	32	9	Old Dominion
14	Jeff Hornacek	G	6-4	190	33	10	Iowa State
31	Adam Keefe	F	6-9	241	26	4	Stanford
32	Karl Malone	F	6-9	256	33	11	Louisiana Tech
43	Chris Morris	F	6-8	220	30	8	Auburn
00	Greg Ostertag	C	7-2	279	23	1	Kansas
34	Bryon Russell	F	6-7	225	25	3	Long Beach State
12	John Stockton	G	6-1	175	34	12	Gonzaga
--	Brooks Thompson	G	6-4	193	26	3	Oklahoma State
15	Jamie Watson	F	6-7	190	24	2	South Carolina

Rd.	Rookies	Sel.No.	Pos.	Ht.	Wt.	College
2	Shandon Anderson	54	F-G	6-6	205	Georgia

DEFENSE: The reflex after seeing that the Jazz allowed just 95.9 points last season is to say it's all because its own halfcourt offense cuts down on scoring opportunities for the other team. Not so. Led by the aggressive guards that give opponents trouble just getting into sets, Utah finished seventh in shooting percentage-against.

OUTLOOK: Jerry Sloan's veteran team shows no signs of slowing down, even peaking last spring by torturing the SuperSonics into a Game 7 of the Western Conference finals. It's just that getting over the hump will be difficult because Salt Lake City doesn't attract impact free agents and the Jazz can't make a major trade without giving up one of the Big Three, which usually results in offseason tinkering while others can make major moves.

The X-factor this fall, for those who are convinced that they will start showing their age (we say don't count on it) is that Stockton will be 34 and Malone 33 on opening night and neither had a full summer of rest because of the Olympics.

JAZZ PROFILES

KARL MALONE 33 6-9 256   Forward

Really showing a lot of signs of breaking down from all the pounding and all the years. Hah ... All he did in his 11th season was finish fourth in the league in scoring (25) and 11th in rebounding (9.8) ... Not known for his defense, but also was 13th in steals (1.68) because of quick hands inside ... Topped 2,000-point plateau for the ninth consecutive year ... If that's not enough, recorded first triple-double of career ... Moved into 11th place on all-time scoring list with 23,343 points ... Has played in 898 of a possible 902 regular-season games ... A steal as the 13th pick in the 1985 draft after a career at Louisiana Tech ... Born July 24, 1963, in Summerfield, La. ... Made $3.676 million.

Year	Team	G	FG	FG Pct.	FT	FT Pct.	Reb.	Ast.	TP	Avg.
1985-86	Utah	81	504	.496	195	.481	718	236	1203	14.9
1986-87	Utah	82	728	.512	323	.598	855	158	1779	21.7
1987-88	Utah	82	858	.520	552	.700	986	199	2268	27.7
1988-89	Utah	80	809	.519	703	.766	853	219	2326	29.1
1989-90	Utah	82	914	.562	696	.762	911	226	2540	31.0
1990-91	Utah	82	847	.527	684	.770	967	270	2382	29.0
1991-92	Utah	81	798	.526	673	.778	909	241	2272	28.0
1992-93	Utah	82	797	.552	619	.740	919	308	2217	27.0
1993-94	Utah	82	772	.497	511	.694	940	328	2063	25.2
1994-95	Utah	82	830	.536	516	.742	871	285	2187	26.7
1995-96	Utah	82	789	.519	512	.723	804	345	2106	25.7
	Totals	898	8646	.525	5984	.722	9733	2815	23343	26.0

JOHN STOCKTON 34 6-1 175   Guard

Dallas coach Dick Motta: "Malone may be the Mailman, but John Stockton's the stamp." ... We couldn't have said it any better ... No. 1 in the league in assists for the ninth consecutive season in 1995-96 ... Already the all-time leader in that category, he also moved past Maurice Cheeks for top spot in steals ... Now at 2,365 in 12 seasons since Jazz got the relative unknown out of Gonzaga with 16th pick in 1984 ... Still most dangerous when he breaks down the defense and gets into the lane, allowing him to use great vision and passing skills to find someone for a lay-in ... Good three-point shooter, though

... Has started 527 straight games, the longest active run in NBA and the fourth-best streak ever ... In all, has played in 980 of a possible 984 games as a pro ... Two-time Olympian was born March 26, 1962, in Spokane, Wash. ... Made $2.8 million.

Year	Team	G	FG	FG Pct.	FT	FT Pct.	Reb.	Ast.	TP	Avg.
1984-85	Utah	82	157	.471	142	.736	105	415	458	5.6
1985-86	Utah	82	228	.489	172	.839	179	610	630	7.7
1986-87	Utah	82	231	.499	179	.782	151	670	648	7.9
1987-88	Utah	82	454	.574	272	.840	237	1128	1204	14.7
1988-89	Utah	82	497	.538	390	.863	248	1118	1400	17.1
1989-90	Utah	78	472	.514	354	.819	206	1134	1345	17.2
1990-91	Utah	82	496	.507	363	.836	237	1164	1413	17.2
1991-92	Utah	82	453	.482	308	.842	270	1126	1297	15.8
1992-93	Utah	82	437	.486	293	.798	237	987	1239	15.1
1993-94	Utah	82	458	.528	272	.805	258	1031	1236	15.1
1994-95	Utah	82	429	.542	246	.804	251	1011	1206	14.7
1995-96	Utah	82	440	.538	234	.830	226	916	1209	14.7
	Totals	980	4752	.517	3225	.821	2605	11310	13285	13.6

JEFF HORNACEK 33 6-4 190   Guard

If he's the third wheel, that's a hell of a tricycle ... Doesn't get the attention of his two superstar teammates, but certainly well-respected throughout the league ... Fifth in three-point shooting last season at 46.6 percent ... Starting shooting guard also versatile enough to play behind John Stockton at the point ... He should be. Was the the primary ball-handler for many of his six seasons in Phoenix, after the Suns got him with the 46th pick in 1986 ... Jazz rescued him from Philadelphia on Feb. 24, 1994, for Jeff Malone ... All-Star in 1992 ... Was a walk-on at Iowa State ... Born May 3, 1963, in Elmhurst, Ill. ... Made $2.121 million.

Year	Team	G	FG	FG Pct.	FT	FT Pct.	Reb.	Ast.	TP	Avg.
1986-87	Phoenix	80	159	.454	94	.777	184	361	424	5.3
1987-88	Phoenix	82	306	.506	152	.822	262	540	781	9.5
1988-89	Phoenix	78	440	.495	147	.826	266	465	1054	13.5
1989-90	Phoenix	67	483	.536	173	.856	313	337	1179	17.6
1990-91	Phoenix	80	544	.518	201	.897	321	409	1350	16.9
1991-92	Phoenix	81	635	.512	279	.886	407	411	1632	20.1
1992-93	Philadelphia	79	582	.470	250	.865	342	548	1511	19.1
1993-94	Phil.-Utah	80	472	.470	260	.878	279	419	1274	15.9
1994-95	Utah	81	482	.514	284	.882	210	347	1337	16.5
1995-96	Utah	82	442	.502	259	.893	209	340	1247	15.2
	Totals	790	4545	.500	2099	.867	2793	4177	11789	14.9

Karl Malone delivered again . . . and had first triple-double.

BRYON RUSSELL 25 6-7 225   Forward

Came up big in the playoffs last season, especially in the Western Conference finals against Seattle . . . Good timing—that was just before he became a free agent . . . May have earned a new contract with that series alone . . . Otherwise, 1995-96 was a struggle . . . Kind of like walking across the Sahara Desert on your hands and knees with no water to drink is a struggle . . . Shot woeful 39.4 percent and had 23 DNP-CDs . . . Almost cut before injuries to teammates saved his job . . . Second-round pick in 1993 out of Cal State-Long Beach . . . Born Dec. 31, 1970, in San Bernardino, Cal. . . . Made $300,000.

Year	Team	G	FG	FG Pct.	FT	FT Pct.	Reb.	Ast.	TP	Avg.
1993-94	Utah	67	135	.484	62	.614	181	54	334	5.0
1994-95	Utah	63	104	.437	62	.667	141	34	283	4.5
1995-96	Utah	59	56	.394	48	.716	90	29	174	2.9
	Totals	189	295	.448	172	.659	412	117	791	4.2

CHRIS MORRIS 30 6-8 220   Forward-Guard

Surprise 1: Jazz already had Jeff Hornacek and still wanted another shooting guard ... Surprise 2: Jazz wanted Morris ... Notorious for being part of the Nets' wild bunch, and a wild, undisciplined shooter, so not exactly a Utah kind of guy ... Jazz realized the same thing, but pulled the trigger anyway when Morris hit the free-agent market ... Playing in the same division as Clyde Drexler, Jim Jackson and Isaiah Rider, they wanted to be able to match up in the backcourt with bigger, stronger guards ... Eventually moved back to his more natural role at small forward ... Second-team All-Rookie after New Jersey took him with fourth overall pick in 1988, out of Auburn ... Born Jan. 20, 1966, in Atlanta ... Made $2.5 million.

Year	Team	G	FG	FG Pct.	FT	FT Pct.	Reb.	Ast.	TP	Avg.
1988-89	New Jersey	76	414	.457	182	.717	397	119	1074	14.1
1989-90	New Jersey	80	449	.422	228	.722	422	143	1187	14.8
1990-91	New Jersey	79	409	.425	179	.734	521	220	1042	13.2
1991-92	New Jersey	77	346	.477	165	.714	494	197	879	11.4
1992-93	New Jersey	77	436	.481	197	.794	454	106	1086	14.1
1993-94	New Jersey	50	203	.447	85	.720	228	83	544	10.9
1994-95	New Jersey	71	351	.410	142	.728	402	147	950	13.4
1995-96	Utah	66	265	.437	98	.772	229	77	691	10.5
	Totals	576	2873	.443	1276	.736	3147	1092	7453	12.9

GREG OSTERTAG 23 7-0 279   Center

Jazz got what it expected when drafting him: a project ... Sometimes effective, sometimes, uh, a rookie ... Missed 17 contests because of a broken right hand ... Did provide a much-needed inside presence by averaging a team-best 1.11 blocked shots an outing ... Not overwhelming by league standards, but pretty good considering it came while getting just 11.6 minutes a game ... If he develops in that area, he'll be a keeper in Utah ... Top shot-blocker in Big Eight history ... He and Danny Manning are the only Kansas players to ever collect 700 rebounds and 200 blocks ... No. 28 pick in 1995 from there ... Born March 6, 1973, in Dallas ... Made $498,000.

Year	Team	G	FG	FG Pct.	FT	FT Pct.	Reb.	Ast.	TP	Avg.
1995-96	Utah	57	86	.473	36	.667	175	5	208	3.6

ADAM KEEFE 26 6-9 241 Forward

Mostly a power forward during his first two seasons as a pro in Atlanta, he came to a team that had Karl Malone, Antoine Carr and Tom Chambers and started to play a lot of small forward ... That versatility increased his worth ... Always was a very good athlete ... Two-sport star in high school was held in such regard as a volleyball player that many thought he could one day make the national team ... Instead, he went to Stanford and was drafted 10th overall by Hawks in 1992 ... Might as well have been playing volleyball. Never panned out in Atlanta, so he was traded to Utah for Tyrone Corbin and a second-round pick on Sept. 16, 1994 ... By last season, he had become David Benoit's backup at small forward much of the way while also seeing time at his natural spot ... Born Feb. 22, 1970, in Irvine, Cal. ... Made $1.65 million.

Year	Team	G	FG	FG Pct.	FT	FT Pct.	Reb.	Ast.	TP	Avg.
1992-93	Atlanta	82	188	.500	166	.700	432	80	542	6.6
1993-94	Atlanta	63	96	.451	81	.730	201	34	273	4.3
1994-95	Utah	75	172	.577	117	.676	327	30	461	6.1
1995-96	Utah	82	180	.520	139	.692	455	64	499	6.1
	Totals	302	636	.516	503	.697	1415	208	1775	5.9

BROOKS THOMPSON 26 6-4 193 Guard

Came to Jazz last summer from Magic with Kenny Gattison and future first-round pick for Felton Spencer ... Still trying to prove he belongs. Age-old problem: is he a one, is he a two or is he a CBA All-Star? ... Defense not at the top of his strengths list ... Doesn't handle the ball well enough for the point and can't create his shot well enough for the two ... Leave him open, though, and he can kill you ... Career-high 21 points against Detroit March 9 ... Herniated disc didn't help his quest for time ... Rewrote three-point shooting record book at Oklahoma State, where he was first-team All-Big Eight choice as a senior ... Began college at Texas A&M ... Works well on perimeter when post is double-teamed. One problem, though: by the time he got in, Shaq was usually showered and dressed ... A lefty

... Selected No. 27 by Magic in 1994 ... Born July 19, 1970, in Dallas ... Made $825,000.

Year	Team	G	FG	FG Pct.	FT	FT Pct.	Reb.	Ast.	TP	Avg.
1994-95	Orlando	38	45	.395	8	.667	23	43	116	3.1
1995-96	Orlando	33	48	.466	19	.704	24	31	140	4.2
	Totals	71	93	.429	27	.692	47	74	256	3.6

GREG FOSTER 28 6-11 240   Forward-Center

Have size, will travel ... The 73 appearances lats season was a career high for one team ... Played in 78 games in 1994-95, but that was with Chicago and Minnesota ... Jazz signed him as a free agent Oct. 5, 1995, then watched him disappear near the end of the bench ... Not much playing time left at the big spots after Karl Malone, Felton Spencer, Antoine Carr and Greg Ostertag ... Started college career at UCLA, then transferred to Texas-El Paso ... Bullets took him 35th in 1990 ... Born Oct. 3, 1968, in Oakland ... Made $350,000.

Year	Team	G	FG	FG Pct.	FT	FT Pct.	Reb.	Ast.	TP	Avg.
1990-91	Washington	54	97	.460	42	.689	151	37	236	4.4
1991-92	Washington	49	89	.461	35	.714	145	35	213	4.3
1992-93	Wash.-Atl.	43	55	.458	15	.714	83	21	125	2.9
1993-94	Milwaukee	3	4	.571	2	1.000	3	0	10	3.3
1994-95	Chi.-Minn.	78	150	.472	78	.703	259	39	385	4.9
1995-96	Utah	73	107	.439	61	.847	178	25	276	3.8
	Totals	300	502	.459	233	.737	819	157	1245	4.2

ANTOINE CARR 35 6-9 225   Forward-Center

Crowd favorite and not too far down on Jerry Sloan's list, either ... Didn't post impressive numbers, but provided veteran toughness off the bench ... Either that or he went in and leaned on guys—had a team-high 245 fouls while getting 19.2 minutes a game ... Good in the playoffs ... The Big Dawg before the Big Dog hit Milwaukee ... Utah got him as a free agent at the end of training camp in 1994 ... Wichita State product was No. 8 pick overall by Detroit in 1983, but played that next season in Italy . . . Born July 23, 1961, in Oklahoma City . . . Made $2.525 million.

Year	Team	G	FG	FG Pct.	FT	FT Pct.	Reb.	Ast.	TP	Avg.
1984-85	Atlanta	62	198	.528	101	.789	232	80	499	8.0
1985-86	Atlanta	17	49	.527	18	.667	52	14	116	6.8
1986-87	Atlanta	65	134	.506	73	.709	156	34	342	5.3
1987-88	Atlanta	80	281	.544	142	.780	289	103	705	8.8
1988-89	Atlanta	78	226	.480	130	.855	274	91	582	7.5
1989-90	Atl.-Sac.	77	356	.494	237	.795	322	119	949	12.3
1990-91	Sacramento	77	628	.511	295	.758	420	191	1551	20.1
1991-92	San Antonio	81	359	.490	162	.764	346	63	881	10.9
1992-93	San Antonio	71	379	.538	174	.777	388	97	932	13.1
1993-94	San Antonio	34	78	.488	42	.724	51	15	198	5.8
1994-95	Utah	78	290	.531	165	.821	265	67	746	9.6
1995-96	Utah	80	233	.457	114	.792	200	74	580	7.3
	Totals	800	321	.508	1653	.780	2995	948	8081	10.1

HOWARD EISLEY 23 6-2 177   Guard

Jazz can't shake him . . . For that, they were happy in the playoffs . . . Cut at the end of training camp, so he hooked on with Rockford of the CBA . . . Barely got into the season with the Lightning when Utah called again . . . Signed as a free agent Dec. 7, then played in all 65 games the rest of the way . . . From nowhere to everywhere . . . Had some especially nice stretches behind John Stockton in the postseason . . . Boston College product went 30th overall to the Timberwolves in '94 draft . . . Born Dec. 4, 1972, in Detroit.

Year	Team	G	FG	FG Pct.	FT	FT Pct.	Reb.	Ast.	TP	Avg.
1994-95	Minn.-S.A.	49	40	.328	31	.775	48	95	120	2.4
1995-96	Utah	65	104	.430	65	.844	78	146	287	4.4
	Totals	114	144	.396	96	.821	126	241	407	3.6

JAMIE WATSON 24 6-7 190   Forward

So much for that encouraging rookie season in 1994-95 . . . Shooting percentage dropped way down (from 50 to 41.9) . . . The only thing that went up was his medical insurance . . . Played in just 16 games before going on the injured list because of a sprained left ankle and calcium deposits . . . Underwent surgery to remove the deposits and missed the final 66 games . . . Left off the playoff roster . . . At least they didn't make him buy tickets to watch . . . Second-round pick, No. 47 overall, in 1994 out of South Carolina . . . Born Feb. 23, 1972, in Elm City, N.C. . . . Makes an average of $1 million annually.

Year	Team	G	FG	FG Pct.	FT	FT Pct.	Reb.	Ast.	TP	Avg.
1994-95	Utah	60	76	.500	38	.679	74	59	195	3.3
1995-96	Utah	16	18	.419	9	.692	27	24	48	3.0
	Totals	76	94	.482	47	.681	101	83	243	3.2

THE ROOKIE

SHANDON ANDERSON 22 6-6 205   **Forward-Guard**
Brother of Willie Anderson . . . Only player in Georgia history to accumulate 1,500 points, 500 rebounds and 300 assists . . . But just third-team All-Southeastern Conference as a junior and senior . . . Tied for first in conference in steals last season . . . The only pick Utah made for itself. Martin Muursepp was taken at No. 25 and then immediately traded to the Heat . . . Born Dec. 31, 1973, in Atlanta . . . Went 54th.

COACH JERRY SLOAN: You'd win a lot of bets by asking people which coach has the longest active tenure with one team . . . It's Sloan . . . Has been with the Jazz for eight seasons . . . Since taking over 17 games into 1988-89, has won at least 50 games in seven of his eight full seasons . . . Jazz have been in the Western Conference finals in three of those, including 1996 . . . Got all the way to late in the fourth quarter of Game 7 on the road . . . Owns 419-220 record (65.6 percent) with Utah . . . Lifetime: 513-341 (60.1 percent) . . . Assistant coach on Lenny Wilkens' staff for Dream Team III at the 1996 Olympics . . . First three seasons as a head coach were with Chicago, the team he is most identified with as a player . . . The first Bull to have his uniform retired (No. 4) . . . Became a Chicago scout and took over as head coach in '79 . . . Two-time All-Star and six-time member of the All-Defensive team in a career that included Baltimore . . . Came to the NBA after leading Evansville to a pair of Division II titles . . . Intense as a player to the point of maniacal . . . Joined Jazz as a scout, then became an assistant to Frank

Layden in 1984-85 ... Took over for Layden on Dec. 8, 1988 ... Jazz players respect his straight-forward approach ... Born March 14, 1946, in Louisville, Ky.... Grew up in McLeansboro, Ill., and still has a home there.

BIGGEST BLUNDER

This was a team going nowhere fast in the spring of 1982, having just completed a 25-57 season that included an 18-game losing streak near the end. Then came the good news: With the No. 3 pick in the draft, the Jazz took Georgia's Dominique Wilkins.

But before the season began, they traded him to Atlanta for John Drew, Freeman Williams and a bundle of cash. Drew and Williams combined to play 162 games for Utah, while Wilkins took off on a spectacular career with the Hawks.

Imagine what might have been: Wilkins and Karl Malone at forward, Mark Eaton at center, John Stockton at point guard. All were draftees in a four-year span.

ALL-TIME JAZZ LEADERS

SEASON

Points: Karl Malone, 2,540, 1989–90
Assists: John Stockton, 1,164, 1990–91
Rebounds: Len Robinson, 1,288, 1977–78

GAME

Points: Pete Maravich, 68 vs. New York, 2/25/77
Assists: John Stockton, 28 vs. San Antonio, 1/15/91
Rebounds: Len Robinson, 27 vs. Los Angeles, 11/11/77

CAREER

Points: Karl Malone, 23,343, 1985–96
Assists: John Stockton, 11,310, 1984–96
Rebounds: Karl Malone, 9,733, 1985–96

VANCOUVER GRIZZLIES

TEAM DIRECTORY: Chairman: Arthur Griffiths; Pres.-GM: Stu Jackson; Exec. VP: Tod Leiweke; Dir. Scouting: Larry Riley: VP-Pub. Rel./Communications: Tom Mayenknecht; Dir. Media Rel.: Steve Frost; Media Rel. Coordinator: Debby Butt; Head Coach: Brian Winters; Asst. Coaches: Rex Hughes, Lionel Hollins, Jimmy Powell. Arena: General Motors Place (20,004). Colors: Turquoise, bronze and red.

SCOUTING REPORT

SHOOTING: It's not just that they can't shoot, having finished last in scoring during 1995-96, next-to-last in three-point shooting and second-to-last in overall accuracy while breaking 50 percent just nine times.

It's that "as a team, we turn down more good shots than any team I've ever played with," point guard Greg Anthony says. "We work hard to get guys shots, and if you don't take it, now you've got to take a forced shot or you get a turnover." Not that this was much of a surprise. The Grizzlies were an expansion team. They're *supposed* to get everyone else's leftovers.

The good news is that there's plenty of room for improvement. The better news is that Shareef Abdur-Rahim is coming to town. The third pick in the draft arrives as a 19-year-old with just one year of college experience, but a pretty polished game and tons of superstar potential.

If the lottery pick of '95, Bryant Reeves, continues to develop at the rate of his second half of last season, Vancouver will have two big men capable of working from the post or stepping out for medium-range jumpers. Put them on opposite sides and suddenly defenses have a problem.

Now to do something about the backcourt. The starters there, Anthony and Blue Edwards, went 41.5 and 41.9 percent, respectively. Key backup Byron Scott, since released, was 40.1. Getting Anthony Peeler from the Lakers may help.

PLAYMAKING: By selecting Abdur-Rahim, the Grizzlies passed on Stephon Marbury. No doubt aware that point guards of his caliber don't come along by the dozen, this indicated a level of satisfaction with Anthony. Shooting accuracy aside, it's a fair assessment.

Anthony finished 13th in the league in assists despite playing

Grizzlies hope Cal rookie Shareef Abdur-Rahim can do it.

GRIZZLIES ROSTER

No.	Veterans	Pos.	Ht.	Wt.	Age	Yrs. Pro	College
2	Greg Anthony	G	6-1	176	28	5	UNLV
—	Tim Breaux	F	6-7	215	26	2	Wyoming
—	Pete Chilcutt	F	6-11	235	28	5	North Carolina
30	Blue Edwards	G	6-4	229	31	7	East Carolina
32	Doug Edwards	F	6-7	235	25	3	Florida State
—	George Lynch	F	6-8	223	26	3	North Carolina
15	Rich Manning	C	6-11	260	26	1	Washington
—	Lee Mayberry	G	6-2	175	26	4	Arkansas
52	Eric Mobley	C	6-11	257	26	2	Pittsburgh
7	Lawrence Moten	G	6-5	185	24	1	Syracuse
—	Anthony Peeler	G	6-4	212	26	4	Missouri
50	Bryant Reeves	C	7-0	280	23	1	Oklahoma State

Rd.	Rookies	Sel.No.	Pos.	Ht.	Wt.	College
1	Shareef Abdur-Rahim	3	F	6-10	220	California
1	Roy Rogers	22	F	6-10	238	Alabama
2	Chris Robinson	51	G	6-5	205	Western Kentucky

for a team that only looks like it's shooting with a bowling ball. They're in even better shape if Peeler can contribute, giving Vancouver better depth at point guard than some long-established teams.

REBOUNDING: So how 'bout that seafood around town? Hey, nice arena. People sure are nice in Canada.

Keep the conversation on anything but rebounding and the Grizzlies are happy, perhaps because they looked like a team that would prefer anything but rebounding. They finished last by percentage. Suddenly, though, size is everywhere: Reeves at 7-0, Abdur-Rahim at 6-11 and the late first-rounder, Roy Rogers, at 6-10. Reeves' 7.4 boards a game in 1995-96 is somewhat misleading because that jumped to 8.5 in the 63 outings after he moved into the starting lineup, a decent start to a career but still in need of improvement.

DEFENSE: The Grizzlies forced the second-most turnovers in the league last season. Seriously. Only Seattle was better, so maybe it's a Pacific Northwest thing. Or maybe it had something to do with Eric Murdock, since released, getting one steal every

Bryant Reeves is expected to sustain late-season surge.

11.5 minutes, the best average in the NBA, and finishing seventh overall.

That helped cut down on shots for opponents, which is important for a defense that was otherwise pourous in allowing the opposition to make 47.5 percent of its attempts. The end result was surrendering an encouraging 99.8 points a game, the second-best mark for an expansion team ever, a number that should improve in 1996-97 with the new size imports, Rogers in particular. He's very raw and has limited offensive moves beyond a jump hook, but could make an immediate impact as a shot-blocker.

OUTLOOK: Everything is pointing up, which is about all any team can hope for heading into its second season. They still have the same coach, Brian Winters, unlike the other newcomer across the country. They got production from the first draft (Reeves) and by all indications did very well the second time around (Abdur-Rahim and Rogers). Even with another last-place finish in the Midwest Division, still the likely ending, the Grizzlies could have reason to feel good about the new season.

GRIZZLIES PROFILES

BRYANT REEVES 23 7-0 280 — Center

Big Foreign Country ... Made nice improvements as rookie season went on, especially after Grizzlies committed all the minutes to him by trading Benoit Benjamin ... Averaged just 13.1 minutes the first 14 games before the deal, but finished at 31.9 ... The 2,460 minutes in all was exactly the same number he played in his final two years at Oklahoma State. Scores from the perimeter ... Good hands ... First draft pick in franchise history, No. 6 overall ... Born June 8, 1973, in Fort Smith, Ark. ... Made $1.474 million.

Year	Team	G	FG	FG Pct.	FT	FT Pct.	Reb.	Ast.	TP	Avg.
1996-96	Vancouver	77	401	.457	219	.732	570	109	1021	13.3

GREG ANTHONY 28 6-1 176 — Guard

Good expansion pickup: a young player with decent talent ... Finished 13th in the league in assists ... Not bad for a guy surrounded by teammates who can't shoot ... After starting 74 times in his first four seasons as a pro, all with the Knicks, he was in the opening lineup 69 times in 1995-96 ... Set single-season bests in most categories, including points, assists and minutes ... Received one vote for Most Improved Player ... Shooting remains a problem ... Just 35.8 percent the final two months of the season ... No. 12 pick by New York in 1991 ... Born Nov. 5, 1967, in Las Vegas and stayed home to star at UNLV ... Made $1.673 million.

Year	Team	G	FG	FG Pct.	FT	FT Pct.	Reb.	Ast.	TP	Avg.
1991-92	New York	82	161	.370	117	.741	136	314	447	5.5
1992-93	New York	70	174	.415	107	.673	170	398	459	6.6
1993-94	New York	80	225	.394	130	.774	189	365	628	7.9
1994-95	New York	61	128	.437	60	.789	64	160	372	6.1
1995-96	Vancouver	69	324	.415	229	.771	174	476	967	14.0
	Totals	362	1012	.405	643	.749	733	1713	2873	7.9

THEODORE (BLUE) EDWARDS 31 6-4 229   G-F

Expansion pickup provided scoring punch . . . Led Grizzlies in total points and minutes . . . Started every game . . . Hit team's first three-pointer ever . . . Well-traveled swingman . . . Usually pretty accurate, but shooting has dropped the last five consecutive seasons since the 52.6 percent of 1990-91 . . . That wasn't a problem when it was 52.2, then 51.2 and even 47.8 . . . At 41.9 in 1995-96, that's a problem . . . Originally picked 21st in 1988 by Utah, out of East Carolina . . . Nicknamed "Blue" by an older sister who found him choking on his bottle in the crib . . . Born Oct. 31, 1965, in Washington, D.C. . . . Made $1.9 million.

Year	Team	G	FG	FG Pct.	FT	FT Pct.	Reb.	Ast.	TP	Avg.
1989-90	Utah	82	286	.507	146	.719	251	145	727	8.9
1990-91	Utah	62	244	.526	82	.701	201	108	576	9.3
1991-92	Utah	81	433	.522	113	.774	298	137	1018	12.6
1992-93	Milwaukee.......	82	554	.512	237	.790	382	214	1382	16.9
1993-94	Milwaukee.......	82	382	.478	151	.799	329	171	953	11.6
1994-95	Bos.-Utah	67	181	.461	75	.833	130	77	459	6.9
1995-96	Vancouver.......	82	401	.419	157	.755	346	212	1043	12.7
	Totals	538	2481	.487	961	.767	1937	1064	6158	11.4

GEORGE LYNCH 26 6-7 223   Forward

What the Lakers always expected, even though they picked him 12th in 1993. A usually solid player off the bench . . . Two inches bigger and he could be a real factor on the boards . . . Great work ethic inside, but just doesn't have the size to clear everyone out of his way . . . Came to Grizzlies from Lakers with Anthony Peeler for 1998 and '99 second-rounders . . . Played well at power forward when the Lakers went with a small lineup . . . Struggles with his shot, even medium-range jumpers small forwards should be able to hit . . . Won an NCAA championship with North Carolina in 1993 . . . Born Sept. 3, 1970, in Roanoke, Va. . . . Made $1.76 million.

Year	Team	G	FG	FG Pct.	FT	FT Pct.	Reb.	Ast.	TP	Avg.
1993-94	L.A. Lakers	71	291	.508	99	.596	410	96	681	9.6
1994-95	L.A. Lakers	56	138	.468	62	.721	184	62	341	6.1
1995-96	L.A. Lakers	76	117	.430	53	.663	209	51	291	3.8
	Totals	203	546	.479	214	.645	803	209	1313	6.5

PETE CHILCUTT 28 6-11 235   Forward

Came to Rockets as a free agent early in 1994-95, then became starting power forward, if only by default, during much of those playoffs for the eventual champions . . . That earned him a four-year deal heading into last season . . . He repaid them by becoming one of the most disappointing players on the team . . . Rockets repaid him by shipping him to an expansion team, Vancouver, after last season along with Tim Breaux for draft picks . . . Maybe too much was expected. After all, he hadn't done anything the first four years as a pro after being picked 17th in the 1991 draft by Sacramento . . . College teammate of Rick Fox, Hubert Davis, J.R. Reid and Scott Williams at North Carolina . . . Born Sept. 14, 1968, in Sumter, S.C. . . . Makes an average of $700,000 per on his deal.

Year	Team	G	FG	FG Pct.	FT	FT Pct.	Reb.	Ast.	TP	Avg.
1991-92	Sacramento	69	113	.452	23	.821	187	38	251	3.5
1992-93	Sacramento	59	165	.485	32	696	194	84	362	6.2
1993-94	Sac.-Det.	76	203	.453	41	.631	371	86	450	5.9
1994-95	Houston	68	146	.445	31	.738	317	66	358	5.3
1995-96	Houston	74	73	.408	17	.654	156	26	200	2.7
	Totals	346	700	.453	144	.696	1225	280	1621	4.7

TIM BREAUX 26 6-7 215   Guard-Forward

Once an inspiration to many dreamers, he now just tries to hang on . . . Grizzlies got him in an offseason deal along with Pete Chilcutt and a first-round pick as multiple second-rounders went to Houston in exchange . . . Rockets got him out of nowhere . . . They stumbled on to him in a pro-am league in town, then gave him a try in a real summer league . . . Work there earned him an invitation to training camp. That became a roster spot for the regular season, then a championship ring . . . Needs to either start defending like Dennis Rodman or learn to shoot better . . . Showed good range in four seasons at Wyoming . . . Undrafted . . . Born Sept. 19, 1970, in Baton Rouge, La. . . . Made $225,000.

Year	Team	G	FG	FG Pct.	FT	FT Pct.	Reb.	Ast.	TP	Avg.
1994-95	Houston	42	45	.372	32	.653	34	15	128	3.0
1995-96	Houston	54	59	.366	28	.622	60	24	161	3.0
	Totals	96	104	.369	60	.638	94	39	289	3.0

ANTHONY PEELER 26 6-4 212   Guard

Traded to Grizzlies by Lakers with George Lynch for 1998 and '99 second-rounders... Known for scoring off the bench... Was a Jerry West favorite... An open-court player when he came out of Missouri as the No. 15 pick in 1992, he has developed into a three-point shooter that defenses must respect... His 41.3 percent from behind the arc easily led the team and was 19th in the league... He and Byron Scott are the only Lakers ever to break 40... At his best down the stretch before a strained right hamstring hampered him for the playoffs ... Big Eight Player of the Year in 1991-92... Born Nov. 25, 1969, in Kansas City, Mo.... Made $1.33 million.

Year	Team	G	FG	FG Pct.	FT	FT Pct.	Reb.	Ast.	TP	Avg.
1992-93	L.A. Lakers	77	297	.468	162	.786	179	166	802	10.4
1993-94	L.A. Lakers	30	176	.430	57	.803	109	94	423	14.1
1994-95	L.A. Lakers	73	285	.432	102	.797	168	122	756	10.4
1995-96	L.A. Lakers	73	272	.452	61	.709	137	118	710	9.7
	Totals	253	1030	.447	382	.778	593	500	2691	10.6

DOUG EDWARDS 25 6-7 235   Forward

Former first-round bust gets another chance... Hawks took him 15th in 1993, then left him unprotected in the expansion draft... Vancouver got him there... Turned in his best game as a pro on Feb. 16 vs. Atlanta—11 points and seven rebounds, both career highs... Came off the bench in all 31 appearances... But played more minutes the second half of last season, when Chris King began to struggle... Didn't even make his Grizzlies debut until Dec. 15, having missed all of preseason and the first 21 games of the regular season because of shin splints ... Born Jan. 21, 1971, in Miami... Standout at Florida State... Made $1.04 million.

Year	Team	G	FG	FG Pct.	FT	FT Pct.	Reb.	Ast.	TP	Avg.
1993-94	Atlanta	16	17	.347	9	.563	18	8	43	2.7
1994-95	Atlanta	38	22	.458	23	.719	48	13	67	1.8
1995-96	Vancouver	31	32	.352	29	.763	87	39	93	3.0
	Totals	85	71	.378	61	.709	153	60	203	2.4

LAWRENCE MOTEN 24 6-5 185   Guard

Led Grizzlies in points per minute last season ... So impressed were coaches that they played him 13 minutes a game, the second-fewest on the team ... And that was with him getting 19.9 in April, when the staff was getting a last evaluation before the end of the season and start of his free-agency ... Made 10 of his appearances the opening month, then just 34 the rest of the way ... Signed a one-year contract as a second-round pick, No. 36 overall, in summer of '95 ... Career scoring leader by the time he left Syracuse, ahead of Derrick Coleman and Sherman Douglas ... Not only that, but No. 1 in Big East history ... Born March 25, 1972, in Washington, D.C. ... Made $280,000.

Year	Team	G	FG	FG Pct.	FT	FT Pct.	Reb.	Ast.	TP	Avg.
1995-96	Vancouver.......	44	112	.453	49	.653	61	50	291	6.6

LEE MAYBERRY 26 6-1 175   Guard

May be too low-key to run a team ... But Grizzlies think otherwise and signed him as a Milwaukee free agent last summer ... Rarely makes mistakes (he had an excellent assist-turnover ratio of 3.39), but doesn't create ... Not as good a defender as advertised, but a better shooter (.388 on three-pointers for career) ... Solid, durable, reliable ... Hasn't missed a game in NBA, college or high-school career ... Holds Bucks' record with 328 straight games played ... Started 50 games two years ago; that dropped to 20 last year as Sherman Douglas took over ... Drafted 23rd out of Arkansas in 1992 ... His sister is married to Hogs' assistant Nolan Richardson III ... Earned $965,000 last year ... Born June 12, 1970, in Tulsa, Okla.

Year	Team	G	FG	FG Pct.	FT	FT Pct.	Reb.	Ast.	TP	Avg.
1992-93	Milwaukee.......	82	171	.456	39	.574	118	273	424	5.2
1993-94	Milwaukee.......	82	167	.415	58	.690	101	215	433	5.3
1994-95	Milwaukee.......	82	172	.422	58	.699	82	276	474	5.8
1995-96	Milwaukee.......	82	153	.420	41	.603	90	302	422	5.1
	Totals	328	663	.428	196	.647	391	1066	1753	5.3

RICHARD MANNING 26 6-11 260   Center

Two things keep the NBA interested: he can shoot and he can be tall . . . Hard worker, too . . . Two things keep the NBA barely interested: he's not strong enough and he doesn't have good enough footwork . . . Originally drafted 40th overall by the Hawks in 1993 . . . Vancouver signed Washington product as a free agent after he spent the previous two seasons in the CBA . . . Opened on the injured list, but at least it was an NBA injured list . . . Cut before the end of the first month, but preferred to stay in British Columbia and work out on his own rather than return to the minors . . . Grizzlies then re-signed him on Jan. 12 . . . Born June 23, 1970, in Tacoma, Wash. . . . Made $225,000.

Year	Team	G	FG	FG Pct.	FT	FT Pct.	Reb.	Ast.	TP	Avg.
1995-96	Vancouver.......	29	49	.434	9	.643	55	7	107	3.7

ERIC MOBLEY 26 6-11 257   Center

Hey, at least he's not Benoit Benjamin . . . Backup center arrived at the end of the first month of 1995-96 along with Eric Murdock from the Bucks in exchange for Benjamin . . . Milwaukee was probably saying, hey, at least he's not Eric Mobley . . . Didn't impress Bucks much in the one-plus season since he was the No. 18 pick in the 1994 draft . . . His 53.6 percent from the field was the best on the Grizzlies, although he didn't meet the qualifying minimum to rank among the league leaders . . . One start . . . Heading into the last year on his contract . . . Attended Pittsburgh . . . Born Feb. 1, 1970, in the Bronx, N.Y. . . . Made $1.328 million.

Year	Team	G	FG	FG Pct.	FT	FT Pct.	Reb.	Ast.	TP	Avg.
1994-95	Milwaukee.......	46	78	.591	22	.489	153	21	180	3.9
1995-96	Mil.-Van........	39	74	.536	39	.448	140	22	188	4.8
	Totals	85	152	.563	61	.462	293	43	368	4.3

THE ROOKIES

SHAREEF ABDUR-RAHIM 19 6-10 220   Forward
He's in the draft. He's out. He's back in . . . Grizzlies thrilled he didn't change his mind again and return to Cal for sophomore season . . . More size for a frontline that already includes Bryant Reeves . . . Star potential at the No. 3 pick . . . First freshman to ever be named Player of the Year in the Pac-10 Conference . . . Jason Kidd is the only other Golden Bear to win the award . . . Julius Shareef Abdur-Rahim was born Dec. 11, 1976, in Marietta, Ga.

ROY ROGERS 23 6-10 238   Center-Forward
With good knees, he goes a lot higher . . . May still have been a steal at No. 22 . . . Raw, with only one offensive move, a jump hook . . . The upside: a shot-blocker . . . Hard worker . . . Played on same frontline as a junior at Alabama with a pair of 1995 first-rounders, Antonio McDyess and Jason Caffey . . . Born Aug. 19, 1963, in Linden, Ala.

CHRIS ROBINSON 22 6-5 205   Guard-Forward
Sun Belt Conference Player of the Year went 51st . . . All-Conference his final three years at Western Kentucky . . . Pretty good shooter . . . Some scouts wonder about his desire . . . Born April 2, 1974, in Columbus, Ga.

COACH BRIAN WINTERS: It's OK to feel sorry for him . . .

But also give him his due . . . Grizzlies couldn't score, but played hard all the time . . . That's why they forced the fifth-most steals in the league last season and why opponents averaged less than 100 points a game . . . Also did a good job of keeping spirits alive during long losing streaks . . . The enthusiasm was expected—this was his first stint as a head coach at any level . . . Had spent the previous nine years as an assistant to Lenny Wilkens, seven with the Cavaliers and the most recent two with the Hawks . . . That was after two years on the bench at Princeton . . . Nine-year playing career included trips to the All-

Star Game in 1976 and '78, representing the Bucks in both . . . Joined the NBA as a first-round pick, No. 12 overall, by the Lakers in 1974 and was named to the All-Rookie team . . . After one season there, was sent to Milwaukee as part of the trade for Kareem Abdul-Jabbar, arguably the biggest deal in league history . . . Averaged 16.2 points in eight years with the Bucks . . . They eventually retired his uniform No. 32 . . . College star at South Carolina . . . Queens, N.Y., native played high-school ball at Archbishop Molloy, which also produced Kenny Smith, Kenny Anderson and Stephon Marbury . . . Born March 1, 1952, in Rockaway, N.Y.

Away from Knicks, Greg Anthony experienced expansion.

BIGGEST BLUNDER

Truth is, there's really nothing to rip these guys for after just one season of operation. Unlike expansion partner Toronto, they didn't fire their coach. Their lottery pick, Bryant Reeves, labored at the start but had a second half full of promise. Heck, the Grizzlies even got rid of Benoit Benjamin before he could become a veteran influence on the young players.

But since the rules say everyone gets dinged for something, the Grizzlies get theirs for taking Gerald Wilkins in the expansion draft and then expecting him to carry a bulk of the offensive load. That would be the same Gerald Wilkins who had been decimated by injuries the previous two seasons.

So what happens? It took him all the way until training camp to suffer a serious back injury. Wilkins played just 28 games last season, 14 in his projected role as starter, and shot 37.6 percent.

ALL-TIME GRIZZLIES LEADERS

SEASON

Points: Blue Edwards, 1,043, 1995–96
Assists: Greg Anthony, 476, 1995–96
Rebounds: Blue Edwards, 570, 1995–96

GAME

Points: Greg Anthony, 32 vs. Philadelphia, 1/5/96
Assists: Greg Anthony, 15 vs. L.A Clippers, 1/7/96
Rebounds: Bryant Reeves, 18 vs. Orlando, 3/15/96

CAREER

Points: Blue Edwards, 1,043, 1995–96
Assists: Greg Anthony, 476, 1995–96
Rebounds: Blue Edwards, 570, 1995–96

GOLDEN STATE WARRIORS

TEAM DIRECTORY: Owner: Christopher Cohan; GM: Dave Twardzik; VP/Asst. GM: Al Attles; Dir. Player Personnel: Ed Gregory; Dir. Media Rel.: Julie Marvel; Head Coach: Rick Adelman; Asst. Coaches: Rod Higgins, George Irvine, John Wetzel. Arena: San Jose Arena (18,500). Colors: Gold and blue.

SCOUTING REPORT

SHOOTING: They do a fine job of generating enough shots. Making them, that's the problem, the Warriors having dropped all the way to 22nd in the league last season in accuracy. Encouragement comes in Joe Smith's 45.8 percent during his rookie campaign, and it's logical to expect improvement. Latrell Sprew-

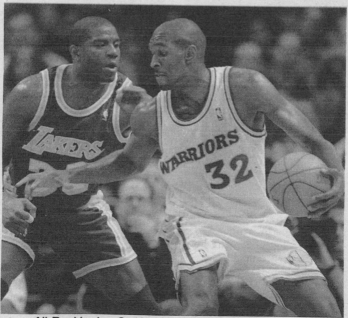

All-Rookie Joe Smith drives against Magic Johnson.

ell, on the other hand, seems stuck at sub-43 percent, troublesome for the Warriors since he got more shots than any other player and shows no sign of getting back anywhere close to the 46.4 of his first year.

It helps that they improved so much at the line, little things that make a big difference. Big enough to probably push them into a triple-digit scoring average, at 101.6. The specific payoff from going from the third-worst team in the league in 1994-95 to the eighth-best last season was about two points a game, one reason the Warriors, 10 games below .500 in all, went 8-6 in those decided by three points or less.

Why the turnaround at the line? They added B.J. Armstrong and had Chris Mullin for 55 games (30 more than the year before) while losing free-throw liabilities like Carlos Rogers, Victor Alexander and Tom Gugliotta. Now to just extend the improvement to when defenders are running at them.

PLAYMAKING: Armstrong is, as he always has been, a shooter who happens to play point guard. It's great that he finished fourth in the league in three-point accuracy in his first season as a Warrior. Not so great is that he averaged just 4.9 assists, a number that became all the more glaring after Tim Hardaway was traded to Miami. That's one reason Mark Price was signed as a Bullet free agent.

In the end, the Warriors were 13th in the NBA in assists per game. Not bad. But they were also 19th in turnovers. Bad. So a new rule: Rony Seikaly (with an assist-to-turnover ratio of 1-2.5) doesn't get to touch the ball unless it's to shoot or rebound. Smith, at 1-1.7, also does his part, but we'll cut him some slack for now because of age. But consider yourself on warning, Joe.

REBOUNDING: The problem of old has become a strength of the present. Sort of. The Warriors were No. 5 in the league by percentage on the offensive boards . . . and No. 24 on the defensive end. That was worth No. 12 overall.

For only the second time in the last 14 seasons, they outrebounded the opposition, and that was after losing the battle of the boards in each of the first 11 games. From there: 42-29. Another boost came not long after, when the first-round draft pick was spent on Todd Fuller, a 6-11, 255-pounder from North Carolina State.

WARRIOR ROSTER

No.	Veterans	Pos.	Ht.	Wt.	Age	Yrs. Pro	College
11	B.J. Armstrong	G	6-2	185	29	7	Iowa
F-21	Robert Churchwell	G-F	6-7	195	24	1	Georgetown
12	Bimbo Coles	G	6-2	186	28	6	Virginia Tech
55	Andrew DeClercq	F	6-10	230	23	1	Florida
F-43	Geert Hammink	C	7-0	262	27	3	LSU
3	Donyell Marshall	F	6-9	218	23	2	Connecticut
17	Chris Mullin	F	6-7	215	23	11	St. John's
—	Mark Price	G	6-0	180	32	10	Georgia Tech
44	Clifford Rozier	C-F	6-11	255	24	2	Louisville
4	Rony Seikaly	C	6-11	253	31	8	Syracuse
32	Joe Smith	F	6-10	225	21	1	Maryland
15	Latrell Sprewell	G	6-5	190	26	4	Alabama

F-Free agent

Rd.	Rookies	Sel.No.	Pos.	Ht.	Wt.	College
1	Todd Fuller	11	C	6-11	255	North Carolina State
2	Marcus Mann	40	F	6-8	245	Miss. Valley State

DEFENSE: They were 22nd in points allowed during 1995-96. Of course, that's cause for celebration around these parts—the team before allowed eight points more a game, 111.1. The 103.1 was the lowest for the Warriors in 20 seasons.

It's not impressive compared to everyone else, but it's a start. To make another jump, they need to get some of those defensive boards, which will then deny the opposition chances at second-chance baskets, especially the easy ones that come directly from the rebound.

OUTLOOK: They're heading in the right direction under Rick Adelman. It's just that the road is so long—they improved by 10 games last season and still finished next-to-last in the Pacific Division. Another 10-game jump gets them into the playoffs, but probably not a home-court edge in the first round.

Time is still on their side, though. The two best players, Sprewell and Smith, are 26 and 21, respectively. Another starter, Armstrong, is 29. And Fuller may move into the opening lineup at center.

WARRIOR PROFILES

LATRELL SPREWELL 26 6-5 190   Guard

Stock has dropped around the league after much-publicized past disputes with Tim Hardaway and Don Nelson, but he remains integral for the Warriors... Played the 10th-most minutes in the league last season by average, at 39.3... Led team in scoring for third straight season... At his best during playoff drive of March... Continues to struggle with his shot... Headed into the summer as a free agent and bound for a big raise after making $975,000 last season... Became a team captain, along with Chris Mullin, after Hardaway was traded to Miami... An indication from the Warriors they were committed to having him around long term?... Golden State used the No. 24 pick to get him from Alabama in 1992... Born Sept. 8, 1970, in Milwaukee.

Year	Team	G	FG	FG Pct.	FT	FT Pct.	Reb.	Ast.	TP	Avg.
1992-93	Golden State	77	449	.464	211	.746	271	295	1182	15.4
1993-94	Golden State	82	613	.433	353	.774	401	385	1720	21.0
1994-95	Golden State	69	490	.418	350	.781	256	279	1420	20.6
1995-96	Golden State	78	515	.428	352	.789	380	328	1473	18.9
	Totals	306	2067	.434	1266	.775	1308	1287	5795	18.9

JOE SMITH 21 6-10 225   Forward

No. 1 pick last year and worth it... "He's a guy you want to focus your team around," Chris Mullin says... Don't worry, they will ... Led all first-year players in rebounds and blocks, tied for first in games and third in scoring... The only rookie and the only Warrior to start all 82... Very sharp. Only needs to be told something once and then it's learned... Should just be entering his senior season at Maryland... Needs to bulk up, but that should come with time... Can hit jump hooks with either hand... Just as impressive, he already has a great court presence... His 14 offensive rebounds Feb. 5 were the most in the league since Dennis Rodman had 18 in overtime

March 4, 1992 . . . Played in the Rookie All-Star Game . . . Born July 26, 1975, in Norfolk, Va. . . . Made $2.473 million.

Year	Team	G	FG	FG Pct.	FT	FT Pct.	Reb.	Ast.	TP	Avg.
1995-96	Golden State	82	469	.458	303	.773	717	79	1251	15.3

RONY SEIKALY 31 6-11 253   Center

Doesn't want to be here . . . But since he was, he averaged 7.8 rebounds in just 28.3 minutes, a decent ratio . . . Would be at 9.7 with the 35 minutes a game some starting centers get . . . Missed the final 15 games because of a torn tendon in his left thumb . . . Underwent surgery March 26 . . . Good shooter, within range . . . Was never under 50 percent from the field after the first week of last season . . . Warriors got him from Miami just before the start of 1994-95 regular season for Billy Owens and the rights to Predrag Danilovic . . . Not a bad trade considering Owens didn't last two seasons with the Heat . . . Born May 10, 1965, in Beirut, Lebanon . . . No. 9 pick by Miami in 1988 after standout career at Syracuse . . . Made $3.532 million.

Year	Team	G	FG	FG Pct.	FT	FT Pct.	Reb.	Ast.	TP	Avg.
1988-89	Miami	78	333	.448	181	.511	549	55	848	10.9
1989-90	Miami	74	486	.502	256	.594	766	78	1228	16.6
1990-91	Miami	64	395	.481	258	.619	709	95	1050	16.4
1991-92	Miami	79	463	.489	370	.733	934	109	1296	16.4
1992-93	Miami	72	417	.480	397	.735	846	100	1232	17.1
1993-94	Miami	72	392	.488	304	.720	740	136	1088	15.1
1994-95	Golden State	36	162	.516	111	.694	266	45	435	12.1
1995-96	Golden State	64	285	.502	204	.723	499	71	776	12.1
	Totals	539	2933	.486	2081	.669	5309	689	7953	14.8

CHRIS MULLIN 33 6-7 215   Forward

Has had so many injuries, they're starting to repeat . . . Suffered torn ligament in his right pinky on March 3 when his hand got caught in Anthony Mason's jersey . . . Missed the final 24 games of the season—the same injury that kept him out the first 20 contests of 1993-94 . . . Before that, had missed only three games, his first season of sustained health since 1991-92 . . . Through it all, remains a valuable weapon as arguably the best outside shooter on the team . . . Isn't asking out of the Bay

Area, but wouldn't mind a trade to a title contender ... Trails only Nate Thurmond on the all-time franchise list for minutes ... A Warrior his entire career since being picked No. 7 out of St. John's in 1985 ... Born July 30, 1963, in Brooklyn, N.Y. ... Is making an average of $2.84 million annually on current contract.

Year	Team	G	FG	FG Pct.	FT	FT Pct.	Reb.	Ast.	TP	Avg.
1985-86	Golden State	55	287	.463	189	.896	115	105	768	14.0
1986-87	Golden State	82	477	.514	269	.825	181	261	1242	15.1
1987-88	Golden State	60	470	.508	239	.885	205	290	1213	20.2
1988-89	Golden State	82	830	.509	493	.892	483	415	2176	26.5
1989-90	Golden State	78	682	.536	505	.889	463	319	1956	25.1
1990-91	Golden State	82	777	.536	513	.884	443	329	2107	25.7
1991-92	Golden State	81	830	.524	350	.833	450	286	2074	25.6
1992-93	Golden State	46	474	.510	183	.810	232	166	1191	25.9
1993-94	Golden State	62	410	.472	165	.753	345	315	1040	16.8
1994-95	Golden State	25	170	.489	94	.879	115	125	476	19.0
1995-96	Golden State	55	269	.499	137	.856	159	194	734	13.3
	Totals	708	5676	.512	3137	.862	3191	2805	14977	21.2

B.J. ARMSTRONG 29 6-2 185   Guard

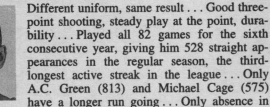

Different uniform, same result ... Good three-point shooting, steady play at the point, durability ... Played all 82 games for the sixth consecutive year, giving him 528 straight appearances in the regular season, the third-longest active streak in the league ... Only A.C. Green (813) and Michael Cage (575) have a longer run going ... Only absence in entire career from the box score was Feb. 7, 1990, when he did not play on a coach's decision as a rookie ... Finished fourth in three-point shooting ... Started each of the final 63 games ... Warriors got him from Toronto in a six-player deal on Sept. 18, 1995 ... Bulls made Iowa product No. 18 pick in 1989 ... Born Sept. 9, 1967, in Detroit ... Made $2.4 million.

Year	Team	G	FG	FG Pct.	FT	FT Pct.	Reb.	Ast.	TP	Avg.
1989-90	Chicago	81	190	.485	69	.885	102	199	452	5.6
1990-91	Chicago	82	304	.481	97	.874	149	301	720	8.8
1991-92	Chicago	82	335	.481	104	.806	145	266	809	9.9
1992-93	Chicago	82	408	.499	130	.861	149	330	1009	12.3
1993-94	Chicago	82	479	.476	194	.855	170	323	1212	14.8
1994-95	Chicago	82	418	.468	206	.884	186	244	1150	14.0
1995-96	Golden State	82	340	.468	234	.839	184	401	1012	12.3
	Totals	573	2474	.479	1034	.856	1085	2064	6364	11.1

North Carolina State's Todd Fuller: No. 11, Warriors.

DONYELL MARSHALL 23 6-9 218   Forward

It's make-or-break time . . . Work ethic still in question . . . That and almost everything else . . . Lottery pick of 1995 managed just 15.1 minutes a game in his second season . . . Continues to struggle to find his shot . . . And his toughness . . . Dueling bad moves: Minnesota used the No. 4 pick to get him in 1994 draft. By midseason of that rookie season, Golden State traded talented Tom Gugliotta to the Timberwolves to get him . . . Born May 18, 1973, in Reading, Pa. . . . Left Connecticut after junior season ... Great uncle is football Hall of Famer Lenny Moore ... Made $2.73 million.

Year	Team	G	FG	FG Pct.	FT	FT Pct.	Reb.	Ast.	TP	Avg.
1994-95	Minn.-G.S.	72	345	.394	147	.662	405	105	906	12.6
1995-96	Golden State	62	125	.398	64	.771	213	49	342	5.5
	Totals	134	470	.395	211	.692	618	154	1248	9.3

BIMBO COLES 28 6-2 186   Guard

The starter in Miami became the reserve in Golden State ... Warriors got him Feb. 22, 1996, along with Kevin Willis for Tim Hardaway and Chris Gatling ... In the opening lineup all 52 appearances with the Heat ... Just three times in 29 games with the new team ... Played behind B.J. Armstrong ... Was averaging 12.8 points with Miami, on pace for a career high ... Ended at 11.0 overall after contributing 7.9 a game as a Warrior ... Did make steady improvement in the months after the trade ... Sacramento picked him 40th in the 1990 draft, then quickly traded the Virginia Tech standout to Miami ... Played on the 1988 Olympic team ... Born April 22, 1968, in Covington, Va. ... Made $1.002 million.

Year	Team	G	FG	FG Pct.	FT	FT Pct.	Reb.	Ast.	TP	Avg.
1990-91	Miami	82	162	.412	71	.747	153	232	401	4.9
1991-92	Miami	81	295	.455	216	.824	189	366	816	10.1
1992-93	Miami	81	318	.464	177	.805	166	373	855	10.6
1993-94	Miami	76	233	.449	102	.779	159	263	588	7.7
1994-95	Miami	68	261	.430	141	.810	191	416	679	10.0
1995-96	Mia.-G.S.	81	318	.409	168	.796	260	422	8929	11.0
	Totals	469	1587	.437	875	.801	1118	2072	4231	9.0

CLIFFORD ROZIER 24 6-11 255   Center-Forward

Longs for the good old days ... The year before, for example ... Went from getting 22.6 minutes as a rookie out of Louisville to just 12.3 minutes in 1995-96 as a second-year player ... Did lead the Warriors in shooting, at 58.5 percent, although that was with just 135 attempts ... Still an encouraging sign considering it was a jump from the 48.5 percent of the season before ... Also increased from 44.7 percent to 47.3 at the line, a step up from real brutal to brutal ... No. 16 pick in

1994 ... Born Oct. 31, 1972, in Bradenton, Fla. ... Made $845,000.

Year	Team	G	FG	FG Pct.	FT	FT Pct.	Reb.	Ast.	TP	Avg.
1994-95	Golden State	66	189	.485	68	.447	486	45	448	6.8
1995-96	Golden State	59	79	.585	26	.473	171	22	184	3.1
	Totals	125	268	.510	94	.454	657	67	632	5.1

ANDREW DeCLERCQ 23 6-10 230   Forward

Runs the floor and rebounds ... In practice ... Games, forget it ... Averaged only 9.2 minutes as a rookie, the fewest of anybody on the team all season ... And that was with getting a "long" look at the end, with 18.3 minutes and even one start in the final seven games ... Warriors love his hustle, work ethic and willingness to do the dirty work ... That was his reputation when they used the 34th pick to get him out of Florida last year ... Set a school record by starting all 128 games during his four-year career ... Born Feb. 1, 1973, in Detroit ... Made $230,000.

Year	Team	G	FG	FG Pct.	FT	FT Pct.	Reb.	Ast.	TP	Avg.
1995-96	Golden State	22	24	.480	11	.579	39	9	59	2.7

ROBERT CHURCHWELL 24 6-7 195   Guard-Forward

Lanky swingman came in on a 10-day contract March 14 and earned a spot for the rest of the season ... He got NBA experience, the Warriors got a practice player ... Totaled just 20 minutes of action ... Started last season with the Chicago Rockers of the CBA ... Ninth in that league in free-throw shooting when Golden State called ... Georgetown standout set a Big East record by starting all 128 games of his college career ... Ranked second on the team in steals and third in assists

B.J. Armstrong has missed only one game in seven years.

and rebounds as a senior in 1994 . . . Born Feb. 20, 1972, in South Bend, Ind.

Year	Team	G	FG	FG Pct.	FT	FT Pct.	Reb.	Ast.	TP	Avg.
1995-96	Golden State	4	3	.375	0	.000	3	1	6	1.5

MARK PRICE 32 6-0 180   Guard

Oops . . . Bullets got the potential Hall of Famer on Sept. 27, 1995, from Cavs for 1996 first-round pick . . . Arrived with sore foot that required surgery. Missed first 32 games . . . Returned, played seven games and broke the left foot. Missed last 43 games . . . Signed by Warriors as free agent last summer . . . Now he must prove he can stay healthy. Played just 55 games in last two seasons . . . When healthy, there are few better . . . NBA's all-time leading free-throw shooter at .907. Also best all-time in playoffs at .944 . . . His 812 three-pointers place him sixth among active NBA players . . . When on his game, he directs an offense to perfection. Kills from the perimeter, penetrates and finds open man . . . During his last six seasons in Cleveland, Cavs were 225-125 with him, 51-81 without him . . . Made $3.687 million last season . . . Son of a college coach . . . Member of Dream Team II . . . Georgia Tech, Class of '86. Left as 10th-best scorer in ACC history . . . Twice won long-distance shootout at All-Star Weekend . . . Born Feb. 15, 1964, in Bartlesville, Okla. . . . Drafted by Dallas, No. 25, on the second round in 1986 . . . Traded to Cavs June 17, 1986, for second-rounder and cash. Oops.

Year	Team	G	FG	FG Pct.	FT	FT Pct.	Reb.	Ast.	TP	Avg.
1986-87	Cleveland	67	173	.408	95	.833	117	202	464	6.9
1987-88	Cleveland	80	493	.506	221	.877	180	480	1279	16.0
1988-89	Cleveland	75	529	.526	263	.901	226	631	1414	18.9
1989-90	Cleveland	73	489	.459	300	.888	251	666	1430	19.6
1990-91	Cleveland	16	97	.497	59	.952	45	166	271	16.9
1991-92	Cleveland	72	438	.488	270	.947	173	535	1247	17.3
1992-93	Cleveland	75	477	.484	289	.948	201	602	1365	18.2
1993-94	Cleveland	76	480	.478	238	.888	228	589	1316	17.3
1994-95	Cleveland	48	253	.413	148	.914	112	335	757	15.8
1995-96	Washington	7	18	.300	10	1.000	7	18	56	8.0
	Totals	589	3447	.477	1893	.907	1540	4224	9599	16.3

GEERT HAMMINK 27 7-0 262   Center

It's Shaquille O'Neal! . . . Big guy . . . Played at LSU . . . Named All-Southeastern Conference . . . First-round pick by the Orlando Magic . . . Then people learned the truth: It's Geert Hammink! . . . Appeared in one game as a rookie, then got cut and played in Italy . . . Magic re-signed him in 1994-95, again made one appearance . . . Was with Omaha of the CBA when Warriors signed him to a 10-day contract March 25 . . . Signed for the rest of the season, or what was left of it, on April 14 . . . Born July 12, 1969, in Arnhem, The Netherlands.

Year	Team	G	FG	FG Pct.	FT	FT Pct.	Reb.	Ast.	TP	Avg.
1993-94	Orlando	1	1	.333	0	.000	1	1	2	2.0
1994-95	Orlando	1	1	.333	2	1.000	2	1	4	4.0
1995-96	Orl.-G.S.	6	2	.500	4	.571	4	0	8	1.3
	Totals	8	4	.400	6	.667	7	2	14	1.8

THE ROOKIES

TODD FULLER 22 6-11 255   Center

Solid pick at No. 11 when many teams expected the Warriors to take one of the European imports . . . Improved all four years at North Carolina State . . . Nice shooting touch out to 15 feet and a pretty good passer . . . No. 1 in ACC in scoring (20.9) and No. 2 in rebounding (9.9) as a senior . . . Born July 25, 1974, in Fayettville, N.C.

MARCUS MANN 22 6-8 245   Forward

Not to be confused with The Man . . . Honorable mention All-American as a senior at Mississippi Valley State . . . No wonder. He averaged 21.6 points and shot 61.8 percent . . . Warriors saw enough to take him 40th . . . Southwestern Conference Player of the Year as a senior . . . Born Dec. 19, 1973, in Carthage, Miss.

COACH RICK ADELMAN: Slowly but surely moving up the  all-time win list ... Returned to the sidelines last season and passed five coaches ... Now ranked 31st, with more room to climb ... No. 6 among all coaches with a .620 winning percentage ... Only Phil Jackson, Pat Riley, Billy Cunningham, K.C. Jones and Red Auerbach are ahead ... Lifetime: 327-200 ... Reached the 300-win plateau in 468 games ... Riley (416), Jackson (419), Cunningham (430), Jones (434), Larry Costello (445) and John Kundla (452) are the only coaches to get there quicker ... First year with the Warriors was also the first year in which he did not get to the playoffs as a head coach ... Six-for-six during tenure with the Trail Blazers ... That includes trips to the Finals in 1990 (a loss to Detroit) and 1992 (a loss to Chicago) ... Runnerup for Coach of the Year in 1991 after Portland finished a league-best 63-19 and ended the Lakers' run of nine straight Pacific Division titles ... Also spent three years with the Trail Blazers as a player, when he was the first team captain in team history, and five as an assistant coach ... Originally made his mark in California, first at Loyola University (now known as Loyola Marymount) and then with San Diego as the 79th pick in the 1968 draft ... Picked by Trail Blazers in the 1970 expansion draft ... Later had stops in Chicago, New Orleans and Kansas City, lasting seven seasons in all before announcing retirement in the summer of 1975 ... Upon returning to Portland in 1983 as an assistant to Ramsay, he worked with Dave Twardzik ... Twardzik, now the Warrior GM, hired him to coach team on May 19 ... Born June 16, 1946, in Lynwood, Cal.

BIGGEST BLUNDER

They coulda been a contender.

Tim Hardaway and Latrell Sprewell in the backcourt. Chris Webber, Chris Mullin, Rony Seikaly up front. A good mix of youth and experience.

But when Don Nelson failed to make an attempt to bridge a

communication gap between himself and Webber in 1994-95, it all crumbled.

Webber, frustrated with his relationship with his coach, was traded to the Washington Bullets. Nelson, who didn't deserve all the blame, became emotionally wounded himself by the events and was eventually replaced. Hardaway and Sprewell were on opposite sides of the affair, causing a gulf there, until Hardaway was also traded. It's been a rebuilding effort ever since.

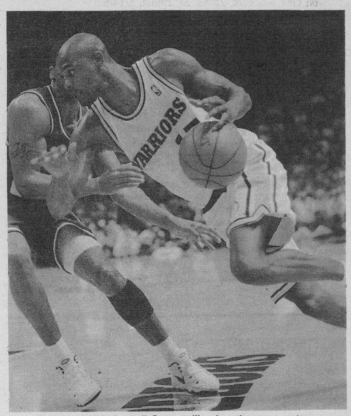

The trouble is Latrell Sprewell's shooting percentage.

ALL-TIME WARRIOR LEADERS

SEASON

Points: Wilt Chamberlain, 4,029, 1961–62
Assists: Eric Floyd, 848, 1986–87
Rebounds: Wilt Chamberlain, 2,149, 1960–61

GAME

Points: Wilt Chamberlain, 100 vs. New York, 3/2/62
Assists: Guy Rodgers, 28 vs. St. Louis, 3/14/63
Rebounds: Wilt Chamberlain, 55 vs. Boston, 11/24/60

CAREER

Points: Wilt Chamberlain, 17,783, 1959–65
Assists: Guy Rodgers, 4,845, 1958–70
Rebounds: Nate Thurmond, 12,771, 1963–74

LOS ANGELES CLIPPERS

TEAM DIRECTORY: Owner: Donald Sterling; Exec. VP: Andy Roeser; VP-Basketball Oper.: Elgin Baylor; VP-Communications: Joe Safety; Dir. of Communications: Jill Wiggins; Coach: Bill Fitch; Asst. Coaches: Jim Brewer, Barry Hecker. Arena: Los Angeles Sports Arena (16,005). Colors: Red, white and blue.

SCOUTING REPORT

SHOOTING: In the old days—the year before—fans who choose to sit in the first four rows around the basket were made

Loy Vaught is joy with his 52-percent shooting.

to sign waivers before they entered the Sports Arena. Just the Clippers wanting to make sure they were not liable in case anyone got hit by those bricks that flew around.

But of all the improvements that came during 1995-96, the most significant—not the 12-game jump in the standings—was that they went from 24th in shooting to 10th, causing a surge in the offense of almost three points a game. They were even decent on three-pointers, another change.

Credit the continued presence of dependable Loy Vaught (52.5 percent), the arrival of Brian Williams (54.3 percent) and Rodney Rogers (47.7) in trade and the emergence of Terry Dehere as a three-point threat, all the way to finishing eighth from behind the arc. That was eighth in the league. There were those who became convinced in his first two seasons that Dehere couldn't even finish eighth on the team in any shooting category.

Now to find some way to light a fire under Lamond Murray, who may be the best shooter on the team, not that you would know it by the 40.2 and 44.7 his first two years as a pro. And to make sure that Williams is back and happy with a new deal after spending part of the summer as a free agent.

PLAYMAKING: Downtown Los Angeles has its smog and traffic. The team of downtown Los Angeles has its point-guard situation.

Pooh Richardson is the starter by default and thus gets most of the blame for the Clippers finishing 26th in the league in assists last season and 21st in turnovers. But it's not all his fault; Dehere, the third guard, was the only teammate to contribute at least four assists a game. Brent Barry, a fine prospect and the guy most fans would like to see replace Richardson, managed all of 2.9 assists in 24 minutes, though, in his defense, not all at the point.

REBOUNDING: Why the Clippers finished last season with 7-0 Stanley Roberts, 6-11 Williams and 6-9 Vaught and then used their lottery pick on another big guy, 6-10 Lorenzen Wright from Memphis: No. 20 in the league in offensive rebounding by percentage, No. 22 on the defensive boards, and No. 23 overall. Any more questions?

Vaught is a terrific worker and finished ninth in the NBA at 10.1 a game, becoming the first Clipper to hit double digits in

CLIPPER ROSTER

No.	Veterans	Pos.	Ht.	Wt.	Age	Yrs. Pro	College
31	Brent Barry	G	6-4	185	24	1	Oregon State
24	Terry DeHere	G	6-4	190	25	3	Seton Hall
F-40	Antonio Harvey	F-C	6-10	245	26	3	Pfeiffer
7	Lamond Murray	F	6-7	236	23	2	California
45	Charles Outlaw	C-F	6-8	210	25	3	Houston
52	Eric Piatkowski	G-F	6-7	215	26	2	Nebraska
2	Pooh Richardson	G	6-1	180	30	7	UCLA
53	Stanley Roberts	C	7-0	295	26	5	Louisiana State
54	Rodney Rogers	F	6-7	255	25	4	Wake Forest
21	Malik Sealy	G	6-8	190	26	4	St. John's
35	Loy Vaught	F	6-9	240	28	6	Michigan
F-8	Brian Williams	C	6-11	260	27	5	Arizona

F-Free agent

Rd.	Rookies	Sel.No.	Pos.	Ht.	Wt.	College
1	Lorenzen Wright	7	F-C	6-11	225	Memphis
2	Doren Sheffer	36	G	6-5	197	Connecticut

this category in eight years. But then, nothing. For all the talk of Williams and his breakthrough 1995-96, he still managed just 7.6 boards in 33.2 minutes. No starting center could be proud of that. And the 4.3 rebounds from Rogers at small forward? Some point guards get as much.

DEFENSE: Where the health of Roberts is most critical. With him, the Clippers have something resembling a deterent inside. Without him, they're a team that can cause turnovers with steals but are in big trouble once the ball gets inside.

Barry needs to improve here, which doesn't make him much different from many second-year players. Williams and Vaught should be able to stumble into more blocks than they've been getting. No wonder Bo Outlaw is never out of the rotation.

OUTLOOK: Sixth place or bust!

The playoffs remain a long shot, seeing as Bill Fitch's team finished three places and 10 games behind No. 8 Sacramento last spring and the Kings and Warriors also have the same plan to improve. Fitch, recovering from triple-bypass surgery, is planning to return.

CLIPPER PROFILES

LOY VAUGHT 28 6-9 240   Forward

If you're doing an all-underrated team, this guy has to be on it . . . Partly because of the team he plays on, partly because of low-key style . . . Just a worker . . . Last season he became the first Clipper to average double-figures in rebounds since Michael Cage in 1987-88 and the first Clipper to average a double-double since Cage that same season . . . No. 9 in the league in rebounding . . . Failed to improve on scoring average for the first time as a pro, but that was nothing major. Still contributed 16.2 points a game, down from the 17.5 of 1994-95 . . . Has a nice medium-range jumper, consistent all the way out to about 15 feet . . . No. 13 pick in 1990 after playing at Michigan . . . Member of the 1989 NCAA championship team . . . Born Feb. 27, 1968, in Grand Rapids, Mich. . . . Made $3 million.

Year	Team	G	FG	FG Pct.	FT	FT Pct.	Reb.	Ast.	TP	Avg.
1990-91	L.A. Clippers	73	175	.487	49	.662	349	40	399	5.5
1991-92	L.A. Clippers	79	271	.492	55	.797	512	71	601	7.6
1992-93	L.A. Clippers	79	313	.508	116	.748	492	54	743	9.4
1993-94	L.A. Clippers	75	373	.537	131	.720	656	74	877	11.7
1994-95	L.A. Clippers	80	609	.514	176	.710	772	139	1401	17.5
1995-96	L.A. Clippers	80	571	.525	149	.727	808	112	1298	16.2
	Totals	466	2312	.515	676	.725	3589	490	4319	11.4

BRIAN WILLIAMS 27 6-11 260   Center

Free spirit, but very costly . . . Had breakthrough season in 1995-96, then went into the summer as a free agent . . . Figured to cash in in a big way, with the Clippers or elsewhere . . . Finished second on the team in scoring (15.8), rebounds (7.6) and shooting (54.3 percent) . . . Only seven players in the league shot better. Only two centers from the Western Conference—David Robinson and Hakeem Olajuwon—averaged more points . . . Received votes for Most Improved Player . . . Spent part of his youth in Southern California, then came back when the Nuggets traded him to the Clippers in 1995-96 as part of the Antonio McDyess deal . . . Born April 6, 1969, in Fresno,

Cal.... Started college career at Maryland, then transferred to Arizona... Orlando took him 10th in 1991... Made $2.2 million.

Year	Team	G	FG	FG Pct.	FT	FT Pct.	Reb.	Ast.	TP	Avg.
1991-92	Orlando	48	171	.528	95	.669	272	33	437	9.1
1992-93	Orlando	21	40	.513	16	.800	56	5	96	4.6
1993-94	Denver	80	251	.541	137	.649	446	50	639	8.0
1994-95	Denver	63	196	.589	106	.654	298	53	498	7.9
1995-96	L.A. Clippers	65	416	.543	196	.734	492	122	1029	15.8
	Totals	277	1074	.547	550	.686	1564	263	2699	9.7

LAMOND MURRAY 23 6-7 236   Forward

Time to show what you're made of... Started great last season, then eventually lost time to Rodney Rogers at small forward and became unhappy with his role... Blamed it on a poor relationship with coach Bill Fitch... Not a talkative guy among teammates to begin with, but seemed to withdraw even more after that ... The question has always been the level of his desire... Some within the organization still feel he can blossom, but this is probably the make-or-break season for ex-California star... No. 7 pick in 1994... Played in Rookie All-Star Game and scored the winning basket in overtime... Cousin of Bullets' Tracy Murray... Born April 20, 1973, in Pasadena, Cal.... Made $2.4 million.

Year	Team	G	FG	FG Pct.	FT	FT Pct.	Reb.	Ast.	TP	Avg.
1994-95	L.A. Clippers	81	439	.402	199	.754	354	133	1142	14.1
1995-96	L.A. Clippers	77	257	.447	99	.750	246	84	650	8.4
	Totals	158	696	.417	298	.753	600	217	1792	11.3

JEROME (POOH) RICHARDSON 30 6-1 180   Guard

Probably about to become the former starting point guard... Clips listed upgrading there one of their top priorities heading into the summer... Doesn't make a ton of mistakes because he rarely pushes the envelope... There's no thrust to his game... Still a poor shooter, but never more than the last two seasons... Defense almost as suspect... First draft pick in Minnesota history, No. 10 overall in 1989 after starring at UCLA..: Grandmother gave him the nickname "Pooh" as a baby, based on the storybook character... Came to L.A.

along with Malik Sealy and Eric Piatkowski for Mark Jackson and Greg Minor in the summer of 1994 . . . Born May 14, 1966, in Philadelphia . . . Made $2.521 million.

Year	Team	G	FG	FG Pct.	FT	FT Pct.	Reb.	Ast.	TP	Avg.
1989-90	Minnesota.......	82	426	.461	63	.589	217	554	938	11.4
1990-91	Minnesota.......	82	635	.470	89	.539	286	734	1401	17.1
1991-92	Minnesota.......	82	587	.466	123	.691	301	685	1350	16.5
1992-93	Indiana.........	74	337	.479	92	.742	267	573	769	10.4
1993-94	Indiana.........	37	160	.452	47	.610	110	237	370	10.0
1994-95	L.A. Clippers	80	353	.394	81	.648	261	632	874	10.9
1995-96	L.A. Clippers.....	63	281	.423	78	.743	158	340	734	11.7
	Totals	500	2779	.452	573	.650	1600	3755	6436	12.9

BRENT BARRY 24 6-6 185 — Guard

Not just Rick's kid . . . A talent loaded with potential . . . Began what could be a long career by being named for Rookie All-Star Game and playing both spots in the backcourt . . . Says his dad: "Brent can do some things I never dreamed of doing. All my kids can pass and see the floor, but Brent does things that truly amaze you. He has a real flair for the game."
. . . Showed good composure for a rookie and a willingness to take the tough shots . . . Needs to improve defense . . . Has long arms and quick hands, so he could be pretty good in that department some day . . . Will probably always have trouble with small, quick point guards . . . A fan favorite . . . Oregon State product opened season as the point, ended as the starting shooting guard . . . No. 15 pick by Nuggets in June 1995, then sent to Clippers in Antonio McDyess/Brian Williams deal . . . Born Dec. 31, 1971, in Hempstead, N.Y. . . . Made $833,000.

Year	Team	G	FG	FG Pct.	FT	FT Pct.	Reb.	Ast.	TP	Avg.
1995-96	L.A. Clippers	79	283	.474	111	.810	168	230	800	10.1

RODNEY ROGERS 25 6-7 255 — Forward

A nice talent, but needs to become more consistent and more intense . . . Went from Denver to Los Angeles along with Brian Williams and Brent Barry for Antonio McDyess in June 1995 . . . Then went from reserve role to the opening lineup . . . Had 51 starts in his 67 appearances . . . Missed about a month—15 games—because of a badly sprained right ankle ... Spent almost all last season at small forward, but played plenty of power forward with the Nuggets ... Can handle some bigger players on defense because he is so strong ... Uses the same to manhandle small forwards down on the blocks ... Versatile offensive weapon who will shoot three-pointers ... ACC Player of the Year at Wake Forest in 1993, just before leaving school after junior season and going ninth in the '93 draft ... Born June 20, 1971, in Durham, N.C. ... Made $1.92 million.

Year	Team	G	FG	FG Pct.	FT	FT Pct.	Reb.	Ast.	TP	Avg.
1993-94	Denver.........	79	239	.439	127	.672	226	101	640	8.1
1994-95	Denver.........	80	375	.488	179	.651	385	161	979	12.2
1995-96	L.A. Clippers.....	67	306	.477	113	.628	286	167	774	11.6
	Totals	226	920	.471	419	.651	897	429	2393	10.6

STANLEY ROBERTS 26 7-0 295   Center

Is the weight finally over? ... After missing most or all of the two previous seasons because of blown Achilles' tendons in both legs, he lasted 51 games in 1995-96 ... As always, his health is a key to the Clippers' success ... They need his size as a defensive presence and his offense as a low-post weapon ... It's easy to forget amidst all the injuries and battles with the diet, but this is a talented player ... His own worst enemy because he's so often out of shape ... Has a lot of support from teammates because he's such a good guy ... Orlando used the 23rd pick in 1991 to take him out of LSU ... Teammate at both places with Shaquille O'Neal ... When the Magic got Shaq, Roberts, usually expandable, became expendable, so Orlando sent him to the Clippers as part of a three-team deal that included the Knicks' Mark Jackson and the Clippers' Doc Rivers, Charles Smith and Bo Kimble ... Born Feb. 7, 1970, in Hopkins, S.C. ... Made $3 million.

Year	Team	G	FG	FG Pct.	FT	FT Pct.	Reb.	Ast.	TP	Avg.
1991-92	Orlando	55	236	.529	101	.515	336	39	573	10.4
1992-93	L.A. Clippers.....	77	375	.527	120	.488	478	59	870	11.3
1993-94	L.A. Clippers.....	14	43	.430	18	.409	93	11	104	7.4
1994-95	L.A. Clippers.....					Injured				
1995-96	L.A. Clippers.....	51	141	.464	74	.556	162	41	356	7.0
	Totals	197	795	.509	313	.506	1069	150	1903	9.7

MALIK SEALY 26 6-8 190   Guard-Forward

Can't shoot, a bit of a problem if you're a shooting guard . . . Brutal from three-point range: 21 percent last season . . . Did work to improve his range and ball-handling . . . Clippers were 25-36 when he played, 4-17 when he didn't . . . Made transition from seldom-used small forward to sometime-starter at shooting guard, but will he become effective enough to salvage his career? . . . Heads clothing company called Malik Sealy XXI—as in his uniform No. 21 . . . Nice defender, especially with big body . . . Clippers got him with Pooh Richardson and Eric Piatkowski in the summer of 1994 from Indiana for Mark Jackson and Greg Minor . . . No. 14 pick by Pacers in 1992 after a standout career at St. John's . . . Born Feb. 1, 1970, in the Bronx, N.Y. . . . Made $1.495 million.

Year	Team	G	FG	FG Pct.	FT	FT Pct.	Reb.	Ast.	TP	Avg.
1992-93	Indiana	58	136	.426	51	.689	112	47	330	5.7
1993-94	Indiana	43	111	.405	59	.678	118	48	285	6.6
1994-95	L.A. Clippers	60	291	.435	174	.780	214	107	778	13.0
1995-96	L.A. Clippers	62	272	.415	147	.799	240	116	712	11.5
	Totals	223	810	.423	431	.759	684	318	2105	9 4

CHARLES (BO) OUTLAW 25 6-8 210   Forward-Center

Blocks a lot of shots for small guy . . . Please, just make him stop taking shots beyond three feet . . . Gives team a spark with hustle . . . Gives team nightmares with lousy free-throw shooting . . . Led the Clippers in blocked shots last season despite averaging just 12.3 minutes, which says plenty about his success and their lack of inside threat . . . But how many others in the NBA play center at 6-8? . . . Will help his future by developing at least a credible offensive game . . . Undrafted out of the University of Houston, he played in the CBA before Clippers signed him as a free agent midway through 1993-94 . . . Born April 13, 1971, in San Antonio . . . Made $500,000.

Year	Team	G	FG	FG Pct.	FT	FT Pct.	Reb.	Ast.	TP	Avg.
1993-94	L.A. Clippers	37	98	.587	61	.592	212	36	257	6.9
1994-95	L.A. Clippers	81	170	.523	82	.441	313	84	422	5.2
1995-96	L.A. Clippers	80	107	.575	72	.444	200	50	286	3.6
	Totals	198	375	.553	215	.477	725	170	965	4.9

TERRY DEHERE 25 6-4 190   Guard

Probably the most improved Clipper last season ... Some perspective: He had a lot of room to improve ... Finished eighth in the league in three-point shooting and set franchise record for attempts from behind the arc (316), made (139) and percentage (.439) ... Even with that, struggles some times at shooting guard (.459 overall), where he has matchup problems with stronger opponents ... Clippers would like him to become better ball-handler so they could use him at the point, but he could turn out to be a good third guard, a backup at both ... Streak shooter who had some big fourth quarters ... Tries on defense, but is a liability ... High-school teammate of Bobby Hurley ... Seton Hall product was drafted 13th in 1993 ... Born Sept. 12, 1971, in New York ... Made $1.68 million.

Year	Team	G	FG	FG Pct.	FT	FT Pct.	Reb.	Ast.	TP	Avg.
1993-94	L.A. Clippers	64	129	.377	61	.753	68	78	342	5.3
1994-95	L.A. Clippers	80	279	.407	229	.784	152	225	835	10.4
1995-96	L.A. Clippers	82	315	.459	247	.755	143	350	1016	12.4
	Totals	226	723	.422	537	.767	363	653	2193	9.7

ANTONIO HARVEY 26 6-10 245   Forward-Center

No shortage of people out there willing to give him a chance ... That's what having size and athleticism will do for you ... Just doesn't have much else to go with it ... Undrafted out of tiny Pfeiffer College in North Carolina, but signed by the Lakers and lasted two years, albeit mostly at the end of the bench ... Vancouver took him in the expansion draft ... When cut by the Grizzlies on Dec. 28, he was signed by Clippers ... Started in nine of his 37 appearances in second L.A. stint ... Carolina Conference Player of the Year as a senior ... Born July 6, 1970, in Pascagoula, Miss.... Made $400,000.

Year	Team	G	FG	FG Pct.	FT	FT Pct.	Reb.	Ast.	TP	Avg.
1993-94	L.A. Lakers	27	29	.367	12	.462	59	5	70	2.6
1994-95	L.A. Lakers	59	77	.438	24	.533	102	23	179	3.0
1995-96	Van.-LAC	55	83	.371	38	.458	200	15	204	3.7
	Totals	141	189	.395	74	.481	361	43	453	3.2

ERIC PIATKOWSKI 26 6-7 215   Guard-Forward

The Polish rifle gets jammed ... A major disappointment ... Question before last season: Would he get major minutes at small forward or shooting guard? ... The answer: Neither ... Averaged just 12.1 minutes ... Good shooter, but has tendency to pass up the jumpers to try and drive ... It's always good to be aggressive and go to the basket, never good to lose scoring opportunities ... Bill Fitch said he envisions the former Nebraska standout as an off-guard similar to Dan Majerle ... Indiana took him at No. 15, then traded him to L.A. as part of the Mark Jackson-Pooh Richardson deal ... His father, Walt, played for Fitch at Bowling Green and then played four seasons in the ABA (1968-72) with Denver, Florida and Kentucky ... Born Sept. 30, 1970, in Steubenville, Ohio ... Made $1.138 million.

Year	Team	G	FG	FG Pct.	FT	FT Pct.	Reb.	Ast.	TP	Avg.
1994-95	L.A. Clippers	81	201	.441	90	.783	133	77	566	7.0
1995-96	L.A. Clippers	65	98	.405	67	.817	103	48	301	4.6
	Totals	146	299	.428	157	.797	236	125	867	5.9

THE ROOKIES

LORENZEN WRIGHT 20 6-11 225   Forward-Center

Cutting right to the chase, the Clippers draft someone who's injured ... Wright's stress fracture of the foot was expected to be a memory by camp, though ... Good quickness to the basket and a good rebounder ... Not a true center, but could see time there if Stanley Roberts goes down again ... No. 6 pick left Memphis after sophomore season ... Born Nov. 4, 1975, in Memphis,

DORON SHAFFER 24 6-5 197   Guard

Drew comparisons as a Jeff Hornacek-type player—a big point guard who makes good decisions ... Nice ball-handler ... Played in native Israel before arriving at Connecticut in 1993 ... Second-team All-Big East as a junior and senior ... Conference Rookie of the Year as a sophomore ... Went 36th ... Played on Israeli national team with another former UConn standout, Nadav Henefeld ... Born March 12, 1972, in Petch-Tikra, Israel.

COACH BILL FITCH: "When people ask me while I'm still around, I tell them it's because I'm not finished yet. Bill Fitch is doing what he wants to do. Not many people can say that." . . . His health permitting, after triple-bypass surgery in August, he heads into a third season with the Clippers . . . Lifetime: 891-995 (47.2 percent) . . . No. 1 all-time in games coached (1,886), No. 4 all-time in wins . . . Has 23 years experience as an NBA head coach . . . Two-time Coach of the Year . . . Has 12 winning seasons and five division titles to his credit . . . They have come in the Central (Cleveland), Atlantic (Boston) and Midwest (Houston), so he's only missing the Pacific for the grand slam . . . Started coaching career at age 24 with 10 seasons at alma mater Coe College, then went to North Daokta . . . Next stop was Bowling Green, where one of his players was Walt Piatkowski, father of current Clipper Eric Piatkowski . . . Last college stop was Minnesota, before moving to the NBA with the Cavaliers . . . Went to the playoffs three times in nine seasons with Cleveland, then went to Boston . . . Coached the 1980-81 Celtics to the championship . . . Moved to Houston for 1983-84 and three years later had the Rockets in the Finals . . . They made the playoffs four of his five seasons . . . Coached Nets for two seasons, then figured he had retired for good . . . Master of rebuilding projects came back for the challenge of all challenges: the Clippers . . . They don't always win, but they always play hard . . . Born May 19, 1934, in Davenport, Iowa . . . Makes permanent residence in Houston.

BIGGEST BLUNDER

What do you mean pick *one* blunder?

Amazingly, the one we chose was not a bad draft pick, of which there have been many, a bad coaching hire, of which they have been almost as many, or a bad trade, where there is no shortage of choices either. It's a bad non-signing.

Danny Manning, an all-star, was willing to stay and even began talking contract. But when the Clippers, having already agreed to the basic price tag, started nit-picking on relatively minor matters, Manning was reminded why he thought about leaving in the first place and announced he would become a free agent. At that point, in February 1986, the Clippers were forced to trade him—to Atlanta for Dominique Wilkins—and start the process in which a once-promising team would be torn apart.

ALL-TIME CLIPPER LEADERS

SEASON

Points: Bob McAdoo, 2,831, 1974–75
Assists: Norm Nixon, 914, 1983–84
Rebounds: Swen Nater, 1,216, 1979–80

GAME

Points: Bob McAdoo, 52 vs. Boston, 2/22/74
Bob McAdoo, 52 vs. Seattle, 3/17/76
Charles Smith, 52 vs. Denver, 12/1/90
Assists: Ernie DiGregorio, 25 vs. Portland, 1/1/74
Rebounds: Swen Nater, 32 vs. Denver, 12/14/79

CAREER

Points: Randy Smith, 12,735, 1971–79, 1982–83
Assists: Randy Smith, 3,498, 1971–79, 1982–83
Rebounds: Bob McAdoo, 4,229, 1972–76

LOS ANGELES LAKERS

TEAM DIRECTORY: Owner: Jerry Buss; Exec. VP: Jerry West; GM: Mitch Kupchak; Dir. Pub. Rel.: John Black; Coach: Del Harris; Asst. Coaches: Bill Bertka, Larry Drew, Michael Cooper. Arena: The Great Western Forum (17,505). Colors: Royal purple and gold.

Shaq O'Neal brings his thunder to land of make-believe.

SCOUTING REPORT

SHOOTING: They're good—No. 6 in the league during 1995-96—but lack the killer three-point bomber, or at least someone with consistent 20-foot range, that becomes so critical in the play-offs. That's a big deal for a team that considers itself challengers for the Western Conference title.

The Lakers did have two players hit at least 100 three-pointers in the same season for the first time ever (Nick Van Exel at 144 and Anthony Peeler at 105), but Peeler was traded just after finishing 19th among individuals. Van Exel remains streaky from everywhere, good enough some nights, or weeks, to carry the team on his 6-1 frame or other times to ride the down escalator all the way to the 41.7 percent of last season.

Cedric Ceballos is terrific at getting his own shots, either by offensive rebound or after slipping away from his defender inside to receive a quick pass that becomes a layup; he is a top-15 regular here. Shaquille O'Neal should be a top-five guy for the next eight years, but his presence may also take away some of Ceballos' inside opportunities.

PLAYMAKING: For all Van Exel's inconsistencies as a shooter, which becomes especially significant when noted that he took the second-most shots on the team last season. He is usually very much under control as a ball-handler. Always has been in the pros, even as a rookie running an uptempo offense. Last season, his assist-to-turnover ratio was a good 3.3-1.

That helped the Lakers commit the third-fewest turnovers in the league in 1995-96, behind only Cleveland and Orlando. It wasn't just Van Exel, either. Eddie Jones, though rarely in charge of the offense, makes few mistakes when he does handle the ball and even impressed last season when forced into emergency duty at the point.

The only backup with any pro experience is Rumeal Robinson, and he has spent most of the last three seasons in the CBA. Beyond that, there are rookies Derek Fisher and Kobe Bryant. Bryant doesn't even have any college experience.

REBOUNDING: Decent on the offensive boards, largely due to the impact of Ceballos, annually one of the best rebounders at small forward. Brutal on the defensive boards, the Lakers were all the way down at 27th by percentage. Only Vancouver and

LAKER ROSTER

No.	Veterans	Pos.	Ht.	Wt.	Age	Yrs. Pro	College
43	Corie Blount	F	6-10	242	27	3	Cincinnati
41	Elden Campbell	F	6-11	250	28	6	Clemson
23	Cedric Ceballos	F	6-7	225	27	6	Cal-Fullerton
6	Eddie Jones	G	6-6	190	25	2	Temple
--	Jerome Kersey	F	6-7	225	34	12	Longwood
34	Shaquille O'Neal	C	7-1	303	24	4	LSU
--	Rumeal Robinson	G	6-2	195	30	5	Michigan
45	Sean Rooks	C	6-10	260	27	4	Arizona
9	Nick Van Exel	G	6-1	170	24	3	Cincinnati

Rd.	Rookies	Sel.No.	Pos.	Ht.	Wt.	College
1	Kobe Bryant	13	G	6-6	200	Lower Merion HS
1	Derek Fisher	24	G	6-1	200	Ark.-Little Rock
1	Travis Knight	29	C	7-0	235	Connecticut

Philadelphia, the two losingest teams in the league, were worse.

The Grizzlies were in their first year, the 76ers in the midst of an overhaul. The Lakers' excuse? Just having a center and power forward who too often played like they were wearing 30-pound ankle weights. So Vlade Divac, the starting center, was traded. Elden Campbell, the power forward, got a seven-year, $49-million deal as a free agent and now must live up to it. Then again, O'Neal must live up to $120 million, but he will make an impact.

DEFENSE: They set Los Angeles-era records in two categories, holding 47 opponents to less than 100 points and allowing just 98.5 points a game. The 13th-place finish in the latter category was a significant improvement from Del Harris' first season as coach, when the Lakers were 21st.

All those block parties they threw helped. While sometimes hurt by going for swats too often, the Lakers also had a worthwhile weapon in finishing fourth in blocked shots. Campbell was sixth. O'Neal isn't known for his defense, but he was ninth.

OUTLOOK: O'Neal, Campbell, Ceballos, Jones, Van Exel. A starting five that will concern every opponent and convince many to make the Lakers the favorite to win the West. It wouldn't be a crazy pick, but the true success of this team will depend on the development of what could be a poor bench, depending on who comes on board late in the summer and in training camp. Bryant, for example, may be a star, but he may also be a year away. Kind of like his team.

Nick Van Exel takes off vs. Houston in '96 playoffs.

LAKER PROFILES

SHAQUILLE O'NEAL 24 7-1 303   Center

Lakers lured him from Disney World to Disneyland with seven-year, $121-million contract ... Labored for a mere $5.7 million in final year of Magic pact ... Summer Olympian ... Missed first 22 games after he suffered a fractured right thumb in preseason game with Miami ... Later sat four games with a bruised quad ... Third in the league in scoring, third in field-goal percentage, ninth in blocked shots, about 291st in free-throw percentage ... Has ranked among top 10 in scoring, shooting and blocks in each of his four seasons. Didn't qualify for rebounds because of games missed. Would have been sixth ... Was first Magic player ever to lead the league in a stat category when his 29.3 took scoring honors in 1994-95 ... Dipped from rancid to putrid in free-throw shooting. Was .487 at the line. Terrific for dead men, bad for All-Stars . . . Still needs some maturity . . . And some legit system defense . . . Too many turnovers, too . . . Remains the most dominating inside force in the game . . . Averaged 27 points, 10 rebounds—but 4.3 turnovers—during Eastern sweep by Bulls . . . Second starring role: a Disney flick, *Kazaam*, about a rapping genie . . . Has own video game, rap albums and numerous commercial endorsements . . . All-Star Game starter again . . . Born March 6, 1972, in Newark, N.J. . . . Left LSU after junior year . . . No. 1 pick in 1992.

Year	Team	G	FG	FG Pct.	FT	FT Pct.	Reb.	Ast.	TP	Avg.
1992-93	Orlando	81	733	.562	427	.592	1122	152	1893	23.4
1993-94	Orlando	81	953	.599	471	.554	1072	195	2377	29.3
1994-95	Orlando	79	930	.583	455	.533	901	214	2315	29.3
1995-96	Orlando	54	592	.573	249	.487	596	155	1434	26.6
	Totals	295	3208	.581	1602	.546	3691	716	8019	27.2

JEROME KERSEY 34 6-7 225   Forward

Free agent signed with Lakers in August after unexpected season as Warrior starter . . . Longtime Trail Blazer was left unprotected in the expansion draft, so Toronto grabbed him, with the provision that Portland would pay his $4.4 million contract last season . . . Eventually cut by the Raptors, signed by the Warriors and reunited with Rick Adelman . . . Went into the opening lineup at small forward in December to add defense and rebounding; stayed there for 58 games . . . Third-leading scorer in Trail Blazer history when he left . . . Born June 26, 1962, in Clarksville, Va., and stayed close to home to attend tiny Longwood College.

Year	Team	G	FG	FG Pct.	FT	FT Pct.	Reb.	Ast.	TP	Avg.
1984-85	Portland	77	178	.478	117	.646	206	63	473	6.1
1985-86	Portland	79	258	.549	156	.681	293	83	672	8.5
1986-87	Portland	82	373	.509	262	.720	496	194	1009	12.3
1987-88	Portland	79	611	.499	291	.735	657	243	1516	19.2
1988-89	Portland	76	533	.469	258	.694	629	243	1330	17.5
1989-90	Portland	82	519	.478	269	.690	690	188	1310	16.0
1990-91	Portland	73	424	.478	232	.709	481	227	1084	14.8
1991-92	Portland	77	398	.467	174	.664	633	243	971	12.6
1992-93	Portland	65	281	.438	116	.634	406	121	686	10.6
1993-94	Portland	78	203	.433	101	.748	331	75	508	6.5
1994-95	Portland	63	203	.415	95	.766	256	82	508	8.1
1995-96	Golden State	76	205	.410	97	.660	363	114	510	6.7
	Totals	907	4186	.472	2168	.697	5441	1876	10577	11.7

NICK VAN EXEL 24 6-1 170   Guard

The breakthrough became a breakdown... Went into last season looking like he was ready to become one of the league's bright young stars, then struggled with his emotions and his shot... Neither should be much of a surprise... Recognized as the team leader before Magic Johnson returned, he was sometimes slow to take responsibility for mistakes on the court... Near the end of the season, he earned a seven-game suspension and $25,000 fine from the league for giving referee Ron Garretson a forearm shove, no doubt solidifying his reputation as a hothead... He's a smart kid, so may be able to overcome that in time... No. 13 in the NBA in assists and No. 9 in assist-to-turnover ratio... In other words, he's not out of control with the ball... Fan favorite in L.A. arrived as second-round pick in 1993... Played at Cincinnati... No. 37 in 1993 draft... Born Nov. 27, 1971, in Kenosha, Wis.... Made $1.9 million.

Year	Team	G	FG	FG Pct.	FT	FT Pct.	Reb.	Ast.	TP	Avg.
1993-94	L.A. Lakers	81	413	.394	150	.781	238	466	1099	13.6
1994-95	L.A. Lakers	80	465	.420	235	.783	223	660	1348	16.9
1995-96	L.A. Lakers	74	396	.417	163	.799	181	509	1099	14.9
	Totals	235	1274	.410	548	.787	642	1635	3546	15.1

CEDRIC CEBALLOS 27 6-7 225   Forward

That's Spring Break Ceballos to you... Became the first Laker since James Worthy in 1989-90 and 1990-91 to average at least 20 points in back-to-back seasons, but all people will remember is his bolting from the team... Missed one game while AWOL, then another while on the suspended list after his return... Never a favorite among teammates; this didn't exactly help... Still appeared in a career-best 78 games... No. 13 in the league in scoring, No. 12 in shooting (53 percent)... The latter was the best for a Laker since A.C. Green's 53.7 three years earlier... Creates many of his scoring opportunities by getting free inside, leading to passes and offensive rebounds... Very good on the boards for a small forward... L.A. got him from the

Suns in the summer of 1994 for a first-round pick ... He was 48th pick in 1990 draft, out of Cal-Fullerton ... Born Aug. 2, 1969, in Maui, Hawaii ... Made $2.245 million.

Year	Team	G	FG	FG Pct.	FT	FT Pct.	Reb.	Ast.	TP	Avg.
1990-91	Phoenix	63	204	.487	110	.663	150	35	519	8.2
1991-92	Phoenix	64	176	.482	109	.736	152	50	462	7.2
1992-93	Phoenix	74	381	.576	187	.725	408	77	949	12.8
1993-94	Phoenix	53	425	.535	160	.724	344	91	1010	19.1
1994-95	L.A. Lakers	58	497	.509	209	.716	464	105	1261	21.7
1995-96	L.A. Lakers	78	638	.530	329	.804	536	119	1656	21.2
	Totals	390	2321	.525	1104	.739	2054	477	5857	15.0

EDDIE JONES 25 6-6 190   Guard

Growing into a fine player ... May never be a monster scoring threat, but shows terrific versatility ... A shooting guard, but has moved to the frontcourt with success when Del Harris goes with a small lineup and even held his own when forced into emergency duty at the point ... No. 3 in the league in steal-to-turnover ratio ... Good defender ... Finished eighth in the league in steals and has led the Lakers in that category both seasons since they used the No. 10 pick in the 1994 draft to get him ... Was MVP at Rookie All-Star Game in 1995 ... Temple product was born Oct. 20, 1971, in Toledo, Ohio ... Made $1.6 million.

Year	Team	G	FG	FG Pct.	FT	FT Pct.	Reb.	Ast.	TP	Avg.
1994-95	L.A. Lakers	64	342	.460	122	.722	249	128	897	14.0
1995-96	L.A. Lakers	70	337	.492	136	.739	233	246	893	12.8
	Totals	134	679	.475	258	.731	482	374	1790	13.4

ELDEN CAMPBELL 28 6-11 250   Forward

Coming off his best season as a pro ... Of course that had nothing to do with the fact that it was the final year of his contract ... Naaaaaah ... Lakers were impressed enough to bring him back ... Blessed with a mix of size and athletic ability ... Uses that on offense to create shots from the low post ... On defense, that makes him an inside factor as a shot-blocker, all the way to finishing sixth in the league ... Posted career highs in nine categories ... Scoring average has improved each of the last six years ... Only 19 players in NBA history had done that prior to 1995-96 . . . Clemson product came as the No. 27 pick in 1990 . . . Born July 23, 1968, in Inglewood, Cal. . . . Made $2.2 million.

Year	Team	G	FG	FG Pct.	FT	FT Pct.	Reb.	Ast.	TP	Avg.
1990-91	L.A. Lakers	52	56	.455	32	.653	96	10	144	2.8
1991-92	L.A. Lakers	81	220	.448	138	.619	423	59	578	7.1
1992-93	L.A. Lakers	79	238	.458	130	.637	332	48	606	7.7
1993-94	L.A. Lakers	76	373	.462	188	.689	519	86	934	12.3
1994-95	L.A. Lakers	73	360	.459	193	.666	445	92	913	12.5
1995-96	L.A. Lakers	82	447	.503	249	.713	623	181	1143	13.9
	Totals	443	1694	.469	930	.670	2438	476	4318	9.7

SEAN ROOKS 27 6-10 250   Center

Was closest thing to a post-up center the Hawks which tells you something about their inside game . . . And now he has a free-agent contract with the Lakers . . . Averaged 11.9 points and 6.4 rebounds his first three seasons but a little better than half that last year . . . Dallas drafted him 32nd out of Arizona in 1992, then sent him to Minnesota for a first-round pick (a likely lottery choice in '96, '97 or '98) in '94 . . . Came to Hawks with Christian Laettner from the Wolves in exchange for Andrew Lang and Spud Webb in February . . . Averaged 5.8 points and 3.2 rebounds in 16 games with the Hawks . . . Made $1.2 million last year . . . Born Sept. 9, 1969, in New York.

Year	Team	G	FG	FG Pct.	FT	FT Pct.	Reb.	Ast.	TP	Avg.
1992-93	Dallas	72	368	.493	234	.602	536	95	970	13.5
1993-94	Dallas	47	193	.491	150	.714	259	49	536	11.4
1994-95	Minnesota.	80	289	.470	290	.761	486	97	868	10.9
1995-96	Minn.-Atl.	65	144	.505	135	.668	255	47	424	6.5
	Totals	264	994	.487	809	.684	1536	288	2798	10.6

CORIE BLOUNT 27 6-10 242   Forward

Lakers got him for the dreaded "future considerations" in summer of '95, then discovered why the Bulls were willing to let him go so easily despite their own hole at power forward at the time . . . Emerged as the backup to Elden Campbell, a key spot, then lost the job once Derek Strong got in shape . . . When Magic Johnson arrived, he dropped to fourth-string . . . Runs the floor well for a big guy . . . Started out as an L.A.

guy, having been born (Jan. 4, 1969) and raised in suburban Monrovia . . . Teammate of Nick Van Exel for two years at Cincinnati . . . Chicago used the 25th pick to draft him in 1993 . . . Made $1.235 million.

Year	Team	G	FG	FG Pct.	FT	FT Pct.	Reb.	Ast.	TP	Avg.
1993-94	Chicago	67	76	.437	46	.613	194	56	198	3.0
1994-95	Chicago	68	100	.476	38	.567	240	60	238	3.5
1995-96	L.A Lakers	57	79	.473	25	.568	170	42	183	3.2
	Totals	192	255	.463	109	.586	604	158	619	3.2

RUMEAL ROBINSON 30 6-2 195   Guard

Free-agent Trail Blazer became a Laker last summer . . . Once the 10th overall pick in 1990, by the Hawks . . . Bounced from Atlanta to New Jersey to Charlotte to the CBA . . . was No. 4 in that league in scoring when the Trail Blazers called Jan. 10 . . . Filled the hole at point guard when Rod Strickland walked out and was suspended . . . Got 14 starts . . . Key member of Michigan's 1990 NCAA championship team . . . Born Nov. 13, 1966, in Mandeville, Jamaica.

Year	Team	G	FG	FG Pct.	FT	FT Pct.	Reb.	Ast.	TP	Avg.
1990-91	Atlanta	47	108	.446	47	.588	71	132	265	5.6
1991-92	Atlanta	81	423	.456	175	.636	219	446	1055	13.0
1992-93	New Jersey	80	270	.423	112	.574	159	323	672	8.4
1993-94	N.J.-Char.	31	55	.362	13	.448	32	63	131	4.2
1995-96	Portland	43	92	.416	33	.647	78	142	247	5.7
	Totals	282	948	.435	380	.603	559	1106	2370	8.4

THE ROOKIES

KOBE BRYANT 18 6-6 200   Guard-Forward

Lakers think he has superstar potential . . . They're not the only ones . . . Makes the jump from Lower Merion High School in Ardmore, Pa., to the NBA . . . "I think there's a real good chance this kid is ready to play before people think," one scout says . . . Hornets used the 13th pick to take him for the Lakers. L.A. then sent Vlade Divac to Charlotte in exchange . . . Son of former pro Joe (Jellybean) Bryant was born Aug. 23, 1978, in Philadelphia.

DEREK FISHER 22 6-1 200   Guard

Jerry West goes small school for the second year in a row to try and find a young backup for Nick Van Exel and a replacement for Sedale Threatt . . . But unlike Frankie King, the No. 1 in '95, Arkansas-Little Rock product is a true point guard . . . Not big and not quick, but very solid . . . Helped stock with showings at predraft camps . . . Went 24th . . . Good defender . . . Born Aug. 9, 1974, in Little Rock, Ark.

TRAVIS KNIGHT 22 7-0 235   Center

Bulls made UConn center the 29th pick, last one in the first round . . . But Bulls gave up their rights and he wound up signing with Lakers . . . Fairly effective rebounder and shot-blocker who still is growing into his frame . . . Averaged 9.1 points and 9.3 rebounds as a senior, then boosted his stock with strong showing in the Desert Classic . . . Born Sept. 13, 1974, in Salt Lake City, Utah.

COACH DEL HARRIS: From getting accolades to getting blame . . . Took some of the heat for the early exit from the playoffs . . . Some also from within . . . But owner Jerry Buss immediately came out and gave him a vote of confidence . . . They were talking contract extension early in the summer . . . Heading into the final season of his original three-year deal . . . Got the 400th win of his NBA career Jan. 15 . . . Only six active coaches are ahead of him on the all-time win list: Lenny Wilkens, Bill Fitch, Pat Riley, Larry Brown, Jerry Sloan and Mike Fratello . . . Coach of the Year in 1994-95, named by the media for the NBA's official award and by his peers for *The Sporting News'* honor . . . Has done great work before . . . Took Houston to the Finals in 1980-81 after a 40-42 regular season . . . Spent eight seasons with Milwaukee and Houston before coming to Los Angeles . . . Has also been a consultant with Sacramento . . . Best season, playoff-wise, was 1980-81, when he guided the Rockets to the Western Conference title . . . Last season was best in victories, 53 . . . Took over Bucks in the summer of 1987 and made the playoffs in all four years . . . Son, Larry, is a scout/video coordinator with Bucks . . . Played baseball and basketball at Milligan College (Tenn.), where he graduated cum laude . . . Born June 18, 1937, in Orleans, Ind.

BIGGEST BLUNDER

Strange that the man they called "Big Game James" because he seemed to play his best during the playoffs would also be the big culprit.

It was the 1984 Finals at Boston Garden. The Lakers had won the opener, then had a two-point lead in Game 2 with about 15 seconds left, and their chances improved dramatically when Kevin McHale missed two free throws. L.A. got the rebound, then called timeout. When play resumed, the ball went to James Worthy, who then attempted a cross-court pass to Byron Scott.

That's when things turned bad. Gerald Henderson intercepted the pass and went in for a layup, forcing overtime. The Celtics won it there, making what could have been an 0-2 start a tied series at 1-1, and eventually claimed the title 4-3.

ALL-TIME LAKER LEADERS

SEASON

Points: Elgin Baylor, 2,719, 1962–63
Assists: Earvin (Magic) Johnson, 989, 1990–91
Rebounds: Wilt Chamberlain, 1,712, 1968–69

GAME

Points: Elgin Baylor, 71 vs. New York, 11/15/60
Assists: Earvin (Magic) Johnson, 24 vs. Denver, 11/17/89
          Earvin (Magic) Johnson, 24 vs. Phoenix, 1/9/90
Rebounds: Wilt Chamberlain, 42 vs. Boston, 3/7/69

CAREER

Points: Jerry West, 25,192, 1960–74
Assists: Earvin (Magic) Johnson, 10,141, 1980–96
Rebounds: Elgin Baylor, 11,463, 1958–72

PHOENIX SUNS

TEAM DIRECTORY: Pres./CEO: Jerry Colangelo; Sr. VP-Head Coach: Cotton Fitzsimmons; VP-Dir. Player Personnel: Dick Van Arsdale; VP-Dir. Pub. Rel.: Tom Ambrose; Dir. Media Rel.: Julie Fie; Asst. Coaches: Paul Silas, Donn Nelson, Danny Ainge. Arena: America West Arena (19,023). Colors: Purple, orange and copper.

Kevin Johnson soared after injury-wracked beginning.

SCOUTING REPORT

SHOOTING: The Suns averaged 104.3 points a game last season, the fourth-most in the league but also their lowest since 1974-75. They kept talking about the loss of Dan Majerle, apparently forgetting his gunner instincts from behind the arc. They got only 33 games from Danny Manning and 56 from Kevin Johnson, key offensive weapons both. And they backed off the three-pointers once Cotton Fitzsimmons replaced Paul Westphal.

For 1996-97, they will have a training camp under Fitzsimmons, who will allow them to run, an experienced Michael Finley (he already contributed 15 points a game as a rookie), a healthy Manning, maybe even a healthy Johnson. What they will not have, for the first time since 1991-92, is Charles Barkley, losing a sure 20-plus points a game.

With him in Phoenix, the Suns had a go-to guy, an impact player for the scoreboard who demands double-team coverage on the post and someone who gets the calls from referees. Without him, they have a bunch of good offensive weapons—KJ, Manning and Finley. Fewer headaches off the court, but maybe more problems on.

PLAYMAKING: For all the talk about KJ and his injuries, ongoing conversation that exists for a reason, there remains a good player beneath all the medical charts, although one who sometimes is a shoot-first point guard. Two seasons ago the Suns committed the fewest turnovers in the league and in 1995-96 were seventh-best, while he averaged 9.2 assists and 18.7 points and shot 50.7 percent.

Backup Elliot Perry did his part with a pretty good assist-to-turnover of 2.4-1, but he was reportedly on the way to Milwaukee at press time. Now the Suns have Sam Cassell from Houston and a very promising rookie, Steve Nash from Santa Clara, who should have the benefit of being brought along slowly. Beyond that, Manning handles the ball very well for a big man.

REBOUNDING: They finished 10th in the league by percentage last season, but drop with the departure of Barkley. John Williams averaged all of six boards a game his first campaign in Phoenix. Take away Barkley, fourth at 11.6 a game, and the leading

SUN ROSTER

No. Veterans	Pos.	Ht.	Wt.	Age	Yrs. Pro	College
8 Mario Bennett	F	6-9	235	23	1	Arizona State
52 Chucky Brown	F	6-8	215	28	7	North Carolina State
— Mark Bryant	F-C	6-9	245	31	8	Seton Hall
F-43 Chris Carr	G	6-6	207	22	1	Southern Illinois
10 Sam Cassell	G	6-3	195	26	3	Florida State
40 John Coker	C	7-1	253	25	1	Boise State
4 Michael Finley	F	6-7	215	23	1	Wisconsin
45 A.C. Green	F	6-9	225	33	11	Oregon State
25 Robert Horry	F	6-10	220	26	4	Alabama
7 Kevin Johnson	G	6-1	190	30	9	California
35 Joe Kleine	C	7-0	271	34	11	Arkansas
15 Danny Manning	F-C	6-10	234	30	8	Kansas
11 Wesley Person	G	6-6	195	25	2	Auburn
F-14 Terrence Rencher	G	6-3	185	23	1	Texas
23 Wayman Tisdale	C-F	6-9	260	32	11	Oklahoma
18 John Williams	C-F	6-11	245	34	10	Tulane

F-Free agent

Rd. Rookies	Sel.No.	Pos.	Ht.	Wt.	College
1 Steve Nash	15	G	6-3	195	Santa Clara
2 Russ Millard	39	F	6-8	240	Iowa
2 Ben Davis	43	F	6-9	240	Arizona

returnee for the Suns here is A.C. Green, he of the 6.8. Good for someone coming off the bench, bad if that has to set the pace this season.

DEFENSE: Where?

The Suns were a poor 19th in shooting-percentage against, so it's not just that opponents averaged 104 points because they played a running game. It helps that Finley showed good skills as a defender, not just a scorer, and that another forward, Robert Horry, also brings something from Houston.

OUTLOOK: Are they coming or going, or about to get caught in that dangerous no-man's land, good enough to stay out of the lottery but not good enough to be a serious playoff threat? Time to either make a bold move for a big man or prepare for the future that already includes a good foundation with Finley, Wesley Person, Cassell, Horry and (based on scouting reports) Nash.

SUN PROFILES

KEVIN JOHNSON 30 6-1 190   Guard

Limped—of course—through a good 1995-96 ... Sidelined for chunks of first half of season by strained hamstring ... The left leg? The right? Doesn't matter. It'll be the other one next time around ... Put up big numbers after the All-Star break: 19.8 points, 10.3 assists, 52.7 percent ... Finished at 18.7, 9.2 and 50.7 ... The 9.2 was good for No. 6 in league in assists ... Career average of 9.55 assists is fourth all-time among those with at least 400 games experience ... The only ones ahead on the list are Oscar Robertson, Magic Johnson and John Stockton ... One of six active players to have 11,000 points and 5,000 assists ... Member of Dream Team II that won a gold medal at 1994 World Championships in Toronto ... Suns got him from Cavaliers midway through rookie season along with Mark West, Tyrone Corbin and picks for Larry Nance, Mike Sanders and a pick ... Born March 4, 1966, in Sacramento ... Made $2.9 million.

Year	Team	G	FG	FG Pct.	FT	FT Pct.	Reb.	Ast.	TP	Avg.
1987-88	Clev.-Phoe.	80	275	.461	177	.839	191	437	732	9.2
1988-89	Phoenix	81	570	.505	508	.882	340	991	1650	20.4
1989-90	Phoenix	74	578	.499	501	.838	270	846	1665	22.5
1990-91	Phoenix	77	591	.516	519	.843	271	781	1710	22.2
1991-92	Phoenix	78	539	.479	448	.807	292	836	1536	19.7
1992-93	Phoenix	49	282	.499	226	.819	104	384	791	16.1
1993-94	Phoenix	67	477	.487	380	.819	167	637	1340	20.0
1994-95	Phoenix	47	246	.470	234	.810	115	360	730	15.5
1995-96	Phoenix	56	342	.507	342	.859	221	517	1047	18.7
	Totals	609	3900	.494	3335	.837	1971	5789	11201	18.4

DANNY MANNING 30 6-10 234   Forward

In two seasons with Suns, he has yet to play one ... Just 79 appearances because of the torn ligament in his left knee, suffered at practice Feb. 6, 1995 ... Spent first 42 games of 1995-96 on injured list, then made a nice comeback ... No one should be surprised, even if it was his second major knee operation ... Led Suns' bench in scoring in 18 of last 22 games ... That 45.9 percent should go back up to 50 range he's used to ...

Soft touch around the basket gives him a great knack to score at different angles ... Quick release with medium-range jumpers or jump hook ... College Player of the Year in 1988 while at Kansas ... No. 1 pick overall later that year with Clippers ... The first part of that was an honor, the second a disaster ... Born May 17, 1966, in Hattiesburg, Miss. ... Top-paid Sun last season at $6.833 million.

Year	Team	G	FG	FG Pct.	FT	FT Pct.	Reb.	Ast.	TP	Avg.
1988-89	L.A. Clippers	26	177	.494	79	.767	171	81	434	16.7
1989-90	L.A. Clippers	71	440	.533	274	.741	422	187	1154	16.3
1990-91	L.A. Clippers	73	470	.519	219	.716	426	196	1159	15.9
1991-92	L.A. Clippers	82	650	.542	279	.725	564	285	1579	19.3
1992-93	L.A. Clippers	79	702	.509	388	.802	520	207	1800	22.8
1993-94	LAC-Atl.	68	586	.488	228	.669	465	261	1403	20.6
1994-95	Phoenix	46	340	.547	136	.673	276	154	822	17.9
1995-96	Phoenix	33	178	.459	82	.752	143	65	441	13.4
	Totals	478	3543	.515	1685	.733	2987	1436	8792	18.4

ROBERT HORRY 26 6-10 220   Forward

Dealt by Rockets to Suns in August with Chucky Brown, Sam Cassell and Mark Bryant for Charles Barkley ... Decent scorer and versatile since he can cause size problems for defenders at small forward or move to power forward and then start hitting three-pointers ... But especially valuable for his work on the other side of the ball ... Having a shot-blocker at small forward is a unique weapon ... Starred in 1995 championship series versus Orlando ... No. 11 pick in 1992 after teaming with Latrell Sprewell and James Robinson at Alabama ... All-Rookie second team ... Born Aug. 25, 1970, in Andalusia, Ala. ... Made $1.601 million.

Year	Team	G	FG	FG Pct.	FT	FT Pct.	Reb.	Ast.	TP	Avg.
1992-93	Houston	79	323	.474	143	.715	392	191	801	10.1
1993-94	Houston	81	322	.459	115	.732	440	231	803	9.9
1994-95	Houston	64	240	.447	86	.761	324	216	652	10.2
1995-96	Houston	71	300	.410	111	.776	412	281	853	12.0
	Totals	295	1185	.447	455	.742	1568	919	3109	10.5

A.C. GREEN 33 6-9 225   Forward

Not the defender he used to be, but still the same effort... Has played in 813 consecutive games, best among the active players and No. 3 all-time... Only Randy Smith (906) and John Kerr (844) have had longer runs... Will move past Kerr the first half of this season if he stays healthy... Maybe even if he doesn't ... Kept streak alive in 1995-96, after all, while wearing a mask for 12 games after two bottom front teeth were knocked out by J. R. Reid's cheap-shot elbow Feb. 25... Born Oct. 4, 1963, in Portland and played at Oregon State... First-round pick by the Lakers from there... Member of championship teams in L.A. in 1987 and '88... Earns an average of $6.473 million annually on his contract.

Year	Team	G	FG	FG Pct.	FT	FT Pct.	Reb.	Ast.	TP	Avg.
1985-86	L.A. Lakers	82	209	.539	102	.611	381	54	521	6.4
1986-87	L.A. Lakers	79	316	.538	220	.780	615	84	852	10.8
1987-88	L.A. Lakers	82	322	.503	293	.773	710	93	937	11.4
1988-89	L.A. Lakers	82	401	.529	282	.786	739	103	1088	13.3
1989-90	L.A. Lakers	82	385	.478	278	.751	712	90	1061	12.9
1990-91	L.A. Lakers	82	258	.476	223	.738	516	71	750	9.1
1991-92	L.A. Lakers	82	382	.476	340	.744	762	117	1116	13.6
1992-93	L.A. Lakers	82	379	.537	277	.739	711	116	1051	12.8
1993-94	Phoenix	82	465	.502	266	.735	753	137	1204	14.7
1994-95	Phoenix	82	311	.504	251	.732	669	127	916	11.2
1995-96	Phoenix	82	215	.484	168	.709	554	72	612	7.5
	Totals	899	3643	.505	2700	.743	7122	1064	10108	11.2

MICHAEL FINLEY 23 6-7 215   Forward

A steal last season with the 21st pick... Speaking of which, he made an impact with his defense... That it came while averaging 15 points a game makes his rookie campaign all the more impressive... Led the Suns at 39.2 minutes per outing... One of only three first-year players in team history to score at least 1,000 points... Walter Davis and Alvan Adams are the other two... Started in the Rookie All-Star Game ... Finished second to Brent Barry in the slam-dunk contest... High-school teammates in Maywood, Ill., with Sherrell Ford of SuperSonics and Donnie Boyce of Hawks... Leading scorer in

Wisconsin history . . . Born March 6, 1973, in Melrose Park, Ill.
. . . Made $628,000.

Year	Team	G	FG	FG Pct.	FT	FT Pct.	Reb.	Ast.	TP	Avg.
1995-96	Phoenix	82	465	.476	242	.749	374	289	1233	15.0

JOHN WILLIAMS 34 6-11 245   Center

Next! . . . Not the answer at center . . . First
season with the Suns was limited by injuries
to 62 games, his fewest in five seasons . . . Bigger
problem was his inability to provide much
of a defensive presence inside . . . Averaging
just 0.9 blocks his first 42 outings? Centers
should get more by accident . . . Did improve
to 2.7 over the last 20 . . . Finished at 1.45
overall . . . Suns sent fan favorite Dan Majerle to Cleveland to get
him in summer of '95 . . . No. 1 in Cavaliers' history in blocks,
No. 2 in rebounds and No. 5 in points . . . They took him 45th in
1985 draft out of Tulane . . . Born Aug. 9, 1962, in Sorrento, La.
. . . Made $4.151 million.

Year	Team	G	FG	FG Pct.	FT	FT Pct.	Reb.	Ast.	TP	Avg.
1986-87	Cleveland	80	435	.485	298	.745	629	154	1168	14.6
1987-88	Cleveland	77	316	.477	211	.756	506	103	843	10.9
1988-89	Cleveland	82	356	.509	235	.748	477	108	948	11.6
1989-90	Cleveland	82	528	.493	325	.739	663	168	1381	16.8
1990-91	Cleveland	43	199	.463	107	.652	290	100	505	11.7
1991-92	Cleveland	80	341	.503	270	.752	607	196	952	11.9
1992-93	Cleveland	67	263	.470	212	.716	415	152	738	11.0
1993-94	Cleveland	76	394	.478	252	.728	575	193	1040	13.7
1994-95	Cleveland	74	366	.452	196	.685	507	192	929	12.6
1995-96	Phoenix	62	180	.453	95	.731	372	62	455	7.3
	Totals	723	3378	.481	2201	.730	5041	1428	8959	12.4

WESLEY PERSON 25 6-6 195   Guard

Shooter . . . Just not always a maker . . . Went
from very promising 48.4 percent of rookie
campaign to 44.5 last season, including a drop
in three-pointers from 43.6 to 37.4 . . . Would
have been worse if not for strong finish—48.9
overall and 45.0 from behind the arc in the 11
games of April . . . Started 10 of those when
Mario Bennett went out . . . Second-team All-
Rookie after Suns grabbed him with 23rd pick . . . Chuck's
younger brother . . . Four-year starter at Auburn . . . Left school as
third on career scoring list behind Chuck Person and Mike Mitch-

ell . . . Born March 28, 1971, in Crenshaw, Ala. . . . Made $845,000.

Year	Team	G	FG	FG Pct.	FT	FT Pct.	Reb.	Ast.	TP	Avg.
1994-95	Phoenix	78	309	.484	80	.792	201	105	814	10.4
1995-96	Phoenix	82	390	.445	148	.771	321	138	1045	12.7
	Totals	160	699	.461	228	.778	522	243	1859	11.6

WAYMAN TISDALE 32 6-9 260   Forward-Center

Still capable of making a decent contribution off the bench . . . Low-post scoring threat . . . Best at power forward, but has played some center in a pinch . . . Ended last season three rebounds shy of becoming only the 14th active player to record 12,000 points and 5,000 rebounds . . . Early-entry candidate from Oklahoma went second overall to Indiana in 1985 . . . Suns signed him as free agent Sept. 16, 1994 . . . Won gold medal with U.S. Olympic team in 1984 . . . Accomplished bass player . . . Born June 9, 1964, in Tulsa, Okla. . . . Made $3.475 million.

Year	Team	G	FG	FG Pct.	FT	FT Pct.	Reb.	Ast.	TP	Avg.
1985-86	Indiana	81	516	.515	160	.684	584	79	1192	14.7
1986-87	Indiana	81	458	.513	258	.709	475	117	1174	14.5
1987-88	Indiana	79	511	.512	246	.783	491	103	1268	16.1
1988-89	Ind.-Sac.	79	532	.514	317	.773	609	128	1381	17.5
1989-90	Sacramento	79	726	.525	306	.783	595	108	1758	22.3
1990-91	Sacramento	33	262	.483	136	.800	253	66	660	20.0
1991-92	Sacramento	72	522	.500	151	.763	469	106	1195	16.6
1992-93	Sacramento	76	544	.509	175	.758	500	108	1263	16.6
1993-94	Sacramento	79	552	.501	215	.808	560	139	1319	16.7
1994-95	Phoenix	65	278	.484	94	.770	247	45	650	10.0
1995-96	Phoenix	63	279	.495	114	.765	214	58	672	10.7
	Totals	787	5180	.508	2172	.762	4997	1057	12532	15.9

JOE KLEINE 34 7-0 271   Center

Depth at center, here or elsewhere . . . Still has some years ahead of him in this league . . . Can't play if you can't stand, though . . . Fainted during national anthem in April game at the Forum . . . Scary moment, but battery of tests found nothing abnormal . . . No truth to the rumor the league office fined him for trying to show support for Mahmoud Abdul-Rauf . . .

The 56 games last season was the low for a career that started in 1985, when the Kings used the No. 6 pick to draft him out of Arkansas . . . Came to Phoenix as a free agent June 17, 1993 . . . Gold medal-winning Olympian in 1984 . . . Born Jan. 4, 1962, in Colorado Springs, Colo. . . . Made $1.04 million.

Year	Team	G	FG	FG Pct.	FT	FT Pct.	Reb.	Ast.	TP	Avg.
1985-86	Sacramento	80	160	.465	94	.723	373	46	414	5.2
1986-87	Sacramento	79	256	.471	110	.786	483	71	622	7.9
1987-88	Sacramento	82	324	.472	153	.814	579	93	801	9.8
1988-89	Sac.-Boston	75	175	.405	134	.882	378	67	484	6.5
1989-90	Boston	81	176	.480	83	.830	355	46	435	5.4
1990-91	Boston	72	102	.468	54	.783	244	21	258	3.6
1991-92	Boston	70	144	.491	34	.708	296	32	326	4.7
1992-93	•Boston	78	108	.404	41	.707	346	39	257	3.3
1993-94	Phoenix	74	125	.488	30	.769	193	45	285	3.9
1994-95	Phoenix	75	119	.449	42	.857	259	39	280	3.7
1995-96	Phoenix	56	71	.420	20	.800	132	44	164	2.9
	Totals	822	1760	.458	795	.797	3638	543	4326	5.3

CHRIS CARR 22 6-5 207   Guard

Has three-point range and also the ability to post up against some defenders . . . Very good leaper, so a pretty good rebounder for his size . . . Gets out of control at times, going up with the ball and then trying to make a play in mid-air . . . Needs to develop . . . Decent contribution last season from a late second-round pick (No. 56), despite unimpressive numbers—41.5 percent shooting and 4.0 points a game . . . Left Southern Illinois after his junior season . . . And after being named Missouri Valley Conference Player of the Year . . . Youngest of 10 kids was born March 12, 1974, in Ironton, Mo. . . . Made $200,000.

Year	Team	G	FG	FG Pct.	FT	FT Pct.	Reb.	Ast.	TP	Avg.
1995-96	Phoenix	60	90	.415	49	.817	102	43	240	4.0

SAM CASSELL 26 6-3 195   Guard

Most people couldn't understand why he wasn't in the Rockets' opening lineup, but there's no denying the spark he supplied off the bench . . . Suns got him in August with Robert Horry, Mark Bryant and Chucky Brown in the deal with Rockets for Charles Barkley . . . Never has shown fear in crashing through the lane . . . Would have received plenty of consideration last season as Sixth Man of the Year if not for missing 19 games with elbow injury... Teammate of Charlie Ward at Florida State before coming to Rockets as No. 24 pick in 1993... Immediately played key role in their winning NBA championships the next two seasons... Born Nov. 18, 1969, in Baltimore... Made $1.04 million.

Year	Team	G	FG	FG Pct.	FT	FT Pct.	Reb.	Ast.	TP	Avg.
1993-94	Houston	66	162	.418	90	.841	134	192	440	6.7
1994-95	Houston	82	253	.427	214	.843	211	405	783	9.5
1995-96	Houston	61	289	.439	235	.825	188	278	886	14.5
	Totals	209	704	.430	539	.834	533	875	2109	10.1

MARIO BENNETT 23 6-9 235   Forward

Suns' executive ripped the guy before the draft, and before Suns took him in the first round, No. 27 overall... Knees were a big question mark after his career down the street at Arizona State... Oh, and he missed the first 55 games of rookie season while recovering from surgery on his left knee... But not only eventually made it into the rotation, he got 14 starts... Has big arms and moves pretty well for big man... Provides much-needed shot-blocking ability... No. 1 all-time in that category at Arizona State despite turning pro after junior season... Born Aug. 1, 1973, in Denton, Tex.... Made $480,000.

Year	Team	G	FG	FG Pct.	FT	FT Pct.	Reb.	Ast.	TP	Avg.
1995-96	Phoenix	19	29	.453	27	.643	49	6	85	4.5

MARK BRYANT 31 6-9 245   Forward-Center

After one season in Houston he landed in Phoenix with Robert Horry, Sam Cassell and Chucky Brown in the Charles Barkley trade... Prefers to avoid attention... Proceeded to take care of that last season by going from someone expected to challenge for the starting job at power forward to a role player on the bench... Was in opening lineup for nine games at center while Hakeem Olajuwon was injured... Versatility is one of his strengths... So is ability to run the floor with a big body... Developed a nice hook shot from the middle of the lane... Had tinkered with it a bit while at Seton Hall, then shelved it after coming to the pros . . . Especially useful at center because he can get it off over bigger opponents . . . Rockets got him as a free agent in summer of '95 . . . Born April 25, 1965, in Glen Ridge, N.J. . . . Made $1 million.

Year	Team	G	FG	FG Pct.	FT	FT Pct.	Reb.	Ast.	TP	Avg.
1988-89	Portland	56	120	.486	40	.580	179	33	280	5.0
1989-90	Portland	58	70	.458	28	.560	146	13	168	2.9
1990-91	Portland	53	99	.488	74	.733	190	27	272	5.1
1991-92	Portland	56	95	.480	40	.667	201	41	230	4.1
1992-93	Portland	80	186	.503	104	.703	324	41	476	6.0
1993-94	Portland	79	185	.482	72	.692	315	37	442	5.6
1994-95	Portland	49	101	.526	41	.651	161	28	244	5.0
1995-96	Houston	71	242	.543	127	.718	351	52	611	8.6
	Totals	502	1098	.501	526	.681	1867	272	2723	5.4

CHUCKY BROWN 28 6-8 215   Forward

Only Rocket to play all 82 games last season, . . . Became a Sun last summer when he was traded with Robert Horry, Sam Cassell and Mark Bryant for Charles Barkley . . . Hard worker, but can't really hang with the bangers inside . . . In truth, a 'tweener . . . Of course, it didn't hurt to play alongside Hakeem Olajuwon . . . Finished ninth in league by shooting 54.1 percent . . . Arrived in Houston as a free-agent signee out of the CBA on Feb. 24, 1995 . . . Cleveland originally got North Carolina State product as the 43rd player drafted in 1989 . . . Born Feb. 29, 1968, in New York . . . Made $425,000.

Year	Team	G	FG	FG Pct.	FT	FT Pct.	Reb.	Ast.	TP	Avg.
1989-90	Cleveland	75	210	.470	125	.762	231	50	545	7.3
1990-91	Cleveland	74	263	.524	101	.701	213	80	627	8.5
1991-92	Clev.-LAL	42	60	.469	30	.612	82	26	150	3.6
1992-93	New Jersey	77	160	.483	71	.724	232	51	391	5.1
1993-94	Dallas	1	1	1.000	1	1.000	1	0	3	3.0
1994-95	Houston	41	105	.603	38	.613	189	30	249	6.1
1995-96	Houston	82	300	.541	104	.693	441	89	705	8.6
	Totals	392	1099	.514	470	.704	1389	326	2670	6.8

JOHN COKER 25 7-1 260   Center

Like you didn't already know the Suns were desperate for size? . . . Had five appearances last season, but Phoenix saw enough to re-sign him early in the summer . . . Spent the first 59 games of 1995-96 on the injured list because of a lingering foot injury . . . Had originally suffered a stress fracture to the left foot as a sophomore at Boise State, then again as a senior . . . Two-time All-

Big Sky Conference in college...Born Oct. 28, 1971, in Bremerton, Wash.

Year	Team	G	FG	FG Pct.	FT	FT Pct.	Reb.	Ast.	TP	Avg.
1995-96	Phoenix	5	4	.800	0	.000	2	1	8	1.6

THE ROOKIES

STEVE NASH 22 6-3 195   Guard
Not flashy like Allen Iverson or Stephon Marbury, but a lot of teams liked this guy...Handles the ball well and plays with a lot of smarts...Showed leadership skills at Santa Clara...With Kevin Johnson thinking about retiring after this season, Suns got the two-time West Coast Conference Player of the Year at No. 15...Born Feb. 7, 1974, in Johannesburg, South Africa, but is a Canadian from British Columbia.

RUSS MILLARD 23 6-8 240   Forward
Good perimeter shooter goes 39th...Helped his standings with nice showings at predraft camps in Portsmouth and Phoenix...Led Iowa in shooting, three-point shooting, free-throw percentage and blocks as a senior...Born March 1, 1973, in Cedar Rapids, Iowa.

BEN DAVIS 23 6-9 240   Forward
Good athlete runs the floor and has range out to about 17 feet...Shot 53.8 and 54.6 percent in two seasons at Arizona...Started college career at Kansas, transferred to a JC after one year, then landed in Tucson...First-team All-Pac 10 as a senior after leading conference in rebounding at 9.5 a game...Suns got him at No. 43...Born Dec. 26, 1972, in Vero Beach, Fla.

COACH COTTON FITZSIMMONS: You again...When Paul Westphal was shown the door, Lowell Fitzsimmons returned for his third stint on the sidelines...That's three stints just with the Suns...First was 1970-72, his initial dip into NBA coaching after nine years at Moberly Junior College (Mo.) and Kansas State...Went from Phoenix to Atlanta Hawks, then Buffalo Braves, then Kansas City Kings...Took over Spurs for two seasons...Went back to Suns in 1988-89 and stayed four seasons, highlighted by 55-27 finish that first season that included the third-biggest improvement in league history at the time and Coach of the Year honors...Retired to the front office as senior executive vice president and chipped in as color commentator . . . Summoned again to replace Westphal on Jan. 17 and went 27-22 . . . Lifetime: 832-767 (52.1 percent) . . . No. 7 in league history in wins . . . No. 3 among active coaches, behind only Lenny Wilkens and Bill Fitch . . . Even though he's had veteran teams in Phoenix, works well with young players . . . And the older guys? "He grates on our nerves," Charles Barkley says, probably kidding. "I've never been around anybody who can talk that much. I think he's a good man. I respect him as a coach and as a person. But that man never shuts up." . . . Son, Gary, is director of player personnel for the Cavaliers . . . Born Oct. 7, 1931, in Hannibal, Mo.

BIGGEST BLUNDER

The 50-50 chance that changed a league: In 1969, the Suns, the worst team in the West, and the Milwaukee Bucks, the least of the East, took part in a coin toss to determine who would have the No. 1 pick in the draft.

Phoenix called heads.

It came up tails.

The Bucks chose UCLA's Lew Alcindor and in his second season, Milwaukee won the NBA championship. Later, as Kareem Abdul-Jabbar with the Lakers, he would become the greatest scorer in NBA history.

The Suns' pick? Neal Walk, a 6-10 forward-center from Florida who had a seven-year career with Phoenix, New Orleans and the Knicks.

ALL-TIME SUN LEADERS

SEASON

Points: Tom Chambers, 2,201, 1989–90
Assists: Kevin Johnson, 991, 1988–89
Rebounds: Paul Silas, 1,015, 1970–71

GAME

Points: Tom Chambers, 60 vs. Seattle, 3/24/90
Assists: Kevin Johnson, 25 vs. San Antonio, 4/6/94
Rebounds: Paul Silas, 27 vs. Cincinnati, 1/18/71

CAREER

Points: Walter Davis, 15,666, 1977–88
Assists: Kevin Johnson, 5,596, 1987–96
Rebounds: Alvan Adams, 6,937, 1975–88

PORTLAND TRAIL BLAZERS

TEAM DIRECTORY: Governor: Paul Allen; Pres.-GM: Bob Whitsitt; Dir. Sports Communications: John Christensen; Coach: P.J. Carlesimo; Asst. Coaches: Rick Carlisle, Dick Harter. Arena: Rose Garden (22,000). Colors: Red, black and white.

SCOUTING REPORT

SHOOTING: Blazing down the wrong trail. In recent years, they could at least be counted on to take a lot of shots, if not make a lot of shots. But that's how Portland put points on the board, going with quantity and not quality.

So last season, when the Trail Blazers dropped all the way down to a little less than 82 attempts a game, the end result was no surprise. They were again a poor-shooting club (at 45.8 percent just 19th in the league), but also a low-scoring club (99.3 points) after falling all the way to 11th in tries, this after finishing first and second the previous two campaigns. It was the first full season without Clyde Drexler and it showed.

The problem before was a lack of weapons with just Rod Strickland (now a Bullet) and Cliff Robinson. So the addition of free-agent Hornet point guard Kenny Anderson and ex-Timberwolf shooting guard Isaiah Rider will help in this area. Robinson is terrific, especially now that he's added the three-point shot to his arsenal. Anderson should provide about 15 points a game as Strickland's replacement. Offcourt problems aside, Rider is a talent with a potential to score 20 points a game at shooting guard.

Arvydas Sabonis did finish seventh in shooting as a rookie (54.5 percent), but that's only worth so much when a guy plays only 24 minutes because the weld joints in his legs might come apart.

PLAYMAKING: Strickland is now with Washington, for which the Trail Blazers can be thankful and concerned. Thankful because it will end the feud with coach P.J. Carlesimo that had become such a distraction. Concerned because Strickland, when you get right down to talent, was good. Better than Anderson.

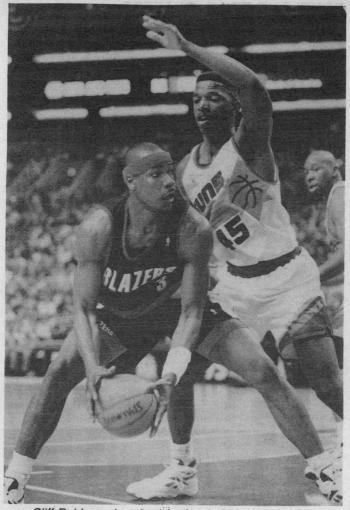

Cliff Robinson is poised for fourth 20-ppg campaign.

REBOUNDING: Now we're talking. The Trail Blazers are one of the league's best every season, at No. 3 by percentage in 1995-96, including No. 1 on the defensive boards. The No. 6 on the

TRAIL BLAZER ROSTER

No.	Veterans	Pos.	Ht.	Wt.	Age	Yrs. Pro	College
—	Kenny Anderson	G	6-1	168	26	5	Georgia Tech
—	Mitchell Butler	G	6-5	210	25	3	UCLA
24	Chris Dudley	C	6-11	240	31	9	Yale
23	Aaron McKie	G	6-5	209	24	2	Temple
3	Clifford Robinson	F	6-10	225	29	7	Connecticut
—	Isaiah Rider	G	6-5	215	25	3	UNLV
11	Arvydas Sabonis	C	7-3	219	31	1	Lithuania
22	Gary Trent	F	6-8	240	22	1	Ohio
—	Rasheed Wallace	F-C	6-10	225	22	2	North Carolina
10	Dontonio Wingfield	F	6-8	256	22	2	Cincinnati

Rd.	Rookies	Sel. No.	Pos.	Ht.	Wt.	College
1	Jermain O'Neal	17	F	6-11	226	Eau Claire H.S. (S.C.)
2	Jason Sasser	41	F	6-7	225	Texas Tech
2	Marcus Brown	46	G	6-3	185	Murray State

offensive boards would make most any team happy, but consider the extra importance of the second-chance baskets here since it comes on a club that can't count on accuracy the first time around.

Actually, no player finished in the top 20 among individuals and no one even broke double-figures on the boards; Chris Dudley led at 9.0 a game. The compensation is that so many Blazers crash the boards: Dudley, Sabonis (8.1), and the new big body, ex-Bullet Rasheed Wallace.

DEFENSE: If the offensive numbers are in decline, at least the defensive are, too. The 97 points allowed last season was a franchise record, by better than two points. Likewise, the 44.2 percent by opponents was an all-time best, erasing a mark that had stood for 18 years.

It shows a commitment by Carlesimo to make this an area of strength. More inside help could come from the first-round pick, 6-11 Jermaine O'Neal, just maybe not this season. He's coming

J.R. Rider brings his scowls and skills to Blazers.

right from high school and, unlike Kevin Garnett and maybe even Kobe Bryant, is very raw.

OUTLOOK: Give the Trail Blazers this much. At a time when they easily could have been playing out the string, they instead became one of the feared underdog opponents of the playoffs. So they got eliminated in the first round. A lot of people didn't even expect them to get that far.

The danger is in getting stuck in that no-man's land—good enough to be respectable but not good enough to make a serious run in the postseason and then always drafting in the 14-15-16 range. A lot of average first-round picks makes you an average team.

TRAIL BLAZER PROFILES

KENNY ANDERSON 26 6-1 168   Guard

Hornet free agent signed seven-year pact with Trail Blazers estimated at $45 million . . . Had been a good producer (15.2 points, 8.6 assists) in 38 games with the Hornets, who traded Kendall Gill and Khalid Reeves to the Nets for him and Gerald Glass last season . . . One of a long line of Georgia Tech point guards, following Mark Price and preceding Travis Best and Stephon Marbury . . . Still carries the same rap from college, that he can't shoot well enough to keep defenses honest (.414 career, .318 on three-pointers) . . . Great penetrator who can be unstoppable in traffic . . . Uses his quickness on offense, but not defense . . . Nets used No. 2 pick in 1991 on him . . . Made All-Star team in 1993-94 . . . Earned $3.898 million last year . . . Born Oct. 9, 1970, in Queens, N.Y.

Year	Team	G	FG	FG Pct.	FT	FT Pct.	Reb.	Ast.	TP	Avg.
1991-92	New Jersey	64	187	.390	73	.745	127	203	450	7.0
1992-93	New Jersey	55	370	.435	180	.776	226	449	927	16.9
1993-94	New Jersey	82	576	.417	346	.818	322	784	1538	18.8
1994-95	New Jersey	72	411	.399	348	.841	250	680	1267	17.6
1995-96	N.J.-Char.	69	349	.418	260	.769	203	575	1050	15.2
	Totals	342	1893	.414	1207	.802	1128	2691	5232	15.3

CLIFFORD ROBINSON 29 6-10 225   Forward

A star, if not a regular All-Star . . . Has averaged at least 20 points each of the last three seasons and continues to work to improve his game . . . Addition of reliable three-point shot gives him another dimension, especially when playing power forward . . . After making 51 from behind the arc the first five years after he was drafted out of Connecticut, it jumped to 142 in 1994-95 and then 178 last season . . . That was a Blazers record and the sixth-most in the league . . . Not just a gunner—the 37.8 percent there is respectable for a big man . . . Versatility to play both forward spots and he spent plenty of time at center earlier in his career . . . A joke that he lasted all the way to No.

36 in the 1989 draft . . . Sixth Man of the Year in 1992-93 . . . Born Dec. 16, 1966, in Albion, N.Y. . . . Made $3.04 million.

Year	Team	G	FG	FG Pct.	FT	FT Pct.	Reb.	Ast.	TP	Avg.
1989-90	Portland	82	298	.397	138	.550	308	72	746	9.1
1990-91	Portland	82	373	.463	205	.653	349	151	957	11.7
1991-92	Portland	82	398	.466	219	.664	416	137	1016	12.4
1992-93	Portland	82	632	.473	287	.690	542	182	1570	19.1
1993-94	Portland	82	641	.457	352	.765	550	159	1647	20.1
1994-95	Portland	75	597	.452	265	.694	423	198	1601	21.3
1995-96	Portland	78	553	.423	360	.664	443	190	1644	21.1
	Totals	563	3492	.449	1826	.678	3031	1089	9181	16.3

ARVYDAS SABONIS 31 7-3 279   Center

Worth the wait . . . And then some . . . That is tempered by talk of what could have been . . . Drafted by the Blazers in 1986 (No. 24 overall), but didn't sign with the NBA until last season . . . Became an impact player even though his legs were shot from injuries while playing in Europe . . . Fabulous passing big man . . . Very smart . . . "He writes a book when he's out there," Clippers coach Bill Fitch says. "He's a guy that's playing with one leg. You can imagine what he was when he was in his prime. Even with all the injuries, he's still a great player. He's like a 7-3 point guard." . . . Well, maybe not a great player. But still good enough . . . European players who saw him healthy—Dino Radja, Vlade Divac, etc.—insist he'd be on the Olajuwon-O'Neal-Robinson level with good wheels . . . Named to the All-Rookie team . . . Born Dec. 19, 1964, in Kaunas, Lithuania . . . Made $2.28 million.

Year	Team	G	FG	FG Pct.	FT	FT Pct.	Reb.	Ast.	TP	Avg.
1995-96	Portland	73	394	.545	231	.757	588	130	1058	14.5

CHRIS DUDLEY 31 6-11 240   Center

Laugh at his free-throw shooting if you must, but respect what he does best . . . Averaged 9.0 rebounds last season in just 24.1 minutes a game . . . In 1994-95, he got 9.3 boards in 27.3 minutes . . . Would be in double figures with the 33-35 minutes a lot of starting centers get . . . Real factor on the offensive boards . . . Without the second-shot opportunities he created, the Blazers' poor 99.3 points a game would have been even worse ... Also 21st in league in blocked shots ... Started 61 times ... Yale product was fourth-round pick by Cleveland in 1987 ... Came to Portland as free agent in the summer of '93 ... Born Feb. 22, 1965, in Stamford, Conn. ... Made $3.8 million.

Year	Team	G	FG	FG Pct.	FT	FT Pct.	Reb.	Ast.	TP	Avg.
1987-88	Cleveland	55	65	.474	40	.563	144	23	170	3.1
1988-89	Cleveland	61	73	.435	39	.364	157	21	185	3.0
1989-90	Clev.-N.J.	64	146	.411	58	.319	423	39	350	5.5
1990-91	New Jersey	61	170	.408	94	.534	511	37	434	7.1
1991-92	New Jersey	82	190	.403	80	.468	739	58	460	5.6
1992-93	New Jersey	71	94	.353	57	.518	513	16	245	3.5
1993-94	Portland	6	6	.240	2	.500	24	5	14	2.3
1994-95	Portland	82	181	.406	85	.464	764	34	447	5.5
1995-96	Portland	80	162	.453	80	.510	720	37	404	5.1
	Totals	562	1087	.411	535	.461	3995	270	2709	4.8

AARON McKIE 24 6-5 209   Guard

Made nice improvement from the first season to the second ... Starting shooting guard not much of a three-point threat, but improved overall from 44.4 percent to 46.7 ... Got the top job there after Clyde Drexler was traded midway through 1994-95 ... Teammate of Rasheed Wallace in high school and Lakers' Eddie Jones at Temple ... Grew up eight blocks from Temple ... Pretty good defender ... No. 17 pick in the 1994 draft ... Born Oct. 2, 1972, in Philadelphia ... Made $845,000.

Year	Team	G	FG	FG Pct.	FT	FT Pct.	Reb.	Ast.	TP	Avg.
1994-95	Portland	45	116	.444	50	.685	129	89	293	6.5
1995-96	Portland	81	337	.467	152	.764	304	205	864	10.7
	Totals	126	453	.461	202	.743	433	294	1157	9.2

ISAIAH (J.R.) RIDER 25 6-5 215   Guard

One more outburst and it's to your room without supper ... Continues to have problems keeping his emotions in check ... Too bad, since the attitude overshadows the considerable talent, which he will now display at Portland ... Was traded by Minnesota last summer for Bill Curley and James Robinson and a future first-rounder ... One game last season, when he was slow to leave the court after being ejected, his mom came out and ordered him to the locker room . . . Tough to handle on the blocks while also having the ability to step outside for medium-range jumpers . . . Led Timberwolves in scoring last two years . . . No. 1 in team history in three-pointers . . . Minnesota made him No. 5 pick in 1993 . . . Standout at UNLV before that . . . Born March 12, 1971, in Oakland . . . Made $3.01 million.

Year	Team	G	FG	FG Pct.	FT	FT Pct.	Reb.	Ast.	TP	Avg.
1993-94	Minnesota	79	522	.468	215	.811	315	202	1313	16.6
1994-95	Minnesota	75	558	.447	277	.817	249	245	1532	20.4
1995-96	Minnesota	75	560	.464	248	.838	309	213	1470	19.6
	Totals	229	1640	.459	740	.822	873	660	4315	18.8

GARY TRENT 22 6-8 240   Forward

Known as Shaq of the MAC in college, when he was an inside force for Ohio University in the Mid-American Conference . . . Known as a reserve in the NBA . . . Averaged 17.7 minutes last season . . . Did get 10 starts . . . His 51.3 percent from the field was No. 2 on the team, behind Arvydas Sabonis, and No. 2 among all rookies . . . Milwaukee used the 11th pick to get him, then quickly packaged him to the Trail Blazers for Shawn Respert . . . Three-time MAC Player of the Year . . . He and Ron Harper are the only players in conference history to get 2,000 points and 1,000 rebounds in a career . . . Set national prep record by making an astounding 81.4 percent of his shots—and we don't mean from the line—as a senior at Hamilton Township High School in Columbus, Ohio . . . Born Sept. 22, 1974, in Columbus . . . Made $1.022 million.

Year	Team	G	FG	FG Pct.	FT	FT Pct.	Reb.	Ast.	TP	Avg.
1995-96	Portland	69	220	.513	78	.553	238	50	518	7.5

DONTONIO WINGFIELD 22 6-8 256   Forward

Let's see. Two pro seasons, three teams. Yeah, nice decision to leave school early . . . Actually, he may have been a trend-setter . . . Declared for the draft after his freshman season at Cincinnati, back when turning pro that soon wasn't the trend . . . College teammate of Nick Van Exel . . . SuperSonics took him with 37th pick in 1994, played him 81 minutes and left him unprotected in expansion draft . . . Raptors grabbed him there, then cut him . . . Trail Blazers made the minor investment with a $225,000 free-agent contract on Oct. 5, 1995 . . . Teams always interested in at least a look because of his athleticism . . . Born June 23, 1974, in Albany, Ga.

Year	Team	G	FG	FG Pct.	FT	FT Pct.	Reb.	Ast.	TP	Avg.
1994-95	Seattle	20	18	.353	8	.800	30	3	46	2.3
1995-96	Portland	44	60	.382	26	.765	104	28	165	3.8
	Totals	64	78	.375	34	.773	134	31	211	3.3

RASHEED WALLACE 22 6-10 225   Forward-Center

Will somebody please slap this guy? . . . Showed the emotional stability of Hitler during the bunker days . . . Drew 19 technical fouls. Lost his temper at the drop of a hat . . . Work habits of a cadaver . . . And he's a trash-talker . . . Sad part is, he has talent. Lots of it. Can post up, can shoot the jumper . . . Some scouts insist he has more natural talent than incoming wunderkind Marcus Camby. But they question if he'll last because of temperament . . . Needs to get stronger . . . Came to Portland with Michael Butler last summer from Washington for Rod Strickland and Harvey Grant . . . Not much of a rebounder as a rookie, but he can block shots . . . Missed last 15 games with a fractured thumb . . . Left North Carolina after two seasons. Most refs and half the league wish he'd go back . . . Finished as leading field-goal shooter in ACC history at .635 . . . Was picked No. 4 overall by Bullets . . . Born Sept. 17, 1974, in Philadelphia . . . Made $1.493 million.

Year	Team	G	FG	FG Pct.	FT	FT Pct.	Reb.	Ast.	TP	Avg.
1995-96	Washington	65	275	.487	78	.650	303	85	655	10.1

MITCHELL BUTLER 25 6-5 210   Guard

Joins Trail Blazers with Rasheed Wallace in deal that sent Rod Strickland and Harvey Grant to the Bullets . . . His shooting regressed. From pathetic (.421) to pitiful (.384). That was the lowest mark on the Bullets by anyone who stayed around for more than the morning coffee break . . . Makes some really bad plays, too . . . Allegedly, he reportedly plays defense . . . Didn't show that last season, although that is his strength . . . Can handle the ball better than most two guards and gets some time at the point . . . He is durable, missing only seven games in three years . . . Bullets signed him as free agent Oct. 5, 1993, after he went undrafted out of UCLA . . . Born Dec. 15, 1970, in Los Angeles . . . Made $500,000.

Year	Team	G	FG	FG Pct.	FT	FT Pct.	Reb.	Ast.	TP	Avg.
1993-94	Washington	75	207	.495	104	.578	225	77	518	6.9
1994-95	Washington	76	214	.421	123	.665	170	91	597	7.9
1995-96	Washington	61	88	.384	48	.578	118	67	237	3.9
	Totals	212	509	.441	275	.614	513	235	1352	6.4

THE ROOKIES

JERMAINE O'NEAL 18 6-11 226   Forward
The Trail Blazers dip into the kiddie litter . . . Attempting to make the jump from Eau Claire High School in Columbia, S.C., to the NBA, sans college . . . Very raw . . . Offensive game is not ready, but this pick at No. 17 was obviously based on potential . . . Quiet and shy, so will need some hand-holding . . . Anyone volunteering in the locker room? . . . Mr. Basketball in South Carolina last season . . . Born Oct. 23, 1978, in Columbia, S.C.

JASON SASSER 22 6-7 225   Forward
Texas Tech product runs the floor well . . . Impressed scouts with how hard he plays . . . Drafted 41st by Sacramento, then was traded to Portland . . . Third-team All-American and Southwest Conference Player of the Year as a senior . . . Helped lead Red Raiders to 30-2 record and Sweet Sixteen before losing to Georgetown . . . No. 2 all-time scoring at Tech . . . Born Jan. 13, 1974, in Denton, Tex.

MARCUS BROWN 22 6-3 185   Guard
Will probably have to make the sometimes difficult transition from shooting guard to point guard . . . Did play some there last season . . . Good shooter . . . Dropped to the Trail Blazers at No. 46 after a poor set of postseason workouts . . . No. 2 scorer in the nation as a senior at Murray State (26.4) . . . Ohio Valley Conference Player of the Year as a junior and senior . . . Born April 3, 1974, in West Memphis, Ark.

COACH P.J. CARLESIMO: Two seasons with the Trail Blazers, two 44-38 finishes, but 1995-96 was anything but average ... Apart from the obligatory battles with point guard Rod Strickland, at least ... Steered Trail Blazers to end-of-season recovery and into the playoffs when the lottery looked like a good bet ... Won 18 of last 22 in the regular season while using seven different starting lineups involving nine of the 12 players ... Intrigue of the summer was to see whether he would get the door or Strickland would get the trade ... It was the latter ... This town ain't big enough for the both of them ... Came to the Trail Blazers, and the NBA, after 12 seasons at Seton Hall ... Was 212-166 (56.1 percent) in that time with the Pirates ... When he went 44-38 in 1994-95, that made him the first coach in 25 years to go directly from college to the pros and post a winning mark ... Cotton Fitzsimmons (Kansas State to Phoenix) was the last to accomplish that ... Only the second coach in school history to break 200 wins, joining Hall of Famer John (Honey) Russell ... Had five 20-win seasons and best year was 1989, when Seton Hall reached the championship game before losing to Michigan ... Coached at New Hampshire College and Wagner before Seton Hall ... Assistant coach for Chuck Daly at the 1992 Olympics ... Graduated from Fordham in 1971 ... Born May 30, 1949, in Scranton, Pa.

BIGGEST BLUNDER

We can at least understand the thinking. They already had a young Clyde Drexler and needed a big man, not another shooting guard. Sam Bowie had just starred at the University of Kentucky, at least on those occasions when he was healthy. There was one problem, though: Michael Jordan was also available.

When the Trail Blazers took Bowie with the second pick in the 1984 draft, after the Houston Rockets selected Hakeem Olajuwon at No. 1, the man who would become the greatest player in NBA history was allowed to slip to the Chicago Bulls at No. 3. And neither franchise would ever be the same.

Bowie was a talent blessed with size, a soft touch and skills as a shot-blocker and was one of the best-passing big men of his generation. But he was also burdened by a series of injuries that made reaching his potential impossible. Jordan, of course, set new standards.

ALL-TIME TRAIL BLAZER LEADERS

SEASON

Points: Clyde Drexler, 2,185, 1987–88
Assists: Terry Porter, 831, 1987–88
Rebounds: Lloyd Neal, 967, 1972–73

GAME

Points: Geoff Petrie, 51 vs. Houston, 1/20/73
Geoff Petrie, 51 vs. Houston, 3/16/73
Assists: Rod Strickland, 20 vs. Phoenix, 4/4/94
Rod Strickland, 20 vs. Houston, 3/30/96
Rebounds: Sidney Wicks, 27 vs. Los Angeles, 2/26/75

CAREER

Points: Clyde Drexler, 18,040, 1984–95
Assists: Terry Porter, 5,319, 1985–95
Rebounds: Clyde Drexler, 5,339, 1984–95

SACRAMENTO KINGS

TEAM DIRECTORY: Managing General Partner: Jim Thomas; Pres.: Rick Benner; VP-Basketball Oper.: Geoff Petrie; Dir. Basketball Services: Wayne Cooper; Dir. Player Personnel: Jerry Reynolds; Dir. Media Rel.: Travis Stanley; Coach: Garry St. Jean; Asst. Coaches: Eddie Jordan, Mike Bratz, Pete Carril. Arena: ARCO Arena (17,317). Colors: Purple, silver and black.

SCOUTING REPORT

SHOOTING: Sorry, one ball per team per possession. We double-checked the rules, and we're pretty sure the Kings have, too. They traded for Mahmoud Abdul-Rauf, a point guard in name only, and will put him in the same backcourt as superstar Mitch Richmond.

Richmond took an astounding 515 three-pointers last season, more than twice as many as the league champion from behind the arc, Washington's Tim Legler. That's OK, though, since Richmond finished ninth. Now comes Abdul-Rauf, who had 309 tries from downtown last season—more than seven of the same top-10 finishers.

The Kings were fifth in the league in that category and second in the Western Conference, behind only San Antonio, so they are dangerous. They just aren't so feared in general after finishing 20th from the field overall. The draft would normally bring an encouraging sign in this area because Predrag Stojakovic is said to be a very good shooter, but he may also return to play another season in Greece.

PLAYMAKING: Abdul-Rauf as the starting point guard? See above. But before passing judgment, we should also note that he does pass, too, averaging 6.8 assists in his last go-round with the Nuggets. OK, so one small forward (Grant Hill) did better, but that was still ahead of noted counterparts like Terrell Brandon and Mookie Blaylock.

And Tyus Edney, at a respectable 6.1 for rookies. Bobby Hurley? Don't ask. If Edney still gets at least decent playing time—he probably won't get close to the 31 minutes a a game last season while starting 60 times—he could continue to develop into a dependable backup at the point and a great spark off the bench at any position.

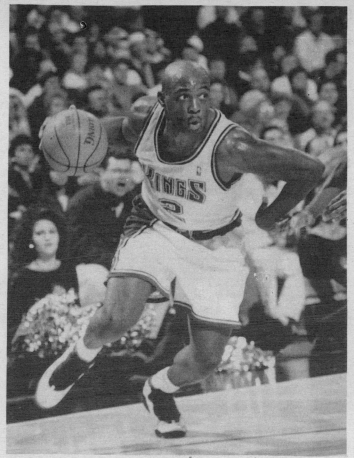

Olympian Mitch Richmond has had eight 20 ppg seasons.

REBOUNDING: Much the way the Kings' defense has made great strides over the last few years, the rebounding game is also improving. Last season was the most dramatic jump yet, from 18th by percentage to ninth.

Things could get even better this season. Of course, they could also get worse. Brian Grant is too much of a talent to get just seven boards a game, as was the case in 1995-96, but, then again,

KING ROSTER

No.	Veterans	Pos.	Ht.	Wt.	Age	Yrs. Pro	College
3	Mahmoud Abdul-Rauf	G	6-1	162	27	6	LSU
31	Duane Causwell	C	7-0	240	28	6	Temple
5	Tyus Edney	G	5-10	152	23	1	UCLA
40	Kevin Gamble	F-G	6-6	235	30	9	Iowa
33	Brian Grant	F	6-9	254	24	2	Xavier
35	Byron Houston	F	6-5	250	26	4	Oklahoma State
7	Bobby Hurley	G	6-0	165	25	3	Duke
20	Clint McDaniel	G	6-4	180	24	1	Arkansas
30	Billy Owens	F-G	6-9	225	27	5	Syracuse
0	Olden Polynice	F-C	7-0	250	31	9	Virginia
2	Mitch Richmond	G	6-5	215	31	8	Kansas State
22	Lionel Simmons	F	6-7	210	27	6	LaSalle
34	Michael Smith	F	6-8	230	24	2	Providence
4	Corliss Williamson	F	6-7	245	22	1	Arkansas

Rd.	Rookie	Sel.No.	Pos.	Ht.	Wt.	College
1	Predrag Stojakovic	14	F-G	6-9	229	PAOK (Greece)

that was a drop from the 7.5 of his rookie season. Corliss Williamson may also be able to make a contribution this campaign after making just 53 appearances last year because of injuries.

DEFENSE: "I see a team that understands what defense is all about," Heat coach Pat Riley says. "They've made a commitment to that end of the floor. They're learning that everything in this league begins and ends with defense. They look like they got tired of what was going on."

After posting significant gains, not coincidentally at the same time they were climbing in the standings, the Kings dropped from second in the league in shooting percentage-against in 1994–95 to 17th last season. That's almost back to where they started. They were 20th in points allowed (102.3) and tied for 17th in steals.

OUTLOOK: Garry St. Jean's team is young for the most part, but their star, Richmond, is 31, and the starting center, Olden Polynice, turns 32 on Nov. 21, so the window of opportunity is not exactly limitless. They can't spend another two seasons just trying to reach the second round. Or even one more season straining to reach .500.

KING PROFILES

MITCH RICHMOND 31 6-5 215   Guard

Continues to carry the load on offense, with no sign of breaking down under the pressure . . . Offseason arrival of another scorer in the backcourt, Mahmoud Abdul-Rauf, could take off some of the weight . . . Could also give defenses somebody else to worry about, creating more chances for the four-time All-Star . . . Member of Dream Team III at the Atlanta Olympics . . . Also played in the 1988 Games in Seoul, making him one of only 12 men to be on a U.S. Olympic basketball team twice . . . Rookie of the Year in 1989 . . . Even with that extensive resume, may still make an all-underrated team . . . Most fans don't realize his ability to hit the three-point or power a defender inside . . . The 23.1 points a game last season was No. 8 in the league and No. 2 among guards, behind only Michael Jordan . . . Starred at Kansas State, then went fifth overall to the Warriors in 1988 . . . Golden State made a big mistake by trading him to Sacramento for Billy Owens . . . Born June 30, 1965, in Ft. Lauderdale, Fla. . . . Made $3.5 million.

Year	Team	G	FG	FG Pct.	FT	FT Pct.	Reb.	Ast.	TP	Avg.
1988-89	Golden State	79	649	.468	410	.810	468	334	1741	22.0
1989-90	Golden State	78	640	.497	406	.866	360	223	1720	22.1
1990-91	Golden State	77	703	.494	394	.847	452	238	1840	23.9
1991-92	Sacramento.	80	685	.468	330	.813	319	411	1803	22.5
1992-93	Sacramento.	45	371	.474	197	.845	154	221	987	21.9
1993-94	Sacramento.	78	635	.445	426	.834	286	313	1823	23.4
1994-95	Sacramento.	82	668	.446	375	.843	357	311	1867	22.8
1995-96	Sacramento.	81	611	.447	425	.866	269	255	1872	23.1
	Totals	600	4962	.466	2963	.840	2665	2306	13653	22.8

MAHMOUD ABDUL-RAUF 27 6-1 162   Guard

Scoring ability amidst all the controversy . . . Suspended last season by the league for refusing to stand during the national anthem . . . The former Chris Jackson said his Muslim religion did not permit it. Fans around the country said it was about disrespecting the flag. Either way, it became an issue that transcended sports . . . It will follow him the rest of his career . . .

Those who pay attention to his game instead of his beliefs will see a shooter with one of the quickest releases in the game... But he doesn't have the size to play shooting guard, so he has been a point guard without true point-guard skills... Kings got him during the offseason for Sarunas Marciulionis... Born March 9, 1969, in Gulfport, Miss., and attended Louisiana State, before Nuggets took him third overall in 1990... Made $2.6 million.

Year	Team	G	FG	FG Pct.	FT	FT Pct.	Reb.	Ast.	TP	Avg.
1990-91	Denver	67	417	.413	84	.857	121	206	942	14.1
1991-92	Denver	81	356	.421	94	.870	114	192	837	10.3
1992-93	Denver	81	633	.450	217	.935	225	344	1553	19.2
1993-94	Denver	80	588	.460	219	.956	168	362	1437	18.0
1994-95	Denver	73	472	.470	138	.885	137	263	1165	16.0
1995-96	Denver	57	414	.434	146	.930	138	389	1095	19.2
	Totals	439	2880	.443	898	.916	903	1756	7029	16.0

OLDEN POLYNICE 31 7-0 250   Center

Runs on emotion... No star, but continues to post decent numbers... Last season he was 14th in the league at 52.7 percent, 17th at 9.4 rebounds a game and established a career high with 12.2 points an outing... No skills as a shot-blocker, so he tries to be a deterent inside by putting a body on anyone who comes down the lane... Originally No. 8 pick by the Bulls out of Virginia in 1987, then traded to Seattle for Scottie Pippen... Sonics' reaction today: "Oops"... Kings got him from Detroit for Pete Chilcutt and a second-round pick Feb. 20, 1994... Since then has become fourth in franchise history—and second in the Sacramento era—in shooting percentage... Born Nov. 21, 1964, in Port-au-Prince, Haiti... Made $2.52 million.

Year	Team	G	FG	FG Pct.	FT	FT Pct.	Reb.	Ast.	TP	Avg.
1987-88	Seattle	82	118	.465	101	.639	330	33	337	4.1
1988-89	Seattle	80	91	.506	51	.593	206	21	233	2.9
1989-90	Seattle	79	156	.540	47	.475	300	15	360	4.6
1990-91	Sea.-LAC	79	316	.560	146	.579	553	42	778	9.8
1991-92	L.A.Clippers	76	244	.519	125	.622	536	46	613	8.1
1992-93	Detroit	67	210	.490	66	.465	418	29	486	7.3
1993-94	Det.-Sac.	68	346	.523	97	.508	809	41	789	11.6
1994-95	Sacramento	81	376	.544	124	.639	725	62	877	10.8
1995-96	Sacramento	81	431	.527	122	.601	764	58	985	12.2
	Totals	693	2288	.525	879	.576	4641	347	5458	7.9

BRIAN GRANT 24 6-9 254   Forward

Great some nights, gone other nights . . . Needs to become a more consistent rebounder to take the next step—just 7.0 last season . . . That's a drop from his rookie numbers (7.5) . . . Second on the Kings in rebounding and scoring in 1995-96 . . . Could become real good . . . One of only eight players in Kings-Royals history to top 2,000 points and 1,000 boards the first two seasons as a pro . . . Among the others: Oscar Robertson, Jerry Lucas and Sam Lacey . . . Good quickness . . . Led Xavier in rebounding all four years and became two-time Midwestern Collegiate Conference Player of the Year . . . No. 8 pick in 1994 . . . Born March 5, 1972, in Columbus, Ohio . . . Made $1.05 million.

Year	Team	G	FG	FG Pct.	FT	FT Pct.	Reb.	Ast.	TP	Avg.
1994-95	Sacramento	80	413	.511	231	.636	598	99	1058	13.2
1995-96	Sacramento	78	427	.507	262	.732	545	127	1120	14.4
	Totals	158	840	.509	493	.684	1143	226	2178	13.8

MICHAEL SMITH 24 6-8 230   Forward

Brings toughness and intensity . . . Probably a backup as long as Brian Grant is around, but developing into a nice player himself . . . Does a lot of the dirty work . . . The 6.0 rebounds a game last season were tops in the league among players with no starts . . . In fact, has never started in first two seasons as a pro . . . Free-throw shooting remains a major weakness . . . Better from close range: his 60.5 percent led the Kings last season . . . Came to the Kings the same time as Grant—the 1994 draft . . . Smith was picked 35th overall, after leading Big East Conference in rebounding all three years at Providence . . . Born March 28, 1972, in Washington, D.C. . . . Made $1.34 million.

Year	Team	G	FG	FG Pct.	FT	FT Pct.	Reb.	Ast.	TP	Avg.
1994-95	Sacramento	82	220	.542	127	.485	486	67	567	6.9
1995-96	Sacramento	65	144	.605	68	.384	389	110	357	5.5
	Totals	147	364	.565	195	.444	875	177	924	6.3

BILLY OWENS 27 6-9 225   Forward-Guard

Back where he started... Sort of... Sacramento originally took Syracuse star with the No. 3 pick in 1991, then traded him to Golden State for Mitch Richmond after a holdout... Kings coach Garry St. Jean was an assistant with the Warriors during that time... Returned to Sacramento last season just before the trade deadline along with Kevin Gamble for Walt Williams and Tyrone Corbin... Hobbled by a bad right foot for much of the time in Sacramento, missing nine games and playing less than 30 minutes in 14 of the 22 appearances... Occasionally used at point forward... Born May 1, 1969, in Carlisle, Pa.... Made $3.32 million.

Year	Team	G	FG	FG Pct.	FT	FT Pct.	Reb.	Ast.	TP	Avg.
1991-92	Golden State	80	468	.525	204	.654	639	188	1141	14.3
1992-93	Golden State	37	247	.501	117	.639	264	144	612	16.5
1993-94	Golden State	79	492	.507	199	.610	640	326	1186	15.0
1994-95	Miami	70	403	.491	194	.620	502	246	1002	14.3
1995-96	Mia.-Sac.	62	323	.480	157	.636	411	204	808	13.0
	Totals	328	1933	.502	871	.631	2456	1108	4749	14.5

LIONEL SIMMONS 28 6-7 210   Forward

The name sounds familiar... Oh, yeah. Small forward. Once considered a cornerstone to the Kings' future. Big contract... And now, a non-factor... Averaged just 15 minutes last season... Shooting hit a career-low 39.6 percent... Limited athletic ability and lack of a consistent outside game hurt... No. 1 in team's Sacramento-era history in games played (413) and career rebounds (2,729)... He and Duane Causwell ended last season with the longest active tenure on the Kings... La Salle product was No. 7 pick in 1990... Born Oct. 14, 1968, in Philadelphia... Made $2.676 million.

Year	Team	G	FG	FG Pct.	FT	FT Pct.	Reb.	Ast.	TP	Avg.
1990-91	Sacramento	79	549	.422	320	.736	697	315	1421	18.0
1991-92	Sacramento	78	527	.454	281	.770	634	337	1336	17.1
1992-93	Sacramento	69	468	.444	298	.819	495	312	1235	17.9
1993-94	Sacramento	75	436	.438	251	.777	562	305	1129	15.1
1994-95	Sacramento	58	131	.420	59	.702	196	89	327	5.6
1995-96	Sacramento	54	86	.396	55	.733	145	83	246	4.6
	Totals	413	2197	.436	1264	.768	2729	1441	5694	13.8

DUANE CAUSWELL 28 7-0 240   Center

Role player . . . When he is a player at all, that is . . . Averaged just 14.3 minutes a game last season . . . Did start 26 times . . . Defensive specialist . . . The 1.07 blocks was second on the club . . . No. 3 in franchise history in blocks (657), behind Sam Lacey (1,098) and LaSalle Thompson (697) . . . Also No. 7 in shooting percentage (51.6) . . . So how to explain the disaster of last season: 41.7 percent? . . . Did set a personal best from the line at 72.9 percent . . . Only Lionel Simmons has played more games in the Sacramento era . . . Played at Temple with Tim Perry, Mark Macon and Donald Hodge . . . Born May 31, 1968, in Queens Village, N.Y. . . . Made $1.83 million.

Year	Team	G	FG	FG Pct.	FT	FT Pct.	Reb.	Ast.	TP	Avg.
1990-91	Sacramento......	76	210	.508	105	.636	391	69	525	6.9
1991-92	Sacramento......	80	250	.549	136	.613	580	59	636	8.0
1992-93	Sacramento......	55	175	.545	103	.624	303	35	453	8.2
1993-94	Sacramento......	41	71	.518	40	.588	186	11	182	4.4
1994-95	Sacramento......	58	76	.517	57	.582	174	15	209	3.6
1995-96	Sacramento......	73	90	.417	70	.729	248	20	250	3.4
	Totals	383	872	.516	511	.628	1882	209	2255	5.9

BOBBY HURLEY 25 6-0 165   Guard

Kings handed him the starting point-guard job by trading away Spud Webb, then he lost it . . . Rookie Tyus Edney passed him by, though Hurley later got the gig back when the Kings looked for a spark during a second-half swoon . . . In the opening lineup 22 times in all . . . Lottery pick in 1993, No. 7 overall, also had nine DNP-CDs . . . Outside game still a big problem . . . Won two national titles at Duke and left as the NCAA's all-time assist leader . . . Born June 28, 1971, in Jersey City, N.J. . . . Made $2.584 million.

Year	Team	G	FG	FG Pct.	FT	FT Pct.	Reb.	Ast.	TP	Avg.
1993-94	Sacramento......	19	54	.370	24	.800	34	115	134	7.1
1994-95	Sacramento......	68	103	.363	58	.763	70	226	285	4.2
1995-96	Sacramento......	72	65	.283	68	.800	75	216	220	3.1
	Totals	159	222	.336	150	.785	179	557	639	4.0

TYUS EDNEY 23 5-10 152   Guard

Second-round success . . . Was a sparkplug in the Kings' 19-9 start . . . Then the scouting reports came in: play for the drive and let him shoot from the outside . . . Teams started to double off him regularly whenever he would spot up . . . Provided toughness and intensity . . . No. 47 pick became first rookie to lead Kings in assists since Phil Ford in 1978-79 . . . His 6.1 was also No. 2 among all first-year players . . . Participated in Rookie All-Star Game . . . Winner of 1995 Francis Pomeroy Naismith Award while at UCLA, given to the top college senior under six feet tall . . . Born Feb. 14, 1973, in Gardena, Cal. . . . Made $210,000.

Year	Team	G	FG	FG Pct.	FT	FT Pct.	Reb.	Ast.	TP	Avg.
1995-96	Sacramento	80	305	.412	197	.782	201	491	860	10.8

KEVIN GAMBLE 30 6-6 225   Forward-Guard

Decent range . . . Usually a better shooter than the 40.1 percent of last season . . . Had never been worse than 45.5 before that . . . No. 1 in playoff experience among all Kings, thanks to his six seasons with the Celtics . . . Versatile swingman . . . Originally third-round pick by Portland out of Iowa in 1987 . . . Came to Sacramento along with Billy Owens from Miami just before the trading deadline last season for Walt Williams and Tyrone Corbin . . . Started 13 times, all as a member of the Heat . . . Born Nov. 13, 1965, in Springfield, Ill. . . . Made $845,000.

Year	Team	G	FG	FG Pct.	FT	FT Pct.	Reb.	Ast.	TP	Avg.
1987-88	Portland	9	0	.000	0	.000	3	1	0	0.0
1988-89	Boston	44	75	.551	35	.636	42	34	187	4.3
1989-90	Boston	71	137	.455	85	.794	112	119	362	5.1
1990-91	Boston	82	548	.587	185	.815	267	256	1281	15.6
1991-92	Boston	82	480	.529	139	.885	286	219	1108	13.5
1992-93	Boston	82	459	.507	123	.826	246	226	1093	13.3
1993-94	Boston	75	368	458	103	.817	159	149	864	11.5
1994-95	Miami	77	220	.489	87	.784	122	119	566	7.4
1995-96	Mia.-Sac.	65	152	.401	38	.792	113	100	386	5.9
	Totals	587	2439	.506	795	.811	1350	1223	5847	10.0

CORLISS WILLIAMSON 22 6-7 245   Forward

Is he a power forward or small forward? ... Style says power game, size says the opposite ... Didn't help that he missed his entire rookie preseason and the first 17 games of the regular season while rehabilitating from surgery on his lower back ... The operation was on July 18, about a month after the Kings picked him 13th ... Then he also had 11 DNP-CDs ... Started three times ... Left Arkansas after his junior year ... Member of the Razorbacks' national-championship team as a sophomore ... MVP of that 1994 Final Four ... Born Dec. 4, 1973, in Russellville, Ark. ... Made $923,000.

Year	Team	G	FG	FG Pct.	FT	FT Pct.	Reb.	Ast.	TP	Avg.
1995-96	Sacramento	53	125	.466	47	.560	114	23	297	5.6

BYRON HOUSTON 26 6-5 250   Forward

Power forward's game in a small forward's body ... At least the height. Except for being 6-5, the rest of his body is all about strength ... Easy-going type off the floor, but bruiser on ... Got opportunity early last season with No. 1 pick Corliss Williamson sidelined ... "He's not going to be a prolific scorer," coach Garry St. Jean says. "But he's going to set the good pick, he's going to make the good pass, he's going to make a good decision within a play, and defensively he's sound." ... No. 27 pick by the Bulls in 1992 after starring at Oklahoma State ... Kings got him along with Sarunas Marciulionis from Seattle for Frank Brickowski in the summer of '94 ... Born Nov. 22, 1969, in Watonga, Kan. ... Made $800,000.

Year	Team	G	FG	FG Pct.	FT	FT Pct.	Reb.	Ast.	TP	Avg.
1992-93	Golden State	79	145	.446	129	.665	315	69	421	5.3
1993-94	Golden State	71	81	.458	33	.611	194	32	196	2.8
1994-95	Seattle	39	49	.458	28	.737	55	6	132	3.4
1995-96	Sacramento	25	32	.500	21	.808	84	7	86	3.4
	Totals	214	307	.456	211	.676	648	114	835	3.9

Mahmoud Abdul-Rauf swears allegiance to the Kings.

CLINT McDANIEL 24 6-4 180 Guard

Kings like his worth ethic and athleticism . . . Needs to improve ball-handling and decision-making to make transition to point guard . . . Good defender . . . Had terrible shooting percentage last season as a rookie—34.8—but unfair to judge off 12 games, usually in garbage time . . . The accomplishment was just making the roster after arriving at training camp as a free-agent invitee . . . Spent most of the season on the injured list with tendinitis in the left knee and spasms in the lower back . . . Strangely, the ailments came and went depending on the health of other Kings . . . College teammate of Corliss Williamson and played on Arkansas' 1994 NCAA championship squad . . . Born Feb. 26, 1972, in Tulsa, Okla. . . . Made $200,000.

Year	Team	G	FG	FG Pct.	FT	FT Pct.	Reb.	Ast.	TP	Avg.
1995-96	Sacramento	12	8	.348	12	.750	10	7	30	2.5

THE ROOKIE

PREDRAG STOJAKOVIC 19 6-9 200   Forward
Arguably the best of the European players in this draft. "By far," one personnel director says . . . Kings may have to work—or pay—to get him out of an existing contract in Greece, but he could be worth the hassle . . . Went 14th . . . Spent the last two seasons with PAOK, where teammates included Nugget draftee Efthimis Retzias and former Indiana center Dean Garrett . . . Born Sept. 6, 1977, in Belgrade, Yugoslavia.

COACH GARRY ST. JEAN: Not just a head coach anymore, but a head coach with playoff experience . . . That's an especially big deal around these parts . . . Last season guided the Kings to their first postseason appearance in 10 years . . . Already the winningest coach in their Sacramento era . . . No. 6 in franchise history . . . Known as "Saint" . . . Credit him for being able to adjust. Took over on May 22, 1992, his first gig as the No. 1 man on the bench, planning to build on an up-tempo style. When that didn't work, put new emphasis on defense . . . That did work . . . The 17th coach in franchise history . . . NBA assistant for 12 years, 10 on Don Nelson's staff, the last four with the Warriors before Sacramento gave him first chance to be head coach . . . The other two years were with Nets . . . Also has front-office experience as assistant director of player personnel at New Jersey and Milwaukee . . . Born Feb. 10, 1950, in Chicopee, Mass., and became a high school star there in basketball and soccer . . . Knee injures ended his career in both sports at Springfield College.

BIGGEST BLUNDER

Proof that being bad is not usually about bad luck: The NBA has held the lottery for 12 years now and never has there been a worse No. 1 pick than Pervis Ellison, the Kings' choice in 1989. None even close.

That it became a brutal top-10 class for almost everyone—

George McCloud, Tom Hammonds, Randy White, Danny Ferry and Stacey King were also included—is no excuse. The lure of the big man obviously got to the Kings, because they could have selected super-shooter Glen Rice or talented Sean Elliott, or even a couple of guards who slipped out of the lottery, Mookie Blaylock and Nick Anderson.

In truth, none of those players could be worth the lofty status that comes with being the No. 1 pick. On the other hand, at least they might still be on the team.

ALL-TIME KING LEADERS

SEASON

Points: Nate Archibald, 2,719, 1972–73
Assists: Nate Archibald, 910, 1972–73
Rebounds: Jerry Lucas, 1,668, 1965–66

GAME

Points: Jack Twyman, 59 vs. Minneapolis, 1/15/60
Assists: Phil Ford, 22 vs. Milwaukee, 2/21/79
      Oscar Robertson, 22 vs. New York, 3/5/66
      Oscar Robertson, 22 vs. Syracuse, 10/29/61
Rebounds: Jerry Lucas, 40 vs. Philadelphia, 2/29/64

CAREER

Points: Oscar Robertson, 22,009, 1960–70
Assists: Oscar Robertson, 7,731, 1960–70
Rebounds: Sam Lacey, 9,353, 1971–82

SEATTLE SUPERSONICS

TEAM DIRECTORY: Owner: Barry Ackerley; Pres./GM: Wally Walker; VP-Basketball Oper.: Billy McKinney; Dir. Pub. Rel.: Cheri White; Coach: George Karl; Asst. Coaches: Bob Weiss, Terry Stotts, Dwane Casey Tim Grgurich. Arena: KeyArena (17,072). Colors: Green, red, yellow and bronze.

SCOUTING REPORT

SHOOTING: All you need to know about the SuperSonics here is that they took the fewest shots in the Western Conference last season—only Indiana, New York, Miami, Detroit and Cleveland had less tries—and still averaged 104.5 points a game. That was the *second*-best output in the league. That's efficiency.

Gary Payton re-signed seven-year, $85-million pact.

SUPERSONIC ROSTER

No.	Veterans	Pos.	Ht.	Wt.	Age	Yrs. Pro	College
—	Craig Ehlo	G-F	6-7	205	35	13	Washington State
1	Sherell Ford	F	6-7	210	24	1	Illinois-Chicago
—	Greg Graham	G	6-4	182	25	3	Indiana
33	Hersey Hawkins	G	6-3	190	30	8	Bradley
40	Shawn Kemp	F	6-10	245	26	7	Trinity JC
—	Jim McIlvaine	C	7-1	240	22	2	Marquette
10	Nate McMillan	G-F	6-5	200	32	10	North Carolina State
20	Gary Payton	G	6-4	190	28	6	Oregon State
14	Sam Perkins	F-C	6-9	245	35	12	North Carolina
55	Steve Scheffler	C	6-9	250	29	6	Purdue
11	Detlef Schrempf	F	6-10	230	33	11	Washington
3	Eric Snow	G	6-3	200	23	1	Michigan State
25	David Wingate	G-F	6-5	185	32	10	Georgetown

Rd.	Rookies	Sel.No.	Pos.	Ht.	Wt.	College
2	Joe Blair	35	F	6-10	251	Arizona
2	Joe Vogel	45	C	6-11	255	Colorado State
2	Drew Barry	57	G	6-5	191	Georgia Tech

That's also a trademark. Three seasons ago, Seattle tied for fourth in the NBA in percentage, then moved up to third in 1994-95. Last season, a drop. All the way back to a fourth-place tie, led by Shawn Kemp at No. 5 among individuals, including No. 1 for Western Conference players.

The success of this season depended on how they came through the free-agent summer. And it all worked out with the re-signing of Hersey Hawkins, their top three-point shooter, and Sam Perkins, whose offensive versatility remains a strength as he launches his 13th season. He's still respected around the league from the post or downtown despite poor numbers last season.

PLAYMAKING: Gary Payton is not to be confused with your prototype point guard. Not when he takes 339 more shots than anybody on the team.

All this means is that the SuperSonics operate without a true distributor. Like it really holds them back. Payton has a right to lean on his shot so much because it has developed into such a dangerous weapon after early struggles out of college. It's one of the things that has made him into one of the best players at his position.

That he averaged 39 minutes last season was also indicative of the Sonics' lack of depth among ball-handlers, seeing as coach George Karl has historically kept his players under wraps (Shawn Kemp: 33.3 minutes in 1995-96). Nate McMillan is still the backup, but is also going to be 32 on opening night. Perhaps with that in mind, management has used a draft pick each of the last two years on point guards, Eric Snow in 1995 and Drew Barry in '96.

REBOUNDING: Kemp can't do it alone. His 11.4 boards a game last season was good for fifth in the league, but Seattle remains average. The new starting center, Jim McIlvaine, should do better here than predecessor Ervin Johnson, although backup Perkins spends so much time away from the basket on offense that he doesn't make much contribution.

For this the 28 other teams should be thrilled. The Sonics create enough havoc with their defense and transition game. Imagine if they also crashed the boards.

DEFENSE: We put the matter to Jerry Sloan, coach of the Utah Jazz. "They take you out of the things you're accustomed to doing," he said. "That's what makes them very effective. If you don't play with intelligence against them, you're going to really have a tough time. Plus, they've got great athletes."

Start with the one in the backcourt. Payton backed up his nick-name—The Glove—by leading the league in steals last season. Hawkins, never known for his defense, was ninth. McMillan didn't rank, but makes a significant contribution. Move up front and the athletic Kemp is waiting.

In the end, the Sonics did such a good job of taking people out of what they're used to doing that no team had more steals, no team forced more turnovers and only one (Miami) held opponents to a lower shooting percentage. And Seattle was able to do it all without the luxury of an inside presence, finishing 18th in blocks during 1995-96 but making up for it with hard rotations. Now they have McIlvaine, who finished 10th among individuals despite averaging just 14.9 minutes with the Bullets.

OUTLOOK: For once, they don't have to live down the past. Now to see how the Sonics live up to it.

This remains a championship contender, but one that spent the

Ageless Sam Perkins is never lost in Seattle.

last couple of months and the next several at something of an intersection. The summer, just after they hung in and forced the Bulls to six games in the Finals, was about deciding which of the many free agents to bring back. The new season could be about seeing if age will finally start to take a toll—Detlef Schrempf turns 34 in January, McMillan is 32 and Perkins 35.

SUPERSONIC PROFILES

SHAWN KEMP 26 6-10 245   Forward

The best player on the court during the 1996 Finals . . . Didn't win MVP because he wasn't on the eventual champion, but won tons of praise . . . Only disappointment around that time was not being picked for Dream Team III, or as a replacement when another forward, Glenn Robinson, dropped out . . . All-Star for the fourth straight season . . . Scoring and rebounding averages have increased each season . . . Great physical specimen who can dominate with the proper focus . . . Never played college ball, but didn't exactly make the jump from high school to the NBA either, having spent one year at Trinity Valley Junior College . . . A steal at No. 17 in 1989 . . . Born Nov. 26, 1969, in Elkhart, Ind. . . . Made $3 million.

Year	Team	G	FG	FG Pct.	FT	FT Pct.	Reb.	Ast.	TP	Avg.
1989-90	Seattle	81	203	.479	117	.736	346	26	525	6.5
1990-91	Seattle	81	462	.508	288	.661	679	144	1214	15.0
1991-92	Seattle	64	362	.504	270	.748	665	86	994	15.5
1992-93	Seattle	78	515	.492	358	.712	833	155	1388	17.8
1993-94	Seattle	79	533	.538	364	.741	851	207	1431	18.1
1994-95	Seattle	82	545	.547	438	.749	893	149	1530	18.7
1995-96	Seattle	79	526	.561	493	.742	904	173	1550	19.6
	Totals	544	3146	.522	2328	.728	5171	940	8632	15.9

GARY PAYTON 28 6-4 190   Guard

A superstar . . . A Dream Teamer in Atlanta . . . Remember when the opposing point guards (Robert Pack, Nick Van Exel) used to give the Sonics so many problems in the playoffs? Payton worked over the prototype, John Stockton, in the Western Conference finals last season . . . This was after being named the league's Defensive Player of the Year . . . They call him The Glove because he's on you like one . . . Tops in steals . . . Tenth in assists . . . Three-time All-Star was the No. 2 overall pick in 1990 . . . Has missed only two games in the six seasons since, and the one from 1995-96 was due to suspension, not injury . . .

Member of the Pac-10 Conference All-Decade team for the 1980s after starring at Oregon State ... Born July 23, 1968, in Oakland ... Signed seven-year, $85-million deal during offseason.

Year	Team	G	FG	FG Pct.	FT	FT Pct.	Reb.	Ast.	TP	Avg.
1990-91	Seattle	82	259	.450	69	.711	243	528	588	7.2
1991-92	Seattle	81	331	.451	99	.669	295	506	764	9.4
1992-93	Seattle	82	476	.494	151	.770	281	399	1110	13.5
1993-94	Seattle	82	584	.504	166	.595	269	494	1349	16.5
1994-95	Seattle	82	685	.509	249	.716	281	583	1689	20.6
1995-96	Seattle	81	618	.484	229	.748	339	608	1563	19.3
	Totals	490	2953	.488	963	.701	1708	3118	7063	14.4

DETLEF SCHREMPF 33 6-10 230   Forward

If he's the third-best player on your team, that says plenty ... May not be The Guy elsewhere because he's not real flashy, but a real talent ... Size makes him a tough matchup at small forward ... But he can also step outside and hit the three-pointer ... Career low in appearances last season was because of fractured left arm that cost him 19 games ... Has represented both West Germany and the unified German teams in the Olympics ... Wife Mary is a former hurdler on the West German national team ... First came to Seattle to attend high school ... Stayed to play at Washington ... Dallas got him from there with eighth pick in 1985 ... Returned to Puget Sound when Sonics sent Derrick McKey and Gerald Paddio to Pacers on Nov. 1, 1993 ... Born Jan. 21, 1963, in Leverkusen, Germany ... Made $5 million.

Year	Team	G	FG	FG Pct.	FT	FT Pct.	Reb.	Ast.	TP	Avg.
1985-86	Dallas	64	142	.451	110	.724	198	88	397	6.2
1986-87	Dallas	81	265	.472	193	.742	303	161	756	9.3
1987-88	Dallas	82	246	.456	201	.756	279	159	698	8.5
1988-89	Dal.-Indiana	69	274	.474	273	.780	395	179	828	12.0
1989-90	Indiana	78	424	.516	402	.820	620	247	1267	16.2
1990-91	Indiana	82	432	.520	441	.818	660	301	1320	16.1
1991-92	Indiana	80	496	.536	365	.828	770	312	1380	17.3
1992-93	Indiana	82	517	.476	525	.804	780	493	1567	19.1
1993-94	Seattle	81	445	.493	300	.769	454	275	1212	15.0
1994-95	Seattle	82	521	.523	437	.839	508	310	1572	19.2
1995-96	Seattle	63	360	.486	287	.776	328	276	1080	17.1
	Totals	844	4122	.497	3534	.797	5295	2801	12077	14.3

HERSEY HAWKINS 30 6-3 190   Guard

One of the differences . . . Contributed emotional stability and outside shooting . . . Appreciated everywhere, they were much-needed ingredients in Seattle . . . Sonics sent disgruntled Kendall Gill to Charlotte to get him in summer of '95 . . . They weren't disappointed . . . Not much of a reputation for defense, but No. 9 in the league in steals in 1995-96 . . . No. 6 in free-throw percentage, too . . . Has 297 consecutive starts, the fourth-longest active streak . . . Has missed just seven games in seven seasons since coming out of Bradley as No. 6 pick in 1988 . . . Clippers did the picking, but sent him to 76ers in a draft-day deal . . . Player of the Year as a college senior by many organizations . . . Born Sept. 29, 1966, in Chicago . . . Made $2.5 million.

Year	Team	G	FG	FG Pct.	FT	FT Pct.	Reb.	Ast.	TP	Avg.
1988-89	Philadelphia	79	442	.455	241	.831	225	239	1196	15.1
1989-90	Philadelphia	82	522	.460	387	.888	304	261	1515	18.5
1990-91	Philadelphia	80	590	.472	479	.871	310	299	1767	22.1
1991-92	Philadelphia	81	521	.462	403	.874	271	248	1536	19.0
1992-93	Philadelphia	81	551	.470	419	.860	346	317	1643	20.3
1993-94	Charlotte	82	395	.460	312	.862	377	216	1180	14.4
1994-95	Charlotte	82	390	.482	261	.867	314	262	1172	14.3
1995-96	Seattle	82	443	.473	247	.873	297	218	1279	15.6
	Totals	649	3854	.467	2749	.867	2444	2060	11288	17.4

SAM PERKINS 35 6-9 245   Center-Forward

Big Smooth had some rough moments in 1995-96 . . . The 40.8 percent from the field was easily a career low . . . So was the 2,169 minutes . . . Bad timing—he was about to become a free agent . . . But he re-signed a two-year contract . . . Love to work from the perimeter, but holds his own on post defense . . . Has to. Plays backup center at 6-9 . . . Also power forward . . . He and Hersey Hawkins were the only Sonics to play all 82 last season . . . Three-time All-American at North Carolina and co-captain of the 1984 Olympic team that steamrolled through Los Angeles . . . Dallas had just picked him fourth overall . . . Born June 14, 1961, in New York . . . Made $3.967 million.

Year	Team	G	FG	FG Pct.	FT	FT Pct.	Reb.	Ast.	TP	Avg.
1984-85	Dallas	82	347	.471	200	.820	605	135	903	11.0
1985-86	Dallas	80	458	.503	307	.814	685	153	1234	15.4
1986-87	Dallas	80	461	.482	245	.828	616	146	1186	14.8
1987-88	Dallas	75	394	.450	273	.822	601	118	1066	14.2
1988-89	Dallas	78	445	.464	274	.833	688	127	1171	15.0
1989-90	Dallas	76	435	.493	330	.778	572	175	1206	15.9
1990-91	L.A. Lakers	73	368	.495	229	.821	538	108	983	13.5
1991-92	L.A. Lakers	63	361	.450	304	.817	556	141	1041	16.5
1992-93	L.A. Lakers-Sea.	79	381	.477	250	.820	524	156	1036	13.1
1993-94	Seattle	81	341	.438	218	.801	366	111	999	12.3
1994-95	Seattle	82	346	.466	215	.799	398	135	1043	12.7
1995-96	Seattle	82	325	.408	191	.793	367	120	970	11.8
	Totals	931	4662	.467	3036	.812	6516	1625	12838	13.8

NATE McMILLAN 32 6-5 200   Guard-Forward

If there was any doubt left how much he means to the Sonics—and there shouldn't have been any—the playoffs took care of that . . . His lower back problems at the end of the Western Conference finals helped send Sonics into the tailspin that required a Game 7 recovery . . . Struggled through the first few games of the Finals against the Bulls, and so did the Sonics . . . Returned for Game 4, and so did the Sonics . . . Emotional leader and stabilizing influence . . . Future in coaching if he wants it . . . Born Aug. 3, 1964, in Raleigh, N.C., and attended North Carolina State . . . No. 30 pick by Seattle in 1986 . . . Made $1.265 million.

Year	Team	G	FG	FG Pct.	FT	FT Pct.	Reb.	Ast.	TP	Avg.
1986-87	Seattle	71	143	.475	87	.617	331	583	373	5.3
1987-88	Seattle	82	235	.474	145	.707	338	702	624	7.6
1988-89	Seattle	75	199	.410	119	.630	388	696	532	7.1
1989-90	Seattle	82	207	.473	98	.641	403	598	523	6.4
1990-91	Seattle	78	132	.433	57	.613	251	371	338	4.3
1991-92	Seattle	72	177	.437	54	.643	252	359	435	6.0
1992-93	Seattle	73	213	.464	95	.709	306	384	546	7.5
1993-94	Seattle	73	177	.447	31	.564	283	387	437	6.0
1994-95	Seattle	80	166	.418	34	.586	302	421	419	5.2
1995-96	Seattle	55	100	.420	29	.707	210	197	275	5.0
	Totals	741	1749	.446	749	.650	3064	4698	4502	6.1

CRAIG EHLO 35 6-7 205   Guard-Forward

Hawks did not pick up his option after he shot .293 in playoffs, so Sonics picked him up as free agent . . . His long, strong relationship with Lenny Wilkens took a hit as the two traded verbal jabs when it was over . . . Had worst shooting percentage (.428) since his first season in Cleveland (.414 in '86-87) . . . Hawks were 19-12 when he scored in double figures . . . Participated in the relay that brought the Olympic Torch to Atlanta . . . Houston's second-round draft pick (40th overall) out of Washington State in 1983, he has Pac-10 rivalry with Byron Scott that has lasted more than a decade . . . Career blossomed under Wilkens in Cleveland and he followed the coach to the Hawks in 1993 . . . Earned $1.855 million . . . Born Aug. 11, 1961, in Lubbock, Tex.

Year	Team	G	FG	FG Pct.	FT	FT Pct.	Reb.	Ast.	TP	Avg.
1983-84	Houston	7	11	.407	1	1.000	9	6	23	3.3
1984-85	Houston	45	34	.493	19	.633	25	26	87	1.9
1985-86	Houston	36	36	.429	23	.793	46	29	98	2.7
1986-87	Cleveland	44	99	.414	70	.707	161	92	273	6.2
1987-88	Cleveland	79	226	.466	89	.674	274	206	563	7.1
1988-89	Cleveland	82	249	.475	71	.607	295	266	608	7.4
1989-90	Cleveland	81	436	.464	126	.681	439	371	1102	13.6
1990-91	Cleveland	82	344	.445	95	.679	388	376	832	10.1
1991-92	Cleveland	63	310	.453	87	.707	307	238	776	12.3
1992-93	Cleveland	82	385	.490	86	.717	403	254	949	11.6
1993-94	Atlanta	82	316	.446	112	.727	279	273	821	10.0
1994-95	Atlanta	49	191	.453	44	.620	147	113	477	9.7
1995-96	Atlanta	79	253	.428	81	.786	256	138	669	8.5
	Totals	811	2890	.456	904	.693	3029	2388	7278	9.0

GREG GRAHAM 25 6-4 182   Guard

They said he was ready to play pro defense when he came out of Indiana as the Big Ten Defensive Player of the Year in '93. They may have fibbed . . . Came to Nets from Sixers as part of the six-player trade involving Derrick Coleman and Shawn Bradley Nov. 30, 1995 . . . Very sporadic playing time . . . Age-old question of what is he best suited for, the point or the two. You know the rest. Doesn't handle ball well enough for one, doesn't shoot well enough for two . . . Still, you could do worse at end of bench . . . Born Nov. 26, 1970, in Indianapolis

... Was No. 17 pick on first round in '93 by Charlotte. Draft rights traded along with Dana Barros and Sidney Green to Sixers for Hersey Hawkins, Sept. 3, 1993 ... Made $1.12 million.

Year	Team	G	FG	FG Pct.	FT	FT Pct.	Reb.	Ast.	TP	Avg.
1993-94	Philadelphia......	70	122	.400	92	.836	86	66	338	4.8
1994-95	Philadelphia......	50	95	.426	55	.753	62	66	251	5.0
1995-96	Phil.-N.J.	53	78	.404	52	.765	57	52	240	4.5
	Totals	173	295	.409	199	.793	205	184	829	4.8

JIM McILVAINE 24 7-1 240   Center

Free-agent Bullet joins Sonics with seven-year, $35-million contract ... One of the best young backup centers in league. Was 10th in blocked shots despite averaging less than 15 minutes a game. Led league in blocks per 48 minutes (6.7) ... Offensive game steadily improving. It has to. Has been invisible for two limited-time seasons ... Figure he'd be adequate offensively given more minutes ... Has developed some low-post moves ... Has come along very quickly ... A second-round find, No. 32, in 1994, out of Marquette ... Can't be all bad: favorite movies are *Caddyshack* and *Spinal Tap* ... Born July 30, 1972, in Racine, Wis. ... Made $525,000.

Year	Team	G	FG	FG Pct.	FT	FT Pct.	Reb.	Ast.	TP	Avg.
1994-95	Washington......	55	34	.479	28	.683	105	10	96	1.7
1995-96	Washington......	80	62	.428	58	.552	230	11	182	2.3
	Totals	135	96	.444	86	.589	335	21	278	2.1

DAVID WINGATE 32 6-5 185   Guard-Forward

Just what the Sonics need, another defensive specialist ... Decent-to-poor shooter, depending on the season, or even the night ... Just 41.5 and 41 percent the last two seasons, and those weren't even career lows ... He'd *better* be a good defender ... Or maybe that's why he has gone through five teams since being drafted in the second round, 44th overall, by Philadelphia in 1986 ... Teammates at Baltimore's Dunbar High School with Muggsy Bogues, Reggie Williams and the late Reg-

gie Lewis . . . Member of Georgetown's 1984 championship team
. . . Born Dec. 15, 1963, in Baltimore . . . Made $560,000.

Year	Team	G	FG	FG Pct.	FT	FT Pct.	Reb.	Ast.	TP	Avg.
1986-87	Philadelphia	77	259	.430	149	.741	156	155	680	8.8
1987-88	Philadelphia	61	218	.400	99	.750	101	119	545	8.9
1988-89	Philadelphia	33	54	.470	27	.794	37	73	137	4.2
1989-90	San Antonio	78	220	.448	87	.777	195	208	527	6.8
1990-91	San Antonio	25	53	.384	29	.707	75	46	136	5.4
1991-92	Washington	81	266	.465	105	.719	269	247	638	7.9
1992-93	Charlotte	72	180	.536	79	.738	174	183	440	6.1
1993-94	Charlotte	50	136	.481	34	.667	134	104	310	6.2
1994-95	Charlotte	52	50	.410	18	.750	60	56	122	2.3
1995-96	Seattle	60	88	.415	32	.780	56	58	223	3.7
	Totals	589	1524	.446	659	.741	1257	1249	3758	6.4

SHERRELL FORD 24 6-7 210   Forward

Not on the playoff roster . . . Hell, barely on
the regular-season roster . . . Averaged just five
minutes a game in 28 appearances . . . Midwestern Collegiate Conference Player of the
Year for 1994-95 while at Illinois-Chicago . . .
Helped draft stock even more by being named
MVP at the Phoenix Desert Classic, a major
predraft camp . . . That got him all the way up
to the first round, to 26th overall . . . Joined in the draft by two
teammates from Proviso East High School in Maywood, Ill., Michael Finley and Donnie Boyce . . . The same school produced
Doc Rivers . . . Born Aug. 26, 1972, in Baton Rouge, La. . . .
Made $500,000.

Year	Team	G	FG	FG Pct.	FT	FT Pct.	Reb.	Ast.	TP	Avg.
1995-96	Seattle	28	30	.375	26	.765	24	5	90	3.2

STEVE SCHEFFLER 28 6-9 250   Forward-Center

The Human Victory Cigar . . . When he plays,
it usually means the game is in hand, or out of
hand . . . Fan favorite at the end of the bench
. . . Banger . . . Hard worker all the time, so a
great practice player . . . Except when he's going at it so hard that teammates are getting hurt
. . . Came into the league as No. 39 pick by
Charlotte in 1990 . . . That was just after being
named Big Ten Player of the Year at Purdue . . . Played on the
Boilermaker teams that won back-to-back conference titles . . .

Arrived in Seattle with a free-agent signing in October 1992 and hasn't left . . . Brother Tom played with Portland in 1984-85 . . . Born Sept. 3, 1967, in Grand Rapids, Mich. . . . Made $250,000.

Year	Team	G	FG	FG Pct.	FT	FT Pct.	Reb.	Ast.	TP	Avg.
1990-91	Charlotte.	39	20	.513	19	.905	45	9	59	1.5
1991-92	Sac.-Den.	11	6	.667	9	.750	14	0	21	1.9
1992-93	Seattle	29	25	.521	16	.667	36	5	66	2.3
1993-94	Seattle	35	28	.609	19	.950	26	6	75	2.1
1994-95	Seattle	18	12	.522	15	.833	23	4	39	2.2
1995-96	Seattle	35	24	.533	9	.474	33	2	58	1.7
	Totals	167	115	.548	87	.763	177	26	318	1.9

ERIC SNOW 23 6-3 200   Guard

Second-round pick got a chance last season . . . Relatively speaking . . . Scrounged up just 389 minutes—an average of nine per outing—but that was also the most by a Sonic rookie since a guy named Gary Payton in 1990-91 . . . Started once . . . Actually selected by Milwaukee at No. 43, but traded to Seattle soon after for the rights to Aurelijius Zukauskas and a future second-rounder . . . Sources say Sonics were forced into the trade by radio announcer and print reporters who knew they had no chance in the world of getting What's-His-Name's name right . . . No. 2 on the all-time assist list behind Scott Skiles at Michigan State . . . Born April 24, 1973, in Canton, Ohio . . . Born $200,000.

Year	Team	G	FG	FG Pct.	FT	FT Pct.	Reb.	Ast.	TP	Avg.
1995-96	Seattle	43	42	.420	29	.592	43	73	115	2.7

THE ROOKIES

JOE BLAIR 22 6-10 251   Forward

Needs to develop a low-post game, but has improved as a rebounder . . . No. 1 all-time at Arizona in shooting, at 61.2 percent . . . Dropped about 20 pounds between the end of the college season and workouts for the pros . . . Only played 14 games as a senior because of academic problems . . . No. 35 pick . . . Born June 12, 1974, in Akron, Ohio.

DREW BARRY 23 6-5 191   **Guard**

Son of Rick, brother of Brent and Jon went 57th . . . Has potential to play either backcourt spot . . . Very good with no-look passes . . . Can hit the three-pointer, though his shooting numbers from behind the arc and overall took a dip his senior season at Georgia Tech . . . Like Muggsy Bogues and Phil Ford, he led the ACC in assists three straight seasons . . . Born Feb. 17, 1973, in Oakland.

JOE VOGEL 23 6-11 255   **Center**

Colorado State product became the 45th pick . . . No wonder most people hadn't heard of him: just 10.1 points, 6.7 rebounds and 48 percent as a senior . . . Born Sept. 15, 1973, in North Platte, Neb.

COACH GEORGE KARL: Hey, we're not the only ones who

owe him an apology . . . Half the free world had him pegged as a goner too, what with those back-to-back first-round losses to lower-ranked teams, and after the Sonics had won the opener . . . Hung in there and bounced back with a vengence last season, guiding the Sonics to their first appearance in the Finals since 1979 . . . That included a franchise-record 64 victories during the regular season, the 10th-most in NBA history . . . Is 266-104 (71.9 percent) in 4½ seasons in Seattle . . . More impressive: Sonics have never lost more than three in a row on his watch . . . Career: 385-280 (57.9 percent) . . . Former point guard at North Carolina and San Antonio . . . Broke into coaching with Spurs as an assistant to Doug Moe . . . Became head coach for the first time with Montana of the CBA, where he spent three years and was Coach of the Year in two of those . . . Returned to NBA as director of player acquisition for Cavaliers in 1983 and a year later became coach. Fired late in 1985-86 . . . The Warriors hired him from there to be their sideline boss. That lasted two seasons . . . Next came stops with Albany of the CBA and Real Madrid of the Spanish League before the Sonics called . . . Born May 12, 1951, in Penn Hills, Pa.

BIGGEST BLUNDER

Remember the big offseason news from Seattle a few years ago? The near-trade of Shawn Kemp for Scottie Pippen?

It shouldn't have been necessary. The SuperSonics would have already had Pippen, if he hadn't been traded to the Bulls in a 1987 draft-day deal with the Sonics for Olden Polynice. Oops.

Imagine Kemp and Pippen along the same frontline today. Imagine teams having to worry about both of them. Now imagine the SuperSonics kicking themselves. OK, so you don't have to imagine that last one.

ALL-TIME SUPERSONIC LEADERS

SEASON

Points: Dale Ellis, 2,253, 1988–89
Assists: Lenny Wilkens, 766, 1971–72
Rebounds: Jack Sikma, 1,038, 1981–82

GAME

Points: Fred Brown, 58 vs. Golden State, 3/23/74
Assists: Nate McMillan, 25 vs. L.A. Clippers, 2/23/87
Rebounds: Jim Fox, 30 vs. L.A. Lakers, 12/26/73

CAREER

Points Fred Brown, 14,018, 1971–84
Assists: Nate McMillan, 4,698, 1986–96
Rebounds: Jack Sikma, 7,729, 1977–86

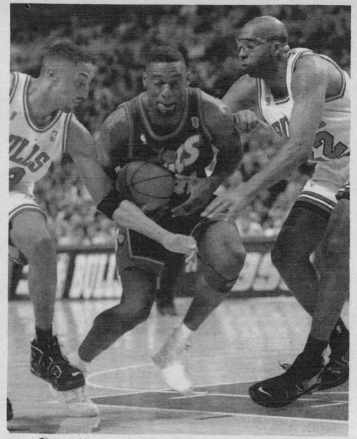

Shawn Kemp starred in losing cause in NBA Finals.

1996 NBA COLLEGE DRAFT

FIRST ROUND

Sel. No.	Team	Name	College	Ht.
1.	Philadelphia	Allen Iverson	Georgetown	6-0
2.	Toronto	Marcus Camby	Massachusetts	6-11
3.	Vancouver	Shareef Abdur-Rahim	California	6-10

Memphis' Lorenzen Wright is a Clipper as No. 7.

Louisville's Samaki Walker got ninth call from Dallas.

Sel. No.	Team	Name	College	Ht.
4.	a-Milwaukee	Stephon Marbury	Georgia Tech	6-2
5.	b-Minnesota	Ray Allen	Connecticut	6-5
6.	Boston	Antoine Walker	Kentucky	6-8
7.	LA Clippers	Lorenzen Wright	Memphis	6-11
8.	New Jersey	Kerry Kittles	Villanova	6-5
9.	Dallas	Samaki Walker	Louisville	6-9
10.	Indiana	Erick Dampier	Mississippi State	6-11

a-Traded to Minnesota
b-Traded to Milwaukee

Mississippi's Eric Dampier was Pacers' pick as No. 10.

Sel. No.	Team	Name	College	Ht.
11.	Golden State	Todd Fuller	North Carolina State	6-11
12.	Cleveland	Vitaly Potapenko	Wright State	6-10
13.	Charlotte	Kobe Bryant	Lower Merion H.S.	6-6
14.	Sacramento	Predrag Stojakovic	PAOK (Greece)	6-9
15.	Phoenix	Steve Nash	Santa Clara	6-2
16.	Charlotte	Tony Delk	Kentucky	6-1
17.	Portland	Jermaine O'Neal	Eau Claire H.S.	6-11

Bucks got UConn's Ray Allen as No. 5 in draft trade.

Sel. No.	Team	Name	College	Ht.
18.	New York	John Wallace	Syracuse	6-8
19.	New York	Walter McCarty	Kentucky	6-10
20.	Cleveland	Zydrunas Ilgauskas	Atletas (Lithuania)	7-3
21.	New York	Dontae Jones	Mississippi State	6-7
22.	Vancouver	Roy Rogers	Alabama	6-10
23.	Denver	Efthimios Rentzias	PAOK (Greece)	6-1
24.	LA Lakers	Derek Fisher	Ark.-Little Rock	6-1

Hornets buzzed Kentucky's Tony Delk with 16th choice.

Sel. No.	Team	Name	College	Ht.
25.	c-Utah	Martin Muursepp	BC Kaleu (Estonia)	6-9
26.	Detroit	Jerome Williams	Georgetown	6-9
27.	Orlando	Brian Evans	Indiana	6-8
28.	Atlanta	Priest Lauderdale	Peristeri (Greece)	7-3
29.	Chicago	Travis Knight	Connecticut	6-11

c-Traded to Miami

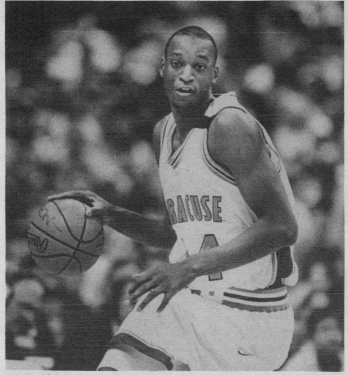

Knicks made Syracuse's John Wallace 18th pick.

SECOND ROUND

Sel. No.	Team	Name	College	Ht.
30.	Houston	Othella Harrington	Georgetown	6-9
31.	Philadelphia	Mark Hendrickson	Washington State	6-9
32.	Philadelphia	Ryan Minor	Oklahoma	6-7
33.	Milwaukee	Moochie Norris	West Florida	6-1
34.	Dallas	Shawn Harvey	West Virginia State	6-4
35.	Seattle	Joseph Blair	Arizona	6-9
36.	LA Clippers	Doron Sheffer	Connecticut	6-5
37.	Denver	Jeff McInnis	North Carolina	6-4
38.	Boston	Steve Hamer	Tennessee	7-0
39.	Phoenix	Russ Millard	Iowa	6-8
40.	Golden State	Marcus Mann	Miss. Valley St.	6-7

Knicks opted for Missippi State's Dontae Jones: No. 21.

Sel. No.	Team	Name	College	Ht.
41.	d-Sacramento	Jason Sasser	Texas Tech	6-7
42.	Houston	Randy Livingston	Louisiana State	6-4
43.	Phoenix	Ben Davis	Arizona	6-9
44.	Charlotte	Malik Rose	Drexel	6-7
45.	Seattle	Joe Vogel	Colorado State	6-11
46.	Portland	Marcus Brown	Murray State	6-2
47.	e-Seattle	Ron Riley	Arizona State	6-5
48.	Philadelphia	Jamie Feick	Michigan State	6-8

d-Traded to Portland
e-Traded to Detroit

Alabama's Roy Rogers went to Vancouver as No. 22.

Sel. No.	Team	Name	College	Ht.
49.	Orlando	Amal McCaskill	Marquette	6-11
50.	Houston	Terrell Bell	Georgia	6-10
51.	Vancouver	Chris Robinson	Western Kentucky	6-5
52.	Indiana	Mark Pope	Kentucky	6-10
53.	Milwaukee	Jeff Nordgaard	Wis.-Green Bay	6-7
54.	Utah	Shandon Anderson	Georgia	6-6
55.	Washington	Ronnie Henderson	Louisiana State	6-4
56.	Cleveland	Reggie Geary	Arizona	6-2
57.	Seattle	Drew Barry	Georgia Tech	6-4
58.	Dallas	Darnell Robinson	Arkansas	6-11

1995-96
NATIONAL BASKETBALL ASSOCIATION

FINAL STANDINGS

EASTERN CONFERENCE

Atlantic Division	Won	Lost	Pct.
Orlando	60	22	.732
New York	47	35	.573
Miami	42	40	.512
Washington	39	43	.476
Boston	33	49	.402
New Jersey	30	52	.366
Philadelphia	18	64	.220

Central Division	Won	Lost	Pct.
Chicago	72	10	.878
Indiana	52	30	.634
Cleveland	47	35	.573
Atlanta	46	36	.561
Detroit	46	36	.561
Charlotte	41	41	.500
Milwaukee	25	57	.305
Toronto	21	61	.256

WESTERN CONFERENCE

Midwest Division	Won	Lost	Pct.
San Antonio	59	23	.720
Utah	55	27	.671
Houston	48	34	.585
Denver	35	47	.427
Dallas	26	56	.317
Minnesota	26	56	.317
Vancouver	15	67	.183

Pacific Division	Won	Lost	Pct.
Seattle	64	18	.780
L.A. Lakers	53	29	.646
Portland	44	38	.537
Phoenix	41	41	.500
Sacramento	39	43	.476
Golden State	36	46	.439
L.A. Clippers	29	53	.354

PLAYOFFS

EASTERN CONFERENCE
First Round
Chicago defeated Miami (3-0)
New York defeated Cleveland (3-0)
Orlando defeated Detroit (3-0)
Atlanta defeated Indiana (3-2)
Semifinals
Chicago defeated New York (4-1)
Orlando defeated Atlanta (4-1)
Finals
Chicago defeated Orlando (4-0)

WESTERN CONFERENCE
First Round
Seattle defeated Sacramento (3-1)
Houston defeated L.A. Lakers (3-1)
San Antonio defeated Phoenix (3-1)
Utah defeated Portland (3-2)
Semifinals
Seattle defeated Houston (4-1)
Utah defeated San Antonio (4-2)
Finals
Seattle defeated Utah (4-2)

CHAMPIONSHIP
Chicago defeated Seattle (4-2)

1995-96 NBA INDIVIDUAL HIGHS

Most Minutes Played, Season: 3,457, Mason, New York
Most Minutes Played, Game: 58, Majerle, Cleveland vs. Seattle 3/5 (2 OT); Mills, Cleveland, vs. Seattle, 3/5 (2 OT); 48, 61 times, most recently by Jackson, Dallas, at San Antonio, 4/21; Perry, Phoenix, at Houston. 4/21
Most Points, Game: 53, Jordan, Chicago, vs. Detroit, 3/7
Most Field Goals Made, Game: 21, O'Neal, Orlando, at Washington, 3/22 (OT); Malone, Utah vs. Portland, 12/26; Jordan, Chicago, vs. Detroit, 3/7
Most Field Goal Attempts, Game: 40, O'Neal, Orlando, at Washington, 3/22 (OT); 37, Olajuwon, Houston, vs. Boston, 1/18
Most 3-Pt. Field Goals Made, Game: 11, Scott, Orlando vs. Atlanta, 4/18
Most 3-Pt. Field Goal Attempts, Game: McCloud, Dallas, vs. New Jersey, 3/5
Most Free Throws Made, Game: 22, Barkley, Phoenix, vs. Washington, 12/20 (OT)
Most Free Throw Attempts, Game: 28, Malone, Utah, vs. Miami, 1/8
Most Rebounds, Game: 31, Mutombo, Denver, vs. Charlotte, 3/26 (2 OT); 28, Jones, Dallas, vs. Indiana, 1/9
Most Offensive Rebounds, Game: 14, Rodman, Chicago, at Detroit, 2/15 (OT); Smith, Golden State, at L.A. Clippers, 2/5
Most Defensive Rebounds, Game: 23, Mutombo, Denver, vs. Charlotte, 3/26 (2 OT); 20, Ewing, New York, at Vancouver, 1/20; Jones, Dallas, vs. L.A. Clippers, 4/6
Most Assists, Game: 25, Kidd, Dallas, vs. Utah, 2/8 (2 OT); 20, Strickland, Portland, at Houston, 3/30
Most Blocked Shots, Game: 12, Bradley, New Jersey, vs. Toronto, 4/17
Most Steals, Game: 7, 11 times, most recently by Johnson, Phoenix, vs. Dallas, 4/19
Most Personal Fouls, Season: 300, Campbell, L.A. Lakers, and Thorpe, Detroit
Most Games Disqualified, Season: 11, Geiger, Charlotte

INDIVIDUAL SCORING LEADERS
Minimum 70 games or 1,400 points

	G	FG	FT	Pts.	Avg.
Jordan, Chicago	82	916	548	2491	30.4
Olajuwon, Houston	72	768	397	1936	26.9
O'Neal, Orlando	54	592	249	1434	26.6
Malone, Utah	82	789	512	2106	25.7
Robinson, San Antonio	82	711	626	2051	25.0
Barkley, Phoenix	71	580	440	1649	23.2
Mourning, Miami	70	563	488	1623	23.2
Richmond, Sacramento	81	611	425	1872	23.1
Ewing, New York	76	678	351	1711	22.5
Howard, Washington	81	733	319	1789	22.1
Hardaway, Orlando	82	623	445	1780	21.7
Rice, Charlotte	79	610	319	1710	21.6
Ceballos, L.A. Lakers	78	638	329	1656	21.2
Miller, Indiana	76	504	430	1606	21.1
Baker, Milwaukee	82	699	321	1729	21.1
C. Robinson, Portland	78	553	360	1644	21.1
Johnson, Charlotte	81	583	427	1660	20.5
Robinson, Milwaukee	82	627	316	1660	20.2
Hill, Detroit	80	564	485	1618	20.2
Elliott, San Antonio	77	525	326	1537	20.0

REBOUND LEADERS
Minimum 70 games or 800 rebounds

	G	Off.	Def.	Tot.	Avg.
Rodman, Chicago	64	356	596	952	14.9
Robinson, San Antonio	82	319	681	1000	12.2
Mutombo, Denver	74	249	622	871	11.8
Barkley, Phoenix	71	243	578	821	11.6
Kemp, Seattle	79	276	628	904	11.4
Olajuwon, Houston	72	176	608	784	10.9
Ewing, New York	76	157	649	806	10.6
Mourning, Miami	70	218	509	727	10.4
Vaught, L.A. Clippers	80	204	604	808	10.1
Williams, New Jersey	80	342	461	803	10.0
Baker, Milwaukee	82	263	545	808	9.9
Malone, Utah	82	175	629	804	9.8
Hill, Detroit	80	127	656	783	8.8
Weatherspoon, Philadelphia	78	237	516	753	9.7
Long, Atlanta	82	248	540	788	9.6
Muresan, Washington	76	248	480	728	9.6
Polynice, Sacramento	81	257	507	764	9.4
Mason, New York	82	220	544	764	9.3
Gilliam, New Jersey	78	241	472	713	9.1
D. Davis, Indiana	78	252	457	709	9.1

FIELD-GOAL LEADERS
Minimum 300 FG Made

	FG	FGA	Pct.
Muresan, Washington . . .	466	798	.584
Gatling, G.S.-Miami	326	567	.575
O'Neal, Orlando.	592	1033	.573
Mason, New York	449	798	.563
Kemp, Seattle	526	937	.561
D. Davis, Indiana.	334	599	.558
Sabonis, Portland	394	723	.545
Williams, L.A. Clippers. . .	416	766	.543
Brown, Houston	300	555	.541
Stockton, Utah	440	818	.538
Geiger, Charlotte	357	666	.536
Ceballos, L.A. Lakers	638	1203	.530
Thorpe, Detroit	452	853	.530
Polynice, Sacramento . . .	431	818	.527
Miller, Toronto	418	795	.526
Vaught, L.A. Clippers	571	1087	.525
Mourning, Miami.	563	1076	.523
Smits, Indiana.	466	894	.521
Malone, Utah	789	1520	.519
Robinson, San Antonio . .	711	1378	.516

3-POINT FIELD-GOAL LEADERS
Minimum 82 Made

	FG	FGA	Pct.
Legler, Washington	128	245	.522
Kerr, Chicago	122	237	.515
Davis, New York	127	267	.476
Armstrong, Golden State . .	98	207	.473
Hornacek, Utah	104	223	.466
B. Price, Washington.	139	301	.462
Phills, Cleveland	93	211	.441
Dehere, LA Clippers.	139	316	.440
Richmond, Sacramento . .	225	515	.437
Houston, Detroit	191	447	.427
Jordan, Chicago	111	260	.427
Wesley, Boston	116	272	.426
Scott, Orlando.	267	628	.425
Rice, Charlotte	171	403	.424
Stockton, Utah	95	225	.422
Murray, Toronto	151	358	.422
Askins, Miami.	99	237	.418
Barry, L.A. Clippers	123	296	.416
Peeler, L.A. Lakers	105	254	.413
D. Ellis, Denver.	150	364	.412

FREE-THROW LEADERS
Minimum 125 FT Made

	FT	FTA	Pct.
Abdul-Rauf, Denver	146	157	.930
Hornacek, Utah	259	290	.893
Brandon, Cleveland	338	381	.887
Barros, Boston	130	147	.884
B. Price, Washington. . .	167	191	.874
Hawkins, Seattle	247	283	.873
Richmond, Sacramento . .	425	491	.866
Miller, Indiana.	430	498	.863
Legler, Washington	132	153	.863
Webb, Atl.-Minn.	125	145	.862
Johnson, Phoenix	342	398	.859
Mullin, Golden State	137	160	.856
Johnson, L.A. Lakers. . . .	172	201	.856
Brown, Boston	135	158	.854
Curry, Charlotte.	146	171	.854
Childs, New Jersey	259	304	.852
Pierce, Indiana	174	205	.849
Pack, Washington	154	182	.846
Stith, Denver	320	379	.844
Armstrong, Golden State	234	279	.839

ASSISTS LEADERS
Minimum 70 games or 400 points

	G	A	Avg.
Stockton, Utah	82	916	11.2
Kidd, Dallas	81	783	9.7
Johnson, San Antonio . . .	82	789	9.6
Strickland, Portland	67	640	9.6
Stoudamire, Toronto	70	653	9.3
Johnson, Phoenix	56	517	9.2
Anderson, N.J.-Char.	69	575	8.3
Hardaway, G.S.-Miami . . .	80	640	8.0
Jackson, Indiana	81	635	7.8
Payton, Seattle	81	608	7.5
Hardaway, Orlando	82	582	7.1
Childs, New Jersey	78	548	7.0
Anthony, Vancouver.	69	476	6.9
Van Exel, L.A. Lakers. . . .	74	509	6.9
Hill, Detroit.	80	548	6.9
Brandon, Cleveland	75	487	6.5
Rose, Denver	80	495	6.2
Edney, Sacramento	80	491	6.1
Blaylock, Atlanta	81	478	5.9
Pippen, Chicago	77	452	5.9

Dikembe Mutombo again topped the NBA in blocked shots.

STEALS LEADERS
Minimum 70 games or 125 steals

	G	St.	Avg.
Payton, Seattle	81	231	2.85
Blaylock, Atlanta	81	212	2.62
Jordan, Chicago	82	180	2.20
Kidd, Dallas	81	175	2.16
Robertson, Toronto	77	166	2.16
Hardaway, Orlando	82	166	2.02
Murdock, Mil.-Van.	73	135	1.85
Jones, L.A. Lakers	70	129	1.84
Hawkins, Seattle	82	149	1.82
Gugliotta, Minneapolis	78	139	1.78
Brandon, Cleveland	75	132	1.76
Pippen, Chicago	77	133	1.73
Stockton, Utah	82	140	1.71
Malone, Utah	82	138	1.68
Hardaway, G.S.-Miami	80	132	1.65
Horry, Houston	71	116	1.63
Sprewell, Golden State	78	127	1.63
Barkley, Phoenix	71	114	1.61
Harper, New York	82	131	1.60
Anderson, Orlando	77	121	1.57

BLOCKED-SHOTS LEADERS
Minimum 70 games or 100 blocked shots

	G	Blk.	Avg.
Mutombo, Denver	74	332	4.49
Bradley, Phil.-N.J.	79	288	3.65
Robinson, San Antonio	82	271	3.30
Olajuwon, Houston	72	207	2.88
Mourning, Miami	70	189	2.70
Campbell, L.A. Lakers	82	212	2.59
Ewing, New York	76	184	2.42
Muresan, Washington	76	172	2.26
O'Neal, Orlando	54	115	2.13
McIlvaine, Washington	80	166	2.08
Miller, Toronto	76	143	1.88
Williams, Dallas	65	122	1.88
Lang, Atl.-Minnesota	71	126	1.77
Divac, L.A. Lakers	79	131	1.66
Garnett, Minneapolis	80	131	1.64
Smith, Golden State	82	134	1.63
Kemp, Seattle	79	127	1.61
Johnson, Seattle	81	129	1.59
Ratliff, Detroit	75	116	1.55
Horry, Houston	71	109	1.54

1995-96 ALL-NBA TEAM

FIRST		SECOND	
Pos.	Player, Team	Pos.	Player, Team
F	Scottie Pippen, Bulls	F	Shawn Kemp, Sonics
F	Karl Malone, Jazz	F	Grant Hill, Pistons
C	David Robinson, Spurs	C	Hakeen Olajuwon, Rockets
G	Michael Jordan, Bulls	G	Gary Payton, Sonics
G	Anfernee Hardaway, Magic	G	John Stockton, Jazz

THIRD	
Pos.	Player, Team
F	Charles Barkley, Suns
F	Juwan Howard, Bullets
C	Shaquille O'Neal, Magic
G	Mitch Richmond, Kings
G	Reggie Miller, Pacers

*1995-96 NBA ALL-ROOKIE TEAM

FIRST	SECOND
Player, Team	Player, Team
Damon Stoudamire, Raptors	Kevin Garnett, Timberwolves
Joe Smith, Warriors	Bryant Reeves, Grizzlies
Jerry Stackhouse, 76ers	Brent Barry, Clippers
Antonio McDyess, Nuggets	Rasheed Wallace, Bullets
Arvydas Sabonis, Blazers (tie)	Tyus Edney, Kings
Michael Finley, Suns (tie)	

*Chosen without regard for position

1995-96 NBA ALL-DEFENSIVE TEAM

FIRST		SECOND	
Pos.	Player, Team	Pos.	Player, Team
F	Scottie Pippen, Bulls	F	Horace Grant, Magic
F	Dennis Rodman, Bulls	F	Derrick McKey, Pacers
C	David Robinson, Spurs	C	Hakeem Olajuwon, Rockets
G	Gary Payton, Sonics	G	Mookie Blaylock, Hawks
G	Michael Jordan, Bulls	G	Bobby Phills, Cavaliers

MOST VALUABLE PLAYER

1955–56	Bob Pettit, St. Louis	1976–77	Kareem Abdul-Jabbar, L.A.
1956–57	Bob Cousy, Boston	1977–78	Bill Walton, Portland
1957–58	Bill Russell, Boston	1978–79	Moses Malone, Houston
1958–59	Bob Pettit, St. Louis	1979–80	Kareem Abdul-Jabbar, L.A.
1959–60	Wilt Chamberlain, Philadelphia	1980–81	Julius Erving, Philadelphia
1960–61	Bill Russell, Boston	1981–82	Moses Malone, Houston
1961–62	Bill Russell, Boston	1982–83	Moses Malone, Houston
1962–63	Bill Russell, Boston	1983–84	Larry Bird, Boston
1963–64	Oscar Robertson, Cincinnati	1984–85	Larry Bird, Boston
1964–65	Bill Russell, Boston	1985–86	Larry Bird, Boston
1965–66	Wilt Chamberlain, Philadelphia	1986–87	Magic Johnson, L.A. Lakers
1966–67	Wilt Chamberlain, Philadelphia	1987–88	Michael Jordan, Chicago
1967–68	Wilt Chamberlain, Philadelphia	1988–89	Magic Johnson, L.A. Lakers
1968–69	Wes Unseld, Baltimore	1989–90	Magic Johnson, L.A. Lakers
1969–70	Willis Reed, New York	1990–91	Michael Jordan, Chicago
1970–71	Lew Alcindor, Milwaukee	1991–92	Michael Jordan, Chicago
1971–72	Kareem Abdul-Jabbar, Milwaukee	1992–93	Charles Barkley, Phoenix
1972–73	Dave Cowens, Boston	1993–94	Hakeem Olajuwon, Houston
1973–74	Kareem Abdul-Jabbar, Milwaukee	1994–95	David Robinson, San Antonio
1974–75	Bob McAdoo, Buffalo	1995–96	Michael Jordan, Chicago
1975–76	Kareem Abdul-Jabbar, L.A.		

ROOKIE OF THE YEAR

1952–53	Don Meineke, Fort Wayne	1974–75	Keith Wilkes, Golden State
1953–54	Ray Felix, Baltimore	1975–76	Alvan Adams, Phoenix
1954–55	Bob Pettit, Milwaukee	1976–77	Adrian Dantley, Buffalo
1955–56	Maurice Stokes, Rochester	1977–78	Walter Davis, Pheonix
1956–57	Tom Heinsohn, Boston	1978–79	Phil Ford, Kansas City
1957–58	Woody Sauldsberry, Philadelphia	1979–80	Larry Bird, Boston
1958–59	Elgin Baylor, Minneapolis	1980–81	Darrell Griffith, Utah
1959–60	Wilt Chamberlain, Philadelphia	1981–82	Buck Williams, New Jersey
1960–61	Oscar Robertson, Cincinnati	1982–83	Terry Cummings, San Diego
1961–62	Walt Bellamy, Chicago	1983–84	Ralph Sampson, Houston
1962–63	Terry Dischinger, Chicago	1984–85	Michael Jordan, Chicago
1963–64	Jerry Lucas, Cincinnati	1985–86	Patrick Ewing, New York
1964–65	Willis Reed, New York	1986–87	Chuck Person, Indiana
1965–66	Rick Barry, San Francisco	1987–88	Mark Jackson, New York
1966–67	Dave Bing, Detroit	1988–89	Mitch Richmond, Golden State
1967–68	Earl Monroe, Baltimore	1989–90	David Robinson, San Antonio
1968–69	Wes Unseld, Baltimore	1990–91	Derrick Coleman, New Jersey
1969–70	Lew Alcindor, Milwaukee	1991–92	Larry Johnson, Charlotte
1970–71	Dave Cowens, Boston	1992–93	Shaquille O'Neal, Orlando
	Geoff Petrie, Portland	1993–94	Chris Webber, Golden State
1971–72	Sidney Wicks, Portland	1994–95	Grant Hill, Detroit
1972–73	Bob McAdoo, Buffalo		Jason Kidd, Dallas
1973–74	Ernie DiGregorio, Buffalo	1995–96	Damon Stoudamire, Toronto

FINALS MVP AWARD

1969	Jerry West, Los Angeles	1983	Moses Malone, Philadelphia
1970	Willis Reed, New York	1984	Larry Bird, Boston
1971	Kareem-Abdul-Jabbar, Milwaukee	1985	K. Abdul-Jabbar, L.A. Lakers
1972	Wilt Chamberlain, Los Angeles	1986	Larry Bird, Boston
1973	Willis Reed, New York	1987	Magic Johnson, L.A. Lakers
1974	John Havlicek, Boston	1988	James Worthy, L.A. Lakers
1975	Rick Barry, Golden State	1989	Joe Dumars, Detroit
1976	Jo Jo White, Boston	1990	Isiah Thomas, Detroit
1977	Bill Walton, Portland	1991	Michael Jordan, Chicago
1978	Wes Unseld, Washington	1992	Michael Jordan, Chicago
1979	Dennis Johnson, Seattle	1993	Michael Jordan, Chicago
1980	Magic Johnson, Los Angeles	1994	Hakeem Olajuwon, Houston
1981	Cedric Maxwell, Boston	1995	Hakeem Olajuwon, Houston
1982	Magic Johnson, Los Angeles	1996	Michael Jordan, Chicago

DEFENSIVE PLAYER OF THE YEAR

1982–83	Sidney Moncrief, Milwaukee	1989–90	Dennis Rodman, Detroit
1983–84	Sidney Moncrief, Milwaukee	1990–91	Dennis Rodman, Detroit
1984–85	Mark Eaton, Utah	1991–92	David Robinson, San Antonio
1985–86	Alvin Robertson, San Antonio	1992–93	Hakeem Olajuwon, Houston
1986–87	Michael Cooper, L.A. Lakers	1993–94	Hakeem Olajuwon, Houston
1987–88	Michael Jordan, Chicago	1994–95	Dikembe Mutombo, Denver
1988–89	Mark Eaton, Utah	1995–96	Gary Payton, Seattle

SIXTH MAN AWARD

1982–83	Bobby Jones, Philadelphia	1989–90	Ricky Pierce, Milwaukee
1983–84	Kevin McHale, Boston	1990–91	Detlef Schrempf, Indiana
1984–85	Kevin McHale, Boston	1991–92	Detlef Schrempf, Indiana
1985–86	Bill Walton, Boston	1992–93	Cliff Robinson, Portland
1986–87	Ricky Pierce, Milwaukee	1993–94	Dell Curry, Charlotte
1987–88	Roy Tarpley, Dallas	1994–95	Anthony Mason, New York
1988–89	Eddie Johnson, Phoenix	1995–96	Toni Kukoc, Chicago

MOST IMPROVED PLAYER

1985–86	Alvin Robertson, San Antonio	1991–92	Pervis Ellison, Washington
1986–87	Dale Ellis, Seattle	1992–93	Chris Jackson, Denver
1987–88	Kevin Duckworth, Portland	1993–94	Don MacLean, Washington
1988–89	Kevin Johnson, Phoenix	1994–95	Dana Barros, Philadelphia
1989–90	Rony Seikaly, Miami	1995–96	Gheorghe Muresan, Washington
1990–91	Scott Skiles, Orlando		

IBM AWARD
Determined by Computer Formula

1983–84	Magic Johnson, Los Angeles
1984–85	Michael Jordan, Chicago
1985–86	Charles Barkley, Philadelphia
1986–87	Charles Barkley, Philadelphia
1987–88	Charles Barkley, Philadelphia
1988–89	Michael Jordan, Chicago
1989–90	David Robinson, San Antonio
1990–91	David Robinson, San Antonio
1991–92	Dennis Rodman, Detroit
1992–93	Hakeem Olajuwon, Houston
1993–94	David Robinson, San Antonio
1994–95	David Robinson, San Antonio
1995–96	David Robinson, San Antonio

COACH OF THE YEAR

1962–63	Harry Gallatin, St. Louis
1963–64	Alex Hannum, San Francisco
1964–65	Red Auerbach, Boston
1965–66	Dolph Schayes, Philadelphia
1966–67	Johnny Kerr, Chicago
1967–68	Richie Guerin, St. Louis
1968–69	Gene Shue, Baltimore
1969–70	Red Holzman, New York
1970–71	Dick Motta, Chicago
1971–72	Bill Sharman, Los Angeles
1972–73	Tom Heinsohn, Boston
1973–74	Ray Scott, Detroit
1974–75	Phil Johnson, Kansas City-Omaha
1975–76	Bill Fitch, Cleveland
1976–77	Tom Nissalke, Houston
1977–78	Hubie Brown, Atlanta
1978–79	Cotton Fitzsimmons, Kansas City
1979–80	Bill Fitch, Boston
1980–81	Jack McKinney, Indiana
1981–82	Gene Shue, Washington
1982–83	Don Nelson, Milwaukee
1983–84	Frank Layden, Utah
1984–85	Don Nelson, Milwaukee
1985–86	Mike Fratello, Atlanta
1986–87	Mike Schuler, Portland
1987–88	Doug Moe, Denver
1988–89	Cotton Fitzsimmons, Phoenix
1989–90	Pat Riley, L.A. Lakers
1990–91	Don Chaney, Houston
1991–92	Don Nelson, Golden State
1992–93	Pat Riley, New York
1993–94	Lenny Wilkens, Atlanta
1994–95	Del Harris, L.A. Lakers
1995–96	Phil Jackson, Chicago

J. WALTER KENNEDY CITIZENSHIP AWARD

1974–75	Wes Unseld, Washington
1975–76	Slick Watts, Seattle
1976–77	Dave Bing, Washington
1977–78	Bob Lanier, Detroit
1978–79	Calvin Murphy, Houston
1979–80	Austin Carr, Cleveland
1980–81	Mike Glenn, New York
1981–82	Kent Benson, Detroit
1982–83	Julius Erving, Philadelphia
1983–84	Frank Layden, Utah
1984–85	Dan Issel, Denver
1985–86	Michael Cooper, L.A. Lakers Rory Sparrow, New York
1986–87	Isiah Thomas, Detroit
1987–88	Alex English, Denver
1988–89	Thurl Bailey, Utah
1989–90	Glenn Rivers, Atlanta
1990–91	Kevin Johnson, Phoenix
1991–92	Magic Johnson, L.A. Lakers
1992–93	Terry Porter, Portland
1993–94	Joe Dumars, Detroit
1994–95	Joe O'Toole, Atlanta
1995–96	Chris Dudley, Portland

NBA CHAMPIONS

Season	Championship	Eastern Division	W.	L.		Western Division	W.	L.	
1946–47	Philadelphia	35	25	Philadelphia		39	22	Chicago	
1947–48	Baltimore	27	21	Philadelphia		28	20	Baltimore	
1948–49	Minneapolis	38	22	Washington		44	16	Minneapolis	
1949–50	Minneapolis	51	13	Syracuse		51	17	Minneapolis	
1950–51	Rochester	36	30	New York		41	27	Rochester	
1951–52	Minneapolis	37	29	New York		40	26	Minneapolis	
1952–53	Minneapolis	47	23	New York		48	22	Minneapolis	
1953–54	Minneapolis	42	30	Syracuse		46	26	Minneapolis	
1954–55	Syracuse	43	29	Syracuse		43	29	Ft. Wayne	
1955–56	Philadelphia	45	27	Philadelphia		37	35	Ft. Wayne	
1956–57	Boston	44	28	Boston		34	38	St. Louis	
1957–58	St. Louis	49	23	Boston		41	31	St. Louis	
1958–59	Boston	52	20	Boston		33	39	Minneapolis	
1959–60	Boston	59	16	Boston		46	29	St. Louis	
1960–61	Boston	57	22	Boston		51	28	St. Louis	
1961–62	Boston	60	20	Boston		54	26	Los Angeles	
1962–63	Boston	58	22	Boston		53	27	Los Angeles	
1963–64	Boston	59	21	Boston		48	32	San Francisco	
1964–65	Boston	62	18	Boston		49	31	Los Angeles	
1965–66	Boston	54	26	Boston		45	35	Los Angeles	
1966–67	Philadelphia	68	13	Philadelphia		44	37	San Fran.	
1967–68	Boston	54	28	Boston		52	30	Los Angeles	
1968–69	Boston	48	34	Boston		55	27	Los Angeles	
1969–70	New York	60	22	New York		46	36	Los Angeles	
1970–71	Milwaukee	42	40	Baltimore		66	16	Milwaukee	
1971–72	Los Angeles	48	34	New York		69	13	Los Angeles	
1972–73	New York	57	25	New York		60	22	Los Angeles	
1973–74	Boston	56	26	Boston		59	23	Milwaukee	
1974–75	Golden State	60	22	Washington		48	34	Golden State	
1975–76	Boston	54	28	Boston		42	40	Phoenix	
1976–77	Portland	50	32	Philadelphia		49	33	Portland	
1977–78	Washington	44	38	Washington		47	35	Seattle	
1978–79	Seattle	54	28	Washington		52	30	Seattle	
1979–80	Los angeles	59	23	Philadelphia		60	22	Los Angeles	
1980–81	Boston	62	20	Boston		40	42	Houston	
1981–82	Los Angeles	58	24	Philadelphia		57	25	Los Angeles	
1982–83	Philadelphia	65	17	Philadelphia		58	24	Los Angeles	
1983–84	Boston	62	20	Boston		54	28	Los Angeles	

Season	Championship	Eastern Division W. L.			Western Division W. L.		
1984–85	L.A. Lakers	63	19	Boston	62	20	L.A. Lakers
1985–86	Boston	67	15	Boston	51	31	Houston
1986–87	L.A. Lakers	59	23	Boston	65	17	L.A. Lakers
1987–88	L.A. Lakers	54	28	Detroit	62	20	L.A. Lakers
1988–89	Detroit	63	19	Detroit	57	25	L.A. Lakers
1989–90	Detroit	59	23	Detroit	59	23	Portland
1990–91	Chicago	61	21	Chicago	58	24	L.A. Lakers
1991–92	Chicago	67	15	Chicago	57	25	Portland
1992–93	Chicago	57	25	Chicago	62	20	Phoenix
1993–94	Houston	57	25	New York	58	24	Houston
1994–95	Houston	57	25	Orlando	47	35	Houston
1995–96	Chicago	72	10	Chicago	64	18	Seattle

NBA SCORING CHAMPIONS

Season	Pts./Avg.	Top Scorer	Team
1946–47	1389	Joe Fulks	Philadelphia
1947–48	1007	Max Zaslofsky	Chicago
1948–48	1698	George Mikan	Minneapolis
1949–50	1865	George Mikan	Minneapolis
1950–51	1932	George Mikan	Minneapolis
1951–52	1674	Paul Arizin	Philadelphia
1952–53	1564	Neil Johnston	Philadelphia
1953–54	1759	Neil Johnston	Philadelphia
1954–55	1631	Neil Johnston	Philadelphia
1955–56	1849	Bob Pettit	St. Louis
1956–57	1817	Paul Arizin	Philadelphia
1957–58	2001	George Yardley	Detroit
1958–59	2105	Bob Pettit	St. Louis
1959–60	2707	Wilt Chamberlain	Philadelphia
1960–61	3033	Wilt Chamberlain	Philadelphia
1961–62	4029	Wilt Chamberlain	Philadelphia
1962–63	3586	Wilt Chamberlain	San Francisco
1963–64	2948	Wilt Chamberlain	San Francisco
1964–65	2534	Wilt Chamberlain	San Fran.-Phila.
1965–66	2649	Wilt Chamberlain	Philadelphia
1966–67	2775	Rick Barry	San Francisco
1967–68	2142	Dave Bing	Detroit
1968–69	2327	Elvin Hayes	San Diego

Season	Pts./Avg.	Top Scorer	Team
1969–70	*31.2	Jerry West	Los Angeles
1970–71	*31.7	Lew Alcindor	Milwaukee
1971–72	*34.8	K. Abdul-Jabbar	Milwaukee
1972–73	*34.0	Nate Archibald	K.C.-Omaha
1973–74	*30.6	Bob McAdoo	Buffalo
1974–75	*34.5	Bob McAdoo	Buffalo
1975–76	*31.1	Bob McAdoo	Buffalo
1976–77	*31.1	Pete Maravich	New Orleans
1977–77	*27.2	George Gervin	San Antonio
1978–79	*29.6	George Gervin	San Antonio
1979–80	*33.1	George Gervin	San Antonio
1980–81	*30.7	Adrian Dantley	Utah
1981–82	*32.3	George Gervin	San Antonio
1982–83	*28.4	Alex English	Denver
1983–84	*30.6	Adrian Dantley	Utah
1984–85	*32.9	Bernard King	New York
1985–86	*30.3	Dominique Wilkins	Atlanta
1986–87	*37.1	Michael Jordan	Chicago
1987–88	*35.0	Michael Jordan	Chicago
1988–89	*32.5	Michael Jordan	Chicago
1989–90	*33.6	Michael Jordan	Chicago
1990–91	*31.2	Michael Jordan	Chicago
1991–92	*30.1	Michael Jordan	Chicago
1992–93	*32.6	Michael Jordan	Chicago
1993–94	*29.8	David Robinson	San Antonio
1994–95	*29.3	Shaquille O'Neal	Orlando
1995–96	*30.4	Michael Jordan	Chicago

*Scoring title based on best average with at least 70 games played or 1,400 points

ALL-TIME NBA
REGULAR-SEASON RECORDS

INDIVIDUAL
Single Game
Most Points: 100, Wilt Chamberlain, Philadelphia vs. New York, at Hershey, Pa., March 2, 1962
Most FG Attempted: 63, Wilt Chamberlain, Philadelphia vs. New York, at Hershey, Pa., March 2, 1962
Most FG Made: 36, Wilt Chamberlain, Philadelphia vs. New York, at Hershey, Pa., March 2, 1962

Most Consecutive FG Made: 18, Wilt Chamberlain, San Francisco vs. New York, at Boston, Nov. 27, 1963; Wilt Chamberlain, Philadelphia vs. Baltimore, at Pittsburgh, Feb. 24, 1967

Most 3-Pt FG Attempted: 20, Michael Adams, Denver vs. L.A. Clippers, at L.A. Clippers, April 12, 1991

Most 3-Pt FG Made: 11, Dennis Scott, Orlando vs. Atlanta, at Orlando, April 18, 1996

Most FT Attempted: 34, Wilt Chamberlain, Philadelphia vs. St. Louis, at Philadelphia, Feb. 22, 1962

Most FT Made: 28, Wilt Chamberlain, Philadelphia vs. New York, at Hershey, Pa., March 2, 1962; Adrian Dantley, Utah vs. Houston, at Las Vegas, Nev., Jan. 4, 1984

Most Consecutive FT Made: 19, Bob Pettit, St. Louis vs. Boston, at Boston, Nov. 22, 1961; Bill Cartright, New York vs. Kansas City, at New York, Nov. 17, 1981; Adrian Dantley, Detroit vs. Chicago, at Chicago, Dec. 15, 1987 (OT)

Most FT Missed: 22, Wilt Chamberlain, Philadelphia vs. Seattle, at Boston, Dec. 1, 1967

Most Rebounds: 41, Wilt Chamberlain, Philadelphia vs. Boston, at Philadelphia, April 5, 1967

Most Assists: 30, Scott Skiles, Orlando vs. Denver, at Orlando, Dec. 30, 1990

Most Blocked Shots: 17, Elmore Smith, Los Angeles vs. Portland, at Los Angeles, Oct. 28, 1973

Most Steals: 11, Larry Kenon, San Antonio vs. Kansas City, at Kansas City, Dec. 26, 1976

Most Personal Fouls: 8, Don Otten, Tri-Cities vs. Sheboygan, at Sheboygan, Nov. 24, 1949

Season

Most Points: 4,029, Wilt Chamberlain, Philadelphia, 1961–62

Highest Average: 50.4, Wilt Chamberlain, Philadelphia, 1961–62

Most FG Attempted: 3,159, Wilt Chamberlain, Philadelphia, 1961–62

Most FG Made: 1,597, Wilt Chamberlain, Philadelphia, 1961–62

Highest FG Percentage: .727, Wilt Chamberlain, Los Angeles, 1972–73

Most 3-Pt. FG Attempted: 678, George McCloud, Dallas, 1995–96

Most 3-Pt FG Made: 267, Dennis Scott, Orlando, 1995–96

Most FT Attempted: 1,363, Wilt Chamberlain, Philadelphia, 1961–62

Most FT Made: 840, Jerry West, Los Angeles, 1965–66

Highest FT Percentage: .958, Calvin Murphy, Houston, 1980–81

Most Assists: 1,164, John Stockton, Utah, 1990–91
Most Blocked Shots: 456, Mark Eaton, Utah, 1984–85
Most Steals: 301, Alvin Robertson, San Antonio, 1985–86
Most Personal Fouls: 386, Darryl Dawkins, New Jersey, 1983–84
Most Disqualifications: 26, Don Meineke, Fort Wayne, 1952–53

Career
Most Games: 1,568, Robert Parish, Golden State, Boston, Charlotte, 1976–96
Most Minutes: 57,446, Kareem Abdul-Jabbar, Milwaukee and Los Angeles Lakers, 1969–89
Most Points Scored: 38,387, Kareem Abdul-Jabbar, Milwaukee and Los Angeles Lakers, 1969–89
Highest Scoring Average: 32.2, Michael Jordan, Chicago, 1984–95
Most FG Attempted: 28,307, Kareem Abdul-Jabbar, Milwaukee and Los Angeles Lakers, 1969–89
Most FG Made: 15,837, Kareem Abdul-Jabbar, 1969–89
Highest FG Percentage: .599, Artis Gilmore, Chicago, San Antonio, Boston, 1976–88
Most 3-Pt FG Attempted: 2,816, Michael Adams, Sacramento, Denver, Washington, 1985–95
Most 3-Pt FG Made: 1,119, Dale Ellis, Dallas, Seattle, Milwaukee, San Antonio, 1983–95
Most FT Attempted: 11,862, Wilt Chamberlain, 1960–73
Most FT Made: 8,531, Moses Malone, Buffalo, Houston, Philadelphia, Washington, Atlanta, Milwaukee, San Antonio, 1976–95
Highest FT Percentage: .906, Mark Price, Cleveland, 1986–95
Most Rebounds: 23,924, Wilt Chamberlain, 1960–73
Most Assists: 10,394, John Stockton, Utah, 1984–95
Most Blocked Shots: 3,190, Hakeem Olajuwon, Houston, 1984–96
Most Steals: 2,311, John Stockton, Utah, 1984–96
Most Personal Fouls: 4,657, Kareem Abdul-Jabbar, Milwaukee and Los Angeles Lakers, 1970–89
Most Times Disqualified: 127, Vern Mikkelsen, Minneapolis, 1950–59

TEAM RECORDS
Single Game
Most Points, One Team: 173, Boston, vs. Minneapolis at Boston, Feb. 27, 1959; Phoenix, vs. Denver at Phoenix, Nov. 10, 1990; 186, Detroit, vs. Denver at Denver, Dec. 13, 1983 (3 overtimes)

Most Points, Two Teams: 320, Golden State 162 vs. Denver 158 at Denver, Nov. 2, 1990; 370, Detroit 186 vs. Denver 184 at Denver, Dec. 13, 1983 (3 overtimes)

Most FG Attempted, One Team: 153, Philadelphia, vs. Los Angeles at Philadelphia (3 overtimes), Dec. 8, 1961; 150, Boston, vs. Philadelphia at Philadelphia, March 2, 1960

Most FG Attempted, Two Teams: 291, Philadelphia 153 vs. Los Angeles 138 at Philadelphia (3 overtimes), Dec. 8, 1961; 274, Boston 149 vs. Detroit 125 at Boston, Jan. 27, 1961; Philadelphia 141 vs. Boston 133 at Boston, March 5, 1961

Most FG Made, One Team: 74, Denver, vs. Detroit at Denver, Dec. 13, 1983 (3 overtimes); 72, Boston, vs. Minneapolis at Boston, Feb. 27, 1959

Most FG Made, Two Teams: 142, Detroit 74 vs. Denver 68 at Denver, Dec. 13, 1983 (3 overtimes); 134, San Diego 67 vs. Cincinnati 67 at Cincinnati, March 12, 1970

Most FT Attempted, One Team: 86, Syracuse, vs. Anderson at Syracuse (5 overtimes), Nov. 24, 1949; 71, Chicago, vs. Phoenix at Chicago, Jan. 8, 1970

Most FT Attempted, Two Teams: 160, Syracuse 86 vs. Anderson 74 at Syracuse (5 overtimes), Nov. 24, 1949; 127, Fort Wayne 67 vs. Minneapolis 60 at Fort Wayne. Dec. 31, 1954

Most FT Made, One Team: 61, Phoenix, vs. Utah, April 4, 1990 (1 overtime); 60, Washington, vs. New York at New York, Nov. 13, 1987

Most FT Made, Two Teams: 116, Syracuse 59 vs. Anderson 57 at Syracuse (5 overtimes), Nov. 24, 1949; 103, Boston 56 vs. Minneapolis 47 at Minneapolis, Nov. 28, 1954

Most Rebounds, One Team: 109, Boston, vs. Denver at Boston, Dec. 24, 1960

Most Rebounds, Two Teams: 188, Philadelphia 98 vs. Los Angeles 90 at Philadelphia, Dec. 8, 1961 (3 overtimes); 177, Philadelphia 104 vs. Syracuse 73 at Philadelphia, Nov. 4, 1959; Boston 89 vs. Philadelphia 88 at Philadelphia, Dec. 27, 1960

Most Assists, One Team: 53, Milwaukee, vs. Detroit at Milwaukee, Dec. 26, 1978

Most Assists, Two Teams: 93, Detroit 47 vs. Denver 46 at Denver, Dec. 13, 1983 (3 overtimes); 88, Phoenix 47 vs. San Diego 41 at Tucson, Ariz., March 15, 1969; San Antonio 50 vs. Denver 38 at San Antonio, April 15, 1984

Most Blocked Shots, One Team: 22, New Jersey, vs. Denver at New Jersey, Dec. 12, 1991

Most Blocked Shots, Two Teams: 34, Detroit 19 vs. Washington 15 at Washington, Nov. 19, 1981

Most Steals, One Team; 25, Golden State, vs. San Antonio at Golden State, Feb. 15, 1989

Most Steals, Two Teams: 40, Golden State 24 vs. Los Angeles 16 at Golden State, Jan. 21, 1975; Philadelphia 24 vs. Detroit 16 at Philadelphia, Nov. 11, 1978; Golden State 25 vs. San Antonio 15 at Golden State, Feb. 15, 1989

Most Personal Fouls, One Team: 66, Anderson, vs. Syracuse at Syracuse (5 overtimes), Nov. 24, 1949; 55, Milwaukee vs. Baltimore at Baltimore, Nov. 12, 1952

Most Personal Fouls, Two Teams: 122, Anderson 66 vs. Syracuse 56 at Syracuse (5 overtimes), Nov. 24, 1949; 97, Syracuse 50 vs. New York 47 at Syracuse, Feb. 15, 1953

Most Disqualifications, One Team: 8, Syracuse, vs. Baltimore at Syracuse (1 overtime), Nov. 15, 1952; 6, Syracuse vs. Boston at Boston, Dec. 26, 1950

Most Disqualifications, Two Teams: 13, Syracuse 8 vs. Baltimore 5 at Syracuse (1 overtime), Nov. 15, 1952; 11, Syracuse 6 vs. Boston 5, Dec. 26, 1950

Most Points in a Losing Game: 184, Denver, vs. Detroit at Denver Dec. 13, 1983 (3 overtimes); 158, Denver vs. Golden State at Golden State, Nov. 2, 1990

Widest Point Spread: 68, Cleveland 148 vs. Miami 80 at Miami, Dec. 17, 1991

Season

Most Games Won: 72, Chicago, 1995–96

Most Games Lost: 73, Philadelphia, 1972–73

Longest Winning Streak: 33, Los Angeles, Nov. 5, 1971 to Jan. 7, 1972

Longest Losing Streak: 20, Philadelphia, Jan. 9, 1973 to Feb. 11, 1973; Dallas, Nov. 13 to Dec. 22, 1993

Most Points Scored: 10,731, Denver, 1981–82

Most Points Allowed: 10,723, Denver, 1990–91

Highest Scoring Average: 126.5, Denver, 1981–82

Highest Average, Points Allowed: 130.8, Denver, 1990–91

Most FG Attempted: 9,295, Boston, 1960–61

Most FG Made: 3,980, Denver, 1981–82

Highest FG Percentage: .545, Los Angeles, 1984–85

Most FT Attempted: 3,411, Philadelphia, 1966–67

Most FT Made: 2,313, Golden State, 1989–90

Highest FT Percentage: .832, Boston, 1989–90

ALL-TIME NBA
PLAYOFF RECORDS

INDIVIDUAL
Single Game

Most Points: 63, Michael Jordan, Chicago, at Boston, April 20, 1986 (2 overtimes); 61, Elgin Baylor, Los Angeles, at Boston, April 14, 1962

Most FG Attempted; 48, Wilt Chamberlain, Philadelphia, vs. Syracuse, at Philadelphia, March 22, 1962; Rick Barry, San Francisco, vs. Philadelphia at San Francisco, April 18, 1967

Most FG Made: 24, Wilt Chamberlain, Philadelphia, vs. Syracuse, at Philadelphia, March 14, 1960; John Havlicek, Boston, vs. Atlanta, at Boston, April 1, 1973; Michael Jordan, Chicago, vs. Cleveland, at Chicago, May 1, 1988

Most 3-Point FG Attempted: 15, Dennis Scott, Orlando, vs. Indiana, at Orlando, May 25, 1995; Nick Van Exel, Los Angeles Lakers, vs. Seattle, at Los Angeles, May 4, 1995

Most 3-Point FG Made: 8, Dan Majerle, Phoenix, vs. Seattle, at Phoenix, June 1, 1993

Most FT Attempted: 32, Bob Cousy, Boston, vs. Syracuse, at Boston, March 21, 1953 (4 overtimes); 28, Michael Jordan, Chicago, vs. New York, at Chicago, March 14, 1989

Most FT Made: 30, Bob Cousy, Boston, vs. Syracuse, at Boston, March 21, 1953 (4 overtimes); 23, Michael Jordan, Chicago, vs. New York, at Chicago, March 14, 1989

Most Rebounds: 41, Wilt Chamberlain, Philadelphia, vs. Boston, at Philadelphia, April 5, 1967

Most Blocked Shots: 10, Mark Eaton, Utah, vs. Houston, at Utah, April 26, 1985; Hakeem Olajuwon, Houston, vs. Los Angeles Lakers, at Los Angeles, April 29, 1990

Most Assists: 24, Magic Johnson, L.A. Lakers vs. Phoenix, at Los Angeles, May 15, 1984; John Stockton, Utah, vs. Los Angeles Lakers, at Los Angeles, May 17, 1988

Most Steals: 8, done 7 times, most recently by Mookie Blaylock, Atlanta, vs. Indiana, at Atlanta, April 29, 1996

Most Personal Fouls: 8, Jack Toomay, vs. New York, at New York, March 26, 1949 (overtime)

TEAM
Single Game

Most Points, One Team: 157, Boston, vs. New York, at Boston, April 28, 1990

Most Points, Two Teams: 304, Portland 153 vs. Phoenix 151, at Phoenix, May 11, 1992 (2 overtimes); 285, San Antonio 152 vs. Denver 133, at San Antonio, April 26, 1983; Boston 157 vs. New York, 128, at Boston, April 28, 1990

Fewest Points, One Team: 64, Portland vs. Utah, at Utah, May 5, 1996

Fewest Points, Two Teams: 145, Fort Wayne 74 vs. Syracuse 71, at Indianapolis, April 7, 1955

Most FG Attempted, One Team: 140, Boston, vs. Syracuse, at Boston, March 18, 1959; San Francisco, vs. Philadelphia, at Philadelphia, April 14, 1967 (overtime)

Most FG Attempted, Two Teams: 257, Boston 135 vs. Philadelphia 122, at Boston, March 22, 1960

Most FG Made, One Team: 67, Milwaukee, vs. Philadelphia, at Philadelphia, March 30, 1970; San Antonio, vs. Denver, at San Antonio, May 4, 1983; Los Angeles Lakers, vs. Denver, at Los Angeles, May 22, 1985

Most FG Made, Two Teams: 119, Milwaukee 67 vs. Philadelphia, at Philadelphia, 52, March 30, 1970

Most 3-Point FG Attempted, One Team: 34, Houston, vs. Seattle, at Houston, May 12, 1996

Most 3-Point FG Attempted, Two Teams: 62, Houston 32, vs. Orlando, at Orlando 30, June 7, 1995

Most 3-Point FG Made, One Team: 20, Seattle, vs. Houston, at Seattle, May 6, 1996

Most 3-Point FG Made, Two Teams: 33, Seattle 20 vs. Houston 13, at Seattle, May 6, 1996

Most FT Attempted, One Team: 70, St. Louis, vs. Minneapolis, at St. Louis, March 17, 1956

Most FT Attempted, Two Teams: 128, Syracuse 64, at Boston 64, March 21, 1953 (4 overtimes); 122, St. Louis 70 vs. Minneapolis 52, at St. Louis, March 17, 1956; Minneapolis 68 vs. St. Louis 54, at Minneapolis, March 21, 1956

Most FT Made, One Team: 57, Boston, vs. Syracuse, at Boston, March 21, 1953 (4 overtimes); Phoenix, vs. Seattle, at Phoenix, June 5, 1993

Most FT Made, Two Teams: 108, Boston 57 vs. Syracuse 51, at Boston, March 21, 1953 (4 overtimes); 91, St. Louis 54 vs. Minneapolis 37, at St. Louis, March 17, 1956

Most Rebounds, One Team: 97, Boston, vs. Philadelphia, at Boston, March 19, 1960

Most Rebounds, Two Teams; 169, Boston 89 vs. Philadelphia, 80, at Boston, March 22, 1960; San Francisco 93 vs. Philadelphia 76, at Philadelphia 76, April 16, 1967

Most Assists, One Team: 51, San Antonio, vs. Denver, at San Antonio, May 4, 1983

Most Assists, Two Teams: 79, Los Angeles Lakers 44, vs. Boston 35, at Los Angeles, June 4, 1987

Most Blocked Shots, One Team: 20, Philadelphia, vs. Milwaukee, at Philadelphia, April 5, 1981

Most Blocked Shots, Two Teams: 29, Philadelphia 20 vs. Milwaukee 9, at Philadelphia, April 5, 1981

Most Steals, One Team: 22, Golden State, vs. Seattle, at Golden State, April 14, 1975

Most Steals, Two Teams: 35, Golden State 22, vs. Seattle 13, at Golden State, April 14, 1975

Most Personal Fouls, One Team: 55, Syracuse, vs. Boston, at Boston, March 21, 1953 (4 overtimes); 45, Syracuse, vs. New York, at New York, April 8, 1952

Most Personal Fouls, Two Teams: 106, Syracuse 55, vs. Boston 51, at Boston, March 21, 1953 (4 overtimes); 82, Syracuse 45, vs. New York 37, at New York, April 8, 1952

Most Disqualifications, One Team: 7, Syracuse, vs. Boston, at Boston, March 21, 1953 (4 overtimes)

Most Disqualifications, Two Teams: 12, Syracuse 7, vs. Boston 5, at Boston, March 21, 1953 (4 overtimes); 7, Los Angeles 4, vs. Detroit 3, at Detroit, April 3, 1962

Widest Point Spread: 58, Minneapolis 133 vs. St. Louis 75, at Minneapolis, March 19, 1956

Official 1996-97 NBA Schedule

*Afternoon (Local Time)

Fri Nov 1
Chi at Bos
Cle at NJ
Mil at Phil
Wash at Orl
Atl at Mia
NY at Tor
Ind at Det
SA at Minn
Sac at Hou
Dal at Den
Sea at Utah
Phoe at LAL
LAC at GS
Port at Van

Sat Nov 2
Cle at Wash
Tor at Char
Det at Atl
Mia at Ind
Phil at Chi
Bos at Mil
Sac at Dal
Hou at Phoe
Utah at LAC
Port at Sea

Sun Nov 3
Char at NY
Den at SA
Minn at LAL
GS at Van

Mon Nov 4
Hou at Utah
Atl at Port

Tues Nov 5
LAL at NY
Det at Phil
Dal at Tor
SA at Cle
Van at Chi
LAC at Den
Minn at Phoe
Port at GS

Hou at Sac
Atl at Sea

Wed Nov 6
Ind at Bos
SA at Wash
Chi at Mia
LAL at Char
Dal at Det
Van at Mil

Thu Nov 7
*Orl vs NJ
in Japan
Hou at Den
Sea at Phoe
NY at GS
Atl at Sac
Minn at Port

Fri Nov 8
Phil at Bos
Char at Wash
NJ vs Orl
in Japan
Mil at Mia
LAL at Tor
Van at Cle
Chi at Det
Sea at SA
GS at Den
NY at LAC

Sat Nov 9
Phoe at Phil
Mil at Char
Wash at Ind
Bos at Chi
Mia at Dal
Utah at Hou
Port at Sac

Sun Nov 10
*Den at Cle
Minn at LAC
Atl at LAL

SA at Port
NY at Van

Mon Nov 11
Den at Tor
Phoe at Chi
SA at Utah
Sea at Sac

Tue Nov 12
Phil at NY
Det at Wash
Char at Mia
Cle at Atl
Phoe at Mil
Port at Minn
Ind at Dal
LAL at Hou
GS at Sea
LAC at Van

Wed Nov 13
Atl at Bos
Wash at NJ
Phil at Tor
Port at Cle
Den at Det
Mia at Chi
LAL at SA
Sac at Utah

Thu Nov 14
Tor at NY
Char at Orl
Dal at Minn
Ind at Hou
Sea at LAC
Mil at GS
Phoe at Van

Fri Nov 15
Den at Bos
Port at NJ
Cle at Phil
Chi at Char
Mia at Atl
Wash at Det

Ind at SA
Van at Utah
LAC at LAL
Mil at Sac

Sat Nov 16
*Minn at NY
Den at NJ
Bos at Wash
Tor at Orl
Phil at Mia
Det at Cle
Atl at Chi
Utah at Dal
GS at Hou
Sac at Sea

Sun Nov 17
Port at Ind
GS at SA
LAL at Phoe
Mil at LAC
Van at Sea

Mon Nov 18
Sac at Van

Tue Nov 19
NY at Orl
Sea at Tor
Atl at Cle
Dal at Mil
Minn at Hou
Mia at Den
LAL at GS
Sac at Port

Wed Nov 20
Det at Bos
Ind at Phil
Sea at Wash
NY at Char
LAC at SA
Chi at Phoe
Utah at LAL
Mia at Van

Thu Nov 21
Minn at Orl
Cle at Tor
NJ at Det
Char at Ind
Atl at Mil
LAC at Dal
Phoe at Hou
Chi at Den
GS at Utah

Fri Nov 22
Sea at Bos
Phil at Wash
SA at LAL
Mia at Sac

Sat Nov 23
Dal at NJ
NY at Phil
Det at Char
*Atl at Tor
Orl at Ind
Wash at Mil
LAC at Minn
Chi at Utah
*Hou at GS
Den at Port

Sun Nov 24
Dal at Bos
Sea at NY
*Sac at Cle
Mia at Phoe
Hou at LAL
SA at Van

Mon Nov 25
Minn at Wash
Mil at Orl
NJ at Utah
Chi at LAC

Tue Nov 26
LAL at Phil
Sea at Char
Van at Atl
Sac at Tor
SA at Dal
Port at Hou
Phoe at Den
Mia at GS

Wed Nov 27
LAL at Bos

Atl at Orl
Char at Tor
Van at Det
Cle at Mil
Sea at Minn
Port at SA
Den at Utah
NJ at Phoe
Mia at LAC

Thu Nov 28
Sac at Ind
NJ at GS

Fri Nov 29
Hou at Bos
Orl at Phil
Wash at Atl
LAL at Det
Van at Ind
Chi at Dal
Minn at Den
LAC at Utah
GS at Port
Phoe at Sea

Sat Nov 30
*Sac at NY
Van at Phil
Hou at Wash
Bos at Mia
Orl at Cle
Char at Mil
Tor at Minn
Chi at SA
NJ vs LAC
  at Anaheim

Sun Dec 1
Sac at Det
Den at LAL
*Port at GS
Utah at Sea

Mon Dec 2
Dal at Orl
Hou at Tor
Char at Utah

Tue Dec 3
Mia at NY
Bos at Atl
Tor at Cle
Chi at Mil
Sac at Minn

Char at LAC
Sea at LAL
Den at GS
Ind at Port

Wed Dec 4
NY at NJ
Cle at Orl
Dal at Mia
Atl at Det
Bos at Hou
Phil at SA
LAL at Utah
GS at Phoe
Ind at Van

Thu Dec 5
Wash at Tor
LAC at Chi
Phil at Dal
Port at Den
Minn at Sea

Fri Dec 6
NJ at Bos
NY at Mia
Cle at Det
Van at SA
Minn at Utah
Orl at LAL
Ind at GS
Phoe at Sac
Char at Port

Sat Dec 7
LAC at NY
Det at NJ
Mil at Wash
Tor at Atl
Mia at Chi
Van at Dal
Phil at Hou
Utah at Den
Char at Sea

Sun Dec 8
Chi at Tor
LAC at Cle
Bos at Mil
Ind at Phoe
Minn at LAL
SA at GS
Orl at Sac

Mon Dec 9
Sea at Phil
Char at Van

Tue Dec 10
Wash at NY
Den at Atl
GS at Tor
Mia at Cle
Det at Mil
Hou at Minn
Ind at Utah
SA at Phoe
Dal at LAC
LAL at Sac
Orl at Port

Wed Dec 11
Tor at Bos
Sea at NJ
Mia at Phil
Cle at Wash
Den at Char
Minn at Chi
Ind at LAL

Thu Dec 12
GS at NY
Sea at Mil
Det at Hou
Phoe at Utah
SA at LAC
Dal at Sac
Van at Port

Fri Dec 13
Chi at NJ
Den at Wash
Phil at Char
GS at Cle
Bos at Ind
Phoe at Minn
Port at LAL
Orl at Van

Sat Dec 14
Den at NY
*Tor at Mia
Phil at Atl
Char at Chi
NJ at Mil
Cle at Minn
Dal at SA
Orl at Utah

Sac at LAC
Hou at Sea

Sun Dec 15
Bos at Det
Van at Phoe
Wash at GS
Hou at Port

Mon Dec 16
Mil at Bos
Det at Tor
Phoe vs LAC
  at Anaheim
Wash at Sac

Tue Dec 17
Utah at NY
Tor at NJ
Char at Phil
Ind at Mia
LAL at Chi
Atl at Dal
GS at Sea
Hou at Van

Wed Dec 18
Ind at Orl
NJ at Cle
NY at Det
LAL at Mil
Sac at Den
Wash at Phoe
Minn at GS
Sea at Port

Thu Dec 19
Utah at Mia
Chi at Char
Mil at Tor
SA at Hou
Wash at LAC
Minn at Sac
Dal at Van

Fri Dec 20
NY at Phil
Utah at Orl
NJ at Atl
Tor at Cle
Det at Ind
Van at Den
Dal at Port
LAC at Sea

Sat Dec 21
Det at NY
Bos at NJ
Chi at Phil
Atl at Char
Orl at Mil
LAL at Minn
Mia at Hou
Phoe at SA
Port at Sac

Sun Dec 22
Char at Bos
*Utah at Cle
Tor at Ind
LAC at GS
Dal at Sea
Wash at Van

Mon Dec 23
Atl at NY
Cle at Orl
NJ at Chi
Utah at Minn
Mil at Hou
Mia at SA
Den at Phoe
LAC at Sac
Wash at Port

Wed Dec 25
*LAL at Phoe
Det at Chi

Thu Dec 26
Orl at Mia
Chi at Atl
*NJ vs Tor
  in Hamilton
Ind at Det
Hou at Mil
NY at Minn
GS at Dal
Phil at Den
Port at Utah
Van at Sac
SA at Sea

Fri Dec 27
Ind at NJ
Tor at Wash
Mia at Char
Mil at Cle
Port at LAC
Bos at LAL

Sat Dec 28
*Orl at NY
Atl vs Wash
  at Baltimore
Char at Det
Cle at Chi
Den at Minn
Sea at Dal
GS at Hou
*Phil at Utah
Bos at Sac
Phoe at Van

Sun Dec 29
*NJ at Ind
Mia at Mil
Phil at LAL
SA at Port

Mon Dec 30
NJ at NY
Char at Wash
Minn at Cle
Orl at Det
Ind at Chi
Sea at Hou
Bos at Den
Sac at Phoe
Utah at LAC
SA at Van

Thu Jan 2
NY at Wash
Tor at Orl
NJ at Mia
Dal at Char
Phoe at Cle
Bos at Det
Port at Hou
Utah at SA
LAL at Sac
Phil at Sea

Fri Jan 3
Minn at Bos
Atl at NJ
Phoe at Ind
Orl at Chi
SA at Den
Sac at LAL
Phil at GS
Sea at Van

Sat Jan 4
Wash at Char

NY at Atl
Ind at Cle
Tor at Det
Minn at Mil
Port at Dal
LAC at Hou
Mia at Utah

Sun Jan 5
Phoe at Bos
Mil at NY
LAC at SA
Phil at Sac
LAL at Van

Mon Jan 6
Utah at Chi
Char at GS
LAL at Port

Tue Jan 7
Dal at NY
SA at NJ
Phil at Orl
Phoe at Atl
LAC at Tor
Mil at Det
Cle at Ind
Hou at Minn
Den at Sac
Mia at Sea

Wed Jan 8
SA at Bos
Dal at Phil
Phoe at Wash
Hou at Cle
Utah at Mil
Sea at Den
Char at LAL
Van at GS
Mia at Port

Thu Jan 9
Minn at NJ
Atl at Orl
Utah at Tor
GS at Van

Fri Jan 10
NY at Bos
Hou at Phil
LAC at Wash
SA at Det
Chi at Mil
Ind at Den

Char at Phoe
Mia at LAL

Sat Jan 11
Bos at NY
Tor at NJ
SA at Atl
Wash at Cle
Utah at Det
Hou at Chi
LAC at Minn
Den at Dal
Ind at Sea
Sac at Van

Sun Jan 12
Orl at Tor
GS at Mil
Char at Sac

Mon Jan 13
Orl at NJ
Utah at Phil
Wash at Mia
Atl at Cle
Phoe at Dal
Char at Den

Tue Jan 14
GS at Bos
Minn at Atl
Wash at Chi
NY at Hou
Den at Phoe
Van at LAL
Ind at Sac
Det at Port

Wed Jan 15
GS at Phil
NJ at Char
Chi at Minn
Orl at Dal
NY at SA
Ind at LAC
Tor at Sea
Det at Van

Thu Jan 16
Mia at Bos
Orl at Atl
Sac at Hou
Cle at Den
Phoe at Utah
Port at LAL

Fri Jan 17
NJ at Phil
Mia vs Wash
  at Baltimore
GS at Ind
Mil at Chi
Hou at Dal
Sac at SA
Tor at Port
Cle at Sea
Utah at Van

Sat Jan 18
Wash at Bos
Char at NJ
Mil at Atl
GS at Minn
Dal at Den
NY at Phoe
Det at LAL

Sun Jan 19
*Orl at Mia
*Phil at Ind
*Chi at Hou
Cle at LAC
Utah at Port
*Tor at Van

Mon Jan 20
*Wash at NY
*Mil at Phil
*Char at Atl
*SA at Minn
NJ at Den
Cle at Utah
Det at Phoe
*Dal at LAL
Van at Sea

Tue Jan 21
Wash at Orl
Atl at Mia
Hou at Char
Minn at Tor
NY at Chi
Ind at Mil
Dal at GS
LAC at Port

Wed Jan 22
Phil at Bos
NJ at SA
Van at Den
Utah at Phoe

Det at Sac
Port at Sea

Thu Jan 23
Mil at Orl
Mia at Tor
Chi at Cle
NY at Ind
NJ at Hou
Sea vs LAC
  at Anaheim
Det at GS
Minn at Van

Fri Jan 24
Orl at Bos
Sac at Phil
NY at Char
Wash at Atl
Dal at SA
Port at Phoe
Den at LAC
GS at LAL

Sat Jan 25
Sac at Wash
Bos at Atl
Char at Cle
Phil at Det
*Mil at Ind
*Tor at Chi
NJ at Dal
Utah at Hou
Minn at Port
Den at Van

Sun Jan 26
*Mia at NY
*SA at Mil
*LAL at Sea
Mon Jan 27
Phoe at Mia
Van at GS

Tue Jan 28
Bos at NY
Cle at NJ
Orl at Wash
Port at Tor
Char at Ind
Det at Mil
Sac at Minn
LAL at Dal
Den at Utah

Atl at LAC
Chi at Van

Wed Jan 29
Tor at Phil
Phoe at Orl
Bos at Mia
Ind at Char
NY at Cle
Port at Det
LAL at SA
Sea at GS

Thu Jan 30
Phoe at NJ
Minn at Dal
Den at Hou
Atl at Utah
Van at LAC
Chi at Sac

Fri Jan 31
Port at Bos
Orl at Phil
Mil at Char
Hou at Ind
Minn at SA
Chi at GS
Wash at Sea
Atl at Van

Sat Feb 1
*Det at NJ
*Phoe at Tor
Mia at Cle
Phil at Mil
Utah at Dal
Sac at Den
GS at LAC

Sun Feb 2
Van at Bos
*Char at NY
*Hou at Orl
Cle at Mia
Phoe at Det
*NJ at Ind
*Port at Minn
Atl at Den
Wash at LAL
*Chi at Sea

Mon Feb 3
Bos at Tor

Sac at SA
Wash at Utah

Tue Feb 4
Hou at NY
Van at NJ
Ind at Orl
Minn at Char
Cle at Mil
Sac at Dal
LAL vs LAC
   at Anaheim
Atl at GS
Chi at Port

Wed Feb 5
Mia at Bos
SA at Phil
Cle at Tor
Wash at Den
Atl at Phoe
Chi at LAL
Utah at Sea

Thu Feb 6
SA at NY
Ind at NJ
Bos at Orl
Mil at Mia
Sac at Char
Hou at Det
Van at Minn

Sun Feb 9
All-Star Game
   at Cleveland

Tue Feb 11
NY at Wash
NJ at Orl
Det at Mia
Phil at Cle
Char at Chi
Tor at Mil
SA at Dal
Van at Hou
Bos at LAC
Utah at Sac
Phoe at Port
Den at Sea

Wed Feb 12
NJ at Char
Tor at Atl
Orl at Det
Cle at Ind

LAL at Minn
Van at SA
Bos at Phoe

Thu Feb 13
Phil at NY
Ind at Mia
GS at Dal
LAL at Den
Port at Utah
LAC at Sac

Fri Feb 14
NJ vs Wash
   at Baltimore
Det at Char
Chi at Atl
Mil at Tor
Orl at Minn
GS at SA
LAC at Phoe
Hou at Sea
Bos at Van

Sat Feb 15
Wash at NJ
Phil at Mia
Den at Mil
Atl at SA
Dal at Utah
Hou at Port

Sun Feb 16
*Ind at NY
Den at Phil
*Det at Tor
*Orl at Chi
*Phoe at Minn
*Sea at LAL
GS at Sac
Bos at Port

Mon Feb 17
*Mil at Wash
Orl at Char
NJ at Cle
Tor at Ind
Atl at Hou
Bos at Sea
Dal at Van

Tue Feb 18
Phoe at NY
Mia at Phil
Den at Chi

SA at Utah
Dal at LAC
Minn at Sac

Wed Feb 19
Port at Orl
Phoe at Char
Ind at Atl
Wash at Det
Tor at SA
Cle at LAL
Bos at GS
Minn at Van

Thu Feb 20
Mia at NJ
LAC at Phil
Den at Ind
Mil at Dal
Tor at Hou
Bos at Utah
NY at Sac

Fri Feb 21
Chi at Wash
Den at Orl
Port at Mia
LAC at Char
Hou at Atl
NJ at Det
GS at Minn
Mil at SA
Cle at Phoe
Van at LAL
NY at Sea

Sat Feb 22
Port at Phil
Char at Atl
GS at Chi
Tor at Dal

Sun Feb 23
*Bos at NJ
*Det at Wash
Den at Mia
Orl at Ind
*LAC at Mil
*SA at Hou
*Sea at Utah
Dal at Phoe
*NY at LAL
*Cle at Van

Mon Feb 24
Det at Orl

GS at Atl
Port at Chi
Char at SA

Tue Feb 25
Sac at NJ
Ind at Wash
Sea at Cle
Char at Dal
LAL at Hou
Tor at Den
NY at Utah
Phil at LAC

Wed Feb 26
Sac at Bos
Mia at Orl
GS at Det
Sea at Ind
Atl at Mil
Minn at SA
Phil at Phoe
NY at Port
LAC at Van

Thu Feb 27
LAL at Wash
Chi at Cle
Minn at Dal
Char at Hou
Tor at Utah

Fri Feb 28
Det at Bos
GS at NJ
SA at Orl
Sea at Mia
LAL at Atl
Mil at Ind
Sac at Chi
NY at Den
Tor at LAC
Utah at Port
Phil at Van

Sat Mar 1
GS at Wash
Bos at Cle
Sac at Mil
Dal at Hou

Sun Mar 2
Cle at NY
*Sea at Orl
*SA at Mia

Atl at Det
*LAL at Ind
*Char at Minn
Phoe at Dal
LAC at Den
Phil at Port
*Utah at Van

Mon Mar 3
*Bos at Tor
Mil at Chi
Utah at GS
NJ at Sac

Tue Mar 4
Mil at NY
Wash at Phil
SA at Char
Cle at Atl
Mia at Det
Bos at Ind
LAL at Dal
Hou at LAC
NJ at Port
Orl at Sea

Wed Mar 5
NY at Tor
Ind at Cle
SA at Chi
Det at Minn
Dal at Utah
Port at Phoe
Hou at GS
Den at Sac

Thu Mar 6
Atl at Phil
Wash at Mia
Bos at Char
Orl vs LAC
 at Anaheim
NJ at Van

Fri Mar 7
NY at Bos
Mia at Wash
Mil at Atl
SA at Tor
Ind at Chi
Den at Minn
Det at Utah
Sac at Phoe
Hou at LAL
Orl at GS

Dal at Port
NJ at Sea

Sat Mar 8
Mil at Cle
SA at Ind
Det at LAC

Sun Mar 9
*Atl at Bos
Chi at NY
*Phil at Wash
*Mia at Char
*Van at Tor
*Utah at Minn
*Hou at Dal
*Orl at Phoe
NJ at LAL
Sac at GS
*Sea at Port

Mon Mar 10
GS at LAC

Tue Mar 11
Chi at Bos
Van at Char
Utah at Atl
Mia at Mil
Phil at Minn
NY at Dal
Hou at SA
Orl at Den
Tor at Phoe
Cle at Sac
LAC at Port
Det at Sea

Wed Mar 12
Utah at NJ
Chi at Phil
Van at Wash
Atl at Ind
Orl at Hou
GS at LAL

Thu Mar 13
Sea at Minn
Bos at Dal
Det at Den
Phoe at LAC
Cle at GS
Tor at Sac

Fri Mar 14
Chi at NJ
Minn at Phil
Char at Orl
Van at Mia
Sea at Atl
Utah at Ind
Wash at Mil
Bos at SA
LAC at LAL
Cle at Port

Sat Mar 15
Char at Phil
Utah at wash
Atl at Chi
SA at Den
Dal at Phoe
*Tor at GS

Sun Mar 16
*NJ at NY
*Van at Orl
*Hou at Mia
Sea at Det
*Ind at Mil
*Bos at Minn
Port at LAC
Tor at LAL
Dal at Sac

Mon Mar 17
Mil at Bos
Utah at Char
Orl at Atl
Det at Cle
Wash at SA
LAL at Den
Phoe at GS

Tue Mar 18
Van at NY
Hou at NJ
Phil at Tor
Minn at Ind
Sea at Chi
Wash at Dal
LAC at Phoe
Sac at Port

Wed Mar 19
Utah at Bos
NY at Phil
GS at Mia
Cle at Char

Ind at Atl
Tor at Det
Van at Minn
Sac at LAC

Thu Mar 20
GS at Orl
LAL at Cle
Port at Mil
Wash at Hou
SA at Phoe
Den at Sea

Fri Mar 21
Orl at Bos
NJ at Phil
LAL at Mia
Dal at Atl
Char at Tor
Minn at Det
Chi at Ind
SA at Sac
Den at Van

Sat Mar 22
Port at Wash
GS at Char
Det at Chi
NY at Mil
Cle at Dal
Phoe at Hou
LAC at Utah
Sac at Sea

Sun Mar 23
*NJ at Bos
Port at NY
*LAL at Orl
*Atl at Tor
*Mia at Minn
Utah at Den
SA at LAC
Sea at Van

Mon Mar 24
LAL at NJ

Tue Mar 25
Sac at Orl
Port at Atl
Ind at Tor
Dal at Chi
Minn at Hou
Cle at SA
Mil at Phoe

Gheorghe Muresan: NBA's Most Improved Player.

Van at LAC
Sea at GS

Wed Mar 26
Det at NY
Phil at NJ
Bos at Wash
Sac at Mia

Port at Char
Dal at Ind
Minn at Den
Mil at LAL
Phoe at Sea

Thu Mar 27
LAC at Atl

Chi at Tor
Cle at Hou
Orl at SA
LAL at Van

Fri Mar 28
NY at NJ
Bos at Phil

Tor at Wash
Cle at Mia
Ind at Char
LAC at Det
Mil at Utah
GS at Phoe
Van at Port
Minn at Sea

Sat Mar 29
Dal vs Wash
  at Baltimore
Sac at Atl
NJ at Chi
Den at Hou
Utah at SA

Sun Mar 30
*NY at Orl
*Mia at Tor
Dal at Cle
Phil at Det
*LAC at Ind
Mil at Den
Sea at Phoe
Minn at GS

Tue Apr 1
Phil at Orl
LAC at Mia
NY at Cle
Wash at Ind
Bos at Chi
Det at Dal
Hou at Den
GS at Port
LAL at Sea
Mil at Van

Wed Apr 2
Cle at Bos
Tor at Phil
Atl at Char
NJ at Minn
Det at SA
Sac at Utah
Hou at Phoe
Den at LAL

Thu Apr 3
Char at NJ
Chi at Wash
LAC at Orl
Mia at Ind
Dal at GS
Mil at Sea

Fri Apr 4
LAC at Bos
Orl at NY
Ind at Phil
Det at Atl
Cle at Chi
Wash at Minn

Phoe at Den
Van at Utah
SA at LAL
Hou at Sac
Mil at Port

Sat Apr 5
Tor at Mia
Phil at Char
NY at Atl
SA at GS
Phoe at Port
*Dal at Sea

Sun Apr 6
*Wash at Bos
*LAC at NJ
Chi at Orl
*Ind at Minn
Dal at LAL
Utah at GS
Sea at Sac
*Hou at Van

Mon Apr 7
Char at Cle
Mia at Det
Phil at Chi
Port at Den

Tue Apr 8
Cle at NY
Mia at NJ
Wash at Tor
Orl at Mil
Port at Dal
Den at SA
Minn at Phoe
Hou at LAC
LAL at GS
Van at Sac

Wed Apr 9
Atl at Phil
Bos at Char
Chi at Ind
LAL at Utah

Thu Apr 10
Chi at NY
Mil at NJ
Det at Mia
Orl at Tor
Sea at Dal
Van at Hou

Port at SA
Minn at LAC
Den at GS
Phoe at Sac

Fri Apr 11
Cle at Bos
NJ at Wash
Char at Det
Atl at Ind
Phil at Mil
Hou at Utah
Phoe at LAL
GS at Sac

Sat Apr 12
Bos at Orl
*NY at Mia
Wash at Char
Ind at Tor
Phil at Cle
Atl at Minn
Van at Dal
*Sea at SA
Den vs LAC
  at Anaheim

Sun Apr 13
*Chi at Det
*NJ at Mil
*Sea at Hou
*Utah at LAL
Phoe at GS

Mon Apr 14
Wash at Phil
Det at Orl
Minn at Mia
Cle at Char
NY at Ind
Tor at Chi
LAC at Dal
GS at Den
SA at Sac

Tue Apr 15
NJ at Atl
Tor at Mil
LAC at Hou
Utah at Phoe
SA at Sea

Wed Apr 16
Char at Bos
Atl at NY

Phil at NJ
Ind at Wash
Chi at Mia
Orl at Cle
Mil at Det
Dal at Minn
Den at Port

Thu Apr 17
Sea at Den
GS at Utah
Sac at LAL
Port at Van

Fri Apr 18
Ind at NY
Bos at Phil
Orl at Wash
NJ at Mia
Tor at Char
Cle at Det
Mil at Minn
Dal at Hou
Phoe at SA
LAL at LAC

Sat Apr 19
Mia at Orl
Phil at Atl
NY at Chi
Den at Dal
Minn at Utah
Van at Phoe
Sac at GS
LAC at Sea

Sun Apr 20
*Tor at Bos
Atl at NJ
*Wash at Cle
*Det at Ind
Char at Mil
*Hou at SA
Utah at Sac
*LAL at Port

1996-97 NBA ON NBC
(Starting Time Eastern)

Day	Date	Game	Time
Wed	Dec 25	LA Lakers at Phoenix	6:00
		Detroit at Chicago	8:30
Sun	Jan 19	Orlando at Miami	Noon
		Chicago at Houston	2:30
Sun	Jan 26	Miami at New York	12:30
		LA Lakers at Seattle	3:00
Sun	Feb 2	Houston at Orlando* or	1:00
		Charlotte at New York*	1:00
		Chicago at Seattle	3:30
Sun	Feb 9	NBA All-Star Game (Cleveland)	6:00
Sun	Feb 16	Seattle at LA Lakers	3:00
		Orlando at Chicago	5:30
Sun	Feb 23	San Antonio at Houston* or	1:00
		Detroit at Washington* or	1:00
		Boston at New Jersey*	1:00
		New York at LA Lakers* or	3:30
		Seattle at Utah*	3:30
Sun	Mar 2	LA Lakers at Indiana	1:00
		Seattle at Orlando* or	3:30
		San Antonio at Miami*	3:30
Sun	Mar 9	Houston at Dallas* or	3:00
		Philadelphia at Washington* or	3:00
		Orlando at Phoenix* or	3:00
		Seattle at Portland*	3:00
		Chicago at New York	5:30
Sun	Mar 16	Houston at Miami* or	Noon
		New Jersey at New York*	Noon
Sun	Mar 23	LA Lakers at Orlando	12:30
Sun	Mar 30	New York at Orlando	12:30
Sun	Apr 6	Chicago at Orlando	5:30
Sat	Apr 12	Seattle at San Antonio* or	3:30
		New York at Miami*	3:30
Sun	Apr 13	Chicago at Detroit	1:00
		Utah at LA Lakers* or	3:30
		Seattle at Houston*	3:30
Sat	Apr 19	New York at Chicago	8:30
Sun	Apr 20	Washington at Cleveland* or	3:30
		Detroit at Indiana* or	3:30
		Houston at San Antonio* or	3:30
		LA Lakers at Portland*	3:30

*Denotes Regional Broadcast
Schedule subject to change

Antonio Davis will leap into next century as Pacer.

1996-97 NBA ON TNT
(Starting Times Eastern)

Day	Date	Game	Time
Fri	Nov 1	New York at Toronto	8:00
		Phoenix at LA Lakers	10:30
Tue	Nov 5	LA Lakers at New York	8:00
Fri	Nov 8	Chicago at Detroit	8:00
		New Jersey at Orlando (Japan)	10:30
Tue	Nov 12	LA Lakers at Houston	8:00
Fri	Nov 15	Chicago at Charlotte	8:00
Tue	Nov 19	New York at Orlando	8:00
Fri	Nov 22	Philadelphia at Washington	8:00
Tue	Nov 26	Portland at Houston	8:00
Fri	Nov 29	LA Lakers at Detroit	8:00
Tue	Dec 3	Miami at New York	8:00
Fri	Dec 6	Phoenix at Sacramento	8:00
		Orlando at LA Lakers	10:30
Tue	Dec 10	Houston at Minnesota	8:00
Fri	Dec 13	Golden State at Cleveland	8:00
Tue	Dec 17	LA Lakers at Chicago	8:00
Fri	Dec 20	Utah at Orlando	8:00
Fri	Jan 3	Orlando at Chicago	8:00
Tue	Jan 7	Miami at Seattle	8:00
Fri	Jan 10	San Antonio at Detroit	8:00
Tue	Jan 14	New York at Houston	8:00
Fri	Jan 17	Utah at Vancouver	9:00
Tue	Jan 21	New York at Chicago	8:00
Fri	Jan 24	New York at Charlotte	8:00
Tue	Jan 28	Detroit at Milwaukee	8:00
Fri	Jan 31	Houston at Indiana	8:00
Tue	Feb 4	Houston at New York	8:00
Sat	Feb 8	NBA All-Star Saturday (Cleveland)	7:00
Tue	Feb 11	Detroit at Miami	8:00
Fri	Feb 14	Chicago at Atlanta	8:00
Tue	Feb 18	San Antonio at Utah	8:00
Fri	Feb 21	Chicago at Washington	8:00
Tue	Feb 25	LA Lakers at Houston	8:00
Fri	Feb 28	Seattle at Miami	8:00
Tue	Mar 4	Orlando at Seattle	8:00
Tue	Mar 11	Houston at San Antonio	8:00
Tue	Mar 18	Seattle at Chicago	8:00
Tue	Mar 25	Cleveland at San Antonio	8:00
Fri	Mar 28	Indiana at Charlotte	8:00
Tue	Apr 1	LA Lakers at Seattle	8:00
Fri	Apr 4	Orlando at New York	8:00
Tue	Apr 8	Cleveland at New York	8:00
Fri	Apr 11	Atlanta at Indiana	8:00
Tue	Apr 15	Utah at Phoenix	8:00
Fri	Apr 18	Phoenix at San Antonio	8:00

Jim Jackson paced Mavs' run-and-gun guys in scoring.

1996-97 NBA ON TBS
(Starting Times Eastern)

Day	Date	Game	Time
Wed	Nov 6	Chicago at Miami	8:00
Wed	Nov 20	New York at Charlotte	8:00
		Chicago at Phoenix	10:30
Wed	Nov 27	LA Lakers at Boston	8:00
		Miami at LA Clippers	10:30
Wed	Dec 4	LA Lakers at Utah	8:00
Wed	Dec 11	Miami at Philadelphia	8:00
Wed	Dec 18	New York at Detroit	8:00
Thu	Dec 26	Orlando at Miami	8:00
Wed	Jan 8	Seattle at Denver	8:00
Wed	Jan 15	Orlando at Dallas	8:00
Wed	Jan 22	Detroit at Sacramento	8:00
Wed	Jan 29	LA Lakers at San Antonio	8:00
Wed	Feb 5	Utah at Seattle	8:00
		Chicago at LA Lakers	10:30
Wed	Feb 12	Orlando at Detroit	8:00
Wed	Feb 19	Portland at Orlando	8:00
Wed	Feb 26	Seattle at Indiana	8:00
Wed	Mar 5	San Antonio at Chicago	8:00
Wed	Mar 12	Orlando at Houston	8:00
Wed	Mar 19	Golden State at Miami	8:00
Wed	Mar 26	Detroit at New York	8:00
Wed	Apr 2	Detroit at San Antonio	8:00
Wed	Apr 9	LA Lakers at Utah	8:00
Wed	Apr 16	Chicago at Miami	8:00

Matchup: Dennis Rodman vs. Sonics' Frank Brickowski.

1996-97 NBA ON CTV

(CTV will carry NBA games in Canada; Starting Times Eastern)

Day	Date	Game	Air Time
Fri	Nov 1	New York at Toronto (E)................	8:00
		Portland at Vancouver (W)...............	10:30
Sun	Dec 8	Chicago at Toronto.....................	8:30
Sun	Jan 5	LA Lakers at Vancouver.................	9:00
Sun	Jan 12	Orlando at Toronto	6:30
Sun	Jan 19	Toronto at Vancouver...................	3:00
Sun	Jan 26	Miami at New York.....................	12:30
		LA Lakers at Seattle...................	3:00
Sat	Feb 1	Phoenix at Toronto....................	3:00
Sun	Feb 2	Chicago at Seattle	3:30
Sun	Feb 9	47th NBA All-Star Game (Cleveland)	6:00
Sun	Feb 16	Detroit at Toronto	12:30
Sun	Feb 23	Cleveland at Vancouver	3:00
Sun	Mar 2	Utah at Vancouver	3:00
Sun	Mar 9	Vancouver at Toronto..................	12:30
Sun	Mar 16	Vancouver at Orlando...................	3:00
Sun	Mar 23	LA Lakers at Orlando	12:30
Sun	Mar 30	Miami at Toronto	3:00
Sun	Apr 6	Houston at Vancouver	3:00
Sun	Apr 13	Chicago at Detroit* or.................	1:00
		Utah at LA Lakers* or.................	3:30
		Seattle at Houston*....................	3:30
Sun	Apr 20	Washington at Cleveland* or	3:30
		Detroit at Indiana* or..................	3:30
		Houston at San Antonio* or	3:30
		LA Lakers at Portland*.................	3:30

E-Regional Coverage in Eastern Canada
W-Regional Coverage in Western Canada
*CTV will select one game on 4/13 and 4/20
Schedule subject to change

Brent Barry showed his budding talent as a rookie.

**Revised and updated FOURTH EDITION
with more than 60
new record-breaking stories!**

THE ILLUSTRATED
SPORTS RECORD BOOK

Zander Hollander
and David Schulz

Setting the record straight, here in a single book are more than 400 records re-created in more than 200 stories. Sports immortals and their feats abound— Cal Ripken, Jr., Michael Jordan, Steffi Graf, Joe DiMaggio, Wayne Gretzky, Muhammad Ali, Jack Nicklaus ... and many more. Perfect for settling living-room or bar-room debates, this fourth edition is illustrated with more than 100 action photos.

* Prices slightly higher in Canada   (0-451-18858-6—$5.99)